T

Cultures of Consumption Series

Forthcoming Titles

Consuming Cultures, Global Perspectives
Historical Trajectories, Transnational Exchanges
Edited by John Brewer & Frank Trentmann

Fashion's World Cities
Edited by Christopher Breward & David Gilbert

The Khat Controversy
Stimulating the Debate on Drugs
David Anderson, Susan Beckerleg, Degol Hailu, Axel Klein

Governing Consumption
New Spaces of Consumer Politics
Clive Barnett, Nick Clarke, Paul Cloke and Alice Malpass

Alternative Food Networks: Reconnecting Producers, Consumers and Food?
Moya Kneafsey, Lewis Holloway, Laura Venn, Rosie Cox, Elizabeth Dowler and
Helena Tuomainen

The Making of the Consumer

Knowledge, Power and Identity in the Modern World

**Edited by
Frank Trentmann**

Oxford • New York

First published in 2006 by
Berg
Editorial offices:
1st Floor, Angel Court, 81 St Clements Street, Oxford OX4 1AW, UK
175 Fifth Avenue, New York, NY 10010, USA

© Frank Trentmann 2006

Berg is the imprint of Oxford International Publishers Ltd.

This book has been produced with the support of the
Economic and Social Research Council and the Arts and Humanities Research Council

Library of Congress Cataloging-in-Publication Data
The making of the consumer : knowledge, power and identity in the modern world /
edited by Frank Trentmann.
    p. cm. — (Cultures of consumption series)
    Includes bibliographical references and index.
    ISBN-13: 978-1-84520-249-1 (pbk.)
    ISBN-10: 1-84520-249-X (pbk.)
    ISBN-13: 978-1-84520-248-4 (cloth)
    ISBN-10: 1-84520-248-1 (cloth)
    1. Consumers. 2. Consumption (Economics) 3. Consumer behavior.
I. Trentmann, Frank. II. Series.

    HC79.C6M35 2005
    339.4'7—dc22

                                                                2005021928

British Library Cataloguing-in-Publication Data
A catalogue record for this book is available from the British Library.

ISBN-13 978 1 84520 248 4 (Cloth)
         978 1 84520 249 1 (Paper)

ISBN-10 1 84520 248 1 (Cloth)
         1 84520 249 X (Paper)

Typeset by JS Typesetting Ltd, Porthcawl, Mid Glamorgan
Printed in the United Kingdom by Biddles Ltd, King's Lynn

www.bergpublishers.com

Contents

List of Illustrations

Acknowledgements

The Making of the Consumer is the result of a dialogue between experts from the humanities and social sciences exploring new approaches to consumption in the modern world. When, why and how did people come to think of themselves as consumers? How have knowledge regimes and economic, cultural and political forces configured this new persona? What can a focus on consumers as subjects and objects reveal about new ways of thinking about cultures of consumption? Contributors were asked to revisit the creation and contestation of consumers in their particular subject area.

Several chapters in this volume developed out of papers first discussed at the international workshop "Knowing Consumers" at the Zentrum für interdisziplinäre Forschung/Centre for Interdisciplinary Research, Bielefeld, Germany, in February 2004. Special thanks must go to Gerhard Haupt, who helped conceive and organize this workshop. The intellectual energy of this project derived additional momentum from those who contributed so much to our discussions: Christina Benninghaus, Maxine Berg, Hartmut Berghoff, Peter Lunt, Paul Nolte, Chris Pole, Michael Prinz, Hannes Siegrist, Jakob Tanner and Claudius Torp. The hospitality and assistance provided by the ZiF and its staff, especially Trixi Valentin and Dr Johannes Roggenhoffer, are gratefully acknowledged. For their generous support of the workshop, I should like to thank the ZiF as well as the Economic and Social Research Council and the Arts and Humanities Research Board, the co-funders of the Cultures of Consumption research programme (L143341003). Finally, I should like to thank everyone at Berg, the anonymous reviewer for comments, Laura Bevir for producing the index, and Stefanie Nixon for her help with preparing the final manuscript.

Frank Trentmann
London
November 2004

List of Contributors

James G. Carrier holds research positions in anthropology at Indiana and Oxford Brookes universities. Publications include *Meanings of the Market: The Free Market in Western Culture* (Oxford: Berg, 1997), *Virtualism: A New Political Economy* (Oxford: Berg, 1998, with Daniel Miller) and *A Handbook of Economic Anthropology* (Cheltenham: Edward Elgar, 2004).

Marie-Emmanuelle Chessel is researcher at the CNRS (Centre de Recherches Historiques, École des Hautes Études en Sciences Sociales, Paris, France). Publications include *La Publicité: Naissance d'une profession* (Paris, CNRS Editions, 1998) and *Au nom du Consommateur* (Paris, La Decouverte, 2004, co-edited with Alain Chatriot and Matthew Hilton).

Michelle Everson is Jean Monnet Senior Lecturer in European Law at Birkbeck College, University of London. She has researched widely in the field of European Law and has particular interests in the areas of European regulatory law, European administrative and constitutional law and European citizenship.

Ben Fine is Professor of Economics at the School of Oriental and African Studies, University of London. His many publications include *The World of Consumption* (second edition London: Routledge, 2002), *The Political Economy of Diet, Health and Food Policy* (London: Routledge, 1998) and *Consumption in the Age of Affluence: The World of Food* (London: Routledge, 1996, with Michael Heasman and Judith Wright).

Jos Gamble is Senior Lecturer in Asia Pacific Business at the School of Management, Royal Holloway, University of London. He is the author of *Shanghai in Transition: Changing Perspectives and Social Contours of a Chinese Metropolis* (London: Routledge Curzon, 2003).

Stephen Kline is Professor in the School of Communications and Director of the Media Analysis Laboratory at Simon Fraser University, Vancouver, Canada. He is the author of *Out of the Garden: Children, Toys and Television in the Age of Marketing* (London: Verso Press, 1993) and *Digital Play: The Interaction of Technology, Culture and Marketing* (Montreal: Queens-McGill, 2003, with Nick Dyer-Witheford and Greig de Peuter).

Ina Merkel is Professor of Cultural Studies at the European Ethnology Institute at Philipps-Universität Marburg, Germany. Her books include *Utopie und Bedürfnis: Die Geschichte der Konsumkultur in der DDR* (Cologne: Böhlau-Verlag, 1999).

Frank Mort is Professor of Cultural Histories and Director of the Institute for Inter-Disciplinary Research in the Arts at the University of Manchester. His publications include *Cultures of Consumption: Masculinities and Social Space in Twentieth Century Britain* (London: Routledge, 1996) and *Dangerous Sexualities: Medico-Moral Politics in England since 1800* (second edition, London: Routledge, 2000). His new book *Origins of the Permissive Society* is forthcoming with Yale University Press.

Erika Rappaport is Associate Professor of History, University of California, Santa Barbara. She is the author of *Shopping for Pleasure: Women in the Making of London's West End* (Princeton: Princeton University Press, 2000).

Uwe Spiekermann is Assistant Professor at the Institute of Economic and Social History, Georg-August-University Göttingen. Publications include *Basis der Konsumgesellschaft: Geschichte des modernen Kleinhandels in Deutschland 1850–1914* (Munich: Beck, 1999).

Vanessa Taylor is an AHRB doctoral student at Birkbeck College, University of London, and is completing a thesis on 'Brewers, Temperance and the Nineteenth-Century Drinking Fountain Movement in Britain'.

Frank Trentmann is Senior Lecturer in Modern History at Birkbeck College, University of London, and Director of the Cultures of Consumption research programme, funded by the UK Economic and Social Research Council (ESRC) and the Arts and Humanities Research Board (AHRB). Recent publications include *Markets in Historical Contexts: Ideas and Politics in the Modern World* (Cambridge: Cambridge University Press, 2004, edited with Mark Bevir) and *Worlds of Political Economy: Knowledge and Power 1700 to the Present* (London: Palgrave Macmillan, 2004, edited with Martin J. Daunton).

Donald Winch is Emeritus Research Professor in the School of Humanities at the University of Sussex. His many publications include *Riches and Poverty: An Intellectual History of Political Economy in Britain, 1750–1834* (Cambridge: Cambridge University Press, 1996) and *That Noble Science of Politics: A Study in Nineteenth-Century Intellectual History* (Cambridge: Cambridge University Press, 1983, with Stefan Collini and John Burrow).

Knowing Consumers – Histories, Identities, Practices

An Introduction

Frank Trentmann

'And what do you mean to be?'
The kind old Bishop said
As he took the boy on his ample knee...

'I want to be a Consumer,'
The bright-haired lad replied
As he gazed up into the Bishop's face
In innocence open-eyed.
'I've never had aims of a selfish sort,
For that, as I know is wrong,
I want to be a Consumer, Sir,
And help the word along.

'I want to be a Consumer
And work both night and day,
For that is the thing that's needed most,
I've heard Economists say.
I won't just be a Producer,
Like Bobby and James and John;
I want to be a Consumer, Sir,
And help the nation on'.[1] (Punch 1934)

Missing Person

The consumer as an engine of wealth and representative of the public interest is an established figure in contemporary politics and discourse. Indeed, the consumer may have become all too familiar, exhorted to keep the American economy moving in the aftermath of 11 September 2001, embraced by communist China in the 1990s and charged with reforming public services in Britain under New Labour. Such is the almost instinctive recourse to this persona in politics, media and academia that the consumer is close to becoming a quasi-natural being. Interestingly, the opening rhyme did not arise from the neoliberal climate of the last two decades, but appeared in the British satirical magazine *Punch* in the early 1930s. It offers a convenient entry into this volume and its line of enquiry. For the increasingly powerful vocabulary of 'the consumer' as a self-evident category or ontological essence has distracted attention from the historical emergence of this creature, its changing shape and values and the different positions it has occupied in politics and society. Rather than using or presuming a consumer in an essentialist or descriptive fashion, *The Making of the Consumer* enquires how and why the consumer developed as an identifiable subject and object in the modern period. Which processes helped and which discouraged the formation of this new social and political category? What has been the relative role of civil society, state and commercial interests in different contexts? What groups and agencies have spoken as consumers or on their behalf, for what reasons and with what implications? Answers to these questions will not only contribute to a richer understanding of the biographies of consumers, but, in turn, prompt new approaches and questions for studies of consumption more generally.

This introduction and the chapters to follow are an attempt to reposition the field of consumption studies by moving beyond an interest in purchase and the practical and symbolic use of *things* to ask about the *subjectivities* of 'the consumer'. The expanding literature on consumption has enriched our understanding of the central role of material culture in the reproduction of social relationships and status, everyday routines and selfhood,[2] but has offered surprisingly little in the way of explaining the evolution of the consumer into a master category of collective and individual identity. Put simply, all human societies have been engaged in consumption and have purchased, exchanged, gifted or used objects and services, but it has only been in specific contexts in the nineteenth and twentieth centuries that some (not all) practices of consumption have been connected to a sense of being a 'consumer', as an identity, audience or category of analysis. To retrieve the making of the consumer as subject and object, it is helpful to turn briefly to the self-limiting assumptions in the current discourse of the 'active consumer'.

If the field of consumption studies originally developed through an emphasis on 'mass consumption' and the passive creature created by culture industries and advertising – the consumer, perpetually unsatisfied, restless, anxious and bored',[3] in Christopher Lasch's words – the last twenty-five years have seen a dramatic turn to the 'active' or 'citizen consumer'– a creative, confident and rational being articulating personal identity and serving the public interest. The 'active consumer' appears everywhere from rational choice economics to environmental discourse and from public policy to marketing and cultural studies. In Britain, New Labour has presented the reform of public services as a self-conscious response to the 'rise of the demanding, sceptical, citizen-consumer'.[4] In Germany, the coalition agreement between Social Democrats and Greens invoked the 'intelligent, well-informed consumer'.[5] Consumer rights have become an expanding point of reference for individuals and public authorities alike. In 2003 'DVD Jon', a Norwegian computer hacker, saw a legal ruling defending his right to crack into legally bought DVDs as a clarification 'that consumers have certain rights that the film industry can't take away from us'.[6] Health care policies in a growing number of countries give recognition to the 'consumer rights' of patients.[7] Instead of a 'passive dupe', the consumer has reappeared as 'co-actor' or 'citizen consumer' in a variety of settings in state, civil society and market, ranging from international organizations discussing environmental policy and Consumers' International agenda of social justice, to the everyday minutiae of monitoring deregulated directory enquiry telephone calls in Britain.[8] In the world of commerce and art, meanwhile, visitors to Eliasson's Weather Project at Tate Modern learnt from Unilever's chairman that its sponsorship 'reflects the commitment to creativity which lies at the heart of Unilever's business, helping us to meet the needs of consumers around the world'.[9] For all its critical stance, academic scholarship has been part of this general discursive shift from 'passive' to 'active consumer', highlighting the agency, resistance and transgression that consumers bring to processes of consumption. Consumers, in the words of the American consumer researcher Russell Belk, must be recognized as 'coproducers of desire and identity and active participant[s] in consumer self-seduction'.[10]

The new orthodoxy of the 'active consumer' in the social sciences has been welcome for retrieving the agency of consumers from relative neglect in the more instrumentalist analyses of mass consumption dominant on both sides of the Atlantic in previous generations. At the same time, this conceptual shift has come with a narrowing of the terrain and temporality in which consumers as agents are seen to live and breathe. Markets, choice and the point of purchase provide the dominant framework for most accounts of agency, be it in economics, political science or sociology and anthropology. Enquiry here starts with individual preferences or what James Carrier in this volume critically terms the 'psycho-cultural orientation' in anthropology.[11] From within this framework it is difficult to approach the prior, larger problem of how 'consumers' develop as an identity and ascriptive category of interest for social movements, states and bodies of commercial and professional experts. Economics, whether in rational choice or more recent behavioural models, takes the consumer as a given. The same is true for most political scientists, whose work focuses on the institutional openings that allow consumers to overcome costs of collective action – rather than explaining how 'the consumer' became an attractive category for mobilization in the first place.[12]

In terms of time, the recent attention given to agency emerged through a self-conscious break with earlier narratives of modernity. Approaches such as post-modernity or late modernity pose a paradigm break with earlier forms of modernity associated with mass production and mass consumption, class or welfarism.[13] It thus involves a temporal distancing from earlier historical formations of consumers and consumption. Attention to the self-reflexive individual, for example, is tied to the study of lifestyles associated with late modernity.[14] Even where the active consumer is seen as 'effect', as in governmentality studies with their emphasis on 'advanced liberal' styles of government seeking to create the habitus of the citizen as entrepreneur, the focus of investigation is a priori limited to the last two decades.[15] The fixation with the consumer as 'effect' ignores not only the diverse workings of the consumer in practice. More generally, it suffers from an in-built temporal ring-fencing of the problem. Whatever their critique of earlier approaches preoccupied with mass production and the power of culture industries and advertisers for ignoring consumers' agency, recent approaches have tended to reinforce an important part of the earlier temporal frame of 'mass consumer society'. Being 'post' requires a clearly defined prior state from which to turn away. In the social sciences, the focus on lifestyle culture and the self-reflexive or 'active' consumer of the late twentieth century acquired its shape in reaction against a prior 'mass consumer society', rather than by interrogating the nature of that earlier configuration.[16] This historical disengagement – and here we are back to the market-centred framework of analysis – was encouraged by an intuitive acceptance of the causal connection between the development of 'modern' consumer culture and commodification, in which markets, shopping and choice appear as dominant drivers.[17] Put differently, the formation of consumers is not much of a problem since it appears as the natural consequence of the growing commodification and creation of desire in market-based capitalism.

The attention given in recent discussions to self and creativity, signs and symbols has significantly enhanced our understanding of the diverse ways in which consumption is tied to people's plural identities, from the creation of subcultures to gay identities.[18] And the sociological tradition of Bourdieu has, of course, been equally influential in analysing the role of consumption practices in creating and recreating distinct status groups. Interestingly, however, neither tradition has been intrigued by the problem of how 'the consumer' arose and acquired its hegemonic status as a master category. Studies of 'consumer culture' have mainly been about the social acts and cultural processes of consumption in market capitalism rather than about the construction of the consumer as an identity and category. The explosion of studies of the 'active consumer' has proceeded with a relative lack of critical reflexivity, which, ironically, has tended to obscure the part played by these very academic studies in constructing and popularizing the consumer as a dominant reference point and object of enquiry. Most analyses start with the consumer as a mature agent, whose genesis is taken as given. The consumer is either presumed to be the product of conditions of 'affluence' in the 1950s–1960s (standardized mass production, advertising, consumer rights),[19] or to lie buried in the distant past, best left to historians of the 'consumer revolutions' of the transatlantic world in the eighteenth century.

Three observations suggest themselves. First, there is an interesting methodological imbalance in mainstream consumption studies between, on the one hand, the recognition of the manipulation and saturation of signs, the economy of symbolic goods and the 'naming' of consumption communities and on the other hand, the relative indifference to the naming and representation of the actors who are speaking as consumers or are being addressed as such. Where identities come into play, enquiries into status formation or subcultures have been better at showing how material culture divides people into distinct status groups than at explaining how and when 'the consumer' provides a shared reference point that can cut across social divides, although we shall soon see that the frequent notion that 'everyone is a consumer' is a historical myth and that the consumer embodied different social groups in different contexts and did not necessarily provide a universal or democratic frame for all private end-users.

Second, the epochal divide running through consumption studies between modernity and late or post-modernity has over-dramatized one particular gulf at the expense of diverse shifts within each formation and developments cutting across them. There is a danger here of assigning the consumer an essential position within these complex large-scale social formations – the modern consumer versus the post-modern active and creative consumer – that erases from view the dynamic process and changing formation of this person in different contexts. Reflexivity and self-reflexivity have rightly become key questions for students of contemporary consumption. It would yield interesting insights to extend this concern to the field of 'consumer culture' and its key categories. These categories have a very recent and troubled history. 'Mass consumption' became a term in the early twentieth century, but the personification of a social system as a 'consumer society' is only a product of the end of the twentieth century – in 1964 George Katona speaks of 'the mass consumption society'. Social scientists and historians alike should be wary when projecting such concepts back into earlier contexts with different social formations, sensibilities and discourses.[20]

Finally, there is the restricting focus on choice and commodity purchase in modern capitalist markets as the natural terrain of studying consuming cultures. This is problematic for several reasons. Not only does it ignore the social significance of consumption in pre-modern, fascist or socialist societies,[21] it also obscures the continuing importance of routine consumption activities (bathing, reading, eating) in the most advanced liberal market societies;[22] in 'affluent' societies like those of Western Europe today, the largest share of people's budget (25 per cent) is dedicated to housing and utilities.[23] Whether their consumption choices have been viewed as authentic expressions of selfhood or as socially constructed, consumers have mainly been approached as moving along an avenue between private domain and market purchase, following their self-interest in ways that stifle civic reflexivity and community engagement, social accountability and citizenship. As this volume will show, much is to be gained from casting our view beyond the market and situating consumers and consumption within their broader social and political spheres. To understand the evolution of the consumer, greater recognition needs to be accorded to processes of identity and knowledge formation that criss-cross the market or occur altogether outside its domain (including law, schools, the home and politics) as well as to those situated in alternative systems of provision or concerning the breakdown of markets (including monopoly provision, planning, rationing). Consumers did not arise effortlessly as an automatic response to the spread of markets but had to be made. And this process of making occurred through mobilization in civil society and the state as well as in the commercial domain, under conditions of deprivation, war and constraint as well as affluence and choice, and articulated through traditions of political ideas and ethics.

Emphasizing the active process in which people create a relationship and an identity with objects, the anthropologist James Carrier has elsewhere written of the act of 'appropriation' that makes consumption always more than a removal of goods from markets: commodities become possessions.[24] We may extend this notion from objects to the consumers themselves and ask who is engaged in an 'appropriation' of the consumer, when and how that knowledge is created, for what purpose and with what implications. In other words, the starting point is not how people have certain bits of information about goods, prices, etc., but when information is processed and systematized in such a way that it creates a sense of being a consumer. It concerns the mutual configuration of knowledge and identity. As we shall see, the appropriation of the consumer is a process drawing on political, intellectual and cultural traditions and processes in which needs and desires, acquisition and use are situated. The following sections offer some pathways to analyse and re-evaluate the formation of the consumer. They will highlight the diverse histories and changing boundaries of the consumer; the dynamic relations between consumers and other social groups; knowledge in use; and the flow of ideas and practices between social systems.

Histories

The starting point for a new approach to the consumer has to be greater engagement amongst social scientists, who have done most of the thinking about consumption, with the current historical rewriting of the subject. An enriched view of the diverse traditions and practices of consumers would not only facilitate understanding of past roads taken or abandoned, but also make available historical and theoretical perspectives to those currently exploring new approaches to consumption, ethics and politics. Just as historians have benefited from enquiries into taste, status and the saturation of signs, so social scientists can now learn from historicizing their fields of enquiry. For the crop of recent historical research challenges the very foundations of the dominant model of 'consumer society' on which social scientists were raised.[25] Historians have moved the goal posts of 'modernity' by discovering supposedly modern or post-modern activities and sensibilities, such as shopping arcades, marketing and luxury fever, in the early modern transatlantic world.[26] More significantly for our immediate purposes, historians have been moving beyond the instinctive causal equation between commodification and the formation of the consumer.[27] If not altogether absent, the consumer was a largely voiceless, marginal figure in the so-called 'consumer revolutions' of the transatlantic world in the eighteenth century. Students of twentieth-century 'consumerism', meanwhile, have explored the expanding language of the consumer prior to the age of affluence and mass marketing.[28]

These accounts unsettle the chronology of consumer society. They also widen the frame of analysis, from market to state and civil society, as well as to ethics and informal life. In her account of the United States' development into a 'consumer's republic', Liz Cohen presents a transition from the public-minded 'citizen consumer' of the 1930s to the 'purchaser citizen' who served the national interest of a mass consumption economy. Importantly, the relative shift in weight between these two porous categories is not entirely a commercial story but also the result of socio-political dynamics, especially in the class and racialized politics of suburban housing, with its spill-over effects on transportation (from public to private), retailing (the rise of the mall) and the substitution of civic with commercial public spaces. The 'citizen consumer' and 'purchasing consumer' are, of course, ideal-typical constructs and do not exhaust the multiple constellations of identities in different settings. They, however, point to the interplay between different traditions and to the shifting discursive politics of the consumer as a necessary first step to any considered debate about the changing place of consumption and consumers in modern societies.

How did the consumer acquire a positive mantle of interests and identities? The negative connotations of consumption as a disease or wasteful practice are well known. These favoured a negative image of 'the consumer' that was easily invoked in debates over luxury: 'unproductive' consumers were seen to undermine the national economy through their selfish and unproductive pursuit of novelties. ' "The consumer (monkey, king or bishop) devours the fruits without return"', as the early cooperator William Thompson put it in 1824.[29] Such negative imagery is echoed in the moralistic and paternalistic outlook of many twentieth-century scholars, social reformers and politicians concerned with consumption.[30] Yet the nineteenth and early twentieth century also witnessed a positive revalorization of the consumer that would carve out new sources of legitimacy, knowledge and identity. In early and mid-nineteenth century Britain and America, political agitation began to assign 'the consumer' a new place as guardian of the public interest. As taxpayers and purchasers, consumers increasingly demanded to be heard and represented and were urged to use their material position to advance moral and public causes, such as the boycott of slave-produced sugar or support for free trade.[31] Political economy, citizenship and ethics were three crucial areas in which the person of the consumer began to take a more defined shape.

Liberal economics, more than any other profession or body of knowledge, has been held responsible for establishing the hegemony of the rational, individualist and utility-maximizing consumer in public discourse. The understandable tendency in cultural studies, sociology and anthropology to turn neo-classical economics into a whipping boy, however, has obscured the rich and complex construction of the consumer in economic knowledge in the first place. The contemporary critique of the rational individualist consumer as insufficiently social or cultural rests on a sharp equation between liberal economics and the marketized consumer. This is commonly traced back to a neoclassical paradigm shift in late nineteenth-century economics and its mathematical fixation with calculating consumer preferences. As Donald Winch shows in his chapter, this textbook story may be a convenient tool in the ongoing battle between culture and rational choice, but fails to capture how the fathers of professional economics understood the consumer. Not only were liberal writers divided over the position of the consumer in political economy and public policy, depending on different theories of value, a division that pitched J.S. Mill against the French *libre échangistes*. The marginalist revolution of the 1870s–1880s also amounted to far less of a sharp break in attitudes to consumers between so-called classical and neoclassical economists than is often presumed. The latter shared many of the same moral and social concerns of the former. Both came to defend the consumer as representative of public interest, but, as Winch shows, initially this had nothing to do with a universally applicable theory of economic maximization and developed out of considerable ambivalence towards the consumer as a subject of economic knowledge. Mill, in fact, rejected any calls to make consumption a distinct subject of economic knowledge and public policy. Where economists, like Mill, turned to the consumer was in conditions of market failure and in the provision of public goods. Nor did the mathematical turn to inter-personal comparisons automatically reduce the consumer to an algebraic sheet of calculations. Marshall and Edgeworth used biology and psycho-physics to offer a picture of the organic adjustment of wants to activities and the generation of new wants. Rather than an intellectual cul-de-sac pointing to methodological individualism, late nineteenth-century economics was a dynamic force behind sociological enquiries into consumers and their changing tastes and wants.[32]

Rationality and knowledge were twin categories central to the expanding debate about consumers in the nineteenth century. Much of the twentieth-century debate has travelled between the opposite camps of consumers as 'dupes' or as those who instinctively know their own interests best. The crystallization and legitimation of the consumer, however, also raised prior questions about the construction and boundaries of this new person's knowledge. In his *Principles of Political Economy* of 1848, Mill wondered whether 'the consumer, or person served, is the most competent judge of the end', unlike the worker and producer, who almost naturally acquired a strong sense of self and interest in their work and were thus held to be 'generally the best selector of means'. At the same time, the uneven distribution of knowledge and reflexivity between these different social actors also attracted particular liberal attention to the consumer. For it marked out consumers – with their underdeveloped sense of reflexivity – as prime objects of a civilizing project. Tellingly, there is a step-change in Mill's excitement about the consumer precisely where the subject moved from 'daily uses of life', with its ministering to existing inclinations, to the consumption of things tending 'to raise the character of human beings'. After all, the 'uncultivated cannot be competent judges of cultivation'.[33]

Before there could be a popular notion of consumer sovereignty, the consumer had to be cultivated. The consumer as a project took different shape in different traditions – in national economics in Imperial Germany the consumer was appropriated for the project of building a strong community and economy, whereas in Britain it fused into a language of liberal self and citizenship. Whether the consumer 'took off' as a social identity, however, was ultimately not determined by academic traditions but by the ability of political languages to provide a synapse between these new analytical categories and social movements and popular politics.[34] It was in Victorian Britain that the 'consumer' first developed this synaptic configuration between political mobilization and a category of knowledge and rights. The chapter by Frank Trentmann and Vanessa Taylor uses metropolitan London as a microcosm to chart the increasingly powerful mobilization of 'the consumer' by users and providers and its widening social frame of reference. In water politics there was a lively flux between the worlds of economic knowledge and law and the mobilization of taxpayers and water users on the streets and in local government. The case of 'water consumers' thus illustrates some of the interconnected conduits involved in the spread of the 'consumer' as a category of identity and ascription. Significantly, consumer consciousness and mobilization developed here in a sphere of private monopoly where payment had nothing to do with either market price or the amount consumed. The advancing contestation and sensibility of the 'water consumer' further illustrate the danger of a stark separation between basic needs and luxuries or ordinary and conspicuous consumption that has informed much of the literature. For water users became consumers precisely on a slippery and evolving path on which the very distinction between what is a necessity and what a luxury was hard fought.

Social accountability, the rights of citizens and political representation were vital ingredients in the mobilization of the consumer in the British metropole. If the consumer was operationalized by these political languages, it was never solely a dependent function or rhetorical device. Contests over needs in the increasingly dynamic arena of radical politics of the 1870s–1890s gradually broadened the social constituency of the consumer from the tax-paying (mainly male) property-owning citizen across class and gender, as users from different classes came together in consumer defence leagues to find their common interest as 'consumers'.

Here was one liberal-radical trajectory, but it would be simplistic to place this story within a linear master narrative linking it to the more recent consumerist pressure groups and legal advice centres associated with Ralph Nader and others. Different traditions and social milieus made for different national and regional stories of the consumer. A universal language of the consumer as private end-user was a particular historical achievement first emerging in liberal, pluralistic societies. The antithetical position of consumer versus producer, so powerful in Anglo-American discourse, required the exclusion of commercial users (gas, coal, water) from that category and a language of the public interest that created an equivalence between private 'consumers' irrespective of their specific position in the economy: wage earners and farmers were consumers as much as middle-class men and women living on a private income. Note the contrast with France and Germany. Here traditions of production, land and corporatism disadvantaged an autonomous language of the consumer as representing the public interest.[35] In Germany consumers were easily portrayed as a sectional interest that could exclude other socio-economic identities (workers and housewives). Conversely, it often were industrial interests which appropriated the language of 'consumers' in battles over corporatist representation, for example heavy industries in Weimar.[36] For the men and women in the consumers' league in early twentieth-century France, consumers were by definition non-producers, as Marie Chessel emphasizes in her chapter. The league sought to educate the middle class as consumers to help workers as producers. Although part of a transatlantic network of consumers' and buyers' leagues that had sprung up in the late nineteenth century, the *Ligue Sociale d'Acheteurs* reflected its distinct cultural roots. While open to non-Catholics, the league evolved from within a milieu of social Catholicism that limited the chance of a broader synapse with other competing moral and social reform movements, such as Gide's cooperatives or secular feminism. Much more than a material revolt of the end-user, in their critique of fashion and the department store women and men in the league developed a vocabulary of the ethical consumer, an emancipatory language that offered both an entry into the public sphere and a way of reconnecting the interests of consumers and producers.

These cases point to the diverse social and ideological roots of the emerging consumer. Rather than thinking in terms of a moment of birth or the progressive unfolding of a universal category, it may be useful to think in terms of the multiple and changing *boundaries* of the consumer. The consumer was *bounded* in terms of ideas, social composition, representation and, significantly, by consuming practices. Differently bounded consumers existed alongside each other – making not only for different formations in different countries, but also separating consumers from other users within countries. The bounded character of consumers is worth emphasizing, since it was vital not only for stabilizing certain meanings but also for delimiting the material and political spheres that were legitimate arenas for consumers. Water consumers or consumer leagues may appeal to a public interest, but before the early and mid-twentieth century there was no shared reference point to 'consumers' connecting diverse consumption practices ranging from utilities and shopping to health care or cultural consumption. There could be connections and exchange between differently bounded consumers, such as between progressive politics and liberal economics concerning monopoly and public goods. But, equally, there were constellations where diverse treatments of the consumer coexisted in virtual silence, as marginalist economics did alongside the moral debate about the department store. Demands for social accountability or political inclusion were thus framed with specific references to specific sites of consumption, not to universal demands for consumer rights or appeals to a generic consumer society. Attention to the simultaneity of differently bounded consumers and users may usefully complement the emphasis in some recent scholarship on the different genealogies informing particular practices and objects of consumption at any given moment.[37]

The bounded nature of consumers was not, of course, fixed or static. But the coexistence of parallel spheres of consumer knowledge and identity means that accounts of the formation of the consumer need to begin from a different starting point than the famous *Making of the English Working Class*.[38] As for E.P. Thompson's working class, the making of the consumer owes as much to agency as to conditioning. Unlike Thompson's story, however, the history of the consumer is neither linear nor unified. There is no single unifying experience or key episode comparable to Thompson's formative 1832. Nor would it be sensible to adopt a view of agency that rested on more or less pure experiences of material reality. Languages of the consumer (like other core identities) are situated in beliefs and practices. In different contexts these can be mobilized in different ways, which, in turn, influence perceptions of the consumer. The inflation of the vocabulary of the consumer has often given it a quasi-natural existence, as when people say 'everyone is a consumer'. Such naturalizing discourse tends to obscure that even in today's 'consumer culture' boundaries and differentiation persist. The export of the language of the consumer to such diverse areas as policing, health care and social services – a key feature of New Labour in Britain – is a political project seeking to complete a long-term trend of loosening boundaries. Political rhetoric and policy initiatives, however, are not the same as social identities and practices.[39] Not only do people continue to have selective notions of themselves as consumers in certain social and commercial contexts (but not others), many informal spheres of social life (such as the home) are frequently bracketed in market-oriented approaches to consumption.

The fundamental change in the twentieth century, therefore, is not that the consumer has become a boundless figure, but rather that the expanding language of the consumer has managed to absorb diverse practices of consumption as commensurate activities (while excluding others). This has involved the unification of consumers initially differentiated and bounded by particular practices – water consumer, the consumer as shopper, the consumer of art. What lay behind this expansive, symmetrical reconfiguration? One conventional answer, encouraged by the initial preoccupation in consumption studies with department stores and marketing, has been to associate this dynamic with the material and symbolic expansion of shopping in people's lives and the dream worlds and desires created around it. Advertisers and psychologists influencing marketing clearly assisted the growing dissemination of the consumer.[40] But on their own they do not offer a satisfactory explanation. Eighteenth-century England was full of shops and had a high degree of commodification without 'the consumer' being a master category. Early twentieth-century China, meanwhile, produced a massive advertising campaign for national products, but the appeal was to 'patriots' and 'citizens', not consumers.[41] Even in continental European societies

good re compare !

it was far from clear on the eve of World War I whether the consumer would be able to assume the more universal persona that was emerging in Britain and the United States. Nationalist parties and corporatist groups portrayed consumers as a sectional interest, while the young advertising profession was fighting an uphill struggle to overcome public scepticism and derision; advertising campaigns directed at 'the consumer' in the inter-war years were partly a legitimating strategy of a young profession to present itself as public servant.[42]

In addition to the commercial sector, there are two relatively neglected agencies that deserve greater recognition for their role in establishing the consumer as a more unifying, universal figure: the state and law. In Europe and America it was war and the constraints that came with it that mobilized the consumer as a social actor and object of state policy. More than choice, affluence and shopping arcades, it was the need to rationalize scarce resources in war-time or to boost demand to overcome economic depression that made states identify consumers as a core target of public policy. Wartime consumer committees provided an umbrella organization for the previously disparate social movements concerned with consumption. States directly promoted consumer action and sensibility by encouraging local bodies of consumers to act as the eyes and ears of state pricing policy, reporting on profiteers and unfair practices in wartime or in the United States during the New Deal.[43] In 1930s Germany, it was the National Socialist state that reinforced a concern with the consumer – not as price-oriented shopper but as an organic member of the racial community, whose consumption preferences and practices needed to be reformed for the sake of the *Volk*. Similarly, in socialist East Germany, consumers emerged not only as the result of a bottom-up process of frustrated individuals but also as a top-down process through state-sponsored consumption programmes.[44] In Japan, after World War II, organized consumers pictured an organic solidarity of producer, consumer and national interests.[45]

If states, then, were as important in popularizing the consumer as commerce and social mobilization from below, the expanding ambition and attractiveness of this new category also created dilemmas for public policy and institutions. The universal, mobile persona of the consumer was not easily grafted on to nation-states, with their respective legal traditions and territorially bounded notions of citizenship. Legal regimes with notions of universal civic rights that presumed the social homogeneity of citizens had no place for special rights for particular groups of its members – nor much for the shared boundary-crossing rights of some general consumer. How the consumer moved from being a problematic and marginal figure to a key category and structuring ideal in European law is the theme of Michelle Everson's chapter. Several general implications emerge. Fields of consumer knowledge do not always converge but can compete or coexist in a functional division of labour. The 'sovereign consumer' in economics initially discouraged a legal recognition of the consumer; instead it privileged aggregate demand and the market as remedies for consumption problems. The eventual construction of the consumer in law (as initially in economics) has resulted from competing visions – suggesting that the formation of the consumer is an ongoing, dynamic process rather than an effect, or past accomplishment. Most significantly, the appropriation of the consumer by law must be located within internal processes of knowledge formation and institutional self-justification. The 'citizen consumer' was tied to internal debates about the social justice function of law. For the European Court of Justice the consumer served as an instrument of securing greater legitimacy for European law. The accelerating privatization of the consumer as a 'market-citizen-consumer' has been part of a supra-national institution's attempt to transcend the nation-state with its territorially rooted law of citizenship.

Recognition of the role of public agencies and forms of knowledge offers an interesting challenge to more linear accounts of consumerism that see a long-term shift either from public spirit to self-centred materialism, or from a defence of the weak to consumer self-responsibility. These narratives may say more about the ongoing and often moralistic concerns of (primarily Anglo-American) scholarship than about the complexity of consumers in the modern period. Much of the current public debate about the civic and ethical dimensions of consumption has posited itself against an ahistorical materialist narrative. Neat clusters of commerce, market and self-regarding individualism, on the one hand and citizenship, public and other-regarding actions, on the other, are, however, problematic. Nineteenth-century appeals to 'conscientious' consumers encouraged individuals to take greater responsibility for their own actions. In 1930s America, choice was defended by some consumer groups and thinkers on moral and public grounds for simultaneously refining people's sense of personal values and leading to higher notions of needs and regard for the community, a position that has some affinities with recent attempts to retrieve alternative and ordinary ethics of consumption.[46] Conversely, social and global justice are dominant concerns for many consumer organizations today. A simple linear transfer model, from citizenship to commerce and from other-regarding to self-regarding actions, altogether ignores the diverse 'collective' forms that an interest in the consumer has taken in the past – from totalitarian policies to liberal radicalism, progressivism to socialism. It also distracts from the ongoing contestation of the 'citizen consumer' in different local, national and supranational arenas of public policy, commercial business and knowledge. In response to public controversies over GM technologies, for example, market researchers and firms like Unilever, in dialogue with NGOs, turned to the 'citizen consumer' as a way of understanding the complex relationships between the civic and ethical values and market preferences of their customers.[47] If liberalization and privatization have extended the scope of the commercial domain in social life, they have been met by a revitalized discourse about consumers' human rights and cosmopolitan citizenship and the emergence of new opportunities for social protest and civic identities at the level of local and global civil society.[48]

Dynamic Relations

Consumers do not emerge on their own but in dynamic relations with other social actors and agencies. These relationships involve uneven access to expertise, authority and power. A psychological focus on individual preferences and motivations or a cultural emphasis on the meaning of objects needs to be broadened to include these dynamic relations in order to understand the changing status and associations of the consumer. The consumer, after all, acquires its normative and analytical power as a collective, shared category that lies beyond explanations at the individual level. Customers and consumer representatives compete with retailers and other experts addressing the consumer over the precise nature and identity of that person. In addition, the consumer can be part of a politics of reputation where different experts are competing for authority and status. The changing relations between consumers and experts is therefore a central strand running through this book.

Research on shopping in Britain in the 1990s highlighted the distinct national, indeed regional, styles of approaching customers.[49] We know little, however, about how these cultures develop. The chapters by Uwe Spiekermann and Jos Gamble contribute to an understanding of these dynamic relations and their significance in shaping the characteristics of consumers in different cultural and economic settings over time. In Germany, in the course of the twentieth century, the changing appeal and characteristics of the consumer constituted part of a transformation of retailing, which itself was conditioned by fundamental changes in political economy and systems of provision in times of war and peace, totalitarianism and liberal democracy. The growing recognition that 'the consumer is king' from the late nineteenth century onwards was in part a step by smaller retailers to reassert their cultural and economic authority vis-à-vis more concentrated department stores and alternative retail networks, like the cooperatives. The retailer, in this discourse, had the necessary expertise to educate shoppers, elevating their tastes and guaranteeing better purchases. 'Personal' relationships were an essential feature in this commercial encounter – an additional dimension of the 'civilizing' project of cultivating consumers noted previously. Emphasis on the personal, more cultured relationship between consumer and retailer was not just a matter of the shop floor, however. It also served larger projects. The 'personal' element in retailer–consumer relations was tied to a defence of German *Kultur* in the battle against 'cheap', materialist American *Zivilisation* in the 1920s, while the Nazis used independent middle-sized retailers as agents to direct and control consumption behaviour for their project of strengthening a racial community. With advancing retail concentration in the second half of the twentieth century, it has become tempting to feel nostalgic about the loss of the 'personal' encounter in shopping. Twentieth-century Germany points to the elements of power and constraint that underwrote this personalized setting. Far from being natural or traditional, the culture of personalized relationships was buttressed by corporate politics and state intervention. For consumers, it was the absence of choice that put a premium on personal relations with local retailers, in times of war and scarcity but also during the inter-war years when the price of many goods remained fixed or regulated.

The independent retailer as expert would be joined and challenged by a host of other experts favouring a more abstract and aggregate approach to the consumer: the centres for consumer and demand research that sprang up on both sides of the Atlantic, including in socialist countries, in the 1930s–1960s. Market research and department stores began to replace the generalizable, uniform consumer with segmented consumer types. Yet these trends in aggregate research and retail concentration should not distract from the continuing significance of cultures of personal relationships. Jos Gamble's contribution is here significant, for it retrieves the ongoing personal dimensions at work in a concentrated and rationalized part of the retail sector: multinational corporations selling to Chinese consumers. More than a transfer of money, the point of purchase is here situated in a broad context of management culture, local knowledge regimes and cultural values. The high expectations placed on customer service result from the interaction of two spheres: the global export of consumer-oriented marketing and training models and local cultures of trust and reciprocal obligations. A focus on interactions provides a useful counter to more instrumentalist analyses in which identities are read off goods or representations. The global language of the 'consumer is king' is modulated by a variety of local cultural norms and understandings, ranging in the Chinese context from the picture of the consumer as a divine figure or family member to the treatment of the consumer as a child or blank sheet. As Gamble's analysis of shopping as a microcosm of cultural relations shows, Chinese consumers are co-producers rather than passive victims of this arrangement. This approach has productive implications for larger narratives in the English-speaking world that have portrayed the consumer as the 'effect' of advanced liberalism activating a novel sense of self-reliance and self-management. In contrast, the case of department stores in China highlights the relational dynamics involved in shaping the consumer. It also points to the contribution of established cultural regimes and values (trust, obligation, family) in shaping the consumer in contemporary societies.

Retailers and department stores have dominated the pages of consumption studies concerned with shopping, but they were not the only experts in pursuit of the consumer. The role of lawyers and social reform movements has already been noted. Scientists and educators shaped the consumer too. Recent public anxieties about GM food have, in part, resulted from a widening credibility deficit of science as authority. Erika Rappaport's discussion of tea in the Victorian Empire offers a provocative counterpoint to the contemporary talk of risk and anxiety. For it was chemists, together with merchants pressing for more standardized and packaged mass marketing, who simultaneously reassured Victorian consumers and shaped anxieties about the physiological and cultural contamination from impure, 'poisoned' Chinese tea. Chemical analysis and advertising offered representations and narratives of production, consumption and digestion that literally fleshed out the body of the consumer in relation to distant, unknown Chinese producers.

The relations between experts and consumers are also dynamic in remoulding the cultural qualities attached to the consumer in discourse and material practices. The changing social boundedness of the consumer involved an ongoing regendering, as well as a broadening across class and income. This volume contributes to a rethinking of the language of separate spheres that dominated an early preoccupation with the consumer as female shopper in contrast to the male citizen and producer.[50] The early political and cultural formation of the consumer suggests a gendering of the consumer that cut across public and private spheres. This involved male, property-owning taxpayers or small traders and producers who spoke as consumers on behalf of their families (the private sphere) and to advance their own claims as citizens (the public sphere). The tension between 'rational' and 'irrational' or impulsive consumers mapped itself out in different gendered ways in different spheres of consumption, such as water or the department store.[51] In inter-war Britain and America, advertisers targeted 'Mr Citizen Consumer' and 'Andy Consumer' as well as female shoppers; audience surveys used by American corporations in the 1930s found that men were as distracted and impulsive as women.[52] In her chapter on tea, Rappaport offers some clues to the dynamics behind such regendering, highlighting the interface between expert representations of the body and nation and the physical qualities and handling of goods. In advertising in the 1870s the growing contrast between an 'impure' foreign product (loose Chinese tea) and the purity of the British nation simultaneously advanced the claims of the new mass retailer and merchant as protector of the domestic sphere: perceptions of the commodity became merged with ideals of female purity.

Rappaport's focus on the battle over the body of the consumer is complemented by Steve Kline's focus on the battle over the mind of the child as consumer. The role of time and ageing across the life cycle of consumers has received less attention than gender.[53] Children are a paradigmatic case for our understanding of consumers as subjects, for they raise the very question of how individuals become socialized as consumers, their knowledge and reflexivity and how much individuals can be trusted to exercise choice safely and responsibly. As Kline shows, current debates about children's competence and literacy as consumers and their implications for commercial freedom or public regulation, are but the latest chapter in a dialectic between rival models of paternalism and pluralism that came to the fore in the Enlightenment. What has changed in the last century is the increasing density of the mediated marketplace, the formation of consumer sensibilities amongst ever younger age groups and the growing prominence of educators, popular psychologists and marketing experts speaking on behalf of children as new consuming subjects.

The dynamic relations between consumers and experts draw attention to the diversity of knowledge practices. Traditions of the consumer are not established and do not evolve unless they are developed through knowledge in practice. Attention to the internal generation of knowledge in fields like economics and law thus needs to be complemented with a discussion of the reception and employment of *knowledge in practice*, that is the diffusion, reception, employment and manipulation of knowledge. There has been considerable interest in the influence of psychology and economics on consumer research and marketing,[54] but we know far less about other types and conduits of consumer knowledge. These include the knowledge in use by retailers and providers – such as notions of how best to address consumers – the aggregate statistical information guiding state policy, the dissemination of home economics and consumer education, the working knowledge of regulatory agencies, surveys used by firms and consumer movements, consumer complaints procedures and consumers' own acquisition and handling of knowledge of goods, services, choices, rights and risks.

Several themes and questions concerning the construction, flow and reception of knowledge emerge. In European and international law, for example, liberal knowledge of a market-based consumer became attractive not simply because of its status within economics but because it served an institutional project of reforming domestic regulation. Similarly, organizations turned to the consumer in the post-Fordist climate of the 1980s–1990s as a vehicle for organizational restructuring and adjusting to more differentiated demand.[55] It may be useful to think about the changing ideological and institutional use value of particularly bounded forms of the consumer in relation to the interest and power of institutions and movements to define what counts as the consumer interest.

Applied knowledge influences the authority and social status of social movements and agencies speaking on behalf of consumers, such as through the use of social surveys, authoritative research, legal advice, or testing information. Certain kinds of knowledge can have a stabilizing effect on certain forms of the bounded consumer, while posing an obstacle for other configurations. Gender and generational categories of marketing and research are one example. Social research and public policy constitute another; Norwegian consumer policy in the 1960s, for example, distinguished between 'producer consumers' and 'mere consumers'.[56] We still know relatively little about the effect of changing communication systems (such as the Internet) on the behavioural and emotional dynamics between customer and corporation and between consumers and providers, especially in areas where new information systems transform social relationships, such as in relationship marketing, or represent a challenge to a profession's established claim of having a monopoly on knowledge, as in healthcare.[57]

Finally, we should recognize that the landscape of different knowledge regimes competing for the consumer and the balance of power between knowledge-holders are changing in the modern period. Compared with the nineteenth century, when knowledge of the consumer was primarily the terrain of social movements and retailers, today consumer advocacy groups are only one player in a crowded field of better resourced and staffed consumer experts in corporations, marketing companies, academia, regulatory agencies and the state.[58] A much greater plurality of knowledges has evolved, but this has also meant that those organizing themselves as consumers have become a voice less easily or clearly heard than previously.

Flow between Systems

The question of how the formation of the consumer relates to other knowledge regimes speaks directly to the long-standing debate about the implications of an expanding consumer identity for public life in general and political culture in particular. Distrust of the new persona, the consumer, was one of the few things uniting religious and intellectual elites, conservatives, communitarians and communists in their fear of 'mass consumption', a trend with roots in the nineteenth century that gathered momentum in the mid-twentieth century. Suspicion of the consumer arose partly from a moralistic distrust of the ability of 'the masses' to handle desire and material pleasures, but it has also drawn on strands of thinking about 'modernity' in terms of the advancing differentiation, distance and rivalry between social systems, or what Frank Mort calls 'competing domains' in his chapter. In this view, the expansion of one system involves the shrinkage of another, or the advancing differentiation of the economy as a separate 'autopoietic' system endangers other social systems.[59] An expanding market culture would result in the commodification of everything, swallowing up civic culture and consumerizing politics.[60] It is not possible here to do justice to the theoretical subtleties of different intellectual projects favouring this general bias, nor their different genealogies. But this short characterization does emphasize a widely shared zero-sum approach to the consumer: the more consumer, the less citizen. Interestingly, one prominent tradition in this mould that is experiencing a recent revival (communitarianism) has its roots in early modern republicanism, which similarly feared that commercial culture would erode civic communities by splitting an active citizenry into separate actors and exclusive identities: the merchant, the soldier, the administrator and so forth. Whatever its intellectual or normative attraction, this picture of a differentiation of identities and systems does not sit easily with the dramatic expansion and energy of political culture in commercial and industrial societies in the modern period. As with eighteenth and nineteenth-century commerce, so with twentieth-century consumption: rather than presuming a zero-sum exchange between consumer and citizen and locating each in separate systems of commerce and politics, it is useful to ask about the flow of knowledge between these systems, the interaction and overlap between ideas and practices of consumption and citizenship and the multiple forms of identities arising therefrom.

This volume points to several ways of remapping the consumer that challenges a narrative of advancing consumerist differentiation. One, already discussed, is to loosen the consumer from a tight mooring in the commercial domain and to recognize that differently bounded consumers have also emerged in civil society and state. Second, it is argued that a less market-oriented focus on individual consumer preferences may restore a sense of the connections that remain in many societies today between consumption and production and between consumption, community and politics, combining self-regarding with other-regarding mentalities and individualist with civic attitudes. James Carrier's discussion of how anthropologists have viewed consumers is instructive here. Critical of a dominant focus on the individual as chooser, Carrier lays out alternative frames of analysis that situate consumers in webs of social relations, political economy and cultural developments, reconnecting consumption to income flows, systems of labour, temporal rhythms and the production of value in tourism and culture industries. Ben Fine starts with the commodity rather than with social groups. But his reconsideration of commodity fetishism also leads him to position the consumer in material and cultural systems of provision that reintegrate production, distribution and marketing. This reframing of the consumer highlights the workings of two types of external constraints – the limits imposed by consumers' position in the economy, class or clan, but also the effects of outside consumers' choices and desires on internal social relations, such as in the case of marketing carnival or anticipating the desire of ecotourists discussed by Carrier.

These approaches embedding consumers in material and cultural systems are complemented by perspectives on the flow of knowledge and social action between systems. Most often commercial culture and political culture have been treated either as separate spheres or in a functional, unilateral relationship, where consumerist knowledge and practices, such as marketing and consumer research, invade political culture (political marketing, opinion polling, focus groups), replacing democratic practices and civic sensibilities with those of commercial culture. Recent research on the 'Americanization' of post-war Europe has begun to complicate this story, suggesting a much more contingent and interactive process, with resistance to political marketing and the relative autonomy of political culture in some countries (France) alongside more enthusiastic uptake in others (Germany).[61] The chapters by Frank Mort and Ina Merkel take us into the *porous* nature of commercial and political spheres in contemporary societies, highlighting the multiple flows between them at the level of both knowledge and social action.

Placing American and British debates about civic culture and consumer culture in the 1950s and 1960s alongside each other, Mort unravels the dynamic inter-actions between the evolving knowledge and discourse about political participation and consumer behaviour. Again, his discussion highlights the contribution of hybrid and eclectic forms of knowledge to the formation of the consumer. The social survey tradition, in particular, provided an important channel linking social action, political analysis and commercial consumer research. Instead of a one-directional flow from commercial knowledge to political knowledge, Mort reveals the reciprocal exchange of information and personnel between these domains, as experts like Lazarsfeld and Abrams moved back and forth between commercial projects and political analysis on both sides of the Atlantic and across it. The mapping of consumer behaviour in this transatlantic project did much to broaden the conception of political culture, not least by moving away from a view of culture as a sphere distinct from politics. Far from being a vehicle of consumerist individualism, to Abrams and Labour party reformers the export of methods like attitudinal research and polling to the political process was part of a social democratic project envisaging a symbiotic relationship between consumer choice and citizenship, private and public sector provision.

The significance of the ongoing reciprocal, interactive relationship between consumption and citizenship becomes even more apparent once we look beyond those established liberal market societies, like the United States and Great Britain, which have been the home of intellectual traditions presenting a paternalistic contrast between noble civic life and selfish or vulgar mass consumerism. It would be difficult not to recognize, for example, the emancipatory and politicizing energy unleashed by the official discourse and recognition of consumer rights in communist China in the 1990s, a reform process that may initially have had an economic rationale but has quickly generated new political sensibilities and demands of citizen consumers, not least in housing and community politics.[62] The political mobilization of commodities is also pronounced in transition economies and those areas within leading capitalist societies undergoing rapid processes of economic and cultural transvaluation and marginalization. East Germany since the collapse of socialism in 1989 is a fertile field for considering the changing meanings and arrangements of commodity culture, collective identity and political subjectivity, as Ina Merkel shows in her chapter. Here is not only a story of the biography of things. Goods from the socialist past, revalued, reappropriated and rebranded, serve as resources of social solidarity and collective memory for East Germans in a battle of cultural and political recognition directed at both the different value system of the more dominant neighbour, West Germany and the rapid process of deindustrialization. More than a cultural process, the revalorization of old brands and commodities and the commercial staging of *Ostalgie* also amounts to a political repositioning of East Germans vis-à-vis their own political past. The focus on consumption in this collective reliving and rewriting of the past is important here. Representing themselves as consumers and rehearsing conditions and practices of consumption under socialism are partly about legitimating a past experienced as an alternative to 'affluent' consumption in the West – and thus about reclaiming the value system attached to alternative systems of provision, such as gifting, cooperation and solidarity. It also offers a civic language of consumption where material culture becomes an arena of quasi-political resistance, distracting from more overt concerns of political guilt and complicity in an oppressive regime: by highlighting their role as consumers in this collective rewriting of the past, East Germans establish their distance from the socialist regime and can even claim an active position in its erosion from within.

What do these interactions between political culture and consumer behaviour mean for the relationship between consumer and citizen? One answer, spelled out by Ben Fine in this volume, is to emphasize the disintegrating forces cutting across consumers. Consumers here appear situated in different material and cultural systems of provision as well as differing in class, gender, race, income and so forth. Consumer issues in this view are likely to become something else in the process of being politicized, as they are pursued along the chain of provision to point to environmental and labour conditions, such as the role of child labour in the manufacture of consumer goods. Clearly there is something to this process of diffusion, as the proliferation of consumer advocacy groups with distinct concerns testifies. A different answer, that favoured by generations of nationalist, conservative, communist or communitarian critics of the consumer, would stress the diffuse and thin identity of the consumer and contrast it with richer, all-encompassing organic identities that tie individuals to collective projects.

There are other ways of approaching this question of diffuseness, however. For one, this volume draws attention to integrative processes and traditions that have enabled consumers or their surrogates to overcome the disintegrative tendencies and develop shared notions of ethics, citizenship and social solidarity. But the diverse and pluralistic formations of the consumer also suggest a more positive political interpretation of this problem of diffuseness. The consumer may be found wanting when it comes to a comparison with the thick, rooted and more ambitious singular claims of other identities. At the same time, it would be historically unwise to imagine a golden age of civic life subsequently eroded by fickle or self-centred consumers. The consumer may be a relatively thin, flexible or diffuse identity, but it is useful to recall that thicker identities have included not only the republican citizen but also more totalizing and brutal projects of nationalism, fascism and communism. An expanding if diffuse and bounded conception of consumers may be a favourable condition for a pluralistic politics recognizing diversity and toleration. The frequent identification of the recent revival of the consumer in public discourse and policy with neoliberalism has tended to obscure the affinities between consumers and civil society. It may be no coincidence that the renaissance of civil society in the last few decades and the growing awareness and recognition of consumers have happened at the same time.

Notes

1. Patrick Barrington, 'I Want to Be a Consumer', *Punch*, 25 April 1934, p. 467.
2. The corpus of books and articles now runs into several thousands. Useful points of entry include D. Miller (ed.) *Acknowledging Consumption: A Review of*

New Studies (London, 1995); J.B. Schor and D.B. Holt (eds), *The Consumer Society Reader* (New York, 2000); A. Appadurai (ed.) *The Social Life of Things: Commodities in Cultural Perspective* (Cambridge, 1986). For a bibliography: www.consume.bbk.ac.uk/worddocuments/consumption20%biblio.doc

3. C. Lasch, *The Culture of Narcissism* (New York, 1978), p. 72.

4. See the green paper by the Secretary of State for Social Security (Frank Field), *New Ambitions for Our Country: A New Contract for Welfare*, Cm 3805 (London, 1998), p. 16.

5. L.A. Reisch, 'Principles and Visions of a New Consumer Policy', *Journal of Consumer Policy*, 27 (2004), pp. 1–42; the German Federal Ministry of Agriculture has been renamed the Federal Ministry of Consumer Protection, Food and Agriculture.

6. *The Guardian*, 8 January 2003, p. 11.

7. M.E. Rider and C.J. Makela, 'A Comparative Analysis of Patients' Rights: An International Perspective', *International Journal of Consumer Studies*, 27(4) (2003), pp. 302–15.

8. The OECD Environment Directorate views 'consumers ... as *co-actors* who interact, shape and are shaped by the way in which systems of production are designed' Environment Policy Committee, Working Party on National Environmental Policy, 'Household Energy and Water Consumption and Waste Generation' (2002), p. 6, emphasis in original. Pamela W.S. Chan, president of CI, at the 2nd annual assembly of NGO consumer associations (1999) on the centrality of a '"citizen consumer movement" [promoting] a fair and just society'; www.europa.eu/int/comm/dgs/health_consumer/events/event17s1_en.html. The British communications regulator Ofcom stressed its role in providing 'neutral and timely information for citizen-consumers'; 'Development of 118 directory enquiries market', www.ofcom.org.uk/media_office/latest_news; 18 June 2004.

9. Niall FitzGerald (Unilever) in the brochure 'The Unilever Series: Olafur Eliasson' accompanying the Tate Modern exhibition, London, 16 Oct. 2003–21 March 2004.

10. R.W. Belk, 'The Human Consequences of Consumer Culture' in K.M. Ekström and H. Brembeck (eds), *Elusive Consumption* (Oxford, 2004), p. 70. See also the contributions in Miller, *Acknowledging Consumption*. Cf. the critique of the overuse of the consumer in Y. Gabriel and T. Lang, *The Unmanageable Consumer: Contemporary Consumption and Its Fragmentations* (London, 1995).

11. James Carrier, p. 274 below.

12. S.K. Vogel, 'When Interests Are Not Preferences: The Cautionary Tale of Japanese Consumers', *Comparative Politics* (January 1999), pp. 187–207; D. Vogel and M. Nadel, 'Who Is a Consumer? An Analysis of the Politics of Consumer Conflict', *American Politics Quarterly*, 5(1) (1977), pp. 27–56; P.L.

Maclachlan, *Consumer Politics in Postwar Japan: The Institutional Boundaries of Citizen Activism* (New York, 2002). For a corrective, see P. Maclachlan and F. Trentmann, 'Civilising Markets: Traditions of Consumer Politics in Twentieth-Century Britain, Japan, and the United States' in M. Bevir and F. Trentmann (eds), *Markets in Historical Contexts: Ideas and Politics in the Modern World* (Cambridge, 2004), pp. 170–201.

13. M. Featherstone, *Consumer Culture and Postmodernism* (London, 1991).
14. A. Giddens, *Modernity and Self-Identity* (Cambridge, 1991).
15. N. Rose, *Powers of Freedom: Reframing Political Thought* (Cambridge, 1999), pp. 164 ff.
16. Noteworthy exceptions include R. Sassatelli, *Consumo, Cultura e Società* (Bologna, 2004); C. Campbell, *The Romantic Ethic and the Spirit of Modern Consumerism* (Oxford, 1987).
17. See D. Slater, *Consumer Culture and Modernity* (Cambridge, 1997).
18. D. Hebdige, *Subculture, the Meaning of Style* (London, 1979); F. Mort, *Cultures of Consumption: Masculinities and Social Space in Late Twentieth-Century Britain* (London, 1996); Celia Lury, *Consumer Culture* (Oxford, 1997).
19. Note the frequent reference to President Kennedy's 1962 speech on consumer rights as a historical signpost, even in innovative approaches seeking to expand the analysis of markets to give greater attention to informal, domestic spheres of consumption, e.g. Reisch, 'Principles and Visions of a New Consumer Policy'.
20. As John Brewer has self-critically noted, historians themselves originally succumbed to this temptation. The influential *Birth of Consumer Society* (London, 1982) by N. McKendrick, J.H. Plumb and Brewer himself mirrored the concerns of the public and academic debates of the 1950s–1970s on the creation of false needs and the power of marketing; 'The Error of Our Ways: Historians and the Birth of Consumer Society', Cultures of Consumption Working Paper no. 12, http://www.consume.bbk.ac.uk/publications.html. See also B. Fine, *The World of Consumption* (London, 2002; 2nd edn), esp. ch. 8.
21. Appadurai, *Social Life of Things*; T. Burke, *Lifebuoy Men, Lux Women: Commodification, Consumption, and Cleanliness in Modern Zimbabwe* (London, 1996); D. Howes (ed.), *Cross-Cultural Consumption: Global Markets, Local Realities* (London, 1996). H. Berghoff (ed.), *Konsumpolitik: Die Regulierung des privaten Verbrauchs im 20. Jahrhundert* (Göttingen, 1999); C. Helstosky, *Garlic and Oil: Food and Politics in Italy* (Oxford and New York, 2004); V. Buchli, *An Archaeology of Socialism* (Oxford and New York, 1999); Ina Merkel, *Utopie und Bedürfnis: Die Geschichte der Konsumkultur in der DDR* (Cologne: Böhlau, 1999).
22. J. Gronow and A. Warde (eds), *Ordinary Consumption* (London, 2001); E. Shove, *Comfort, Cleanliness and Convenience* (Oxford, 2003).
23. Eurostat, *Consumers in Europe* (Luxembourg, 2001), Table 1.14; this number does not include household expenditure on furnishings and household

equipment (another 6%); clothing, by comparison, is on average 6%, food 13%, recreation and culture 10%.

24. J. Carrier, *Gifts and Commodities* (London, 1995).

25. In addition to the below, see esp. M. Daunton and M. Hilton (eds), *The Politics of Consumption: Material Culture and Citizenship in Europe and America* (Oxford, 2001); V. de Grazia and E. Furlough (eds), *The Sex of Things: Gender and Consumption in Historical Perspective* (Berkeley, CA, and London, 1996); S. Strasser, C. McGovern and M. Judt (eds), *Getting and Spending: European and American Consumer Societies in the Twentieth Century* (Cambridge, 1998). Cf. the place of 'consumer society' and 'mass consumption' in H.-G. Haupt, *Konsum und Handel: Europa im 19. und 20. Jahrhundert* (Göttingen, 2002).

26. C. Walsh, 'Social Meaning and Social Space in the Shopping Galleries of Early Modern London'; J. Benson and L. Ugolini (eds), *A Nation of Shopkeepers: Five Centuries of British Retailing* (London, 2003), pp. 52–79; M. Berg, *A Nation of Shoppers: How Georgian Britain Discovered the Delights of Luxury* (Oxford, 2005).

27. For the following, see F. Trentmann, 'The Genealogy of the Modern Consumer: Meanings, Knowledge, and Synapses' in J. Brewer and F. Trentmann (eds), *Consuming Cultures, Global Perspectives* (Oxford and New York, forthcoming).

28. L. Cohen, *A Consumer's Republic: The Politics of Mass Consumption in Postwar America* (New York, 2003); F. Trentmann, 'Beyond Consumerism: New Historical Perspectives on Consumption', *Journal of Contemporary History*, 39(3) (2004), pp. 373–401; M. Hilton, *Consumerism in Twentieth-Century Britain* (Cambridge, 2003); and see the chapters by L. Cohen, M. Jacobs and F. Trentmann in Daunton and Hilton, *Politics of Consumption*. For post-1945, see now S. Kroen, 'A Political History of the Consumer', *The Historical Journal*, 47(3) (2004), pp. 709–36; I. Theien and E. Lange (eds), *Affluence and Activism: Organized Consumers in the Post-War Era* (Oslo, 2004).

29. Cit. in M. Hilton, 'The Legacy of Luxury', *Journal of Consumer Culture*, 4(1) (March 2004), p. 104.

30. D. Horowitz, *The Morality of Spending: Attitudes Towards the Consumer Society in America, 1875–1940* (Chicago, 1992); D. Horowitz, *The Anxieties of Affluence: Critiques of American Consumer Culture, 1939–1979* (Amherst, MA, 2004). Hilton, 'Legacy of Luxury'; L. Black, *The Political Culture of the Left in Affluent Britain, 1951–64: Old Labour, New Britain?* (Basingstoke, 2003).

31. L. Glickman, 'Buy for the Sake of the Slave: Abolitionism and the Origins of American Consumer Activism', *American Quarterly* 56(4) (2004), pp. 889–912; C. Sussman, *Consuming Anxieties: Consumer Protest, Gender and British Slavery, 1713–1833* (Stanford, CA, 2000); F. Trentmann, 'National Identity and Consumer Politics: Free Trade and Tariff Reform', in P.K. O'Brien and

D. Winch (eds), *The Political Economy of British Historical Experience, 1688–1914* (Oxford, 2002), pp. 215–42.

32. As Parsons realized, see Winch below, p. 41. See also H. Pearson, 'Economics and Altruism at the Fin de Siècle' in M. Daunton and F. Trentmann (eds), *Worlds of Political Economy* (Basingstoke, 2004), ch. 2; P. Swann, 'Marshall's Consumer as an Innovator' in S.C. Dow and P.E. Earl (eds), *Economic Organization and Economic Knowledge*, I (Cheltenham, 1999), pp. 98–118.

33. J.S. Mill, *Principles of Political Economy* (1848), book v, ch. XI.

34. An argument developed in Trentmann, 'Genealogy of the Consumer'.

35. See, for example, the influence of Fourierism: E. Furlough, *Consumer Cooperation in France: The Politics of Consumption 1834–1930* (Ithaca, NY, 1991).

36. A. Feiler, 'The Consumer in Economic Policy', *Social Research* 1:1/4 (1934).

37. A. Appadurai, 'Consumption, Duration, and History,' in D. Palumbo-Liu and H. Gumbrech (eds), *Streams of Cultural Capital* (Stanford, CA, 1997); and see Fine's chapter in this volume.

38. E.P. Thompson, *The Making of the English Working Class* (Harmondsworth, 1980; 1st edn 1963); cf. G. Stedman Jones, *Languages of Class* (Cambridge, 1983) and the discussion in M. Bevir and F. Trentmann (eds), *Critiques of Capital in Modern Britain and America: Transatlantic Exchanges, 1800 to the Present Day* (Basingstoke and New York, 2002), ch. 1.

39. For the diverse meanings and practices in different 'consumerist' social services, see J. Clarke, N. Smith and E. Vidler, 'Consumerism and the Reform of Public Services: Inequalities and Instabilities' in M. Powell, L. Bauld and K. Clarke (eds), *Social Policy Review* 17 (Bristol, 2005); J. Clarke, 'Constructing Citizen Consumers' in J. Newman (ed), *Remaking Governance* (forthcoming). See also J. Harris, 'State Social Work and Social Citizenship in Britain: From Clientelism to Consumerism', *British Journal of Social Work*, 29(6) (1999), pp. 915–37.

40. S. Ewen, *Captains of Consciousness* (New York, 1876).

41. K. Gerth, *China Made: Consumer Culture and the Creation of the Nation* (Cambridge, MA, 2003).

42. C. Lamberty, *Reklame in Deutschland, 1890–1914: Wahrnehmung, Professionalisierung und Kritik der Wirtschaftswerbung* (Berlin, 2001). For Britain, see Stefan Schwarzkopf's London PhD in progress on the advertising industry.

43. Robert Schloesser, 'Die Kriegsorganisation der Konsumenten', in *Genossenschaftliche Kultur*, 19/20 (1917); F. Trentmann, 'Bread, Milk and Democracy' in Daunton and Hilton, *Politics of Consumption*; M. Jacobs, '"How About Some Meat"': The Office of Price Administration, Consumption Politics, and State Building from the Bottom up, 1941–1946', *The Journal of American History*, 84(3) (1997), pp. 910–41; M. Jacobs, *Pocketbook Politics: Economic Citizenship in Twentieth-Century America* (Princeton, 2005), pp. 122–35.

44. See U. Spiekermann in this volume; K. Pence 'The Myth of a Suspended Present: Prosperity's Painful Shadow in 1950s East Germany' in P. Betts and

G. Eghigian (eds), *Pain and Prosperity: Reconsidering Twentieth-Century German History* (Stanford, 2003), pp. 137–59.

45. Maclachlan and Trentmann, 'Civilising Markets'.
46. See Trentmann, 'Genealogy of the Consumer'. C. Barnett, P. Cloke, N. Clarke and A. Malpass, 'Consuming Ethics: Articulating the Subjects and Spaces of Ethical Consumption', *Antipodea*, 37(1) (2005), pp. 23–45.
47. R. Doubleday, 'Institutionalising Non-governmental Organisation Dialogue at Unilever: Framing the Public as "consumer citizens"', *Science and Public Policy*, 31/2 (April 2004), pp. 117–26.
48. See B. Morgan, *'Emerging Global Water Welfarism'* in Brewer and Trentmann, *Consuming Cultures.*
49. D. Miller, P. Jackson, N. Thrift, B. Holbrook and M. Rowlands (eds), *Shopping, Place and Identity* (London, 1998), pp. 118ff.
50. For critical discussion, see C. Breward, *The Hidden Consumer: Masculinities, Fashion and City Life 1860–1914* (Manchester, 1999).
51. For the latter, M. Nava 'Modernity tamed?' in M. Andrews and M.M. Talbot (eds), *All the World and Her Husband: Women in Twentieth-Century Consumer Culture* (London and New York, 2000), pp. 47–64; E.D. Rappaport, *Shopping for Pleasure: Women and the Making of London's West End* (Princeton, NJ, 2000); G. Crossick and S. Jaumain (eds), *Cathedrals of Consumption: The European Department Store, 1850–1939* (Aldershot, 1999).
52. R. Marchand, *Creating the Corporate Soul: The Rise of Public Relations and Corporate Imagery in American Big Business* (Berkeley, Los Angeles and London, 1998), pp. 282f.
53. For children, see most recently the special issue of the *Journal of Consumer Culture*, 3/2 (July 2003); and the working papers at www.consume.bbk. For ageing consumers, see J. Vincent, 'Consumers, Identity and Old Age', *Education and Ageing*, 14(2) (1999), pp. 141–58, and the current research by S. Biggs, R. Leach and P. Higgs, www.consume.bbk.
54. E. Carter, *How German is She? Postwar West German Reconstruction and the Consuming Woman* (Ann Arbor, 1997), ch. 3; C. Conrad, 'Observer les consommateurs', *Le Mouvement Social*, 206 (2004), pp. 17–39. P. Miller and N. Rose, 'Mobilizing the Consumer: Assembling the Subject of Consumption', *Theory, Culture and Society*, 14(1) (1997), pp. 1–36.
55. P. du Gay and G. Salaman, 'The Cult[ure] of the Customer', *Journal of Management Studies*, 29(5) (1992), pp. 615–33
56. K. Ilmonen and E. Stø, 'Nordic Consumer Policy' in P. Sulkunen, J. Holmwood, H. Radner and G. Schulze (eds), *Constructing the New Consumer Society* (New York, 1997), p. 210.
57. J. Fitchett and P. McDonagh, 'Relationship Marketing, E-commerce and the Emancipation of the Consumer' in A. Sturdy, I. Grugulis and H. Willmott (eds), *Customer Service: Empowerment and Entrapment* (Basingstoke, 2001),

pp. 191–9; G. Hogg, A. Laing, D. Winkelman, 'The Professional Services Encounter in the Age of the Internet', *Journal of Services Marketing*, 17 (2003), pp. 476–94.

58. See, for example, the case of food, with the widening gulf of adspend and resources available to consumer advocacy groups. By 2003 the food industry's global advertising budget reached $40 billion, an amount exceeding the GDP of 70% of the world's nations, T. Lang and M. Heasman, *Food Wars: The Global Battle for Mouths, Minds and Markets* (London and Sterling, VA, 2004), p. 206.

59. See, for example, N. Luhmann, *Die Wirtschaft der Gesellschaft* (Frankfurt a.M., 1988).

60. For recent statements, see D. Marquand, *Decline of the Public* (Oxford 2004). See also P. Ginsborg, *Il tempo di cambiare: Politica e potere della vita quotidiana* (Torino, 2004). For an argument about the emanationist basis of consumerism that has colonized more and more aspects of social life, see C. Campbell, 'I Shop Therefore I Know that I Am' in Ekström and Brembeck, *Elusive Consumption*, pp. 27–44; it is of course debatable whether shopping (let alone many other consumption practices) can be reduced to this logic – see, for example, D. Miller, *The Dialectics of Shopping* (Chicago, 2001).

61. S. Kroen, 'A Political History of the Consumer'. See also de Grazia, *Sex of Things*; F. Mort, 'Paths to Mass Consumption' in P. Jackson, M. Lowe, D. Miller and F. Mort (eds), *Commerical Cultures: Economies, Practices, Spaces* (Oxford, 2000) pp. 7–13.

62. D.S. Davis (ed.), *The Consumer Revolution in Urban China* (Berkeley, CA, 2000); D. Davis, 'Chinese Homeowners as Citizen-Consumers', in Garon and Maclachlan (forthcoming).

Part I
Defining Consumers: Consumers in Economics, Law and Civil Society

–2–

The Problematic Status of the Consumer in Orthodox Economic Thought
Donald Winch

> Consumption is the sole end and purpose of all production; and the interest of the producer ought to be attended to, only so far as it may be necessary for promoting that of the consumer. The maxim is so perfectly self-evident, that it would be absurd to attempt to prove it.
>
> Adam Smith, *Wealth of Nations*[1]

I

The role of the consumer and of consumption more generally in formal economic analysis has always been a good deal more problematic than Adam Smith's best-known pronouncement on the subject might suggest. Even that statement cannot be taken entirely at face value. For if the maxim was self-evident, why did Smith still feel it necessary to devote a large part of the *Wealth of Nations* to 'a very violent attack' (his description) on those dominant styles of politico-economic thinking that identified prosperity with policies that advanced producers' interests? Smith's maxim does, nevertheless, contain an important clue to a way of thinking that appears quite regularly in the writings of orthodox economists over the next two hundred years or so. Exposing the economic costs of various types of monopoly became a *leitmotif* of post-Smithian political economy and there is a legitimate line of descent from Smith to Alfred Marshall and beyond that accords priority to the interests of unorganized consumers over the organized interests of producers. Indeed, Marshall's concept of 'consumers' surplus' was designed to make articulation of the interests of the 'silent many' a professional duty on the part of economists.[2]

Our experience of modern forms of neoliberalism mostly leads us to identify this concern with the orthodox commitment to cosmopolitan free trade and the benefits of competition in delivering the promise contained in the idea of consumer sovereignty. What modern neoliberalism does *not* prepare us for, and sometimes warns us against, is something equally closely associated with the orthodox viewpoint during the nineteenth century. Competition can only serve the consumer interest when it is a feasible and stable regime; when it is not vitiated by consumer ignorance; and when it does not conflict with collective wants that cannot be registered adequately through market signals. As answers to these problems economists have pioneered regulatory rules for private and public monopolies and proposed other forms of provision derived from the analysis of market failure and the concept of 'public goods', pure or mixed. Behind such modes of analysis and the assessments of the public interest they license, lies the belief that the consumer should not be confined to a passive role similar to that associated with mere constitutional monarchy.

Yet having rescued the consumer as a representative of the public interest that any modern economic system ought to serve, those retrospectively labelled as 'classical' political economists (Smith, Ricardo, J.S. Mill) found it difficult to agree on how important he or she was as an active presence in their scheme of things. With the gradual shift towards what, again retrospectively, became known as 'neoclassical' economics (Jevons, Marshall, Walras, Menger), it might appear that consumer demand, indeed the whole question of choice between alternative economic states or courses of action, had been accorded a more significant role. It will be apparent, however, from other chapters in this book that the consumer, as conceived by orthodox economics, functions as a polar case for many students of the culture of consumption. What they regard as the most interesting variables, the economist takes as given. The utility-maximizing neoclassical economist figures unflatteringly in Ben Fine's chapter and is one of the sources of the concept of 'contractual autonomy' and the 'myth of the individualized consumer' in Michelle Everson's treatment of legal constructions of the consumer.[3] He – it is hard to think of him as a she – also features marginally in Jos Gamble's chapter as the creator of the 'one-dimensional' and thoroughly 'de-contextualized' agent.[4]

This yields a paradoxical outcome. Economists have good claims to have been the first to rescue the consumer from a political economy of power and plenty that only had room for producers' interests; they have also pioneered ways of addressing the central question of how the living standards of the mass of society could be improved. But in the process the choosing agent seems to have achieved sovereignty at the cost of becoming an isolated rational individual whose tastes are given and whose sensitivity to change is limited to the numerical information contained in prices, incomes and estimates of the risks or uncertainties that impinge on his profit-seeking or pleasure and leisure-maximizing goals.

II

We can best consider how this state of affairs has arisen by returning to 'classical' beginnings and to how exchange values were conceived as being determined, a crucial question that remains the special preserve of economists – without which, indeed, it is hard to conceive of any science of economics. Smith's restatement of the scholastic distinction between use value and exchange value hardened in the hands of his Ricardian successors. Utility, usefulness or use value became a mere prerequisite *for* rather than a determinant *of* exchange values. For this purpose it was more important to consider the real costs involved in producing goods, whether measured in money or labour effort. Market values might fluctuate on a day-to-day basis, but under long-run competitive conditions the exchange value of goods whose supply could be augmented would conform to their costs of production. If supply rather than demand was the ultimate determinant of the majority of exchange values (leaving aside uniquely scarce goods and those produced under monopoly conditions), this provided a good reason for not attending to the minutiae of the shifting preferences of consumers between an almost infinite variety of goods and services. It was sufficient to say that markets performed an allocative function, with Ricardo, for example, believing that once the inertia associated with custom or ignorance had been overcome, they usually did so with a high degree of responsiveness to rising or falling profits and prices.

'Luxuries' might come in forms as diverse as human vanity and ingenuity could devise, but for the majority of consumers, those who on any simple utilitarian calculation constituted the public interest, it sufficed to speak collectively of the 'necessaries' and 'conveniences' that comprized the bulk of their budgets. Long and short-term price movements in the key components of such budgets, chiefly food, were central to the question of whether standards of living were rising or falling and the prices that mattered as far as economic growth and employment were concerned were the average wage rate, the prevailing rate of return on capital, and land rents.

The subordinate or passive role of the consumer was further emphasized by the status accorded to consumption in orthodox versions of the macroeconomics of growth and employment. John Stuart Mill, the figure who acted as the last original spokesman for the classical synopsis and also as the bridge to a new generation, gave the following authoritative ruling on the subject:

> we contend that Political Economy ... has nothing to do with the consumption of wealth, further than as the consideration of it is inseparable from that of production, or from that of distribution. We know not of any *laws* of the *consumption* of wealth as the subject of a distinct science: they can be no other than the laws of human enjoyment. Political economists have never treated of consumption on its own account, but always for the purpose of the enquiry into what manner different kinds of consumption affect the production and distribution of wealth.[5]

The most crucial choice facing consumers was that between 'productive' and 'unproductive' consumption, where expenditure of the former type contributed to the accumulation of material wealth and the generation of new forms of employment. It was to this distinction that Mill was referring when speaking of the manner in which 'different kinds of consumption affect the production and distribution of wealth'. Though often presented with neutral analytical intent, the contrast between the two forms of consumption could take on moral and political characteristics when classifying government expenditure alongside wasteful personal indulgence as unproductive. In brief, the position could be characterized as one in which macroeconomic imperatives, sometimes fortified by moral ones, took precedence over those microeconomic concerns that were to preoccupy a later generation of neoclassical economists.

The doctrine underpinning Mill's ruling was Say's Law of Markets, which maintained that, outside conditions of acute monetary disorder, aggregate production always generated enough income to sustain an equivalent level of aggregate consumption. The law was formulated as an answer to under-consumptionist diagnoses and remedies that had gained currency during the prolonged period of post-1815 depression. Such diagnoses were based on the idea that government expenditure, monetary reflation or some other expedient to maintain 'unproductive' spending was necessary to offset a general tendency for capital to accumulate more rapidly than could be absorbed at current levels of aggregate demand. In Mill's day it was a position associated with the names of Malthus, Chalmers and Sismondi and some of his earliest economic writings were devoted to undermining their opinions. He regarded the idea that 'the great end of legislation in matters of national wealth ... was to create consumers' as one of those 'palpable absurdities' that had been unmasked by advances in the science of political economy: '[t]he point is fundamental; any difference of opinion on it involves radically different conceptions of political economy, especially in its practical aspect'.[6] The absurdity was not palpable enough, however, to discourage the formation of a dissident under-consumptionist tradition, one version of which was to be revived by J.A. Hobson at the end of the century and given a measure of academic respectability when John Maynard Keynes mounted his own attack on Say's Law in the 1930s.

Nor did the Ricardian approach to exchange value go unchallenged in its own day. The opposed position was one that defined political economy as 'catallactics', or the science of exchanges and considered utility to be the proper measure and main determinant of exchange values. Although there were British exponents of this view, it was more generally associated with a 'French school' of utility theorists.[7] The economist whose name was attached to the orthodox macroeconomic position, Jean-Baptiste Say, appeared on this occasion within the ranks of the opposition. By stressing the role of utility as a measure of value, Say was able to be more accommodating to non-material goods or services as a source of wealth than many of Smith's British followers were inclined to be. But from the late 1840s onwards, in the eyes of those who later sought to overthrow the cost-of-production approach to exchange value, Say was to be outshone by a more popular French author, Frédéric Bastiat, for whom the slogan *libre échange* combined explanatory power with a normative defence of private property against the claims of protectionists and socialists. Bastiat's writings provided definitive answers of a natural order variety to post-1848 socialists in France – answers that were to be recycled by those who sought to resist the advancing tide of collectivism in late nineteenth-century Britain.[8]

Mill could only be dimly cognizant of this when writing his *Principles* in the 1840s, but he was aware of the catallactic interpretation of the science and the work of some of its French advocates. He thought of it as being 'too confined' to serve as a definition of the science; and it gave too prominent a place to exchange when compared with the two other main branches of political economy concerned with production and distribution. The laws of production, being based on physical laws, did not depend on exchange. Nor was exchange vital to distribution:

> Even in the present system of industrial life, in which employments are minutely sub-divided and all concerned in production depend for their remuneration on the price of a particular commodity, exchange is not the fundamental law of the distribution of the produce, no more than roads and carriages are the essential laws of motion, but merely a part of the machinery for effecting it.[9]

On this matter Mill was speaking with his own voice rather than as a disciple of Ricardo: he was underlining one of his main innovations, the distinction between the laws of production and those regulating distribution. While the former set physical limits to what could be achieved at any given state of the productive arts, the latter were 'a matter of human institution solely'. By introducing this distinction, Mill hoped to achieve two objects: first, to break what had seemed to be an indissoluble link between political economy and a particular set of competitive and capitalistic institutions; and second, to create the necessary space for empirical and speculative enquiry into those modes of distribution that would follow from different types of property relations that included experiments along cooperative lines and peasant proprietorship.

Smith's welfare criteria had made an increase in the absolute share of income going to wage earners an essential ingredient in the definition of opulence or economic growth.[10] In that sense Mill's concern with the future of the labouring classes does not mark a shift of alignment from the consumer to the producer. Mill was going further in the same direction by making *relative* improvement in the condition of these classes a welfare condition based on the standards of distributive justice that ought to be applied to their condition in future. Cooperative enterprises that curbed the conflict between capital and labour, protected under-informed working-class consumers from unscrupulous middlemen and shifted the distribution of income in favour of wage earners became one of his main hopes for the future. It was for this change of emphasis in a 'socialist' direction that Mill became a dangerous influence in the eyes of some contemporary adherents to the French school. Their suspicions were aroused when Mill took the lead in a campaign for the reform of the English system of land tenure and advocated taxation of the 'unearned increment' in rents; and when he defended the cooperative workshop experiments taking place in France after the 1848 revolution. The suspicions were amply confirmed when they learned from his posthumously published *Autobiography* that he and his wife were happy to be classed as 'decidedly under the general designation of Socialists'.[11] What Mill's socialism-of-the-future amounted to and whether it was compatible with his status as the leading exponent of orthodox political economy in Britain, was to preoccupy many of those brought up under his guidance. Short answers are still not easy to formulate, but as far as the role of the consumer is concerned it is important to note one further problematic dimension.

Those followers of the French school who were strongly committed to an approach to the theory of value via utility and were most keen to enthrone the consumer as the ultimate arbiter in economic affairs were also dedicated to the sanctity of private property and the incomes derived from it. It followed from the pre-eminent worth they attached to the individual's freedom to enter into all forms of contractual relationship that they were less inclined to tolerate the kind of interventionist measures designed to protect workers and consumers proposed by more pragmatic exponents of economic liberalism, the category defined by Mill and shared by many of his successors.

The analysis of 'natural' as opposed to 'artificial' monopoly brought the division between Mill and his anti-socialist opponents into sharp contrast. For *libre échangistes*, while 'feudal' restrictions on the commercial availability of land were to be condemned, along with the 'artificial' monopoly created by protectionist policies, the 'natural' monopoly established via exclusive property rights was more akin to fulfilment of a divine plan for making the best use of given resources. The market price or rent that could be earned from such natural monopolies was justified as payment for a valued service. It had the further advantage of setting a scarcity price that induced users of its services to tailor use to need. The products of labour, land and capital possess utility and hence value to us in meeting our needs as consumers. Wages, rent and profits were therefore the effect rather than the cause of value. Free markets provided the incentives necessary to maximize utilities at minimum cost. In doing so, they also generated a just system of rewards to the different contributing factors of production.[12] Laissez-faire, therefore, was more than a general maxim or rule of thumb to which significant exceptions could be made on empirical grounds – the position Mill adopted when surveying the necessary and optional roles of government in Book V of his *Principles*.

Mill thoroughly approved of the attack on Bastiat and the French school mounted by his closest disciple in economic matters, J.E. Cairnes, when divorcing the science of political economy from laissez-faire conclusions and the normative issues involving justice and natural right. The 'plausible optimist falsities' of Bastiat's *Harmonies économiques*, Cairnes maintained, confused the idea that *human* interests were harmonious with the statement that *class* interests were as well. Bastiat and his followers overlooked the powerful part played by 'passion, prejudice, custom, *ésprit de corps,* class interest' in human affairs, all those forces that led interested parties to confuse their interests with the public good.[13] Mill's support for Cairnes on this matter amounts to an explicit denial that the invisible hand was endowed with providential properties for harmonizing human activities. In Mill's words, there were no grounds for believing that 'the economic phenomena of society as at present constituted always arrange themselves spontaneously in the way which is most for the common good or that the interest of all classes are fundamentally the same'.[14]

What makes the conclusion derived from this minor passage of arms of greater significance is that the Mill–Cairnes position describes the basic outlook of the first generation of 'professional' or academic economists in Britain, including such manifestly post-classical authors as Jevons, Sidgwick, Marshall and Edgeworth. It also includes Walras, who had his own scores to settle with the fundamentalist forms of liberalism that dominated the academic life of economists in France.[15] In other words, the classical/neoclassical dividing line, a far more ragged affair on the historical ground than it is in textbooks, does not mark a significant division when considering attitudes towards consumer protection and state intervention more generally.[16]

Mill's brand of cooperative socialism with a hopeful evolutionary twist had to be reconciled with the arguments of his essay *On Liberty*. The kind of cooperative enterprises he favoured competed with one another as well as with other types of enterprise. In this respect Mill remained within the orthodox pro-consumer camp, anxious to protect consumers from becoming the victims of fraudulent traders and the monopolistic and oligopolistic activities of railway companies and those supplying public utilities such as gas and water.[17] Public utilities, notably roads and bridges constructed at public expense and privately financed railways with their 'natural' monopoly features and powers, were both fields in which the new tools of analysis associated with neoclassical economics first showed their paces. Indeed, the new utility theorists of the 1870s and beyond might be said to be engaged in a process of rediscovering what engineer-economists, notably Dupuit, had already established in the 1840s when proposing solutions to the problems of what prices should be charged for the use of public investments in roads and bridges. These methods added considerably to the precision with which the net benefits of public projects could be estimated, with the distinction between average and marginal costs and revenues later providing a more sophisticated way of setting the pricing rules that should be adopted by regulatory regimes. As will be clear from the chapter in this book by Frank Trentmann and Vanessa Taylor, lacking such methods of analysis and measurement did not mean that Mill was incapable of appreciating the basic issues facing the local taxpayer and the consumers of services provided by privately controlled public utilities.[4] But he was cut off from some of these later developments by the dogmatic way in which he maintained that the existing cost-of-production approach to value left nothing more to be said on the subject and by his denial that 'the laws of human enjoyment', the 'laws of the consumption of wealth', were a legitimate part of the economist's province.

The reasons why Mill *qua* economist could find no place for the laws of human enjoyment in his scheme of things and was not impressed by the new generation of utility theorists emerging in the 1870s, go to the heart of his position as an exponent of a 'positive' or experiential methodology for the social sciences.[19] But in essence the answer can be found in Ricardo's blunt rejection of Say's attempt to make utility the measure of value: '[v]alue in use cannot be measured by any known standard; it is differently estimated by different persons'.[20] What appeared to be another palpable absurdity, then, a theory of value built upon foundations that seemed to offer no scope for objective comparisons over time, still less inter-personal ones that could be aggregated, was, of course, to be the challenge taken up by the next generation of utility theorists and all their modern successors working in such fields as consumer choice and welfare economics.

III

Jevons, acting in a spirit of angry iconoclasm, placed himself at the head of this generation in Britain when he published his *Theory of Political Economy* in 1871. Standing the Ricardo–Mill tradition on its head, he maintained that 'value depends entirely on utility'. The laws of human enjoyment explored by Bentham as part of a concern with the intensity, duration, certainty and propinquity of pleasures and pains could provide a psychological foundation for a theory of economic maximization that had universal application. The pure or abstract version of the science of political economy under static conditions turned on 'the mechanics of utility and self-interest'. Pleasure maximization and pain minimization constituted *the* problem for any basic theory of economic life. Hence Jevons's revolutionary manifesto urging the abandonment of the 'mazy and preposterous assumptions' of the Ricardo–Mill theory of value and his plea for a rehabilitation of the French school.[21] With his newly acquired understanding of the pre-history of the utility tradition, he could express his aim as one of making explicit the mathematics that underlay Bastiat's simple harmonious circle of 'wants, efforts, satisfaction'.[22] Reduced to its essence economic behaviour entailed an enquiry into the way in which we achieve an optimal relationship between our efforts and our wants.

Amid the bold programmatics of Jevons's aim to transform economics into a quantitative and hence a mathematical science it is easy to overlook the modesty with which he presented his initial findings. Unlike Mill (and Marshall later) Jevons did not claim to be advancing 'a systematic view of Economics' and was never able to complete a later attempt to do so.[23] He was also frank in conceding that it was not possible to 'weigh, nor gauge, nor test the feelings of the mind: there is no unit of labour, or suffering, or enjoyment'. Nevertheless, even if we had no direct unit of measurement, the feelings that underlay our buying and selling behaviour were quantitative; and they could be estimated by our willingness to pay various prices to meet our needs: '[t]he will is our pendulum and its oscillations are minutely registered in the price lists of the markets'. He conceded, however, that economics only dealt with 'the lowest rank of feelings': it had nothing to say about the 'higher calculus of moral right and wrong' that 'would be needed to show how [man] may best employ that wealth for the good of others as well as himself'.[24]

In saying this Jevons was merely upholding the neutral or amoral stance towards goods and the lifestyles they supported that economists, classical and neoclassical, felt it necessary to sustain when giving formal definitions of wealth-seeking activities.[25] Walter Bagehot, a contemporary of Jevons, though speaking as one of the last of the Ricardians, expressed it more provocatively. The economist did not ask whether only the best of human wants ought to be encouraged: 'He regards a pot of beer and a picture, a book of religion and a pack of cards, as all equally "wealth" and therefore, for his purpose, equally worthy of regard'.[26] Bagehot was partly responding to the vocal moral critics of political economy, notably Ruskin, partly distancing himself from Bastiat's claims that the economics of free markets could deliver the best of all possible worlds.

For a mixture of what might be described as 'professional' reasons, then, the orthodox neoclassical approach to consumer behaviour was exactly what Jevons said it was, the *mechanics* of utility and self-interest. On the basis of the law of diminishing marginal utility, economists could say something about the satiability of wants, those belonging to the lower rank at least and could take a renewed interest in the stock-flow problems posed by durable and perishable consumer goods. Jevons, for example, has some interesting things to say about utilization over time, about the effects of fashion and luxury and about the recycling of discarded goods and waste by-products.[27] After repeating the mantra that 'the economist must take the nature of the man or the woman as he finds it', he found it impossible to 'resist pointing out how slight an alteration of wants and tastes would often result in a great increase of wealth'.[28] In addition to believing that the English prejudice against non-white breads was harmful to working-class budgets and health, he had strong views on the degrading, drink-sodden enjoyments of urban industrial workers. Bagehot's pot of beer, taken in quantity, could not be regarded with moral equanimity. More significantly, despite his acknowledgement of the contribution made by Bastiat and the French school and a general antagonism to socialism, he was well disposed towards a wide range of public goods: '[t]here can be little doubt that, as civilization progresses and the political organization of peoples is gradually developed and perfected, the public expenditure in works of utility will increase to the average advantage of everybody'.[29] If anything, Jevons was more fearful than Mill of the effect of the monopolistic powers of trade unions on consumer interests, but he matched Mill in his support for industrial co-partnership as a solution to industrial strife. His plea was for a series of practical legislative experiments to be undertaken as a pragmatic guide to future intervention.[30]

Jevons's revolution certainly resulted in greater attention being paid to the demand factor and in the hands of Marshall and others it led to greater sophistication in classifying the results that could emerge from various types of market, with the period allowed for adjustment to shifting demands occupying a prominent role. In addition to his distinctions between short and long-run adjustment, Marshall was responsible for forging many of the tools used by future generations of economists when dealing with consumer behaviour empirically: demand schedules, substitution of one good or factor for another at the margin and price elasticities of demand (including oddities such as Giffen goods that could generate upward-sloping demand curves). For purposes of making welfare judgements he combined these tools with consumers' surplus and its producer equivalents. Since consumers' surplus was an attempt to revive Dupuit's measurement of the total as opposed to the marginal utility that consumers derived from their consumption, Marshall was taking the utility approach to exchange value one stage further than Jevons had done; he was also less squeamish about the possibilities for inter-personal comparisons of utility.[31] This remains true even when allowance is made for the restrictive assumptions on which Marshall constructed his partial equilibrium demand schedules – the schedules that encouraged him to believe that under certain conditions the surpluses, or gains and losses in total utility accruing to groups of consumers as a result of price changes, could be estimated.

Once again, however, appearances can be misleading. Marshall deplored Jevons's iconoclastic strategy and was not prepared to publish his *Principles of Economics*, the new 'organon' for the science that would replace Mill, until he had found a way of reconciling the older classical ideas on exchange value (supply-side factors) with the newer ones based on utility theory (demand-side factors). This entailed some over-generous reinterpretation and rehabilitation of the cost-of-production theories advanced by Ricardo and Mill.[32] It also accounts for Marshall's decidedly downbeat treatment of what Jevons had believed to be liberating discoveries or re-discoveries. Since Marshall had good claims to be among the independent discoverers of the significance of marginal utility, his luke-warmness cannot be attributed solely to personal pique at being forestalled by Jevons. Classical economists, he maintained, had said little on the subject because 'they really had not much to say that was not the common property of all sensible people'. The recent revival of interest could be attributed to 'mathematical habits of thought' and the new possibilities for making use of statistical evidence on consumption 'to throw light on difficult questions of great importance to public wellbeing'. Marshall also claimed that 'the spirit of the age' required economists 'to examine how far the exchange value of any element of wealth, whether in collective or individual use, represents accurately the addition which it makes to happiness and wellbeing'.[33]

The greater ease with which economic quantities could be measured via the price mechanism was Marshall's main reason for believing that economics could advance more surely and rapidly than other social sciences. But while measurement as the basis of science was crucial to Marshall's enterprise, he was unhappy with the hedonistic implications of Jevons's approach. This can be gauged by various typically Marshallian attempts to modify linguistic usage. Just as he substituted 'man in the ordinary business of life' for 'economic man', refused to distinguish between 'selfish' and 'altruistic' motives and preferred 'analysis' to 'theory' and 'satisfaction' to 'pleasure', so he also sought to distinguish his version of the science from what he described as Jevons's 'hedonics'.[34] Above all, despite devoting an early section (Book III) of his *Principles of Economics* to 'wants and their satisfaction', he made it clear that wants ruled life only in the animal or lower stages of existence. In more civilized states they played a dependent role when compared with 'efforts and activities', those relations into which people entered in the course of their working or productive lives and by which their 'characters' were formed, for good or ill. The adjustment of wants to activities and the creation of new wants as a result of new activities were the foundation on which he wished to build his own scientific edifice rather than on any theory of consumption alone. Character-formation as a result of quasi-Darwinian processes of adaptation to changes in the work environment lay at the centre of Marshall's contribution to a subject to which he would have loathed to be described as contributing, namely sociology. Although Talcott Parsons was critical of Marshall's labours in this field, he rightly perceived that Marshall's ambitions qualified him to stand beside Durkheim, Pareto and Weber as a sociologist, the only English figure deemed worthy of the appellation.[35] Jevons had recognized the need for a form of economic sociology, but left it for others to achieve. As an economic imperialist, Marshall's own preference was to be regarded as someone who had redrawn the boundaries of economics sufficiently generously to make these larger 'organic' (as opposed to 'mechanical') themes part of the most advanced of the social sciences. Hence, of course, his well-known statement that 'the Mecca of the economist lies in economic biology rather than in economic dynamics'.[36] This Mecca receded with every step Marshall took towards it, but the signs of the search can be found in such concepts as that of 'external economies' and in other ways in which Marshallian firms form supra-market, synergistic relations with each other, their employees and consumers of their products.[37]

Marshall was also opposed to the 'maximum satisfaction' school of thought represented by Bastiat and some more recent continental thinkers.[38] In essence his reasons for rejecting this school do not differ from those given earlier by Mill and Cairnes, though use of the surplus concept provided a more precise way of assisting the 'spirit of the age' in demonstrating that the market price of goods did not always represent the best outcome when viewed from a welfare perspective. The doctrine of maximum satisfaction embodied attitudes of complacency towards economic outcomes that Marshall consistently opposed. Equity, or the distribution of consumers' and producers' incomes, always needed to be considered alongside economic efficiency when making welfare judgements. The satisfactions attached to an additional increment in the income or expenditure of the poor were greater than those of the rich.[39] As Cairnes had argued earlier, conflicts between private and public interests were legion in economic life. Professional students of the science were capable of arbitrating in such conflicts, possibly by means of Marshall's measuring rods.

Beyond these technocratic possibilities, Marshall, in common with Jevons, could not 'resist' recording his judgements (often of a paternalistic kind) on the uses and misuses of wealth by rich and poor consumers alike. Mill had condemned the snobbish aspirations of the English middle classes and had therefore refused to recognize them in his scheme of proportional income taxation: each person or family, regardless of class or income, was to be given the same untaxable allowance to cover 'the requisites of life and health and with protection against habitual bodily suffering, but not with any indulgence'.[40] This reflected his refusal to accept any psychological law sanctioning interpersonal comparisons and progressive taxation of the rich. Marshall, by contrast, accepted the law of diminishing marginal utility as applied to incomes and recognized that 'necessary' expenditures could vary with economic occupation. Some necessaries were essential to the maintenance of 'efficiency' as opposed to mere subsistence; he also recognized a category of consumption goods that could be regarded as 'conventionally necessary'.[41] But such considerations did not prevent him from making adverse comments on mere 'display' and those lifestyles that did not reflect station and economic roles.[42] Indeed, in his effort to convince his late-Victorian public that economics had much to contribute to the attainment of altruistic or 'noble' ends, he refused to concede this territory to such critics of conventional economics as Ruskin and William Morris. He brought this to such a fine art that he was accused by less earnest followers, such as Keynes, of being 'too anxious to do good'.[43]

IV

What has been said so far amounts to little more than a selective narrative of the role assigned to consumer behaviour and consumption generally in the mainstream writings of a sequence of leading British economists considered over a century or more. It suggests why Smith's maxim is by no means self-evident as a guide to the way in which economists have treated the consumer when defining the territory that their science was designed to explore. Though couched mainly in 'internalist' terms, the story also contains some hints that reveal how the economists selected for attention would have approached the larger 'external' issues raised by consumer behaviour when engaged in applied economics and when writing as political economists in the larger sense.

To students of consumer culture and to those who are not especially interested in the formalities of the history of economic thinking, this story may appear bloodless – overly intellectual, lacking a material base and having no obvious material result. One obvious defence would be to say that those about whom I have chosen to speak were in the business of creating or reformulating a science that could support research and be taught to others. Inescapably, that is an *intellectual* activity, even when the results are merely pedagogic aids to clear thinking. Intellectual fashions play a part here. It is not insignificant that the post-1870 generation of economists had mathematical and natural scientific backgrounds. Enthusiasm for the new physics and classical mechanics shaped the thinking of Jevons, Walras, Marshall and Edgeworth. Broadly, it supported the idea that the absence of units of exact measurement was not a barrier to the use of differential calculus in posing and even solving problems that could not be posed in any other way. Other developments in psycho-physics were initially to prove attractive to Edgeworth: for example, the Fechner experiments in establishing the *ebenmärklich* or just perceivable response to sensory stimuli. Differential sensitivity to measured amounts of stimulus confirmed the possibility of measuring the marginal satisfactions or dissatisfactions derived from changes in states of pleasure or pain.[44] But pointing to these ways in which it was possible for an economist to become a mathematical utilitarian of the Edgeworth variety does not shift the problem of interpretation in a markedly materialist direction. Moreover, psychologists have frequently been right to suspect that the appropriation by economists of evidence that appeared to be psychological in character has rarely been a profound form of borrowing. Until fairly recently economists have preferred robust psychological home-brew to more refined imported wines.[45]

Previous attempts to furnish a materialist background to the marginal revolution, linking it with stages in the development of capitalism, have mostly fallen foul of the messy historical contingency of the process. There was nothing sacrosanct about the almost simultaneous publication of the works of Jevons, Walras and Menger in the 1870s, the last of whom was not known to Jevons and only became known to Walras in the subsequent decade. Their discovery of marginal utility was clearly a *re*discovery, with precursors writing in several different languages over the previous century.[46] Moreover, the division between classical and the Jevonian, Walrasian and Marshallian modes of neoclassical thinking does not provide a decisive clue to economists' practical views on consumers and consumption.

It is even harder to link the interest in consumer behaviour with novel developments in material culture centring on the rise of consumer society, a subject on which it is possible for historians to disagree by more than a couple of centuries.[47] Mass consumer society might be a nineteenth and twentieth-century phenomenon connected with urbanization and rising standards of living, but I do not see many signs of its being a major influence on the thinking of professional economists – the ones I have considered at least. If I had chosen to deal with more dissident voices, such as those of Veblen and Patten in the United States, Ruskin and Hobson in Britain and the teleological writings of some members of the German historical school, a very different picture would emerge. Each in their different ways contested the abstract, comparative static and neutral or amoral stance towards the world of goods that orthodox economists, when speaking as scientists at least, attempted to sustain. Thus Ruskin brought Platonic absolutes to bear on judgements of the 'illth' or moral degradation associated with the shoddy quality of goods produced and consumed under capitalism. Hobson could fortify his Ruskinian enthusiasms by following Marshall in employing organic evolutionary perspectives to speculate about future social trends in machine production that might favour a return to more artisanal modes and higher qualitative standards of consumption.[48] Here he came closest to the two American figures he most admired, Patten and Veblen and the treatment of consumer wants over long periods of time.[49] Dissidents were always more attracted to institutionalist and evolutionary approaches to economic behaviour than to the comparative static approaches that were, in defiance of Marshall's hopes, the first fruits of neoclassicism. From a consumer perspective, the heterodox picture would be one in which 'conspicuous consumption', the economics of abundance and the pathology of misdirected consumption and under-consumption were far more central to the functioning of capitalism.

Surveying the scene from an Austrian perspective, with its interest in *Güterqualität* and distinctions between goods of higher and lower order, its opposition to mathematical models based on mutual determination and its Mengerian emphasis on unintended consequences, would yield another very different picture. Judged by what such later exponents as von Mises and Hayek have made of the Austrian inheritance, it would have libertarian features that bring us back to Bastiat and some of his admirers in the Spencerian camp. Alternatively, if I had taken my cue from the work of social and economic statisticians, men of the stamp of Ernst Engel, another set of emphases would have emerged. Engel, after all, successfully measured what the more theoretical, historical and qualitative observers merely made the subject of conjectural history: the income elasticity of household demand over time. Why theory and empirical findings lived separate lives before and even after the advent of econometrics is another problem in the history of economics.[50]

Consumer protection and consumer cooperatives are another matter. Here economists did have some tangible promptings from their material environment. Observations of the comparative 'stickiness' of retail as opposed to wholesale prices stimulated some early attempts to explain this phenomenon and to assess the consequences of over-investment in the distributive trades relative to those engaged in production. Hobson, for example, was to give this a more radical twist by incorporating distributive waste within his more general account of the waste associated with unemployment during depressions.[51] Once more, however, it would be difficult to claim that the more precise methods of analysis associated with neoclassical economics modified the principal conclusions: nineteenth-century inferences that turned on 'social waste' and 'adulteration' emerged in the twentieth century as 'excess capacity' and such non-price forms of competition as the creation of niche markets through advertising and brand names.[52] The record of support for consumer cooperatives is also a fairly consistent one from Mill through Jevons to Marshall. Economists did not create them, but they did more than give them respectability in the eyes of the middle classes. They assessed the strengths and weaknesses of the cooperative movement and were, if anything, over-sanguine about its long-term prospects as a way of organizing retailing.

The cholera outbreaks of the 1840s and 1850s did a great deal to concentrate the mind on the problems of London's water supply and hence on the inadequacies of public utility provision. Regulation of railway pricing was also a response to novel circumstances. And if, like Dupuit, your job description entailed being a civil engineer in the Écoles des Mines et Ponts et Chaussées, finding ways of articulating public benefits was what one got paid for.[53] Nothing could be more crudely materialist than that, though it says little about how Dupuit performed his duties. Marshall's claims on behalf of the professionally trained economist were a good deal more pious-sounding, but that should not lead one to dismiss them on that ground alone. After all, the Marshallian surpluses and concern with externalities, when developed by Pigou, his pupil and successor to the Cambridge Chair, into a full-blown economics of welfare, remains an essential tool in public debate on a wide range of environmental issues.[54] When orthodox economists weighed in on the side of free trade against Joseph Chamberlain's tariff reform campaign at the turn of the century, they were helping to seal the bond between citizenship and being a consumer forged in the anti-Corn Law debates of the 1840s.[55] Many of those who rejected tariff reform by voting Liberal in 1906 were not simply voting with their wallets and shopping baskets: they had become convinced that free trade was an issue that involved their status as citizens and patriots.[56]

If one had to select a concrete historical fact on which to peg such phenomena, it would be political rather than economic: the extension of the suffrage to urban and rural working-class males in 1867 and 1884 respectively. A politics of the consumer – more than the politics of the producer – requires a popular electorate that could be appealed to and manipulated by the new democratic style of politics ushered in by extension of the suffrage. Moments when consumers form movements and assume a collective identity, moments when they cast off the anonymity that attaches to a role that all of us routinely and sometimes playfully perform, are interesting ones – more interesting, in some respects, than those in which we act in our capacity as taxpayers or benefit receivers. Frank Trentmann has convincingly argued that it is only under some rather special conditions and through particular political traditions that material cultures of consumption eventuate in a consumer politics: the former usually comes without the latter.[57]

What, then, is the contribution of modern economics to the understanding of cultures of consumption? Economists have often been accused of favouring Goering's (actually Hanns Johst's) view of 'culture' as something that makes him reach for his revolver. While this may be apocryphal, a great deal of attention has been confined to the mechanics of self-interest and utility, the formal analysis of rational consumer choice under conditions in which tastes and technology can be taken as given. The award of the Nobel Prize in Economics in 2002 to Daniel Kahneman and Vernon L. Smith for work on the borderline between economics and the psychology of decision making and for conducting successful laboratory experiments on market rationality, suggests that crossing disciplinary borders is not taboo for economists. Over a much longer period economists have often been more interesting as students of consumer culture when they have been engaged in extending the boundaries of formal theory or speculating outside them. This is certainly true of Adam Smith, who had a great deal to say about the restless role of social emulation in shaping consumer behaviour and whose models of economic development would not make much sense if he had ducked the problem of long-term shifts in the pattern of consumer behaviour.[58] But those are the very parts of Smith that are of more interest to social psychologists and economic historians than to modern economists and I am sure the same is true of Jevons's and Marshall's Victorian moralizing on the uses and misuses of wealth.

At one time nothing so vulgar as 'marketing' was allowed to sully the purity of textbook treatments of supply and demand, according to which it was essential to stress the independence of the two sets of forces under analysis. Judging quality by price, as in 'snob' markets, posed anomalies similar to those posed by Marshall's Giffen goods: they pointed up more general rules. It was only when he went beyond comparative statics that Marshall was able to confront marketing and mass retailing more frontally. Witness the interesting chapters in his book on *Industry and Trade* that deal with buyers' and sellers' markets, fashion goods, branding, advertising, department stores, chains and cooperatives.[59] But Marshall was exceptional in his anxiety to demonstrate the realism of his grasp on the modern economic world and one of his reasons for favouring 'analysis' over 'theory' was that he wanted a word that united theory with empirical enquiries. As with *maximum* satisfaction, Marshall was not keen to develop models based on *pure* or *perfect* competition. Those who later developed theories of monopolistic competition were not merely being polite in expressing indebtedness to Marshall.

Economists have, of course, made some notable contributions to modern types of neoliberalism, Viennese or Chicago style. The effect of this may have been to suggest that consumers do not need to organize or be given protection outside the usual laws against fraud when their interests are fully catered for under a regime of competitive markets, actual or constructed by means of a judicial rearrangement of property rights. The status of the consumer has been problematic precisely because neoliberalism has never exhausted what economists have wished to say on the subject.

Notes

1. Glasgow edition of the Works and Correspondence of Adam Smith, vol. II, p. 660 (IV.viii. 49).
2. The quoted phrase comes from *Principles of Economics* (London, 1961), 9th variorum edition with annotations by C.W. Guillebaud, 2 vols, vol. I, p. 492. It appears as part of Marshall's discussion of consumers' surplus and the regulation

of monopolies. He hoped that consumers' surplus could be made an operational concept for public administrators charged with calculating the interest of consumers as a supplement to the calculations made by private producers.

3. See B. Fine's and M. Everson's chapters in this volume.
4. See J. Gamble's chapter in this volume.
5. 'On the Definition and Method of Political Economy' in *Essays on Some Unsettled Questions in Political Economy* (London, 1844), as reprinted in *The Collected Works of John Stuart Mill*, 33 volumes (Toronto, 1965–91), vol. IV, p. 318. Future references will be abbreviated to *CW*.
6. For the quoted phrases see 'Of the Influence of Consumption on Production' in *CW*, IV, pp. 262–3, and *Principles* in *CW*, III, p. 575. For his criticisms of Malthus, Chalmers and Sismondi see *CW*, II, pp. 66–8, 75–7, and III, pp. 570–6.
7. Putting 'French school' in quotation marks signals that it was a term of interpretative, even polemical, art arising out of controversies in the second half of the nineteenth century, long after the principles of the supposed 'school' had been founded. Jevons's history of utility theorizing in the preface to the second edition of his *Theory of Political Economy* (London, 1879) lists the following French names: Condillac, Baudeau, Le Trosne, J.-B. Say, Destutt de Tracy, Bastiat and Courcelle-Seneuil. Among mathematical treatments it includes those of Isnard, Cournot and Dupuit, reaching a triumphant conclusion in the work of his contemporary, Walras.
8. For a study of one of these groupings see M.W. Taylor, *Men versus the State: Herbert Spencer and Late Victorian Individualism* (Oxford, 1992). Although this work does not mention Bastiat, it is the best treatment of the anti-étatist ideas of those who publicized extreme laissez-faire ideas and fundamentalist defences of the right to private property in Britain during the final third of the nineteenth century.
9. *Principles* in *CW*, III, p. 455.
10. 'No society can surely be flourishing and happy, of which the far greater part of the members are poor and miserable. It is but equity, besides, that they who feed, cloath and lodge the whole body of the people, should have such a share of the produce of their own labour as to be themselves tolerably well fed, cloathed and lodged.' *Wealth of Nations*, vol. I, p. 96 (I.viii.36).
11. *Autobiography* in *CW*, I, p. 239.
12. The arguments summarized in this paragraph can be found in Bastiat's *Harmonies économiques* (Paris, 1852).
13. See 'Political Economy and Laissez-Faire' and 'Bastiat' in Cairnes's *Essays in Political Economy* (London, 1873).
14. *Later Letters* in *CW*, XVII, p. 1764.
15. See J.-P. Potier, 'Léon Walras, critique de l'école liberale orthodoxe francaise', *Les Cahiers de l'Association Charles Gide pour l'étude de la pensée économique*, II, 1988, 165–90.

16. For Marshall's views on Bastiat see p. 41 above. Sidgwick dismissed the fusion of natural liberty and natural justice, 'of whom Bastiat may be taken as a type', as uncharacteristic of the views of English economists, whose objections to government interference were based on its tendency 'to impair aggregate production more than it could increase the utility of the produce by better distribution'; see his *Principles of Political Economy*, 2nd edn (London, 1887), p. 400. Edgeworth was content to repeat these arguments in his article on Bastiat for the *Palgrave Dictionary of Political Economy* (1926).

17. For Mill's views on socialism see 'Chapters on Socialism' in *CW*, V, pp. 705–53; on public goods and utilities see *Principles* in CW, II, pp. 141–2; III, pp. 803–04, 947, 955–6, 968–71. But see especially his proposals for dealing with the London water supply in *CW*, V, pp. 431–7.

18. Trentmann and Taylor in this volume.

19. For a fuller treatment see N. De Marchi, 'Mill and Cairnes and the Emergence of Marginalism in England' in R.D.C. Black, A.W. Coats and C.D.W. Goodwin (eds), *The Marginal Revolution in Economics* (Durham, NC, 1973), pp. 78–97.

20. For a longer defence of this position see the *Works and Correspondence of David Ricardo*, edited by P. Sraffa, 11 volumes (Cambridge, 1950–73), vol. VIII, pp. 276–7.

21. *Theory of Political Economy*, 2nd edition (London, 1879), p. xlix.

22. *Theory*, p. 44; the other quoted phrases can be found on pp. 2 and 23.

23. The posthumously published work entitled *The Principles of Economics* is better described by the subtitle assigned to it by his editor, H. Higgs: *A Fragment of a Treatise on the Industrial Mechanism of Society and Other Papers* (London, 1905).

24. The quotations come from the *Theory*, pp. 8, 13–15 and 29.

25. As Jevons expressed the limitation in his *Principles of Economics* (London, 1905): '[i]t belongs to other branches of the moral and social sciences to investigate the ultimate effects of actions. In economics we treat only of proximate effects. A revolver is a means of attaining both good and evil, but we have only to consider whether it is wanted, and, if wanted, how it may be obtained with the least cost of labour', p. 12.

26. See *The Collected Works of Walter Bagehot*, edited by N. St John-Stevas, 15 volumes, (London, 1965–86), vol. XI, p. 287.

27. See the opening seven chapters on utility, wealth and consumption in his *Principles*.

28. *Principles*, p. 32, citing his support for the Bread Reform League.

29. *Principles*, p. 41.

30. See *The State in Relation to Labour* (1882, 3rd edition, 1894), p. 171. See also Jevons's *Methods of Social Reform* (London, 1883) for his essays on industrial partnerships, legislation to control the drink trade, and his advocacy of state-controlled and municipal enterprises in the provision of the postal and telegraph services as well as free public libraries, museums and public amusements.

31. Compare the following statements by Jevons and Marshall respectively. 'Every mind is thus inscrutable to every other mind, and no common denominator of feeling seems to be possible' (*Theory*, p. 15). 'It is useless to say that various gains and losses are incommensurable, and cannot be weighed against one another. For they must be, and in fact they are, weighed against one another before any deliberate decision is or can be reached on any issue' (see *Memorials of Alfred Marshall*, edited by A.C. Pigou, London, 1925, p. 302).

32. See D.P. O'Brien, 'Marshall's Work in Relation to Classical Economics', in J.K. Whitaker (ed.), *Centenary Essays on Alfred Marshall* (Cambridge, 1990), pp. 127–63.

33. See *Principles*, vol. I, pp. 84–5.

34. See *Principles*, appendix I, vol. I, pp. 817–21.

35. Parson's seminal articles on Marshall *qua* sociologist were later incorporated in his *Structure of Social Action* (New York, 1937). See also 'A Separate Science: Polity and Society in Marshall's Economics' in S. Collini, D. Winch and J. Burrow, *That Noble Science of Politics* (Cambridge, 1983), pp. 308–37.

36. *Principles*, vol. I, p. xiv.

37. These Marshallian themes have been best explored by his modern editor, John Whitaker, and by Brian Loasby. See, for example, Whitaker's 'Some Neglected Aspects of Alfred Marshall's Economic and Social Thought', *History of Political Economy*, 9 (1977), pp. 161–97; 'The Distribution Theory of Marshall's Principles' in A. Asimakopulos (ed), *Theories of Income Distribution* (Boston, 1988); and Loasby's essay on 'Firms, Markets, and the Principle of Continuity' in J.K. Whitaker (ed.), *Centenary Essays*, pp. 108–26. For attempts to retrieve some of these 'lost' elements in Marshall see W. Lazonick, *Business Organization and the Myth of the Market Economy* (Cambridge, 1991); and G.M. Peter Swann, 'Marshall's Consumer as an Innovator' in S. C. Dow and P.E. Earl (eds), *Economic Organization and Economic Knowledge* (Cheltenham, 1999), pp. 98–118.

38. For Marshall's criticisms of Bastiat see *Principles*, vol. I, p. 763n.

39. *Principles*, vol. I, pp. 17–19, 130–1, 471, 474, 851–2.

40. See *Principles* in *CW*, III, pp. 808–11.

41. See *Principles*, I, pp. 68–70.

42. See *Principles*, I, pp. 134–7, 720; and 'Social Possibilities of Economic Chivalry' in *Memorials of Alfred Marshall*, pp. 324–5.

43. 'Alfred Marshall' in *Essays in Biography* in *The Collected Writings of John Maynard Keynes* (Cambridge, 1971–89), 30 volumes, vol. X, p. 200.

44. This now emerges more clearly from Peter Newman's introduction to the new edition of *F. Y. Edgeworth's Mathematical Psychics and Further Papers on Political Economy* (Oxford, 2003).

45. For a history and commentary on the relationship see G.J. Stigler, 'The Development of Utility Theory' in his *Essays in the History of Economics* (Chicago, 1965), pp. 66–155; and S.B. Lewin, 'Economics and Psychology:

Lessons for Our Own Day from the Early Twentieth Century', *Journal of Economic Literature*, Vol. XXXIV (1996), pp. 1293–1323.

46. See M. Blaug, 'Was There a Marginal Revolution?' in R.D.C. Black *et al.* (eds), *The Marginal Revolution*, pp. 3–14.

47. J. Brewer, 'The Error of Our Ways: Historians and the Birth of Consumer Society', The Royal Society, 23 September 2003, working paper no. 012, www.consume.bbk.ac.uk.

48. These themes appear in his early work on the *Evolution of Industry* of 1894, especially the final chapter on 'Civilization and Industrial Development', and recur in later work.

49. See T. Veblen, *The Theory of the Leisure Class* (London, 1925); and S. Patten, *The Consumption of Wealth* (Philadelphia, 1889) and *The Theory of Dynamic Economics* (Philadelphia, 1892). Both of Patten's works can be read as reasoned rejections of Mill's exclusion of the laws of the consumption of wealth from economic theory; they define the dynamic economy as one in which 'society progresses from a simple, costly and inharmonious consumption to a varied, cheap and harmonious consumption' (*Dynamic Economics*, p. 44).

50. See G.J. Stigler, 'The Early History of Empirical Studies of Consumer Behaviour' in his *Essays on the History of Economics*, pp. 198–233.

51. See the comments on this in the work he wrote with A. Mummery, *Physiology of Industry* (London, 1889), pp. 149–50. It became a running theme in later works; see, for example, *John Ruskin: Social Reformer* (London, 1898), p. 133, and *The Social Problem* (London, 1901), p. 11.

52. The two sentences that precede this note cover a great deal of territory, but the following references illustrate what I have in mind. An indication of classical thinking on retailing can be gleaned from the record of a discussion by members of the Political Economy Club in 1857 on the question 'By What Laws Are Retail Prices and Profits Determined?'. Mill took the lead in this and an account of the discussion was reconstructed by Adelaide Weinberg from Cairnes's unpublished notes; see 'A Meeting of the Political Economy Club' in *The Mill News Letter*, vol. I, Number 2, Spring 1966, pp. 11–16. See also Mill's *Principles* in CW, III, p. 791, and Cairnes's *Some Leading Principles of Political Economy, Newly Expounded* (London, 1874), pp. 128–34. For post-classical treatments along similar lines see an undated manuscript on 'Retail Prices' by Marshall in A.C. Pigou (ed.), *Memorials of Alfred Marshall,* pp. 353–7.

53. For a recent treatment of this see M. Mosca, 'Jules Dupuit, the French "Ingénieurs Économistes" and the Société d'Économie Politique', in G. Faccarello (ed.), *Studies in the History of French Political Economy* (London, 1998).

54. On this see J. Chipman's 'Marshall's Consumer's Surplus in Modern Perspective', in J.K. Whitaker (ed.), *Centenary Essays*, pp. 278–92.

55. For a study of this episode see A.W. Coats, 'Political Economy and the Tariff Reform Campaign of 1903' in his *On the History of Economic Thought: British and American Economic Essays* (London, 1992), vol. I, pp. 284–337.

56. See F. Trentmann, 'National Identity and Consumer Politics: Free Trade and Tariff Reform' in D. Winch and P.K. O'Brien (eds), *The Political Economy of British Historical Experience, 1688–1814* (Oxford, 2002), pp. 215–40.

57. See F. Trentmann, 'The Genealogy of the Modern Consumer: Meanings, Identities, and Political Synapses', in J. Brewer and F. Trentmann (eds), *Consuming Cultures, Global Perspectives* (Oxford and New York, forthcoming), ch. 2.

58. For one economist's reflections on this topic see N. Rosenberg, 'Adam Smith, Consumer Tastes, and Economic Growth' in his *The Emergence of Economic Ideas* (Aldershot, 1994), pp. 42–55.

59. The full title of this work tells its own story; see *Industry and Trade: A study of industrial technique and business organization; and of their influences on the conditions of various classes and nations* (London, 1919). On the subjects listed in the text see Book II, Chapters 5, 6 and 7.

–3–

From Users to Consumers

Water Politics in Nineteenth-Century London*

Frank Trentmann and *Vanessa Taylor*

On Monday 15 July 1895 one and a quarter million inhabitants in the East End of London awoke to a water shortage. Charles Lyel, a householder and member of the Hackney Vestry, complained that the East London Waterworks Company had stopped his constant delivery and switched back to intermittent supply. Water was turned on between 9 and 10 in the morning and flowed for a mere two to three hours, with the result 'that I am deprived of my morning tub, [and] there is no bath for the children in the evening'. To be told by 'the company that the supply "is ample for all legitimate use" is adding insult to injury', Lyel told *The Times*.[1] East Enders without Lyel's benefit of a cistern, or occupying the upper floors of tenements, were still less fortunate. People began to store water in jugs, buckets, basins or any container available. Others began to mobilize consumers against water companies. John B. Kyffin, a draper of Hackney Road, had for some days put up with the 'scant supply of water' for his shop and twenty-six assistants. When the water necessary for domestic purposes 'practically ceased altogether' on 15 and 16 July, he had had enough. Looking at the rates (local taxes) water companies were collecting on his £200 property and at his toilets with 'no flushing remedy' and assistants taken ill while local authorities received a million gallons to water the roads, Kyffin took the company to court for failing to give the statutory 'proper supply of water for domestic purposes'. Kyffin lost but proceeded to mobilize consumers across Hackney with support from the vestry and fellow ratepayers.[2]

The battle between consumers and water companies during the 1895 East London 'water famine' marked a formative stage in the breakthrough of a new consumer identity and politics in the modern period. Water has been mainly understood in the context of public health, urbanization, housing, leisure and the material environment.[3] While building on this research, this chapter seeks to reconnect the contestation of a basic good (water) to central problems of modern consumer society, in particular the formation of the consumer around questions of needs, rights and waste. Whatever their particular inflection, from Veblen to recent post-modern accounts, most seminal texts have structured their narratives of consumer society or consumerism around the expansion of desire, affluence and commercial objects and spaces and their role in creating social distinction, modernity and a liberal self.[4] The literature has largely followed Maslow's chronological hierarchy of needs: consumer societies emerge when humans have advanced from basic needs, like food and shelter, to material wants.

The chapter problematizes this dominant approach by looking at the place of needs and the non-market provision of basic goods in the formation of the consumer. Shopping and the growing mountain of commodities in the eighteenth and nineteenth centuries did not in itself generate reflexive 'consumers'.[5] In Britain, often seen as the birthplace of modern consumer culture, they emerged in battles over 'necessaries', especially bread and water. Until the turn of the twentieth century, 'consumer' still mainly referred to the person 'using up' water, gas and perishable foods. And it was struggles over these particular taxed consumables (rather than commodity culture in general) that fleshed out a new social and political persona: the consumer. Taking water in nineteenth-century London as a case study, we explore the significance of a basic good and questions over access, quantity, quality, price and control in the making of the consumer. Consumers were the agents and products of a shifting contestation of needs, rights, rationality and waste. The nineteenth-century water wars mobilized users and turned them into consumers, defining a new social identity for actors and a category of knowledge and public legitimation. This story broadens our understanding of the evolution of 'active' citizen-consumers associated with Western consumer culture and may also help to reunite the study of consumer societies with that of human development and rights to basic goods.

Water London: Monopolies and Fragmentation

One way of thinking about the modern city has been in terms of the body. Organic 'auto-regulation' became an attractive model for some nineteenth-century engineers and sanitary reformers envisaging, as Patrick Joyce has recently put it, the 'constant circulation of fluids and the continuous replenishment of vital functions'.[6] This model may hold for the sewage system but has less interpretive potential for water supply and consumption. 'Water London' – the metropolitan area covered by the water companies – was less one body with constant circulation than a series of separate monopolistic networks offering mainly inconstant supply, providing uneven access across municipal boundaries and drawing water from different sources and through separate mains systems. Even after the consolidation of metropolitan government in 1889, the territory administered by London County Council (121 square miles) was a mere 14% of Water London (845 square miles). People in neighbouring streets and districts had radically different experiences as users, subject to different hours, quantities, standards of supply and prices. Constant flowing water began to be introduced systematically in the late 1860s but progress was slow and uneven. The number of houses with constant water (482,317) exceeded those with intermittent supply (287,432) only by 1891.[7] Many areas on constant supply suffered repeated water shortages.

Waste was not so much a by-product as a structuring feature of the system. In 1851 it was estimated that 29 million gallons of the 44 million pumped were wasted through the intermittent system.[8] Rather than striving for a closed, self-regulating system, some companies adopted a more open-ended approach. Under constant supply, the Grand Junction Company found it more rational to pump more than to reduce its waste – in 1891 it supplied over 47 gallons daily per head, an extraordinary quantity compared to the London average of 31 gallons at the time, or the average 33 gallons (150 litres) *consumed* in England and Wales today.[9]

Until the 1800s Londoners had drawn water from surface wells, public pumps and limited piped supplies. Although wells continued to be a source for some until the 1870s, the nineteenth century established the dominance of piped water. A period of intense competition between private water companies in the first two decades of the century gave way to an informal 'districted' monopoly that was to last until 1902. The eight dominant companies were the New River Company (established 1619), Chelsea Waterworks (1723), Southwark Waterworks (1760), Lambeth Waterworks (1785), South London Company (1805, from 1845 Southwark and Vauxhall Waterworks), West Middlesex Company (1806), East London Waterworks (1807), Kent Waterworks (1809) and Grand Junction Waterworks (1811).[10] Despite repeated calls for public control and ownership from the 1810s onwards, London resisted the prevailing nineteenth-century trend of municipalization.[11] The arrangement came to an end only with the Conservatives' 1902 Metropolitan Water Act, which bought out the companies for a generous £43 million and transferred control to the Metropolitan Water Board, with local authority representation.

Water London, in brief, lacked a unitary system of supply and consumption. Instead of material auto-regulation and an evacuation of the political, water made for political contestation, its rising cultural status becoming harnessed to the language of liberty, property and civilization.

Cultural Contestation and Early Ratepayer Protests

The first half of the nineteenth century witnessed the transvaluation of water through cultural notions of purity and cleanliness as well as the impact of Chadwickian public health. Water appeared a 'first necessary of life' and, as 'a gift of Heaven', was given to all. Water pollution could affect everyone and reduce even 'splendid mansions' to 'whited sepulchres'.[12] Critics of water companies appealed to the public interest in 'pure water'. What amounted to 'pure' or 'clean' water, however, was subject to interpretation – a field of disagreement that would diminish in time, but not disappear altogether as theories of disease and testing methods continued to compete with each other.[13] Water undertakings had to be justified by public utility and those speaking on the water question had to speak for the public. But if the best way of delivering water for the benefit of the public was open to question, so too was the nature of 'the public'.

In the 1810s and 1820s the status of water as a basic need was mobilized through two complementary liberal languages: liberty vs. slavery and free tax-paying citizens vs. monopoly. In the years following the establishment of monopoly, complaints about the cost, quality, quantity and unreliability of water supplies became common-place. The first issue to galvanize customers was that of escalating prices. Water rates were based on assessments of consumption derived from property size, until the 1850s when they became a percentage of annual property values (like other local taxes). Additional charges were frequently levied for baths and WCs (toilets), or for tall buildings. In 1818 protests arose in various London parishes. The most high profile was the Select Vestry in affluent St Marylebone, a body 'composed of noblemen and gentlemen', which introduced three (unsuccessful) bills for a parochial water supply.[14] The Anti-Water Monopoly Association (AWMA) was established in October 1819 by civil servant James Weale. With the active support of the vestry (the parish-based unit of local government representation), the AWMA canvassed parishes in the West Middlesex and Grand Junction Company districts for a boycott of rate increases considered 'highly illegal, ... prejudicial to the Interests of the public in general, and ... oppressive to a large proportion of the Inhabitant Householders'. Though claiming that the increases were 'felt as a most oppressive burthen by the least wealthy classes of Housekeepers', the AWMA was forced to appeal to 'Gentlemen of rank' to augment its funds. The companies, however, denied they were making profits at the expense of the public and dismissed the campaign as a sectional interest, 'fomented by party, kept by party' and appealing 'naturally' to 'the malcontents of the parish'.[15]

The Association had run out of steam by late 1820, but debate about the rights of householders and the scope of the public continued. The 1821 parliamentary select committee concluded that, given the water companies' high capital outlay, unrestricted competition would be unmanageable and prices were not unreasonably high, for good quality water. Weale, however, protested that '[w]ater must be considered ... one of the elements necessary to existence, the same as light and air...; and therefore, its artificial supply to a great city ought not to be the subject of free trade, nor ... any kind of trade'. Drawing on an older notion of non-commercial public provision, he held that the supply 'should be profuse rather than merely sufficient and gratuitous to the poor'. He tied the interests of ratepayers to ratepayer control. Water supply should be maintained by rates and administered by local bodies.[16]

When criticism of the water companies reignited over a deterioration in water quality in the late 1820s – when WC use was rising[17] – debate again concerned the nature of the public and their rights and duties. In 1827 John Wright published *The Dolphin*, an influential protest against the Grand Junction's new intake opposite the

Common Sewer at Chelsea. For Wright, there was a direct link between the bad state of the water, monopoly and the denial of customers' freedoms. At a time of heated argument over the emancipation of slaves, Wright saw a parallel with water ratepayers: 'those customers ... handed over, by these jobbers in one of God's choicest blessings, from one set of monopolists to another, like so many negroes on a West Indian estate'.[18]

Writing in support of the companies, engineer William Matthews sought to undermine Wright's 'public'. Water users were not synonymous with ratepayers, Matthews emphasized. Nor did local government representatives necessarily have the same interests as their ratepayers. Matthews denied that a parochial water supply would lower the rates, 'the public having experienced many expensive instances of Select Vestry economy'. Private enterprise and public interest need not conflict. Among those undertakings derived from 'a spirit of enterprise' and risk, water companies were 'conspicuous ... for their public and private utility'.[19] Wright, he charged, merely wanted to establish a rival company. On both sides, accusations of sectionalism challenged an essential notion of the public as rational, economizing and free.[20]

The *Westminster Review*, in 1830, offered a third view of the public that showed how difficult it still was to graft the consumer on to the public interest. Embodied here in the figure of John Bull, the public had indeed been represented by Wright, but in the process made a fool of. The concern with water was not the natural priority of a rational householder promoting his family's health, but the result of a herd instinct: '[t]his is the way to govern multitudes. Justification, taxation, emancipation, the nation, or Dolphin and poisonation, it is all one: the halloo is given and the dogs follow'. And while the status of water as a basic need validated calls for reform, the very unpopularity of London water as a beverage could undermine the attempts of water campaigners to speak as consumers. John Bull, the reviewer pointed out, was 'no very violent water drinker', though 'always ready enough to poison himself with gin and compounds'.[21]

Health, Liberty and Civilization: Ignorant and Responsible Consumers

The 1840s saw the establishment of sanitarian priorities associated with Chadwickian public health: a focus on the prevention of epidemic disease through the reform of drainage and water supply. The Public Health Act of 1848 – the year of Britain's second major cholera epidemic – established a General Board of Health with powers to enforce the appointment of local boards of health in crisis areas. While the utilitarian focus on clean and sufficient water contributed to the emergence of a public function for cleanliness, this was often fused with a Christian view of the symbolic properties of water and the moral value of cleanliness. Philanthropic and temperance initiatives, such as the public bath and drinking fountain movements, aimed to promote the consumption of water by the poor, for their 'moral and physical welfare', as well as for a 'future saving' on the poor rate.[22]

Water campaigners exploited the notion that 'cleanliness is next to godliness'.[23] Without cleanliness, Christian Socialist Charles Kingsley emphasized, 'education is half powerless, for self-respect is all but impossible'. He referred not to the 'stains contracted by honest labour, which the butcher ... washes off', returning 'at once to decency and comfort, but ... [to] the habitual ingrained personal dirt, where washing is either impossible or not cared for; ... which extends itself from the body to the clothes, the house, the language, the thoughts' of the many thousands in British cities who 'never dream of washing'. To them, water was no necessity but 'a luxury as impossible as turtle or champagne'.[24] In the wake of cholera, the *Edinburgh Review* argued that 'an abundant supply of water' was needed to 'wash away the causes of those diseases which are silently but incessantly wasting away the health, the morals and the wealth of the community'. Nor did cholera stop at the doors of the rich, whose water had been contaminated by leakage from cesspools and sewer gases. The water question was a reminder of 'the great law which binds the rich and the poor together'. Once the public had a right and a duty to cleanliness, it was a short step to demand that London water 'be placed in the hands of the Government, or some public body responsible to the consumers'.[25]

Empowered consumers, however, were quite specific social and political actors. Water drinkers and users did not yet perfectly map on to water 'consumers'. There was tension between a public health notion of universal needs and the dominant political language promoting a narrower idea of the 'consumer' as a ratepaying citizen, that is, a propertied (mainly male) householder paying local taxes and with rights to local government representation. The payment of water rates legitimated this group of users as 'consumers' and it was in this strictly limited and legally defined sense that we encounter the voice of the consumer in the mid-nineteenth century. Importantly, this initially meant that those speaking as 'water consumers' or 'gas consumers' included commercial users (shopkeepers, warehouses, fishmongers) as well as propertied private users. Consumers, appealing to public opinion or calling for representation of the public interest, tended to invoke a ratepaying public.

Public health discourse promoted a more inclusive, universal notion by linking consumers' interests to those of community welfare. A gulf emerged, however, between consumer interests and consumer knowledge. In contrast to the consumer envisaged by Victorian and Edwardian free traders, or the more familiar recent model of the rational, utility-maximizing individual, the new interest in the consumer in the water debates of the late 1840s and early 1850s had ignorance at its starting point. Consumers allowed themselves to be cheated, Kingsley argued, paying for water the companies wasted. '[P]ure and wholesome water' was the aim, but 'the consumer [was] not the best judge of this', being ignorant of the new science of public health and 'often content for years to drink ... fluids which physicians ... warn ... in vain, to be mere diluted poison'. Kingsley contributed to the broadening of the social persona of the consumer, referring also to users of standpipes. Poor consumers were doubly hurt: not having clean or soft water, they worked longer and wore away more soap and fabric in the process of washing.[26] Yet all consumers shared a common position of ignorance and apathy. Self-interested, short-sighted shopkeepers and middle-class local government representatives deprived the city of the civic-minded leadership found elsewhere. Water company power and the impotent consumer resulted from a materialist culture and its erosion of public spirit.

Such contrasts between consumer (social need and public interest) and materialism (selfish interest and money) are noteworthy for running counter to the individualist and market-based conceptions of the consumer that have structured recent debates about consumption and citizenship.[27] Interestingly, in his appeal to the ignorant consumer Kingsley drew directly on John Stuart Mill's *Principles of Political Economy*. Unlike economists on the continent, Mill was strongly opposed to state attempts 'to create consumers' and overcome 'underconsumption' and thought the discussion of consumption as a separate branch of political economy misguided.[28] Where Mill inspired Kingsley and others was in his connection of consumer knowledge to a moral project of self-cultivation operating beyond the commercial domain. Consumer knowledge here did not concern price awareness but those 'things, ... the worth of which the demand of the market is by no means a test'. The consumer came to be of interest at the point where the issue ceased to be one of serving 'the daily uses of life' or ministering to existing inclinations and became a civilizing project: the consumption of things tended 'to raise the character of human beings'. This developmental view of knowledge and self-formation suggested an immature rather than a sovereign consumer. 'The uncultivated cannot be competent judges of cultivation', as Mill put it characteristically. Put differently, consumers were not a solution, unfolding through the price mechanism of demand and supply, but a problem, a cultural project for civil society. This association – between the consumer, the underdeveloped self and the need for the ethical cultivation of higher sensibilities – would become a prominent theme in late nineteenth and early twentieth-century progressive politics and social philosophy in Europe and America.[29]

Earlier, in 1851, Mill had lent support to a call for a municipal take-over of London water,[30] but his discussion of consumer cultivation in the *Principles* related to education. Kingsley's instinctive connection between Mill's consumer and the need for water reform suggests the fluidity of contemporary conceptions of water as a material and cultural good: water met physiological needs but, equally, cultivated self and moral conscience and socialized individuals as virtuous members of the community. Self-government depended on England showing that 'her boasted civilization and liberty has a practical power of self-development'.[31]

These intertwined themes of self-fashioning and self-government, civic engagement and Christian duty, were not merely literary tropes but provided a language for the political mobilization of water users. The cholera outbreak of 1848–9 – killing

14,000 in London – triggered the formation of the Metropolitan Parochial Water Supply Association (MPWSA).[32] Founded in Southwark, at its peak in 1850–1 the Association attracted representatives from ninety parishes, over an area of 1¼ million people, with forty vestries petitioning Parliament. It brought together local officials, sanitary and housing reformers, surgeons and respectable ratepayers – a broad middle-class alliance pressing for public water management and for a constant supply at high pressure. Economic rationale and Christian teaching were complementary, warning of the 'moral slaughter' as well as 'physical devastation' resulting from poor water. Concern for the poor combined with an increasingly assertive sense of the consumer as taxpayer and representative of the public interest. 'Competition, animated by mere ... gain', the MPWSA argued, 'has totally failed to secure the necessary advantages... The consumer has been sacrificed, that the producer might be enriched'.[33] Here too, the consumer appeared in a narrative of social development that challenges the conventional story in which the material and discursive unfolding of the 'modern' consumer takes place only after the fulfilment of basic needs (characterizing 'traditional' society).[34] The MPWSA took a different view. Although British society was the most affluent in the world – with the 'highest mental and spiritual wants ... satisfied'– 'the necessities of the most elementary animal ... requirements have been neglected'.[35] The consumer was to tame, not to strengthen, Mammon.

These 'consumers' were stirred by recent images of cholera and anxieties of divine retribution, but also by the dramatic increase in local water rates following the renewal of a monopoly agreement between the Southwark and Lambeth companies. Public control would provide better service at a lower price, they hoped. Although they failed to formulate a precise scheme, the principles of consumer representation were clear: a water management board elected by and accountable to ratepayers.[36] The consumer was the water taxpayer not the water user.

The MPWSA's political rationale (and failure) was part of the larger liberal project of creating virtuous citizens by expanding local self-government. Assessments of the capacity for civic-mindedness of local taxpayers inevitably influenced the nature and political appeal of reform schemes. When in the vestry of St Luke's propertied and commercial users of water met in July 1851, W. Horne, 'a large consumer of water in trade', insisted that 'ratepayers are quite competent to the management of the water supply. They are generally willing to ... take part in parish affairs'. In this district of 55,000 people, the vestrymen spoke on behalf of the inhabitants suffering from poor water. In contrast to the vestry's £30 electoral qualification, Horne (a Poor Law Guardian) called for 'some new body..., to be elected by the consumers... [E]very ratepayer should have a voice'.[37] The growing reflexivity of ratepayers as water consumers benefited from parallel debates over gas supply and the representation of the interests of (mainly commercial) gas consumers.[38]

The MPWSA was close to Mill's Athenian vision of representative local government. Other sanitary reformers such as Chadwick, with low expectations of local taxpayers, looked instead to the central state for public investment and services. Both sides shared a view of the water problem as a sign of 'the abdication of the most imperative functions of citizenship', in the words of the MPWSA. Where they differed was in their estimation of a property-owning electorate's ability to overcome this apathy. The rights of the 'consumer' could be invoked to underwrite a more ambitious role for local taxpayers, but there were other ratepayers for whom the prospect of public management raised fears of spiralling costs and risky investments in new technologies.[39] The fragmented nature of London's local government made it easy for opponents of public control to play off the latter against the former.

The select committee on the 1851 Metropolis Water Bill captured this tension and illustrates some of the difficulties faced by advocates of consumer representation. Edward Collinson, an MPWSA supporter and former chairman of the Board of Guardians for St George-the-Martyr, Southwark, faced challenges to the MPWSA's claims to speak for the public. How representative were their gatherings of rate-payers? A meeting in December 1849 brought together 137 parish officers from thirty-three parishes. An 1851 meeting in Southwark produced a unanimous requisition signed by 700 inhabitants, 'the largest ... for a public meeting that ever was known in the borough'. Yet there were 'about 280 parishes in the metropolis', Collinson was reminded by the counsel for the Bill. Nor was it clear that the parish officers attending were elected by their ratepayers. Collinson's was an 'open' vestry (open to all ratepayers), but others were not. And if the Association truly represented the interest of consumers, critics asked, why did it have to cancel its activities in the summer of 1850 because of a lack of funds?[40]

If only supported by a minority of ratepayers, how could the Association justify the potentially ruinous burden of a public take-over of the water companies? Nor was it clear that, once water was in public hands, ratepayers would be willing to spend higher taxes on much-needed investment in new sources of supply, reservoirs and pipes; ratepayers' fiscal conservatism had blocked improvements in Derby, Reading and several other towns.[41] Moreover, as the Lambeth Company engineer emphasized, poor or deficient supply was often the fault of selfish landlords who failed to furnish tenants with butts or repair interior pipes.[42]

Consumers themselves were far from homogeneous. Water districts had different material and natural properties (such as landscape and building height), as well as different water sources, entailing different costs, quantity and quality of water. To amalgamate companies into one public body might pitch consumers against consumers – 'Bethnal Green against Hyde Park Gardens'.[43] Here, then, the asymmetry was not between consumer and monopoly, but between different groups of consumers. Critics of the compulsory rate favoured by the MPWSA were quick to point out that it would adversely affect the many occupiers of houses serving as both shop and home. More generally, such proposals raised fears that public control would exacerbate rather than diminish social polarization. Calls for public control in the name of the consumer, by the MPWSA and in Francis Mowatt's unsuccessful bill for a 'water parliament', might be little more than a scam by better-off citizens to reap disproportionate benefits from public services.

The idea that the water consumer had a right to representative control and ownership had nevertheless by 1850 become an established part of political discourse, though the form and level of representation remained contentious. While some vestries continued to press for local control,[44] municipal control became a real possibility with the establishment of the Metropolitan Board of Works (MBW) in 1855 and was taken up with sustained vigour by the London County Council in the 1890s. The 1880 parliamentary select committee opened its report on London's water purchase in words almost identical to those cited in 1850 by the MPWSA: 'the supply of water to the Metropolis should be placed under the control of some Public Body, which shall represent the interests and command the confidence of the water consumers'.[45]

Expanding Consumers: Identities, Needs and Entitlements

The quality of London's water supply probably improved in the second half of the nineteenth century, following relocation of the companies' intakes, improved storage and filtration and the transformation of the sewerage system, although anxieties about epidemics, eels and microbes persisted; developments in chemistry and bacteriology arguably increased sensibilities of risk.[46] Patrick Joyce has presented the Chadwickian revolution as a paradigmatic development in '[t]he "black boxing" of sanitation as a matter of science and technology, separate from the political'.[47] Water consumption and supply, however, followed a different trajectory. Instead of being part of a general framing of the material world in durable forms, water consumption remained fluid and contentious, fuelling political mobilization and raising questions of political subjectivity and authority. As a political actor, legal entity and part of an imagined community of users, the consumer acquired a new prominence in the 1870s–90s. The water wars of this period continued certain earlier themes – such as monopoly versus consumer – but at the same time expanded the identity of the consumer through a more extensive contestation of its membership, rights and needs. As a concept and identity, the consumer was one of the beneficiaries of the dynamic democratic culture created by the 1867 and 1884 Reform Acts, the extension of the borough franchise (1867, 1869) and the rise of progressive politics in London.[48] We shall focus on three areas of this expansion: consumers' successful challenge of the basis for water rate assessment, the invoking of consumer rights by commercial 'consumers' and the activism of Consumer Defence Leagues.

The mobilization of the consumer as ratepayer needs to be placed in the context both of the changing *basis* on which companies charged consumers and of the disproportionate *increase* in the amount of the water tax relative to other goods. Until the mid-nineteenth century, companies had estimated each household's domestic consumption (counting rooms or chimneys, for example). Legislation in 1847/52 compelled water companies to provide water for domestic supply. At the same time, the companies' Special Acts of 1852 introduced a new regime of maximum legal rates for six of the companies, in the form of a graduated scale of percentages set against 'annual value'.[49] Domestic water rates in London became based on the value of property, not actual use, in contrast to other European capitals like Paris (where it was based on estimated consumption) or Berlin (where private use was metered).[50] Importantly, water-closets, baths and gardens, excluded from 'domestic supply' obligations, remained subject to extra charges. Commercial and industrial properties were also assessed separately and increasingly by meter. The precise meaning of annual value, however, was left underspecified. London water rates may have been below the charges levied in provincial cities, as defenders of the companies stressed. Still, the inequalities in charges faced by householders in different districts were glaring. In 1890, for example, the owner of a house of £50 rateable value paid £2 4s. if supplied by the Chelsea Company, but £3 17s. if dealing with Lambeth.[51]

Charging on the basis of annual value had enormous financial implications, tying water rates to the tremendous property boom. While Londoners saw the price of food fall and enjoyed the declining costs of other utilities like gas, thanks to new technologies, water rates were going up and up. It is doubtful whether water companies reaped sufficient profit from the charging system to meet the ever-expanding needs of a growing city like London – water supply was liable to diminishing returns and benefited less from cost-saving technologies.[52] What is certain is that it made water companies vulnerable to charges of profiteering and inevitably drew them into political debates about the 'unearned increment' and progressive taxation in radical politics. Reformers argued that growth in site value alone gave the companies an annual windfall of some £200,000 (one fifth of their dividends) in 1897, 'for which they have provided no greater advantages to the consumers'.[53]

The post-1852 payment regime became a rich source of consumer protest from the 1870s, as the legitimacy of different versions of annual value came under fire. Controversy over valuation raised fundamental questions. Who was a 'consumer'? Who had the right to compel the companies to provide water? What was 'essential domestic supply' and for what 'domestic' purpose, by what kind of service and on what basis could companies charge or disconnect their customers?

The repercussions of a legal case brought against the Grand Junction Company reveal the development of 'the consumer' as an increasingly contested site between water companies, on the one hand and propertied water users and ratepayers (mainly middle class, but also increasingly clerks and artisans) as well as commercial users, on the other. In 1882 Archibald Dobbs, a barrister with progressive political ambition, decided to do what generations of consumer advocates have done since: he introduced a test case challenging the method of property valuation. The difference to Dobbs, the leaseholder of a modest house in Paddington, was small: £4 per cent on the 'net value' of £118 instead of on the 'gross value' of £140. The difference to the water companies was the potential loss of several hundred thousand pounds and an avalanche of litigation from aggrieved ratepayers seeking to retrieve over-payments. Supported by several vestries, Dobbs pursued the case all the way to the House of Lords and won. [54]

Water companies were quick to decry the Lords' decision, but in most cases decided to abide by the new interpretation, revising their rates. [55] Dobbs became the hero of the 'rate-paying public' and, amidst cheers in public meetings, promised to continue his battle to secure the same advantage for 'every water consumer in London'. [56] A network of Water Consumers' Defence Leagues (WCDLs) sprang up all over London. These leagues had some kinship with earlier ratepayer associations and drew support from prominent vestries, but were not parish-based. Between 1883 and 1885 branches were established in Islington, East London, Clapham and other parts of London; consumer leagues also emerged in other cities, like Sheffield. They held public meetings, distributed leaflets and posters, wrote to the press and had the support of several local MPs. Focused at first on annual value, they were reinvigorated in the mid-1890s by water shortages in south and east London, circulating 'Instructions to Consumers', with advice not to fill in company questionnaires and to pay water rates only on the poor law assessment rateable net value. [57] They set up advice bureaus and provided legal support. Pressure by the Battersea Water Consumers' Defence Association (WCDA) and by East End Leagues led to reduced rates for members and equitable settling of disputes without recourse to litigation. [58] In more affluent areas, like St John's Wood, propertied individuals were emboldened by Dobbs' success and instructed their solicitors against the long-standing 'robbery': by over-charging, the companies were violating the property rights of consumers. [59] In other places, water consumers were less fortunate as water companies successfully objected to 'incorrectly rated' values. [60] Still, the proto-Naderite foundations of consumer advocacy had been laid.

The companies' response to the campaigns only reinforced the centrality of the consumer. In correspondence with the Local Government Board and the Wandsworth District Board of Works in 1884, the secretary of the Southwark and Vauxhall Company was in little doubt of the serious threat represented by these grass-roots consumer associations with their boycotts. One strategy was to turn consumers' public health rights against them: the company stopped the water supply of ratepayers withholding rates, hoping that the sanitary authority would step in, since it could not allow houses to remain occupied without sufficient water. But the Wandsworth Board made it clear it would not do the company's dirty work and its powers 'should not be used as a means of *enforcing payment*'. The company had experienced unprecedented difficulties in collecting rates but also realized that to cut off supply in cases of non-payment could inflame the situation; in a district of 102,781 houses, only 135 had been cut off in the preceding six months. [61]

The weak regulatory setting left, however, plenty of possibilities for the companies. Another strategy was to recoup declining profits from average householders by turning the screw on rich and commercial users. A committee of 'aggrieved occupiers' was quickly formed after the New River Company raised rates in the City. Wealthy firms were consumers too, they argued. The case of Cooke, Sons & Co. versus the New River Company hinged on the very question of who was a consumer and who was not. In his six-storey warehouse in the New River district, Cooke paid by *meter* for a hydraulic lift but by *rate* for 'domestic' uses of water, such as toilet flushing. In 1887 Cooke sought to discontinue his payment of these 'domestic dwelling house' rates, demanding that all his warehouse water be classed as non-domestic and therefore metered. The company, however, argued that if Cooke no longer claimed to be using water for domestic purposes, payable by rate, he ceased to be a consumer under existing legislation and had no right to demand supply or meter.[62]

The New River Company's Act (1852) had left the nature of consumers and their entitlement ambiguous and Cooke eventually lost. What mattered historically, however, was that the dispute over entitlement to metered supply revealed the widening social functions of the rights and expectations of consumers. Effectively, Cooke had turned to the identity of the consumer as a way of extending to commercial users the rights of private consumers to a secure water supply. Against a narrower legal definition, consumer advocates began to champion more 'common sense' definitions of the consumer. Significantly, this involved at first only a partial broadening. The consumer 'may be taken to mean the whole human race', but only if pressed to 'an absurd length', Dobbs felt. Given the necessity of contracting for water supply, it excluded 'infants', 'lodgers', 'non-householders', 'paupers' and 'lunatics' (house-holding women were not mentioned here). Property and ability to pay remained essential.[63]

In the context of continuing fears of epidemic disease and concern over water shortages, the conception of the consumer became more socially inclusive, as questions of private rights fused with concerns for public welfare and consumer mobilization created new social solidarities. When a mechanic walked into the offices of the Water Consumers' Defence League in High Holborn in 1884, it was found that his charges were nearly double the legal rate (at £2 2s. per year on a house rented at £37). '[W]ater consumers [are] placed ... between two fires', one Massey Mainwaring wrote to *The Times*: 'water at an exorbitant rate, or no water and the dread of cholera'. His rates having increased from £16 16s. to over £20 16s., Mainwaring had also consulted the League office and expressed his sympathies with the mechanic. As consumers, rent-paying tenants were now linked to rich inhabitants of Belgravia.[64]

Complaints and legal action by tenants suggest a growing sense of entitlement and consumer awareness amongst social groups not formally qualifying under the dominant rubric of ratepayer consumers. The status of non-ratepaying tenants had always been precarious in the English system, where service depended on the landlord's payment of water rates. In the short term, the Dobbs decision put some vulnerable tenants at risk, where landlords felt encouraged to enter into disputes with companies on precarious grounds. In the long-term, however, such cases helped to disseminate more ambitious views of company obligations to water consumers. R. Hayward of West Ham, for example, rented out 39 houses and, in the eyes of the East London Company, was 'one of those perverse Landlords', with 'passions … enflamed by the Agitators and their "Leagues"', who erroneously believed that the parish assessment was the basis under Dobbs. When the company threatened to disconnect the water because of his year-long refusal to pay on the basis of its valuation, Hayward took his case to court, stressing in a letter to the Home Secretary (Harcourt) that the company threatened to deprive over seventy families, 'no parties to the dispute, of an element alike necessary to health and Existence'.[65] Increasingly, non-ratepaying tenants asserted their own rights. Paulet, a weekly tenant, was given notice to quit by his landlord, who paid the water rate. When he refused to leave, the landlord instructed Chelsea Waterworks to stop his supply. Paulet protested, invoking the Water Companies Act (1887) and had the company fined by the magistrate: 2s. for each day of non-supply. Paulet eventually lost, but there can be little doubt of his own sense of right as a consumer.[66]

The weak formal powers of consumer complaint were increasingly stretched by this expanding social conception of the consumer. A minimum of twenty 'inhabitant' householders' signatures were legally required before the Local Government Board (LGB) could act on a complaint. 'Water famines' from the 1870s onwards produced memorials to the LGB from Kensington to the East End, from householders and tenants. In September 1896, for example, tenants and householders in Lambeth protested against a failure to supply. As the company pointed out in painstaking detail, the protest was invalid; fewer than twenty of the signatories were ratepaying householders. The list included several non-ratepaying tenants – men and women – who nonetheless insisted they should be heard since water rates were included in their rent.[67] Attempts by water companies to exploit such technicalities were increasingly considered in poor taste by government officials.[68]

In 1895, 1896 and 1898 many parts of London were gripped by a series of 'water famines' and protests that crystallized consumer identity. Shortages were most severely felt in East London, where the preponderance of poor and working-class water users ensured the broadening of the terms of water consumer debates. In August 1898 the 700-strong Bromley Branch of the Union of Gasworkers and General Labourers pressed the LGB to compel the East London Company to keep water running for more than six hours a day since the 'poor' had no cisterns to supply WCs without water, 'thereby creating a danger to our wives and children'.[69] In Hackney ratepayers called a meeting in September 1898 to protest against the same company's 'criminal neglect of the consumer' in restricting supply to four hours a day. The chairman 'hoped there would be no deaths … as a result of the … famine', but considered that 'some of the directors (a voice, "All") might be charged with manslaughter'. This agitation attracted an overflow of over 1,000 outdoors.[70] The East London Water Consumers' Defence Association pressed for the municipalization of water and called on consumers to boycott rates for water not supplied. Radical imagery (see Figure 1) showed the water monopoly as a rocky skull propped up by 'Capitalism' and 'Government Acts', with helpless women, men and children, squashed by cholera and typhoid, waiting for Moses to strike water from the rock with his rod, 'Municipal Control'. Moses the 2nd is cheered on by a worker whose pocket holds a paper: 'Public Opinion'.

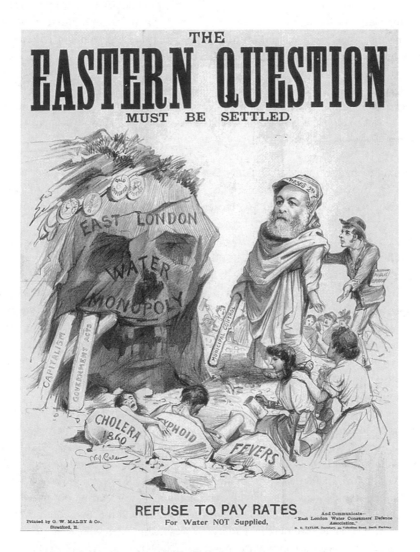

Figure 1 Poster of the East London Water Consumers' Defence Association, 1898

Source: PRO, COPY 1, 143 folio 165. Reproduced with permission of the Public Record Office (PRO), National Archives, United Kingdom.

At the same time that 'the consumer' became socially more inclusive of non-ratepaying working people and the poor, it became newly exclusive in undermining the claims of rich commercial users. The 'famines' pitched unmetered domestic users against metered commercial users suspected of being favoured by water companies at the expense of domestic consumers.[71] Progressive attempts to tax the unearned increment, mirrored in the water rate debates, challenged the claims of ratepaying firms to be fellow consumers. The interest of commercial or rich users in paying only for water used – as in the Cooke case – ran counter to a progressive interest in using the water rate as a tax to provide municipal services. William Torrens, the promoter of the 1885 Water Rate Definition Act, complained of the

> outcry ... lately raised by the owners of luxurious mansions, great warehouses, and improved ... offices, that they should be ... taxed only for ... occasionally washing their hands ... A water-rate according to property and income, not ... poverty and privation, is one of the justest and wisest burthens that any community can bear.[72]

The rich, too, had an interest in healthy tenants, advocates of ground values argued. Defenders of water companies responded that the graduated system of rates in poor areas like east London and Southwark meant that already 'the rich pay for the poor'.[73]

The consumer was now moving towards the private end-user, but this movement was neither linear nor complete by 1900. The poor and working people were not only private end-users, but sometimes ran small businesses from home. *The Times'* Special Correspondent wrote of the hardship of a Jewish family in Whitechapel during the summer of 1896: a 'respectable-looking couple' with 'children, well kept', who filled their baths and additional casks from a tap in the backyard – 'the usual arrangement' – to catch the intermittent supply. Their 'real grievance' was that they needed constant supply for a small lemonade business.[74] Thousands of laundrywomen, fishmongers and other small traders, mixing domestic and commercial premises, were similarly affected by intermittent supply.

The coming of consumer society is conventionally associated with a bifurcation between a domestic, female world of consumption and a public, male sphere of production and commerce.[75] The politics of water are a reminder that, for a significant group, the domestic and the commercial were still fused in the late nineteenth century. Much of the actual consumption of water 'for domestic purposes' taking place in households – cooking, laundry and cleaning – was carried out by women. Like Charles Lyel, whose wife had to save water in the bath for 'the requirements of the servant and her assistant in the scullery', it was mainly men who, as householders and ratepayers, spoke for their wives, mothers, daughters or servants.[76] Female water users might express grievances within memorials to the LGB, but generally it was male ratepayers and tenants who publicly articulated the water consumer's domestic interest.[77]

The Consumer between Waste and Abundance: Rationalities and Responsibilities

Daniel Roche begins his historical discussion of water in France with a passage recalling how, in the 1950s, when a rural area in southern France finally received a modern water supply, an elderly woman responded by keeping the tap on constantly.[78] New technologies require new knowledge and habits and produce new norms, expectations and behaviours.[79] The late nineteenth-century conflicts over 'water famines' in London, Manchester, Liverpool and elsewhere were political manifestations of the growing tension between water consumers' expanding everyday practices and expectations and the companies' uphill struggle to provide constant supply for expanding cities. Between the 1860s and 1890s London water companies almost doubled the amount of water pumped through the system, already supplying 175 million gallons daily (31 gallons per person) by 1890.[80] With the introduction of a 'constant supply' and the diffusion of hot running water and WCs (even if only in shared corridors in working-class housing) came a new sense of entitlement. Indeed, water companies and critics of municipalization argued that the Consumer Leagues had reinforced a dangerous sense of popular entitlement, as if water were a free, natural good. '[G]ood water laid on in the house', the conservative physician Arthur Shadwell emphasized, 'is no more a gift of Nature than loaves of bread brought to the door. And bread is equally one of the necessaries of life'. The 'modern town-dweller' had become so used to 'taps to turn and buttons to press, that he regards them as natural, forget[ting] ... to whom he owes them'.[81]

Water companies and water-advocacy groups today are aware of the difficulties of changing consumer habits. Water-saving is currently promoted through a variety of educational and commercial tools, from *Finding Nemo* stickers and local festivals to trade-in schemes for wasteful garden hoses. In the late-Victorian period, neither water companies nor Consumer Leagues produced anything like the more recent apparatus of governmentality. As detailed as the discussion was about rates, quality, hours and volumes of supply, it was vague about the timing and frequency of water use for different functions in the home, such as the washing of the body or clothes. The topic that did come to the fore with a growing sense of entitlement in the 1880s and 1890s was waste.

The debate about the wasteful water consumer reflects the impact of constant supply on consumer expectations and sensibilities and provides an early commentary on human behaviour under conditions of mass consumption. If, as the companies insisted, an abundant supply of water was pumped through their mains, why the numerous protests about a 'famine'? Where did the water go? The debate about waste laid bare the different rationalities informing the habits of consumption of different groups. In doing so, it raised questions about consumer knowledge and responsibility and about the fractures of a 'public' consumer interest.

Companies controlled the supply of water to the doorstep but had limited powers over the arrangements of pipes, stop-cocks and receptacles on the inside. The role of internal pipes and cisterns was one of the most long-standing issues of public debate. Was company water already polluted in the mains or was it polluted by shared water butts and by consumers who 'will not look after their own affairs' and allowed their cisterns to rot?[82] By the 1880s Consumer Leagues' efforts to create more literate, active consumers met with a concerted counter-attack from companies holding wasteful consumers responsible for shortages and dirt. Constant supply shifted the problem from poor equipment to irresponsible use or waste. During the alleged 'famine' of August 1896, for example, the East London Company continued to pump no less than 154 gallons daily to each house. The problem was, it insisted, that 'consumers took not the slightest interest in the ... careful use of the water, and made no provision against drought, frost, or the breaking of the mains'.[83] The historical emergence of the consumer as a citizen, then, was accompanied by a critique of the apathetic consumer.

Water companies sought to drive a wedge between responsible and irresponsible consumers, reminding those who left their taps running that 'this waste is distinctly illegal, and ... a great source of inconvenience to neighbouring consumers'. In the summer of 1883 alone over 600,000 notices were distributed across London. Water Examiner Frank Bolton criticized the 'apathy and carelessness of a great number of the consumers'.[84] The water famines from 1895 on brought another wave of such communications, hosepipe bans and threats to return to intermittent service.[85] What appeared irrational waste to some, however, was perfectly rational behaviour to others. There is evidence that poor and working-class tenants left water running because of unsatisfactory or non-existent storage facilities and inconvenient or unreliable hours of supply where companies reinstated intermittent supply.[86] *Punch* was quick to caricature the gulf between company attacks on wasteful gardening and the realities of poverty, picturing a company turncock threatening women and children bearing empty pots around a dry standpipe.[87]

In 1851 gas-fitter Edward Collinson had responded to the select committee that 'careful' consumers could be protected from others' wastefulness by home visits, on the gas inspector model, as long as control was with local authorities. By the 1890s the meter had become for many the preferred means by which consumers might internalize more rational and economizing consumption habits.[88] The case for water meters was taken up in 1875 by the MBW and, in the 1880s, by the City Corporation. The dramatic increase in rateable value spread demand for meters well beyond expensive City properties to include middling ratepayers in Consumer Defence Leagues and London County Council (LCC) representatives from the East End. Pointing to the provision of metered commercial users during the 1895/6 famines, some domestic consumers successfully deducted 'a fair sum' from their rates for a lack of 'sufficient' supply.[89]

Metered provision was a legislative failure. Obstacles included cost: an average meter was estimated at almost £5 (twice the annual water charge for a middle-class house). Water companies were not universally opposed to meters, but the gains from charging on a rapidly increasing rateable value provided little incentive. Moreover, as one commentator suggested, meters might reduce waste 'where the consumer pays directly ... but ... in the case of the small houses in East London, where the effects of the late drought have been most severely felt, the landlord almost invariably pays the water rate. Consequently payment by meter would be no deterrent to the consumer (the tenant) and he might go on wasting the water, ... with absolute impunity'.[90] The meter debate of the 1890s reveals the widening social imagery of the consumer – now including non-ratepaying tenants – but also the resulting tensions between consumers in different socio-economic positions.

Companies used meters outside the home, along with 'water stethoscopes', to detect leakage or waste and could cut off offenders for systematic waste. In the increasingly confrontational water politics of the 1880s and 1890s, however, the London companies were loath to force their limited powers on wasteful consumers in general. '[G]oing to law is generally useless', *The Times'* Special Correspondent found, 'because of the universal odium in which the ... companies are held'; magistrates, moreover, were also 'consumers and human'.[91] Recourse to law was reserved for strong cases, which illustrate the extremes of consumer waste confronting the companies. Several East London consumers informed on neighbours during the 1896 drought. On 22 June, after a month in which rainfall had dropped to 4 inches (from an average of 25 inches) and after repeated warnings, J. Wheeler of Leyton was summoned. Wheeler paid for domestic use only but ran a pipe to his backyard, with the tap turned full on, using up to 500 gallons an hour. Such waste, the company charged, made it difficult to provide others with sufficient water and it threatened to shut the mains. The water flowed into a pond in Wheeler's garden, in which 'about 20 ducks' were swimming happily.[92]

Conclusion: Revisiting Consumer Society via Water Consumers

Our analysis of nineteenth-century water politics has implications for both our understanding of the evolution of the consumer and our approach to consumer society more generally. Water politics were fluid in the sense that debates about water – access, needs and rights – created new social needs, sensibilities and political identities. The role of water in refashioning the self and body through new ideas and practices of hygiene and cleanliness is well known. Water played an equally significant role in shaping the new identity of the consumer. A rare and at best descriptive category in earlier centuries, 'the consumer' evolved into a more prominent social and political persona in the nineteenth century. Alongside parallel contests over the taxation of other necessaries (bread and sugar), water played a seminal role in the development of the consumer. Several interrelated features stand out. First, the consumer emerged initially as the voice of male ratepayers and property-owners, before becoming more socially inclusive in the late century. Second, consumers did not begin as private users: the category included propertied private end-users but remained open to commercial users and those freeholders who paid tenants' water-rent but did not themselves consume the water. Third, the central site of contestation was the domestic sphere – the amount, cost, access and quality of water for a household represented by its head, the male propertied consumer – not the world of shops. Finally, the mobilization of the consumer took place over a good located outside a market system of provision. Price was not determined by use or the laws of demand and supply but by property value. Consumption was about using up or wasting a natural resource considered vital for civilized life, not about desire or the utility added in the exchange of a commercially purchased commodity. Politicization was about not only the level or price of consumption but also its changing temporal rhythm and control: constant supply held out to consumers a new sense of freedom – with running water from their domestic tap or external standpipe at any time they chose – that was threatened by the reintroduction of intermittent supply during 'famines'.

That the politics of water played such a large part in the evolution of consumers in a metropole that was the hub of an expanding commercial culture of consumption raises questions for the study of 'consumer society'. For all the subtle and complex understandings of consumption, historians, like sociologists, have tended to project an essential consumer into the past without enquiring into the historically specific formation of the consumer as a distinct category. When Victorians established the consumer, they did so by contesting a distinctive good through a broadly liberal political tradition of ideas and concerns about property, accountability, representation and public service. The consumer was a bounded subject. In the twentieth century, markets and liberal economics came to appropriate and universalize the consumer as the purchaser of any kind of good or service, but the social and political foundations of its identity were laid elsewhere. Many of the key debates associated with twentieth-century 'mass consumer society', and technocratic consumer movements,[93] were introduced by water consumers, consumer defence leagues and their critics. Consumer knowledge versus apathy, the asymmetry between 'impotent' consumers and monopolistic firms, the consumer as citizen, the wasteful versus the conscientious consumer – it was around water consumption that the consumer's characteristics took form.

The study of consumption has been shaped by intellectual currents and projects developed in the generations after the historical birth of the consumer charted here. Whether viewed as a source of social distinction and social solidarity, an instrument of alienation or, more recently, for self-fashioning, irony and resistance, the consumer has predominantly been framed through the study of durables, commercial goods and luxuries and through tastes, desires and signs. 'Basic' goods have been left to those concerned with international development and human rights or historians studying bread riots or subsistence crises. The argument of this chapter has been not only that contestation over necessaries and 'famines' continued in the modern period, but also that it was here that the consumer emerged as a prominent actor, identity and subject of politics. In most human cultures, water carries a variety of attributes, meanings and uses. In the modern period, new technologies, public health and changing bodily practices have transformed perceptions of needs, 'waste', and 'sufficient' supply. Rather than a dichotomy between essential ('basic') and non-essential goods, it was precisely the combination of notions about water as both a 'necessary' vital for health and a precondition for cleaner, more 'civilized' and responsible citizens that propelled the consumer forward. For those metropolitan men who began to agitate as consumers, water was about 'capabilities'.[94] Access to more, better and cheaper water was not merely about fulfilling basic needs but about the capabilities of truly human functioning. Of course, this argument was articulated within a society and political tradition identifying the consumer as a male property-owning citizen, but it provided a basis for a quasi-constitutional argument that consumers as citizens had a right to demand certain services and standards from their governments. At the beginning of the twenty-first century, water remains a contentious issue for users in affluent as well as poor areas of the globe; one in five UK households are in debt to their water company.[95] Water continues to bring together long-standing issues of citizenship, social exclusion, consumer education and human development alongside more recent concerns about sustainability. Historians and social scientists would do well to reintegrate ordinary goods like water into the study of consumer society.

Notes

*Thanks for comments to Martin Daunton, Christopher Hamlin, Anne Hardy, Patrick Joyce, Robert Millward, Elizabeth Shove, Rick Wilk, and to ESRC/AHRC (Res. 154250022) for assistance.

1. C. Lyel, *The Times*, 23 July 1895, 12e. 1 gallon is 4.55 litres.
2. Court report, *The Daily Chronicle*, 22 July 1895.
3. A. Hardy, 'Parish Pump to Private Pipes: London's Water Supply in the Nineteenth Century', in W.F. Bynum and R. Porter (eds), *Living and Dying in London* (London, 1991), pp. 76–93; C. Hamlin, *Public Health and Social Justice in the Age of Chadwick* (Cambridge, 1998); A.K. Mukhopadhyay, *Politics of Water Supply: The Case of Victorian London* (Calcutta, 1981); P. Joyce, *The Rule of Freedom: Liberalism and the Modern City* (London, 2003); S. Halliday, *The Great Stink: Sir Joseph Bazelgette and the Cleansing of the Victorian Metropolis*

(Thrupp, Stroud, 1999); S.C. Anderson and B.H. Tabb (eds), *Water, Leisure and Culture* (Oxford and New York, 2002); J.-P. Goubert, *La conquête de l'eau* (Paris, 1986); R.J. Evans, *Death in Hamburg: Society and Politics in the Cholera Years 1830–1910* (Oxford, 1987); F.M. Snowden, *Naples in the Time of Cholera, 1884–1911* (Cambridge, 1995).

4. T.B. Veblen, *The Theory of the Leisure Class: An Economic Study in the Evolution of Institutions* (New York, 1899); J.K. Galbraith, *The Affluent Society* (Boston, 1958); T. Richards, *The Commodity Culture of Victorian England* (London, 1991); S. Ewen, *Captains of Consciousness: Advertising and the Social Roots of the Consumer Culture* (New York, 1976); J. Baudrillard, *The Consumer Society: Myths and Structures* (London, 1998; orig. Paris, 1970); P. Bourdieu, *La Distinction: Critique sociale du jugement* (Paris, 1979). Notable exceptions include M. Douglas and B. Isherwood, *The World of Goods: Towards an Anthropology of Consumption* (London, 1979); J. Gronow and A. Warde (eds), *Ordinary Consumption* (New York, 2001); H.G. Haupt, *Konsum und Handel: Europa im 19. und 20. Jahrhundert* (Göttingen, 2003); F. Trentmann, 'Beyond Consumerism: New Historical Perspectives on Consumption', *Journal of Contemporary History*, 39(3) (2004), pp. 373–401.

5. F. Trentmann, 'The Genealogy of the Modern Consumer', in J. Brewer and F. Trentmann (eds), *Consuming Cultures, Global Perspectives* (Oxford and New York, forthcoming).

6. Joyce, *Rule of Freedom*, p. 65.

7. Public Record Office (PRO), The National Archives, London, MH 29/15: 'Monthly Report by Colonel Frank Bolton … upon the Water Supplied by Several Metropolitan Water Companies', pp. 7f.

8. *3 Hansard Vol. 117*, c. 465, 5 June 1851.

9. PRO, MH 29/24: *Report of the Royal Commission Appointed to Inquire into the Water Supply of the Metropolis* (1893), p. 15. Office of Water Services (OFWAT), *Security of Supply, Leakage and the Efficient Use of Water, 2002–2003 Report* (2003), p. 39.

10. J. Graham-Leigh, *London's Water Wars: The Competition for London's Water Supply in the Nineteenth Century* (London, 2000), chs 1 and 2.

11. Already 60% of waterworks in Britain were municipalized by the 1870s.

12. J. Wright, *The Dolphin: or, Grand Junction Nuisance* (London, 1827), p. 10, pp. 97f.

13. C. Hamlin, *A Science of Impurity: Water Analysis in Nineteenth Century Britain* (Bristol, 1990).

14. Mins. Evid., House of Commons Select Committee [HCSC] on Supply of Water to the Metropolis, 1821 (706), p. 97, in *Water Supply, 1: Reports and Papers, 1805–1840*; Graham-Leigh, *London's Water Wars*, pp. 65–71.

15. M.K. Knight, HCSC (1821), pp. 97f. London Metropolitan Archives (LMA): Acc/2558/GJ/08/072: 'St Mary-le-bone Anti-Water Monopoly Association

Fund', 14 October 1819; *Report of the Committee appointed by the Meeting of the Inhabitant Householders of the Parish of St Marylebone, … 14ᵗʰ October, 1819.*

16. Weale, HCSC (1821), p. 71.
17. Hardy, 'Parish Pump', pp. 82f. Halliday, *Great Stink,* pp. 28f 42–5.
18. Wright, *Dolphin,* p. 7.
19. W. Matthews, *Hydraulia* (London, 1835), pp. 330–3, pp. 73f.
20. Wright, *Dolphin,* p. 7; Matthews, *Hydraulia,* pp. 332, 350.
21. 'Thames Water Question', *Westminster Review,* 12 (1830), pp. 31, 33.
22. E. Collinson, Mins. Evid., HCSC on Metropolis Water Bill (643), Parliamentary Papers 1851 (XL), Q 5395. LMA: Acc/3168/018: *Metropolitan Drinking Fountain and Cattle Trough Association Annual Report 1866* (Earl of Grosvenor MP), p. 13.
23. LMA: Acc/2558/NR13/22: *The Supply of Water to the Metropolis of the Empire … by the Executive Committee of the Metropolitan Parochial Water Supply Association* [MPWSA] (n.d.), p. 1.
24. C. Kingsley, 'The Water Supply of London', *North British Review,* 15 (May 1851), pp. 231f.
25. W. O'Brien, 'The Supply of Water to the Metropolis', *Edinburgh Review,* 9 (April 1850), pp. 390, 399, 402; MPWSA, *Supply of Water.*
26. Kingsley, 'Water Supply', pp. 231, 234. See also Wright, *Dolphin,* pp. 8–10.
27. A. Blair, *The Courage of Our Convictions* (London, 2002); D. Marquand, *Decline of the Public: The Hollowing Out of Citizenship* (Oxford, 2004).
28. See D. Winch's chapter in this volume.
29. J.S. Mill, *Principles of Political Economy,* quoted in Kingsley, 'Water Supply', p. 231. H. Kyrk, *Economic Problems of the Family* (New York, 1929); C. Gide, *Cours d'économie politique* (Paris, 1909); J.A. Hobson, *The Evolution of Modern Capitalism* (London, 1894). See Trentmann, 'Genealogy of the Modern Consumer'.
30. *Public Agency v. Trading Companies: The Economic and Administrative Principles of Water-Supply for the Metropolis. Correspondence between John Stuart Mill, Esq. And the Metropolitan Sanitary Association on the Proper Agency for Regulating the Water-Supply for the Metropolis* (London, 1851).
31. Kingsley, 'Water Supply', p. 252.
32. For MPWSA, see Collinson, HCSC (1851), Qs 4935–5457. In the Southwark and Vauxhall Co. district, 2,880 died. In London's 1854 cholera outbreak, contamination was traced to water from this district. W. Luckin, *Pollution and Control: A Social History of the Thames in the Nineteenth Century* (Bristol, 1986), pp. 79–81.
33. Collinson, HCSC (1851), Qs 4971–72. MPWSA, *Supply of Water,* p. 13.
34. For a critique, see A. Appadurai (ed.), *The Social Life of Things* (Cambridge, 1986).

35. MPWSA, *Supply of Water*, p. 1.
36. MPWSA, *Supply of Water*, p. 4. Collinson, HCSC (1851), Q 5026, Q 5033.
37. *The Times*, 10 July 1851, 6c.
38. M. Daunton, 'The Material Politics of Natural Monopoly: Consuming Gas in Victorian Britain', in M. Daunton and M. Hilton (eds), *The Politics of Consumption* (Oxford and New York, 2001), pp. 69–88.
39. MPWSA, *Supply of Water*, p. 1. When the MBW introduced water purchase bills in 1878, some parishes joined forces with the water companies in petitioning Parliament, objecting that public management would mean higher charges 'without corresponding benefits'. LMA: Acc/2558/NR13/121: *Metropolis Water Supply Bills: Petition of the Vestry of the Parish of St Pancras*, p. 1. Opposition was especially pronounced amongst lower-middle-class ratepayers who controlled many borough councils, until the reforms of 1867 and 1869 (enfranchizing about 60% of working class men). M. Daunton, 'Taxation and Representation in the Victorian City', in R. Colls and R. Rodger (eds), *Cities of Ideas* (Ashgate, 2004), pp. 33–9; cf. C. Hamlin, 'Muddling in Bumbledom: On the Enormity of Large Sanitary Improvements in Four British Towns, 1855–1885', *Victorian Studies*, 32 (1988), pp. 79–83.
40. Collinson, HCSC (1851), Q 4967, Q 4980, Q 4982, Q 5079, Q 5091, Q 5118.
41. T. Hawksley, HCSC (1851), Q 13549, Q 13552.
42. J. Simpson, HCSC (1851), Q 12825.
43. Hawksley, HCSC (1851), Qs 13571–3.
44. PRO, MH 29/15: London Water Supply, Executive Committee of Vestries and District Boards: Letter, 29 January 1891; Memorandum, January 1891.
45. MPWSA, *Supply of Water*, p. 4 (quoting O'Brien). HCSC Report on London Water Supply (329), PP 1880 (X), p. iii. It recommended placing London water under the control of the City Corporation, MBW and representatives of suburban bodies.
46. B.F.C. Costelloe, 'London v. the Water Companies', *The Contemporary Review*, 67 (June 1895), pp. 811–13. Hamlin, *Science of Impurity*.
47. Joyce, *Rule of Freedom*, p. 69, drawing on B. Latour, *Science in Action: How to Follow Scientists through Society* (Milton Keynes, 1987).
48. J. Davis, *Reforming London: The London Government Problem, 1855–1900* (Oxford, 1988); S. Pennybacker, '"The Millennium by Return of Post": Reconsidering London Progressivism', in D. Feldman and G. Stedman Jones (eds), *Metropolis London: Histories and Representations since 1800* (London, 1989), pp. 129–62; E.F. Biagini and A.J. Reid (eds), *Currents of Radicalism: Popular Radicalism, Organised Labour, and Party Politics in Britain, 1850–1914* (Cambridge, 1991).
49. Simpson, HCSC (1851), Q 12790; A. Dobbs, 'The London Water Companies: A Review and an Impeachment', *The Contemporary Review*, 61 (January 1892), pp. 30–1.

50. Only Southwark and Vauxhall could be compelled to provide water by meter. PRO, MH 29/6: H.J. Smith, Minutes of the Select Committee on Private Bills as to the Southwark and Vauxhall Bill, 8 May 1884, Q 1297. For different pricing regimes on the continent, see Goubert, *Conquête de l'eau*, ch. 7.

51. PRO, MH 29/15: London Water Supply, Executive Committee of Vestries and District Boards, Memorandum, January 1891, p. 19 (evid. of S. Wood, Guildhall, 1890). Between 1851 and 1891 the average rateable value of houses variously increased by between 70% and 270%. In the Grand Junction district, a house with rateable value of £76 went up to £105 in this period; in the New River district, from £37 to £100. W.H. Dickinson, 'The Water Supply of London', *The Contemporary Review*, 71 (February 1897), p. 238. A. Shadwell, *The London Water Supply* (London, 1899), pp. 67f.

52. R. Millward, 'Urban Water Supplies, c. 1820–1950' (forthcoming); J. Cavalcanti, 'Economic Aspects of the Provision and Development of Water Supply in Nineteenth-Century Britain' (unpublished PhD thesis, Manchester University, 1991).

53. Dickinson, 'Water Supply of London', p. 239.

54. 'Dobbs v. Grand Junction Waterworks Company (Nov. 1883)' in F. Bolton and P.A. Scratchley (eds), *The London Water Supply* (London, 2nd edn 1888), pp. 182–8. In the 1889 LCC election, Dobbs stood for South Paddington and was narrowly defeated by a moderate.

55. PRO, MH 29/6: East London Water Works Company Report, 3 April 1884. PRO, MH 29/6: H.J. Smith, Minutes of the Select Committee on Private Bills as to the Southwark and Vauxhall Bill, 8 May 1884, Q 1311.

56. *The Times*, 20 December 1883, 6e: Holloway Hall meeting.

57. PRO, MH 29/6: H. Baines (Battersea Ratepayers' Association) to Local Government Board (LGB), 2 February 1884, and reply, 13 February 1884; Alfred Jelley (Sec., Southwark and Vauxhall Water Company) to LGB, 27 February 1884; Clapham, Stockwell and South Lambeth Water Consumers' Defence Association Notice (n.d.). MH 29/8: T.J. Ewing (Hon. Sec., Bethnal Green Branch WCDL) to Board of Trade, 20 April 1885. MH 29/22: Charles L. Floris (Hon Sec., Clapham WCDA [originally 'Clapham Ratepayers']) to Earl of Dudley, 13 August 1895; PRO, MH 29/27: Floris to LGB, 24 January 1896. MPs included Daniel Grant, Adolphus Morton and Percy M. Thornton. *The Times*, 16 July 1881, 6c; 20 December 1883, 6e; 2 January 1884, 6c; 21 March 1884, 10c.

58. *The Times*, 30 September 1884, 9f.; O. Coope, *The Times*, 9 October 1884, 5f.

59. PRO, MH 29/8: *St. John's Wood and South Hampstead Advertiser*, 29 October 1885.

60. PRO, MH 29/8: Chelsea Water Works Co. objection to St. George's, Hanover Sq. Assessment Committee, 24 June 1885.

61. PRO, MH 29/7: Wandsworth Board of Works to Sir W. Harcourt, 14 October 1884 (emphasis in original). MH 29/7, 10 November 1884: Alfred Jelley (Sec. of Southwark and Vauxhall Co.) to LGB.

62. Judgment in A. Dobbs, *By Meter or Annual Value?* (London, 1890), pp. 12–22, 49.

63. Dobbs, *By Meter*, p. 21, pp. 33f.

64. *The Times*, 17 November 1884, 8a.

65. PRO, MH 29/7: R. Hayward to Sir William Harcourt, 4 October 1884; I.A. Crookenden (Sec., East London Co.) to LGB, 15 October 1884; *The Daily Chronicle*, 16 October 1884; Royal Courts of Justice Judgment, 11 November 1884.

66. Bolton and Scratchley (eds), *London Water Supply*, p. 165.

67. PRO, MH 29/23, W.T. Bruce to LGB, 26 September 1896. Compounded ratepayers had local rates included in the rent.

68. PRO, MH 29/4: W.W.G. (LGB) advice to John Lambert (New Hampton memorial), 7 March 1881.

69. PRO, MH 23/33: Branch Secretary, National Union of Gasworkers and General Labourers, to LGB, 23 August 1898.

70. *The Times*, 6 September 1898, 7f. For ratepayer associations' growing rebelliousness, see A. Offer, *Property and Politics, 1870–1914* (Cambridge, 1981), pp. 295ff.

71. J. Harris, *The Daily Chronicle*, 22 July 1895. Harris offered domestic consumers free legal advice. The East London Company repeatedly rejected this charge, e.g. Crookenden, *The Times*, 31 July 1896, 10e.

72. W.T.M. Torrens, 'Pure Water and Plenty of It', *Macmillan's Magazine*, 63 (December 1890), p. 111. See also B.F.C. Costelloe, Chairman of Local Government and Taxation Committee (LCC), in *The Times*, 24 November 1892, 14d.

73. Shadwell, *London Water Supply*, pp. 68–9.

74. *The Times*, 3 August 1896, 6f.

75. For critical discussion, see C. Breward, *The Hidden Consumer: Masculinities, Fashion and City Life 1860–1914* (Manchester, 1999).

76. C. Lyel, *The Times*, 30 July 1895, 3d.

77. This contrasts with the prominence of women in visual representations of water consumers. Nineteenth-century drinking fountain and temperance imagery drew on traditional associations between water and femininity, but identified female figures, bearing pitchers, more as suppliers than consumers of water.

78. D. Roche, *A History of Everyday Things: The Birth of Consumption in France, 1600–1800* (Cambridge, 2000; orig. Paris, 1997), p. 135.

79. E. Shove, *Comfort, Cleanliness and Convenience: The Social Organization of Normality* (Oxford and New York, 2003).

80. W. Pole, 'Water Supply of London', *The Quarterly Review*, 174 (January 1892), p. 78.
81. Shadwell, *London Water Supply*, p. 13.
82. 'Thames Water Question' (1830), p. 38; Hamlin, *Science of Impurity*, pp. 191f.
83. *The Times*, 25 August 1896, 8a.
84. PRO, MH 29/5: East London Water Works Company, 'Notice to Consumers and Sanitary Authorities', 2 August 1883; Water Examiner's Monthly Report, July 1883, pp. 1–3. Bolton complained that many waste pipes were still linked directly to sewers and allowed gases back into the water.
85. PRO, MH 29/22: East London Water Works Co. Notice, 12 July 1895. *The Times*, 11 Sept. 1896, 4f.
86. A. Walmer, *The Times*, 3 August 1896, 6c.
87. 'East London Water Supply!', *Punch*, 8 August 1896.
88. HCSC (1851), Qs 5318–22. F.C. Rasch MP, *The Times*, 26 August 1896, 4a.
89. H. Buck, *The Times*, 3 August 1896, 6c; PRO, MH 29/22: Correspondence between Clapham Ratepayers and Southwark and Vauxhall Water Co., May–June 1895.
90. L.H., *The Times*, 26 August 1896, 4a.
91. *The Times*, 24 August 1896, 8c.
92. *The Times*, 22 June 1896, 16f.
93. H. Rao, 'Caveat Emptor: The Construction of Nonprofit Consumer Watchdog Organizations', *American Journal of Sociology*, 103 (1998), pp. 912–61; C. Beauchamp, 'Getting Your Money's Worth: American Models for the Re-making of the Consumer Interest in Britain, 1930s–1960s', in M. Bevir and F. Trentmann (eds), *Critiques of Capital in Modern Britain and America: Transatlantic Exchanges 1800 to the Present Day* (Basingstoke, 2002), pp. 127–50; L. Glickman, 'The Strike in the Temple of Consumption: Consumer Activism and Twentieth-Century American Political Culture', *The Journal of American History*, 88 (2001), pp. 99–128; M. Hilton, *Consumerism in Twentieth-Century Britain* (Cambridge, 2003); P. Maclachlan, *Consumer Politics in Postwar Japan* (New York, 2002).
94. A. Sen, *Commodities and Capabilities* (Amsterdam, 1985).
95. G. Klein, *Life Lines: The NCC's Agenda for Affordable Energy, Water and Telephone Services* (London, 2003), p. 2.

–4–

Women and the Ethics of Consumption in France at the Turn of the Twentieth Century

The *Ligue Sociale d'Acheteurs*

*Marie-Emmanuelle Chessel**

The turn of the twentieth century was a crucial period for the mobilization of reformers organizing themselves in the name of the consumer: the flourishing of boycotts, of spontaneous movements and of consumer organizations make it possible to speak of a politicization of consumption in these years, both in the United States and in Europe.[1] One particularly interesting example in this world of consumer activism was that of the consumers' leagues, created by men and women who sought to reform the behaviour of consumers in order to improve the working conditions of workers and employees. These leagues multiplied between 1890 and 1910 and they defined consumption as a mode of public expression and political action.

In Paris, in 1902, a consumers' league of this type was created, alongside the consumer cooperatives: the *Ligue Sociale d'Acheteurs* (the Social League of Buyers, LSA). The founding of this organization took place shortly before that of other consumers' organizations and movements agitating against the *vie chère* (expensive life), which sprang up around the First World War.[2] The LSA was established for the purpose of 'developing a sense of responsibility in buyers for the treatment of workers' and 'bringing about changes in working conditions'. Its members wanted to educate consumers, insisting most importantly on the ethics of consumption. The French consumers' league was influenced by its American counterpart, which had existed in New York since 1890. Starting in 1897, consumers' leagues were created in Philadelphia, Chicago and Boston and a National Consumers' League (NCL) in 1898.[3] The idea spread quickly to Europe: leagues emerged in the Netherlands and France in 1902, in Switzerland in 1903 and Germany in 1907. A *Lega dei compratori lombardi* appeared in Milan from 1906 to 1908, created by the *Società nazionale di patronato e mutuo soccorso per le giovani operaie*. A Spanish *Liga de compradoras* was founded in Barcelona and links existed with other American and European leagues, though we know very little about them. Finally, a consumers' league was created in Belgium in 1911–12, which reappeared in the inter-war period.[4]

The 'transfer' of consumers' leagues from the United States to France took place rapidly, in the context of a reforming elite on both sides of the Atlantic already open to international exchanges.[5] Contacts were secured between the founders of the American leagues – Florence Kelley and Maud Nathan in New York – and Jean and Henriette Brunhes, the couple who founded the first consumers' league in Paris. There is nothing astonishing about this. The founders of American consumers' leagues, like many reformers of the Progressive Era, were inspired by Europe: they had already 'borrowed' the idea of consumers' leagues from England in 1890. They also seemed happy to share their experiences and learn from European initiatives, a fact that favoured transatlantic exchanges among reformist movements in this period. The transfer of consumers' leagues from the United States to Europe was rapid because this common network of reformers already existed. The consumers' leagues constituted but one reform instrument (among many) being proposed as an alternative to economic liberalism and as a response to the social consequences of industrial capitalism then confronting Western societies. The leagues also offered reforming men and women a means of expressing their religious faith in a practical and daily way in secular organizations.

The existence of this broad network of American and European reformers did not preclude national particularities among them, particularly in cultural and religious terms. The founders of the American leagues, like Florence Kelley, belonged to Protestant circles, which had long been actively engaged in social activism in a context in which consumption had been an arena for social protest, from the early days of the American Revolution to the anti-slavery campaigns. Certain Jewish women, such as Maud Nathan, saw consumers' leagues as a personal and political means of engagement, as a way of moving beyond charity to 'preventive charity' by treating the causes rather than the consequences of poverty. In France, by contrast, consumers' leagues were run by Catholics.

The American version of consumers' leagues responded to the particular efforts of a group of Catholics influenced by the writings of John Ruskin – who insisted on the quotidian responsibilities of believers – and by the teachings of Pope Leon XIII. In the encyclical *Rerum Novarum*, Leon XIII enjoined Catholics to integrate evangelical principles into their social and economic activities. This gave rise to a current of 'social Catholicism' and to the creation of several women's organizations devoted to social action, a favourable context for the genesis of the LSA. In the tradition of '*integral*' (complete) Catholicism, these French 'social' Catholics insisted that it was not sufficient that religion remain a personal act, limited to one's individual conscience. Rather religion had to translate into daily practices which would ultimately affect a broader transformation of society according to religious principles. This set them apart from so-called 'liberal' Catholics. '*Integral*' Catholics believed that their faith could not be exclusively personal; through the mediation of the Church their faith would ultimately express itself in the transformation of society. From this principle followed their social activism. It is in this context that Henriette Brunhes' affirmation can be understood : '[We are persuaded] that more than mere discussions and theories it is the strict surveillance of each of our everyday actions and the careful study of our responsibilities that will allow us to spread social Christian principles in the world of work'.[6]

As in the United States, the LSA in France was created by women and women remained very involved until the end. This is why this league has been studied as a female organization.[7] True, women played the most important role in this league, especially at the beginning (1902–08). The role of men, however, became more important from the moment that the organization became national (1909–14). Men became increasingly involved, especially Jean Brunhes and his brothers, but also other 'social' Catholics such as Jacques Tourret from Lyons. This incorporation of men was already presaged at the turn of the century when, as in the United States, consumers' leagues became part of a broader intellectual, religious and political movement that surpassed women's traditional Christian philanthropic activities. In France consumer activism offered opportunities for Catholic intellectuals who were rethinking their role in society and for women seeking new ways to intervene in the public sphere beyond that of mere charity. The LSA offered possibilities that were at once discrete – they did not involve religious proselytizing – and practical, destined simultaneously to resolve the 'social question' and to reform a Catholicism confronted by industrial society and a new consumer culture.

Around 1900 the consumers' leagues in New York and Paris were comparable in terms of their discourse and their practices. The LSA encouraged its members to inform themselves about the working conditions of dressmakers and shop girls in department stores. Members were asked to choose 'correctly' from a 'white list' of 'good dressmakers' who were thought to treat their workers well and who promised not to make them work at night or on Sundays. Consumers in general and women in particular, were encouraged to reform their own shopping habits, particularly regarding when they shopped – on a daily, weekly and annual basis – always in relation to the effects that the timing of their shopping would have on workers. In terms of the shopping 'day', they were expected to refuse to have deliveries made in the evening. In terms of the 'week', they were to refuse to shop on Sunday, in order to allow workers a day of rest. In terms of the 'year', they were to make their Christmas purchases early in December to prevent employees in shops from being overworked during this busy season.[8]

The differences between these American and French organizations, however, increased in the decade before the First World War. The chapters of the LSA in France, whether in Lyons, in Marseilles or in the smaller cities of France, did not limit their attention and their activities to department stores or to the textile industry, as did their American counterparts. The French organizations became increasingly interested in other professions, in particular artisans, small shopkeepers and service employees (pastry makers, hairdressers and servants, for example). Like their counterparts in the United States, French consumers' leagues also tried new forms of action, like lobbying on labour legislation. However, in their discourse the French members of the LSA distanced themselves somewhat from the NCL.

Inspired by 'social Catholicism', the members of the LSA insisted upon the necessary collabouration of the state, businesses and consumers and not on their inevitable opposition; they continued to remind consumers of their responsibility to try to reform the working conditions of workers and employees. The debates which took place between American and French delegates at the first international conference of the LSA in Geneva in 1908 reflected these differences.[9]

Contrary to their counterparts in the United States, the French consumers' league was not a 'mass' organization: the first Parisian league had 250 members in 1902 and only 600 in 1908. In 1909 it became a national organization (the *Ligue Sociale d'Acheteurs de France*) and, by 1914, it had 30 sections and 4,500 individual members. In terms of its membership this organization pales in comparison to French consumer cooperatives (which had around 500,000 members in 1914), or the American National Consumers' League in 1916 (with its 15,000 members).[10] In spite of its small membership, the LSA offers a unique opportunity to think about important questions about consumption and French society at the beginning of the twentieth century. The creation of the LSA took place precisely when French society and consumption, was in the process of transformation, in particular in big cities. The LSA can be seen as one reaction to these changes: people from the LSA began to think about the relationships between bourgeois consumers and workers. Bourgeois consumers and workers were seen as very different groups: workers were not considered 'real' consumers. Middle-class members of the LSA, however, saw their own consumption linked to workers' work ; they tried to build a 'bridge' between these two separate worlds.

In the Heart of the Bourgeoisie

At first glance, the LSA betrays a reaction on the part of the French bourgeoisie and in particular on the part of bourgeois women, to the transformation of consumer society and to the evolution of values and practices which accompanied these changes. Even if one cannot speak of a total democratization of consumption at the beginning of the twentieth century,[11] changes in this direction could be seen in big cities, whether in advertising posters, the range of women in the streets and new types of women (working and consuming) in the shops. These changes were especially felt by men and women of the upper and middle-classes.[12]

Even if Charles Gide – the French promoter of consumer cooperatives who affirmed, in 1898, that the 'reign of the consumer' had arrived[13] – was openly cited by the promoters of the American and French consumers' leagues, the LSA was not at all like the consumer cooperatives. It did not bring together workers in order to buy goods at lower prices; nor did it want to defend the rights of consumers. As in other European countries, such as Germany, the LSA distinguished itself from other consumer associations dedicated to lowering the prices of products.[14] The LSA brought together women and men of the nobility and the upper middle-class trying to educate themselves and their bourgeois neighbours as consumers.

The French consumers' league was created in Paris by middle-class Catholics of good families, accustomed to doing charity work. The founder was Henriette Brunhes (1872–1914). She was the youngest of seven children. Her mother, Elise Weyer, was a fervent Catholic, who died in 1897 in a charity bazaar fire, a major disaster in which a great number of women perished who were of 'good society' and involved in charitable organizations. The sisters of Henriette Brunhes married the Marquis Maurice d'Elbée, Eugène Roland-Gosselin, Camille Bellaigue and the Baron Eugène Bodin de Galembert, Catholics integrated into this 'good society'; they were close to Pope Pius X and the *Action Française*, a political movement of the extreme right.

When she founded the LSA, Henriette Brunhes was surrounded by a small group of women who also came from the upper middle-class, notably the banking community (Henriette's father, Emile Hoskier, was a banker) and the army. In this small 'founding' group, there was a widow of a military man (Mme Klobb), the wife of an old officer (Mme Ludovic de Contenson) and the daughter of the founder of the Crédit Lyonnais (the Baronness Georges Brincard). Henriette Brunhes was thus a member of the *grande bourgeoisie*, a group close to the nobility and for which charity was the principal form of social activism. The list of Parisian members at the beginning of the league's existence confirms this bourgeois origin. One third of the members listed in 1905 (80 out of 251) can be formally identified in the *Bottin Mondain* from Paris (1904), and some of them were noble: the Comtesse Henri de Castries, Mme Charles de la Chapelle, the Comtesse Pierre de Cossee Brissac, the Marquise de Ganay.[15] If the composition of the league reflects a middle-class world, its discourse demonstrates that this world was also concerned with working-class people.

Consumers versus Workers

This bourgeois world saw itself as set apart from 'the people'. The consumers' league did not seek to educate workers, but to educate men and women of the middle-class in order to help workers. At the heart of their practice was a fundamentally paternalistic (or maternalistic) vision. The reigning idea was that bourgeois consumers must, by their purchasing practices, help improve working conditions for workers. They dedicated themselves to protecting workers and employees, who were imagined as fundamentally different from themselves, indeed as 'minors': consumers from the consumers' league and workers stood on either side of a huge divide.[16]

The 'non-working' women of the consumers' leagues thought of themselves as the only existing consumers. They could not imagine that the workers they were trying to protect were also consumers. The advice regarding consumer practices that the LSA gave to fellow members of the league clearly excluded working women. Workers and employees did not order their lingerie six months in advance, since they were paid either daily or weekly; organizing one's self and one's money in such a fashion was a bourgeois practice.[17] Workers were initially opposed to the closing of stores on Sunday because they worked all other days of the week. The opening of stores on Sundays had emerged precisely to accommodate a working class clientele, as well as rural clients who came to the city on Sunday to sell their products and to take advantage of the opportunity to do their own shopping.[18] When someone asked Henriette Brunhes how she might get workers to join her organization, she was unable to give a concrete response.[19] Emma Pieczynska, director of the Swiss League, also received no response when she asked, in the context of the international conference of consumers' leagues in 1908: 'How will female workers manage if the shops close their workshops and their factories, especially on Saturday? They will find themselves in the cruel situation of not being able to procure the most basic necessities!' As in the United States, neither the participation of workers in the organization nor their constraints as consumers were considered by the consumers' leagues. When the league did direct advice at working-class women in the context of home economics (*enseignement ménager*) it was in regard to household budgets. The women of the league counselled them to save (not spend), to find ways to manage their meagre resources and to produce for themselves the items they consumed.[20] Unlike bourgeois women from the LSA, these young workers were not considered capable of controlling their consumer impulses.

The women and men of the LSA did not think that the democratization of consumption was a good thing. Quite the contrary, women of the league criticized the *bon marché* (the bargain) and the *bonnes occasions* (good deals) that shoppers had to avoid if they wanted to ameliorate the conditions of workers.[21] These women also refused to accept the commercial innovations of the department stores because of the feared social consequences. For example, the *rendu* – the possibility of returning an article to a department store if one did not like it – was criticized because it caused the shop girls a loss of money; they lost the commission linked to the sale.[22] The members of the league criticized fashion and preferred the traditional seasonal rhythms of the bourgeoisie. They advised their members to order their dresses from their dressmakers far in advance. That way workers could do such work during periods when they did not have other work to do.[23] The members of the league were also critical towards advertising, considered to be immoral. This position was common among elites at the beginning of the twentieth century: organizations such as the French Society for the Protection of the French Countryside, or the Commission of Old Paris, believed that advertising and in particular posters and banners, disfigured city centres and the countryside and undermined the identity of the country.[24]

These different elements explain why the LSA never obtained Charles Gide's direct support, most notably at the occasion of the first international conference for consumers' leagues in Geneva in 1908.[25] While the LSA shared Gide's belief that consumers had to organize in order to play an active role in negotiating the kinds of changes wrought by the new commercial methods of producers and shopkeepers, their values differed sharply from his. Gide was a defender of the *rights* of consumers (and not of their duties or responsibilities); he thought of consumers and workers at the same time and was interested in problems such as lower prices. In addition, his social Christianity had a socialist tinge; consumer cooperatives were, for Gide, structures that would provide apprenticeship in democracy and economic efficiency. All of this put him at a great distance from liberal and statist solutions circulating in the period.[26] He considered the actions of consumers' leagues to be ineffective due to 'the indifference of the women of good society'. Consumers' leagues could not legitimately regulate working conditions when they 'don't limit themselves to exercising control over stores, or professions involved in selling directly to the public, but extend their efforts to regulate manufacturers which do not have a direct relationship with the consumer'. Gide believed that the details of the organization of production should be dependent on the actions of unions.[27] Clearly, all of those activists who claimed to speak 'in the name of the consumer' in France at the beginning of the twentieth century had neither the same objectives nor the same interests.

A Women's World

The LSA ascribed a special role and responsibility to elites, but especially to women. Women were considered as those principally responsible for conditions of work among the working class. As Henriette Brunhes emphasized: '[i]t is *we* [women] who do the research on a store that sells things most cheaply, it's the love of finery that pushes us, these other women, to buy dresses and hats at very low prices'.[28] From this responsibility was also born a duty to pay attention to the manner in which they bought and in which they organized themselves. 'Social purchasing' required forethought and careful planning. This 'responsibility' was clearly inscribed within a traditional definition of woman as responsible for the organization of the household and the private sphere.

In this sense consumers' leagues in general and the LSA in particular, resemble many other female associations which had been justifying their existence for over a century by virtue of domestic ideology.[29] Of course one must distinguish between rhetoric and social reality when evoking the nineteenth-century domestic ideology's distinction between a masculine public sphere and a private sphere reserved to women. Nonetheless, the rhetoric was powerful enough to be used by the women involved in the consumers' league to justify their activism. The language of Henriette Brunhes and that of Maud Nathan in New York are comparable in this regard: their political involvement derived partly from a critique of modes of consumption of women of the world and partly from the evidence they proffered regarding their responsibility *as women* to respond to this situation.

In relation to other feminine and feminist associations, however, the activities of Maud Nathan and of Henriette Brunhes were quite different, drawing attention to the different trajectories of American and French feminist movements. In 1902, while Maud Nathan also took part in the struggle for the right to vote, Henriette Brunhes did not belong to any feminist organization explicitly calling for the rights of women, or an equal treatment of men and women. Brunhes' position can be explained by the fact that feminism in France was considered by Catholics to be associated with republicanism and libertinism. In the absence of a moderate Catholic feminist movement before 1919, it was virtually unthinkable for Catholic women like Henriette Brunhes to support any feminist cause.[30]

Women of the French LSA appear isolated among the multiple groups of women activists at the beginning of the twentieth century. On the one hand, they situated themselves at a great distance from other feminine and feminist groups (such as liberals and socialists) because of their Catholicism. If one thinks only of the league members' concern for social issues, one could imagine them seeing eye to eye with some socialists; but the league members' Catholic and largely conservative conception of women made them eschew their would-be allies' feminist positions.[31] On the other hand, women in the consumers' league did not get along with moderate female philanthropists, situated at the centre of the political spectrum and tied to Protestant philanthropy, because of their own more progressive position on social issues. Members of the LSA found these moderate women to be too conservative in regard to the conditions of workers.[32] Being both Catholic and socially progressive, members of the LSA therefore found themselves on the margins of other feminine and feminist organizations.[33]

Innovation at the Heart of Social Catholicism

It is particularly in relation to other Catholic organizations that the more radical elements of the LSA become apparent. If compared to the socialist and feminist organizations at the turn of the century, the LSA appeared conservative in its ideas about both class and gender; in the eyes of other Catholics engaged in Belle Epoque politics, the LSA appeared downright subversive. In the Catholic world the LSA was very different from other Catholic organizations and Henriette Brunhes was not a typical Catholic *bourgeoise*.

The LSA was not a typical Catholic organization; it was a 'social' Catholic organization, situated at the progressive extreme of other Catholic organizations. Like feminist or women's groups, Catholic organizations were flowering at the turn of the century, such as the League of French Women (*Ligue des Femmes Françaises*) created in 1901 and the Patriotic League of French Women (*Ligue Patriotique des Françaises*) created in 1902. These organizations were close to politically conservative parties,[34] and were profoundly and overtly anti-feminist.

They considered feminism to be secular, free-thinking and revolutionary.[35] And when these leagues called out to consumers, in order to create Catholic consumers' leagues, this was not to effect social reform.

At Amiens, for example, the Patriotic League of French Women created in 1907 a Catholic Buyers' Association for the Weekly Rest. Like the LSA, this organization fought for the weekly holiday. Its members agreed not to buy anything on Sundays or in stores that were open on Sundays. But they were particularly invited 'never to buy in stores known to be owned by Jews, freemasons or enemies of religion', and instead to favour the opposite: 'stores known as Catholic and in particular owned by members of the Patriotic League of French Women'.[36] No such guidelines can be found in the records of the LSA; indeed it disapproved of such anti-Semitic language and it deliberately distanced itself from such organizations, especially since it accepted the republican state, in contrast to these conservative Catholic associations.

The composition of the LSA underscores its more progressive face. The members of the French consumers' league included middle-class men, but not just any middle-class men; one finds a large number of socially progressive Catholics, including intellectuals. Jean Brunhes (1869–1930), the founder of the LSA with his wife, belonged to that network of 'social' Catholics trying to reform French society. With his brothers, Bernard, a graduate of the Ecole Normale and a professor of science in Clermont-Ferrand, Gabriel, who died as the Bishop of Montpellier and Joseph, a lawyer in Dijon, Jean wrote a work singing the praises of the Encyclical *Rerum Novarum* (*Du Toast à l'Encyclique*), even as he supported the activities of the LSA. After taking a post teaching human geography at the *Collège libre des sciences sociales*, Jean Brunhes became a professor at the Catholic University at Fribourg, which he left to become professor at the Collège de France.[37] Whether in France or in Switzerland, he remained close to the Sillon, a group of young 'Catholic democrats' around Marc Sangnier, who supported the policy of rallying to the Republic and the social policy pronounced by Pope Leon XIII. At Fribourg he was a friend of Max Turmann, a professor also close to the Sillon, a Christian democrat who wrote many works on popular education at the beginning of the century. In France he frequented a circle run by Henri Lorin (1857–1914) and participated in the *semaines sociales,* or 'social weeks', a sort of itinerant university for social Catholicism at which the LSA was often represented.

The '*comité de perfectionnement*' of the LSA and the French section of the international committee responsible for propaganda at the International Conference at Geneva (1908) contained a number of members of Jean Brunhes' university and 'social' Catholic entourage. As was the case for the Social Christian Union and the 'white lists' in Great Britain, one finds among partisans of consumer activism a new generation of economists who were considering new approaches to political economy and in particular imagining state intervention as against the convinced partisans of economic liberalism.[38] This group included: Georges Blondel, professor at the

École des Hautes Études Commerciales (HEC) and at the Collège libre des sciences politiques; Eugène Duthoit, professor at the Catholic University at Lille; Firmin Sauvaire-Jourdan, professor at the law school at the University of Bordeaux; and also Paul Cauwès. This last economist, like Charles Gide professor at the University of Paris, was the founder of the *Société d'économie politique nationale*, which opposed the efforts of the *Société d'économie politique libérale*. Cauwès was also one of the founders of the national French association for the legal protection of workers and presided over the French section of this organization until 1906.[39] Alongside these economists stood lawyers from the *Musée social*, like Maurice Saleille and Raoul Jay, professor of law at the University of Paris, a pillar of the *Revue d'économie politique*, member of the *Conseil supérieur du travail* (Work Council) and of the French section of the Association for the Struggle against Unemployment.[40]

Coming together in the LSA, in sum, was a network of female reformers engaged in charitable Catholic activities and a network of male reformers accustomed to working together, at home and in international organizations. The LSA's place within a network of social Catholic reformers close to the Sillon and the *semaines sociales* was a specificity of the consumers' league of France as opposed to that of the United States and also with regard to the Swiss League (which Jean and Henriette Brunhes contributed to creating, but which placed itself within a feminist Protestant network).[41]

The progressive nature of the French consumers' league becomes particularly apparent when recognizing the 'social' Catholic network of which it was a part. Like other Catholic progressive organizations (the Sillon), the LSA was the object of ferocious criticism on the part of Catholic conservatives close to Pope Pius X, around 1910. The league was harshly criticized in the Catholic milieux as 'modernist' at a moment when such an accusation was considered a crime of *lèse majesté*. The aspects of the LSA most widely criticized by conservative Catholics included its neutrality (the fact that it was not overtly 'Catholic') and the fact that it was explicitly non-sectarian (and accepted non-Catholics in its ranks). The LSA, according to its critics, should have rejected the Protestant influence which came from the United States: 'The European direction could have, should have remained Catholic, [instead of which] it has attained in Europe what it has retained in America, namely a Protestant direction'.[42] In the context of the quarrel around 'modernism', criticism was focused on the links which existed between Catholics and Protestants, or the supposed influence of the United States on this French Catholic association.

These criticisms had serious consequences for women in the LSA. Henriette Brunhes broke permanently with the most conservative part of her family. Indeed, her nephew (Dominique Roland-Gosselin) organized a cabal against the LSA in 1908–10. Henriette's two sisters sent her incendiary letters. According to them, the LSA ought to have been openly Catholic and recruited exclusively from the Catholic community. Henriette Brunhes was wounded by these attacks, which attempted to exclude her from the Catholic world, something that she refused to allow to happen.

She maintained that her action, if influenced by her openness to other cultures, remained at heart consonant with Catholic culture. Yet her conception of 'Catholic culture' was clearly considered revolutionary by many Catholic women around her.[43]

What favoured the evolution in the direction of Henriette's capacious view of Catholic culture? It is important to insist upon the influence of Protestant culture as a factor that encouraged openness and innovation in this French Catholic bourgeois world. Contrary to her sisters, Henriette was in a way being true to a part of her origins, which were quite mixed. Her mother (Elise Weyer) was a fervent Catholic; but she was of Russian Orthodox origin and she converted to Catholicism when Henriette was young. Henriette's father (Emile Hoskier), meanwhile, was a Protestant of Danish and Swedish origin. To this heritage, one must add several other key influences: the intellectual encounter with John Ruskin (a Christian rebelling against his Scottish Presbyterian faith); the encounter with the socially progressive Catholic milieu of her husband Jean Brunhes, which was open to other groups (notably Protestants and socialists); and the encounter with American and European consumers' leagues.

Surveys and Advertising

The characterization of the LSA as 'innovative' and 'progressive' is further supported by the organization's practices. The promoters of the LSA did not hesitate to draw upon new methods and techniques to put their ideas into practice. Two examples stand out: the LSA's use of surveys and advertising.[44]

The practice of doing surveys is particularly interesting because surveys were undertaken not by going to visit the poor in order to do charitable acts but rather to gather 'scientific' data in order to reform society. Indeed, the process of doing surveys was a relatively formal procedure, strongly influenced by the empirical sociology of Frédéric Le Play. The LSA even asked a professor close to the Leplaysiens, Pierre de Maroussem, to give a course to members on the methods of doing surveys. In the archives one can find forms filled out by members of the league, as well as detailed reports on these detailed surveys.[45] In these surveys, LSA people could 'see' and 'study' workers' way of life. This shows the perceived difference between reform-minded consumers and workers.

These surveys had little to do with the consuming habits of workers; in this sense the league did not participate in the efforts to learn about the consumption practices of the popular classes, or in the research on budgets and family expenditures. These were precisely the research agendas inaugurated in the nineteenth century by Le Play and became increasingly important after the First World War, a time when 'surveys on family budgets became a social technique employed by both governments trying to design its social and economic policies and by private groups working to improve the living and working conditions of the poorest members of society'.[46] Yet if the surveys did not participate in this broader project, they did nonetheless have important consequences. The surveys show that the LSA saw itself as a centre for the social education of women, much like the League of Social Action, a women's organization created in 1900 by Jeanne Chenu. Henriette Brunhes was a fan of the 'regime of the continuous survey' and proposed a sort of 'how-to' guide for her collabourators. First, a group leader would gather together some of her collabourators. She would inform herself on the literature available on a specific question. Once the survey began, the surveyors would rely upon 'personal relations' and use 'enormous care'. Finally, the leader of the group would write her report, composed of 'facts and figures supported by serious references'.[47] The methods used had their limits: the surveyors were content to go and question only employers and accepted what they said on faith; often they left their questionnaires and returned later to pick them up; nor did they necessarily think about how representative the shops surveyed were. The surveys, however, changed the way in which they were seen and in which they saw themselves. For the women of the league the surveys constituted a way of getting information, of being introduced to a broader social world, a means of 'stepping out' in the public sphere, of acquiring a certain kind of expertise and of having the experience of speaking out.[48]

Advertising was another interesting 'innovative' practice employed by the LSA, in a manner comparable to American consumer leagues.[49] Even if some members of the LSA railed against advertising, the league eventually used a 'brand name' and advertising to defend its ideas. The league's means of propaganda included printing tracts, posters and exhibitions of objects made by workers in their homes (as a way of struggling against the sweating system). The French consumers' league was in contact with the American league in order to disseminate a list of 'good' Parisian dressmakers and they even published a tract named *International Publicity*. In addition to lectures and articles in the press, they developed calendars that proposed model buying periods, based on the constraints of the working world. Even though it had a discourse that was critical of and offered alternatives to consumer society, the league's use of advertising demonstrates a willingness to employ some of its key practices: they used consumer society's methods against it.

Women in the Public Sphere

The turn of the twentieth century was a key period for the politicization of consumption in both Europe and the United States and consumers' leagues like the LSA were part of that process. The French case was not exceptional: in the context of an international reformist bourgeois world, consumer activism emerged as one response among many to the 'social question'. But it is interesting to examine what the LSA has to teach us about French society. To an astonishing degree consumer activism was taken in hand by social Catholics, women and men alike, who saw in consumers' leagues the opportunity to affect the mentality and social action of Catholics and to build a bridge between workers and consumers.

Henriette Brunhes and fellow women of the LSA occupied an intermediary position between the most radical feminists and the most conservative Catholic women engaged in social causes in the Belle Epoque in France. At the same time that they defended a traditional conception of woman in the family, they proposed a new vision of the appropriate behaviour of women in the public sphere. Like other women activists at the turn of the twentieth century, the women of the LSA transformed a legitimate feminine and domestic responsibility into the basis for a public role for women. What is specific and different about these women is that they did not limit their work to traditionally 'female' concerns like religion, charity, compassion, maternal love and personal sacrifice, but focused their attention on consumption. While consumption can be considered a 'feminine' activity, members of the LSA did not conceive of it as a purely private act (such as provisioning the household, a role traditionally reserved for women). Rather, consumption was seen as participation in the capitalist system and was consistently presented in connection with work in factories, workshops and department stores.

From the beginning the league permitted its members to participate in reforming the world, all the while remaining in 'their' Catholic universe. This reforming spirit might seem a small deviation to us, but it was a giant step for them to take, since doing so carried the risk of exclusion from Catholic society. Alongside traditional charity work and Catholic action, feminist movements and reforming networks, men and women in the French consumers' league explored a new path: towards socially responsible consumption. The innovative nature of the LSA derived from a capacity for alliance, international cultural transfer and an openness to other religions and other social classes.

In the decade before the First World War the LSA, like its American counterparts, engaged increasingly in lobbying, in order to affect social and labour legislation. The women in the league did this in collaboration with fellow male members and with other organizations such as the *Association nationale française pour la protection légale des travailleurs*, the *Musée social*, trade unions and the *Bureau du Travail*. These women participated indirectly in the elaboration and the control of legislation in the social domain. Through its surveys, the LSA collected some information on workers, especially home workers. Lobbying with other associations, it supported the vote and the application of social laws, such as the law of 13 July 1906 'establishing Sunday rest for employees and workers', seats for shop girls in department stores, limiting night work for bread and pastry makers, etc. In addition the league participated alongside 'work inspectors' in the policing of the social regulations, as for instance on work hours.

Women of the consumers' league employed practices that recognized that they had a very public role as consumers. They saw themselves as playing an active role as ethical consumers in shaping mass consumer society as it was coming into being. By insisting on their duties (as consumers) they posed, in fact, as citizens who had rights, in particular the right to intervene in capitalism. Consumption transformed the members of the league into veritable social actresses not merely 'nurses' who distributed bandages in a male capitalist world.[50] They considered themselves as organized and rational actors (like managers correctly treating their own employees). These women acted as citizens, without having the ballot (and without asking for it): this citizenship can be defined as 'social' (as opposed to 'civic' or 'political')[51] and as 'subjective' (they thought that they could intervene in the public sphere and began to behave as citizens and to feel as if they were citizens, even if legally this was not true).[52] Consumption was one tool – there were others – for women to act in the public sphere, in this case as reformers of capitalism.

It is always difficult to evaluate the importance of movements such as the LSA, consumers' leagues or cooperatives, as well as, more broadly, the respective role of men and women in the politics of consumption; the results can easily be characterized as mediocre when compared with the organizers' ambitious dreams.[53] All the same, in addition to their successful campaigns resulting in real changes in legislation regarding work or the control of prices, these leagues offered new roles for women activists in Belle Epoque France. The women of the LSA spoke out and acted in the public sphere in their capacity as consumers with the same 'right' or 'responsibility' to intervene in these realms as men, employers or union organizers. In the context of mixed-sex organizations, the women of the leagues used the tools of capitalism to transform it; they no longer positioned themselves as women of charity standing outside the world of work. They performed acts of citizenship, well before French women secured the right to vote.

Notes

*This text was translated by Sheryl Kroen, whom I thank particularly. Earlier versions of this paper were presented at the University of Florida (Gainesville), at the Center for European Studies at Harvard (Cambridge, MA), at the Institut d'Histoire Moderne et Contemporaine (Ecole Normale Supérieure, Paris) and at the conference 'Knowing Consumers' in Bielefeld. I would like to thank participants for discussion. For additional comments, I am especially grateful to Patrick Fridenson, Heinz-Gerhard Haupt, Matthew Hilton, Sheryl Kroen and Frank Trentmann.

1. L. Cohen, *A Consumers' Republic: The Politics of Mass Consumption in Postwar America* (New York, 2003), pp. 21–2; M. Hilton, *Consumerism in Twentieth-Century Britain: The Search for a Historical Movement* (Cambridge, 2003),

pp. 27–52; P. Maclachlan and F. Trentmann, 'Civilizing Markets: Traditions of Consumer Politics in Twentieth-century Britain, Japan and the United States', in M. Bevir and F. Trentmann (eds), *Markets in Historical Contexts* (Cambridge, 2003), pp. 170–201; S. Kroen, 'A Political History of the Consumer', *Historical Journal*, 47(3) (2004), pp. 709–36.

2. J. Barzman, *Dockers, métallos, ménagères: Mouvements sociaux et cultures militantes au Havre, 1912–1923* (Rouen, 1997); J.-M. Flonneau, 'Crise de vie chère et mouvement syndical, 1910–1914', *Le Mouvement Social*, 72 (1970), pp. 49–81.

3. L.L. Athey, 'The Consumers' Leagues and Social Reform, 1890–1923', (unpublished PhD thesis, University of Delaware, 1964); K.K. Sklar, 'The Consumers' White Label Campaign of the National Consumers' League, 1898–1918', in S. Strasser, C. McGovern and M. Judt (eds), *Getting and Spending: European and American Consumer Societies in the Twentieth Century* (Cambridge, 1999), pp. 17–35.

4. L.L. Athey, 'From Social Conscience to Social Action: The Consumers' League in Europe, 1900–1914', *Social Service Review*, 52(3) (1978), pp. 362–82; M.-E. Chessel, 'Donne ed Etica del Consumo nella Francia della Belle Epoque. A proposito della Lega sociale dei consumatori', *Memoria e Ricerca*, 16 (2004), pp. 114–16; V. Pouillard, 'Catholiques, socialistes et libre-penseurs: Les porte-paroles des consommateurs en Belgique (1880–1940)', in A. Chatriot, M.-E. Chessel and M. Hilton (eds), *Au nom du consommateur: Consommation et politique en Europe et aux Etats-Unis au XXe siècle* (Paris, 2004), pp. 262–76; F. Trentmann, 'The Modern Genealogy of the Consumer: Meanings, Identities and Political Synapses before Affluence', in J. Brewer and F. Trentmann (eds), *Consuming Cultures, Global Perspectives* (Oxford and New York, forthcoming), ch. 2.

5. D.T. Rodgers, *Atlantic Crossings: Social Politics in a Progressive Age* (Cambridge, MA, 1998). See further on the 'transfer' of elements from the United States towards France in M.-E. Chessel, 'Consommation, action sociale et engagement public fin-de-siècle, des Etats-Unis à la France' in *Au nom du consommateur*, pp. 247–61.

6. Archives Nationales (AN), 615 AP 73, H. Brunhes, 'L'éducation du consommateur: Ligues sociales d'acheteurs', draft (n.d.).

7. S. Fayet-Scribe, *Associations féminines et catholicisme, 19ᵉ–20e siècles* (Paris, 1990).

8. Schlesinger Library, Maud Nathan Scrapbooks, A57, vol. 2, 'Women and their Work. Christmas Appeal of the Consumers' League', n.d. [1900]; Bibliothèque Marguerite Durand (BMD), LSA File, Tract No. 3, 'Pour Noël et le jour de l'an', 1904–6.

9. M.-E. Chessel, 'Consommation et réforme sociale à la Belle Epoque: La conférence internationale des Ligues sociales d'acheteurs en 1908', *Sciences de la société*, 62 (2004), pp. 45–67.

10. A. Chatriot, 'Les coopérateurs', in J.-J. Becker and G. Candar (eds), *Histoire des gauches en France, vol. 2: XXe siècle: à l'épreuve de l'histoire* (Paris, 2004), pp. 91–7; J.K. Dirks, 'Righteous Goods: Women's Production, Reform Publicity and the National Consumers' League, 1891–1919', (unpublished PhD thesis, Yale University, 1996), p. 2.

11. L. Auslander, *Taste and Power: Furnishing Modern France* (Berkeley, CA, 1996), p. 256.

12. R. Williams, *Dream Worlds: Mass Consumption in Late Nineteenth-Century France* (Berkeley, CA, 1982); P.G. Nord, *Paris Shopkeepers and the Politics of Resentment* (Princeton, NJ, 1986); L. Tiersten, *Marianne in the Market: Envisioning Consumer Society in Fin-de-Siècle France* (Berkeley, CA, 2001).

13. C. Gide, 'Le règne du consommateur', 1898, in *Coopération et économie sociale 1886–1904* (Paris, 2001), pp. 187–224.

14. W.G. Breckman, 'Disciplining Consumption: The Debate about Luxury in Wilhelmine Germany, 1890–1914', *Journal of Social History*, 24(3) (1991), p. 497.

15. AN, 615 AP 67, List from J. Bergeron, 5 July 1905; *Bottin Mondain*, (Paris, 1904).

16. A. Gueslin, 'Le paternalisme revisité en Europe occidentale (seconde moitié du XIXe, début XXe siècle)', *Genèses*, No. 7 (1992), pp. 201–11.

17. M. Perrot, *Le mode de vie des familles bourgeoises, 1873–1953* (Paris, 1982), p. 4.

18. R. Beck, 'C'est dimanche qu'il nous faut: Les mouvements sociaux en faveur du repos dominical et hebdomadaire en France avant 1906', *Le Mouvement social*, 184 (1998), pp. 23–51.

19. *Musée social*, H. Brunhes, 'La ligue sociale d'acheteurs' (Paris, 1903), pp. 151–3.

20. H. Brunhes, *Le développement et l'organisation de l'enseignement ménager en Suisse, et particulièrement dans le canton de Fribourg*, Circulaire du Musée social, Paris, 1901.

21. Baronness G. Brincard, *Le prix des 'bonnes occasions'* (Blois, 1905).

22. M. Turmann, *Initiatives féminines* (Paris, 1905), p. 282.

23. M. Deslandres, *L'acheteur: Son rôle économique et social* (Paris, 1911). See also M.A. Beale, *The Modernist Enterprise: French Elites and the Threat of Modernity (1900–1940)* (Stanford, 1999), pp. 116–20.

24. M.-E. Chessel, *La Publicité: Naissance d'une profession (1900–1940)* (Paris, 1998), pp. 145–80.

25. AN, 615 AP 80, C. Gide to A. de Morsier, 26 November 1907; A. de Morsier to H. Brunhes, 29 November 1907; AN 615 AP 67, draft of a letter from H. Brunhes to C. Gide, n.d. [1908].

26. E. Furlough, *Consumer Cooperation in France: The Politics of Consumption, 1834–1930* (Ithaca, 1991).

27. Gide, *Coopération et économie sociale*, p. 196; 'Une récente étude de M. Ch. Gide sur les ligues d'acheteurs', *Bulletin des LSA*, 2nd trimester 1907, pp. 54–64.

28. AN, 615 AP 73, H. Brunhes, 'Le sweating system', in *Le travail de la femme et de la jeune fille*, MS October 1901.

29. S.A. Curtis, 'Charitable Ladies: Gender, Class and Religion in Mid-Nineteenth Century Paris', *Past and Present*, 177 (2002), pp. 121–56, and E. Diebolt, *Les femmes dans l'action sanitaire, sociale et culturelle, 1901–2001: Les associations face aux institutions* (Paris, 2001). For comparison, see for instance J.R. Walkowitz, *Prostitution and Victorian Society: Women, Class and the State* (Cambridge, 1980) or M. Ryan, *Cradle of the Middle Class: The Family in Oneida County, New York, 1790–1865* (Cambridge, 1981). Thank you to Sheryl Kroen for comments on this subject.

30. C. Bard, *Les filles de Marianne: Histoire des féminismes 1914–1940* (Paris, 1995), pp. 268–9.

31. A. Cova, *'Au service de l'Eglise, de la patrie et de la famille': Femmes catholiques et maternité sous la IIIe République* (Paris, 2000), p. 88; J. Coffin, *The Politics of Women's Work: The Paris Garment Trades 1750–1915* (Princeton, NJ, 1996), pp. 234–7.

32. AN, 615 AP 71, A. Moreau to H. Brunhes, 20 August, 2 September, 11 November, 1900; Baronness Brincard to H. Brunhes, 19 June 1905 ; Mrs Chalamet to H. Brunhes, 16 June 1905.

33. L. Klejman and F. Rochefort, *L'égalité en marche: Le féminisme sous la Troisième République* (Paris, 1989), p. 108; Cova, *'Au service de l'Eglise'*, pp. 66–8.

34. B. Dumons, 'Mobilisation politique et ligues féminines dans la France catholique du début du siècle. La Ligue des femmes françaises et la Ligue patriotique des Françaises (1901–1914)', *Vingtième siècle*, 73 (2002), pp. 39–50.

35. C. Bard, *Les femmes dans la société française au 20e siècle* (Paris, 2001), pp. 87–8.

36. AN, 615 AP 81, Ligue catholique d'acheteuses pour le repos hebdomadaire. Ligue patriotique des Françaises, *Appel-programme*, Amiens, 1907.

37. C. Charle and E. Telkes, *Les professeurs du Collège de France: Dictionnaire biographique (1901–1939)* (Paris, 1988), pp. 41–3.

38. J. Vincent, 'L'économie morale du consommateur britannique en 1900', in *Au nom du consommateur*, pp. 231–46.

39. B. Dumons and G. Pollet, 'Universitaires et construction de l'Etat providence: La formation économique et juridique des élites françaises (1890–1914)', *Revue d'histoire des facultés de droit et de la science juridique*, 20 (1999), pp. 179–95; R.F. Kuisel, *Capitalism and the State in Modern France* (Cambridge, 1981); C. Topalov (ed.), *Laboratoires du nouveau siècle: La nébuleuse réformatrice et ses réseaux en France, 1880–1914* (Paris, 1999).

40. J.R. Horne, *A Social Laboratory for Modern France: The Musée Social and the Rise of the Welfare State* (Durham, NC, 2002).

41. A.-M. Käppeli, *Sublime croisade: Éthique et politique du féminisme protestant, 1875–1928* (Geneva, 1990).

42. AN, 615 AP 70, Verax, 'Le Congrès international des ligues d'acheteurs', *La semaine de Rome*, No. 27, 3 October 1908.

43. M.-E. Chessel, 'Catholicisme social et éducation des consommateurs: La *Ligue Sociale d'Acheteurs* au coeur des débats (1908–1910)', in M.-E. Chessel and B. Dumons (eds), *Catholicisme et modernisation de la société française (1890–1960)* (Lyon, 2003), pp. 19–39.

44. On surveys and advertising at the LSA, see M.-E. Chessel, 'Aux origines de la consommation engagée: La Ligue sociale d'acheteurs (1902–1914)', *Vingtième siècle*, 77 (2003), pp. 100–6.

45. AN, 617 AP 67, Report from the Baronness Brincard on the 'marmitons-pâtissiers', Third General Assembly, 3 April 1903.

46. A. Savoye, 'Les enquêtes sur les budgets familiaux: La famille au microscope' in Y. Cohen and R. Baudouï (eds), *Les chantiers de la paix sociale* (Fontenay-aux-Roses, 1995), p. 55; M. Halbwachs, *La classe ouvrière et les niveaux de vie* (Paris, 1913). See also M. Bulmer, K. Beale and K. Kish Sklar (eds), *The Social Survey in Historical Perspective, 1880–1940* (Cambridge, 1991) and C. Baudelot and R. Establet, *Maurice Halbwachs: Consommation et société* (Paris, 1994), pp. 22–3.

47. AN, 615 AP 82, H. Brunhes to Mrs Audollent, 10 July 1903.

48. M. Perrot, 'Sortir', in G. Fraisse and and M. Perrot (eds), *Histoire des femmes en Occident*, IV, *Le XIXe siècle* (Paris, 1991), pp. 467–94.

49. Dirks, 'Righteous Goods', pp. 275–304.

50. B.G. Smith, *Ladies of the Leisure Class: The Bourgeoises of Northern France in the Nineteenth Century* (Princeton, NJ, 1981), pp. 123–61.

51. On the three types of citizenship see S. Walby, 'Is Citizenship Gendered?', *Sociology*, 28(2) (1994), pp. 379–95.

52. K. Canning and S.O. Rose (eds), *Gender, Citizenships and Subjectivities* (Oxford, 2002).

53. M. Hilton, 'The Female Consumer and the Politics of Consumption in Twentieth Century Britain', *Historical Journal*, 45(1) (2002), pp. 103–28.

–5–

Legal Constructions of the Consumer
Michelle Everson

Rightly or wrongly, issues of consumption are generally considered to be a modern phenomenon within the law and, further, to be intimately entwined with the notion of 'consumer protection'. Notwithstanding an ancient legal role in the creation of individual patterns of consumption through the imposition of formalized 'contracts' upon social bargaining processes, or the historical opportunities that law gave social groups to form and express a consumer interest,[1] current legal thinking dates the interface between law, consumers and consumption at 1962; more particularly, to a speech by John F. Kennedy which, following the thalidomide crisis, introduced the 1962 Drug Amendments Bill.[2] The sentiments expressed within this speech were reproduced, almost verbatim, by the European Economic Community in a 1975 Council Resolution on a Preliminary Programme for a Consumer Protection and Information Policy:[3] '[t]he consumer is no longer seen merely as a purchaser and user of goods and services for personal, family or group purposes but also as a person concerned with the various facets of society which might affect him directly or indirectly as a consumer'. Public outrage at market failure had coalesced into a demand for government action. The 'consumer' was simultaneously born and reborn. The final addressees of modern production were first identified and named. In the increasingly differentiated society that had developed since the end of the Second World War, a gulf had opened up between the market, the state and 'consumers', who were now to be seen as being distinct from, say, workers, family members or voters.[4] The hitherto passive act of consumption, however, was also immediately to be reshaped by government intervention into an active relationship with the means of production and distribution (the market). Typically, though rarely translated into formal norms, the rhetorical language of interventionist 're-connection' was one of rights, including, in the European example, rights to the protection of 'health and safety' and 'economic interests' and to 'information' and 'representation'. The character of the consumer was to be reconstituted by rights and law and re-embedded within traditional national paradigms of economic-civic (economic interests), political (representation) and social (health and safety) citizenship. The character of the 'citizen consumer' and the law that created and protected it was to be the glue of reintegration within a differentiated world.[5]

The central integrative function of constituting and protecting the citizen consumer that was thus assigned to law perhaps in part justifies the current assumption that law has only been directly concerned with matters of consumption for forty years. Accordingly, although the following analysis also draws upon a longer legal historical framework, the primary focus is the definition and functioning of the notion of consumer protection within the past four decades and, in particular, its use (misuse) and application (misapplication) within the process of European integration.

The post-war period has witnessed a peculiarly intense interaction between law, modes of production/distribution (market), the state and individual consumers. Equally, this period has also seen paradigm shifts in modes of economic and political organization (from national, to supranational, to international), as well as huge upheaval in the manner in which law and legal science views itself (from formal, to substantive, to procedural justice). Seen in this light, it might be argued that law (always only a very blunt instrument with which to tackle the complexities of consumption and its appropriate place within the world)[6] has largely failed, both itself (lacking internal legal coherence) and a wider goal of recivilising or democratizing the market (reintegrating society) through the promotion of the citizen consumer. In short, where the term 'citizen consumer' has given way within legal discourse to legal external notions of 'heightened consumer protection', the 'informed' or 'confident' consumer, the 'sovereign consumer' or the 'market citizen', law has proved remarkably prone to manipulation by varied and conflicting political, philosophical and economic constructions of the consumer, as well as the views implicit within them on the appropriate place of consumption within modern society.

From 'Contract to (Consumer) Status'

Explicit recognition and use of the notion of 'consumer' has come late to law. As an example, consumers were only to appear in the title of UK legislation with the Consumer Protection Act of 1987. A degree of continuing legal ambivalence about the notion of the consumer can also be identified in the 'soft law' status of much modern consumer policy. Consumer 'rights' are rarely formalized and are instead more commonly afforded a declaratory character.[7] The roots of late and cursory recognition, however, lie within a peculiarly legal conundrum: the fixation of 'formal' law with notions of 'contractual equality' that inherently deny the existence of a differentiated group of consumers. Importantly, such formal law continues to influence current legal attitudes to issues of consumption. Much of the past century and the last forty years in particular, have thus also been marked in legal circles by a struggle between formal law and conceptions of substantive justice, which, at least beyond a sphere of 'pure' contract law, has seen (public) regulatory provision implicitly recognize the existence of a differentiated class of consumers and embed them firmly within a national political economy.[8]

A Swiss declaration of 1879, rejecting the introduction of a special law for the sale of goods within Switzerland, provides a key to the longevity of a formal legal paradigm of contractual equality denying the existence of a distinct class of consumers. The Swiss *Bundesrat* found that: 'The refusal to legislate specifically for retailers is in accordance with the democratic institutions of the Swiss state and democratic impulses of the Swiss people'.[9] Granted, the reasons for legal dismissal of the consumer may have been (and to a degree still are) wholly internal to law. Nonetheless, such internal legal reasons were also initially bolstered by nineteenth-century perceptions of the liberal constitutional state and its citizens.

For a post-feudal law, which had won its legitimacy through the granting of 'universal' civic rights, the most important of which was the right to dispose freely of property in a binary contractual relationship, notions of 'particularity' within the market, above all the existence of distinct groups of contractual partners, were to be firmly rejected. The guiding tenet of post-feudal law was a notion of formal civic equality. Intimately connected with maxims of 'contractual freedom' and 'privacy of contract', formal civic equality both founded an apolitical (internal) legitimacy for law and denied the law any social steering function beyond the maintenance of an axiom of personal (contractual) equality. Further, where such a legal perception met with political-philosophical constructions rejecting any form of social differentiation, or particularity within the national polity, legal internal justifications for the rejection of a distinct class of consumers were reinforced as surely as they were subsumed within prevailing national paradigms of liberal citizenship.

From 'status' to 'contract': the famous appellation that located the birth of modern law in its ability to transcend imputed and socially imposed categories of feudal organization through universal equality inevitably formed a barrier to the reintroduction of status within law by means of a recognition that certain classes of contract might share peculiar characteristics, which warranted a preferential treatment for particular groups of contractual partners, or consumers. For the law, consumers could only exist as individual contractual partners, whose interests were to be safeguarded by notions designed to ensure equality, such as 'good faith', 'undue influence' and 'misrepresentation', as well as new forms of law, such as tort, or *Deliktsrecht*, which sought to ameliorate the consequences of 'isolated' harm arising out of a single contract. By the same token, 'citizenship' within the emerging nation-state, with all its connotations of social homogeneity, reinforced legal universalism and mitigated against the division of society into functionally differentiated spheres. The Swiss *Bundesrat* could easily justify its assertion that the sale of goods required no particular regulation, since Switzerland was also characterized by a peculiarly high degree of social and economic cohesion. The unitary conception of contract law 'is justified by the far higher degree of equal access to education in Switzerland than in all other European nations and by the commercial talents of the Swiss people'.[10]

In much the same way as the figure of the 'autonomous contractual partner' precluded legal recognition for consumers, the character of the 'national citizen' and, interestingly enough, the 'national economic citizen', in his duty-filled guise as a cohesive social phenomenon and market-building patriot, was also a bulwark against the recognition of social or economic differentiation within society that a political recognition of the status of the consumer would bring.

In this final respect, the figure of the 'talented' national economic citizen, the entrepreneur who would ensure the cohesion of newly emergent national economies, is also noteworthy. Legal and political disdain for the consumer as a distinct class was thus further bolstered by the classical economic perception of the relationship between addressees of production (consumers), modes of production and distribution, which, informed by the notion of the 'sovereign consumer',[11] again acted to dilute notions of social and economic differentiation, promoting price freedom and market transparency as optimal mechanisms to ensure economic development. Familiar to us and still highly influential in its neoliberal forms, the character of the sovereign consumer reinforced both a legal belief in contractual autonomy and a political faith in an entrepreneurial national economic citizen, as its underlying assumption that consumer demand was a sufficient force to control and direct modes of production and redistribution gave birth to a (largely non-interventionist) regulatory regime founded in informational and market transparency.

From the legal point of view, the sovereign consumer coalesced with notions of contractual autonomy and equality of contractual partners. To be sure, business might initially appear to be a stronger contractual partner than the consumer. However, where the 'hidden regulative hand' of supply and demand dictated that individual consumers would be expressing optimal social demands in their contractual dealings, any personal imbalance was at once negated through *optimal* market direction by the *sum* of consumers. Further, where the character of the 'sovereign consumer' did demand legal or political intervention within the market, such intervention was logically to be framed either in a language of 'information equality' that was remarkably close to the traditional contractual language of 'good faith', or within new forms of public regulatory law, such as anti-trust or competition law. Here, efforts to ensure informational transparency and order within the market might be caste as being wholly within the interests of the sovereign consumer *qua* his appearance as an autonomous contractual party; at the same time, the interventionist character of such policy measures might also be structurally and intellectually isolated from a formalist and apolitically legitimated core of private law (contract).[12]

The relationship between law and consumption established before World War Two, then, was both dominated by a paradox and began to set patterns and raise problems in relation to legal intervention in the sphere of consumption that remain visible to this day. First, the paradox: a private contractual core of formal law was (and partially still is) inherently opposed to the recognition of consumers as a distinct category. And yet, to the degree that legal emphasis upon contractual autonomy conformed to liberal economic models of supply and demand, as well as political notions of entrepreneurial national citizenship, the legal relationship with consumption was undoubtedly also shaped by visions of the 'sovereign consumer' outside law. Whether or not law was aware of this guiding hand, the 'sovereign consumer' and, more particularly, the policy demand that the information deficit between producers and consumers be closed allowed for and justified a degree of 'duality'. For it combined a specific regulation of categories of contract (e.g. insurance contracts) with the argument that such regulation was not intervention, but instead a neutral response to the specificities of particular informational deficits.[13] Equally, however, the pre-war period was also marked by the beginnings of a process of legal differentiation. Within the system of law itself, the position of the consumer was beginning to be shaped by different forms of law (in particular, competition law), with varying guiding philosophies, which might, but which also might not, be congruent with one another.[14]

At first glance, the consumer-oriented political programme laid down by Kennedy and adopted within European rhetoric, might appear to be a simple, if visionary, matter of ironing out imbalances in power between modes of production and addressees of the distributive system. Set against the background of a widespread common experience of catastrophic harm (thalidomide), the myth of the individualized consumer, suffering individual harm and seeking individual redress, was to be set aside in favour of the recognition of the existence of the distinct character of a 'mass' of consumers with a collective interest that required representation vis-à-vis the market. However, as happens time and again within consumer debate (most recently in relation to the BSE crisis), a wholly understandable, if simplistic, perception that 'something must and will be done' feeds the demand for rapid intervention and fuels a misconception that the aims of intervention may be easily drawn up and the goals readily achieved. When the rhetorical character of programmes such as the 1975 European programme for consumer protection is dissected to reveal the radical and emblematic character of the 'citizen consumer', however, it is abundantly clear that action to 'reverse immediate harm' can also mask a mass of philosophical, political and economic controversies and paradoxes.

Thus, for example, the declaration of 'a right to protection of health and safety', the simple impulse to prevent harm, also heralds a fundamental philosophical shift in and a potential conflict between, visions of the individual freedom of citizens and consumers; between the 'freedom to' of the entrepreneurial sovereign consumer and the 'freedom from' (harm) of the citizen consumer.[15] This possible alteration in the character of the consumer from active entrepreneurial sovereign to a potentially more passive recipient of interventionist protection is also matched in its radicality in the political sphere. Here a 'right to representation' (for the consumer within modes of production) both serves as a timely recognition of the functionally differentiated status of modern societies, but also raises coordination difficulties and a danger of conflict between the universal character and interventionist legitimacy of the political citizen (macro-interventionist direction) and the particularist character and interventionist legitimacy of the citizen consumer (micro-interventionist direction).

Perhaps most fundamentally, the coordinating character of a citizen consumer, who at a political level serves as an instrument of market democratization as consumer representatives are integrated into production and distribution processes, also stands in the eye of the storm between liberal economics and interventionist visions of market organization: is demand a neutral economic and self-regulating mechanism, or is it instead to be shaped politically by the addressees of production?[16] From a legal viewpoint, the vital question is one of how and whether the figure of the citizen consumer and contested efforts to reshape relationships between market, state and consumers/citizens, interacted with internal legal debates and conflict on the 'materialization' of law. The appearance of the citizen consumer was largely historically congruent with intensified discussion within the legal system on the nature of law and its role in pursuing and securing a measure of social justice, beyond its traditional (politically neutral) commitment to individual equality and freedom.[17] Seen in this light, the veiled but emblematic character of the citizen consumer became both a hook upon which critical lawyers might hang their campaign to 'socialize' law, pursuing an interventionist and reformist agenda within the market,[18] and a flash point, at which divergent views on the formal and substantive roles of law fought out an internal battle for the soul of law. It would be impossible to give a full review of this extraordinarily intense period of legal interaction. Nevertheless, the major spheres of legal action and conflict may be sketched out in order to furnish an orientating picture of the various (differentiated) spheres of law that have impacted upon prevalent perceptions of the consumer.

A vital mechanism both to ensure informational transparency within consumer transactions and to compensate for any inequalities in bargaining powers, the law of contract remains a bastion of formal dogmatic legal reasoning.[19] This is not to say, however, that contract was not to be influenced by 'materialization' (socialization) efforts. Above all, legislative intervention in the form, say, of the German *Allgemeine Geschäftsbedingungen* (1974) or the UK Unfair Contract Terms Act (1979) did represent institutional efforts to afford contractual recognition to a differentiated mass of consumers. Nonetheless, the tendency remained, both within courtrooms and within dominant legal opinion,[20] to view much modern contractual intervention through the lens of traditional formal dogmatic law, thus casting the issue of consumer transactions in the traditional prism of the combating of informational imbalance and overlaying the character of the citizen consumer with its sovereign counterpart. Alternatively, intervention within contracts was not to be viewed as a matter of introducing the consumer within the distribution system, but was rather a corrective mechanism, dedicated to ensuring contractual balance of power at the point of sale.[21]

The core issues of competition policy, 'price control', 'the misuse of market power' and 'the maintenance of transparency in market transactions' form the primary stage upon which economic theory battles on the nature of supply and demand are fought out. They present law with unparalleled problems of cognitive and institutional transformation and coordination. Between the 'pure' economic theory premise, which argues that sensitive control of market power concentrations is of itself a guarantee and support for the primacy of a sovereign consumer and an extreme interventionist stance, which places its faith in public regulation of price control as a (politically directed) mechanism to ensure the reintegration of addressees of production within the production process, there lie a host of subtle technical considerations and positions.

Although formal law dedicated to the clarity of the application of its vision of individual consumer sovereignty may find it easy to enforce a 'pure', market transparency oriented form of competition law,[22] dedication to the pursuit of substantive price control through law was also a simple legal fact of life throughout most of the post-war years.[23] Sensitive legal treatment of the complex economic consequences of competition policy, as well as an awareness of underlying philosophical positions, are, however, a rarity.[24] Simply stated, law has always had difficulties understanding the complexities of competition policy. In the post-war years it was unable to integrate competition policy across industrial and commercial sectors.[25] It was even less capable of recognizing and integrating competing and complex policy goals, including those goals of industrial or economic policy (e.g. preservation of international economic competitiveness) that had little if anything to do with the position of the consumer.[26] Seen in this light, legal literature dedicated to the protection of the position of the consumer was largely unable to pierce the veil of highly differentiated national competition policy in order to identify and pursue one coherent view of the consumer.

All formalist rearguard action in the sphere of contract and competition law notwithstanding, large sections of post-war national regulation have undoubtedly been marked by a legal materialization triumph in relation to intervention beyond the system of distribution and exchange, in order to reshape modes of production in line with social and cultural demands. Forming a direct opposition to the character of the sovereign individualized consumer, policies of intervention within modes of production assumed a 'collective' character for an inherently 'diffuse' consumer interest,[27] subordinating production processes to political interests, such as health and safety at work criteria, consumer protection interests and end product quality shaping criteria, such as pork content in sausages and cocoa content in chocolate. Such regulatory standards represent an acceptance that transparency of information at the point of sale alone is not enough to secure the protection of the consumer. However, such standards are also an effort to establish representation of the citizen consumer within the modes of production by means of mobilizing the national polity and a public regulatory law dedicated to giving shape to its legal materialization aims.

This issue of ensuring the representation of a 'collective' consumer interest within the market, however, also points to further aspects of legal debate within the national regulatory complex, more particularly the issue of who might represent the consumer interest, where and when, within the law applying to the market. Once again, although a collective interest channelled by means of the national citizen and polity was easily established within public regulatory law, efforts to ensure representation in private spheres such as contract law, or the self-regulatory sphere of private industry standards, were far less clear cut.

In particular, the trend to a materialization of private law through the expansion of general legal protection clauses, such as 'good faith' or 'misrepresentation', to allow for individual consumer actions based within a claim that a general consumer interest was at stake (heightened information demands etc.) was often either hard fought or (perversely) simply accepted within an unreflecting canon of formal dogmatic private law without any thought to the possible fundamental shifts in modes of political representation that such moves entailed.[28] The continuing and vibrant debate about the representation of consumer interest groups within processes of private industry standardization, touching upon such vital issues as who might be fairly said to legitimately represent the collective consumer interest and to be able to assert it above other interests (including, on occasions, the interests of the national polity), was thus, in this latter case, simply overlooked.

If the question to be posed of post-war efforts to ensure a degree of reintegration of consumers within the market and modes of production is one of whether law in this period was consciously working with a coherent construction of the consumer, the answer must be no. Simply stated, various structural constraints within the law joined together to ensure that no single construction of the consumer would be able to establish itself within a private–public regulatory complex of contract law, competition law, regulatory law and procedural law:

- *Formality versus materialization*: a constant disrupting factor continued to be the legal-internal conflict over whether and how the law could or should pursue substantive justice and/or support a collectively defined 'diffuse' consumer interest.
- *The limited cognitive capacity of law*: perhaps fittingly in relation to a problem of consumption in part created by increasing functional societal differentiation, law itself proved to be too self-contained an instrument to allow for the coherent translation of economic and political conceptions and constructions of the consumer into a legal framework of regulation.
- *The limited interventionist steering capacity of law*: closely connected with this final point, differentiation within the legal system itself also limited the overall steering capacity of the public–private regulatory network as incoherence and lack of connection between the individual elements of the network (e.g. between competition policy and private law) restricted the effectiveness of individual consumer policy and protection measures. Clearly this is not to say that the post-war years were devoid of legal visions of the consumer. To the contrary, a materialization momentum meant that legal literature was crowded

with individual efforts to define and promote a collective vision of consumer interest,[29] or, by opposition, to recast (even ignore) materialization developments within the formally flavoured paradigm of the sovereign consumer. However and with all the luxury of hindsight, legal efforts to give form to Kennedy's vision of a democratized market presided over by a citizen consumer appear today only to be so much sound and fury, an inchoate debate in which neither formal nor substantive approaches can claim successfully to have promoted a coherent consumer interest; the former by virtue of their refusal to accept the realities of social differentiation and legal materialization, the latter by virtue of their fatal overestimation of the cognitive and interventionist capacities of law.

Significantly, however, while the post-war legal debate was unable to establish a coherent vision of the consumer, it nevertheless did bequeath us an influential 'real-world' figure of the 'nationally embedded consumer'. Even if material intervention within the market was incoherent, it nonetheless resulted in a veritable avalanche within each national jurisdiction of regulatory standards, competition policy prescriptions, procedural mechanisms to ensure consumer representation, as well as material contract law provisions. The incremental establishment of national frameworks of market regulation accordingly determined that consumers would find themselves in starkly differentiated national markets, where national regulation and law would dictate the mode of national production, the extent and character of goods and services on offer within that market, as well as the terms and conditions under which such goods and services might or might not be purchased.

The Rational European Consumer

This final point is determining for the evolution of a European consumer policy. It is perhaps one of the greatest ironies of European integration that whilst the EEC was never in possession of a competence to intervene in matters of consumer protection or consumer policy,[30] the figure of the 'European consumer' was itself pivotal within the history of the creation of the European market. A clear European competence in consumer matters was established only with the Single European Act (1987) and the introduction of Article 100(s), guaranteeing a 'high level of protection' for European consumers, into the European Treaty. Nonetheless, consumer policy had exercized the Community long prior to this date, as the figure of the nationally embedded consumer and the complex of national regulation and law that secured its position, proved to be the major obstacle to the process of European market integration.

The integrationist interest, the desire to make one market out of disparate national economies, perforce led European law into a tangential relationship with nationally embedded concepts of the consumer as the national regulatory law that sustained them fell under the rationalizing gaze of the demand that all barriers to trade within the Community be dismantled. Primary, 'judge-made' European law, though not inherently concerned with visions of the consumer, was thus forced both to confront embedded national attitudes to consumer law and culture and also 'explicitly' to investigate the character and nature of the European consumer in order to justify its deregulatory interventions. This unique engagement of a judiciary with the concept of the consumer, alone, makes the European integration experiment a fascinating area for study. The completion of the internal market and the recognition of a European competence for consumer protection heralded an era of re-regulation during which European policy makers (European Commission) and lawyers began to sketch out the positive contours and characteristics of the future European consumer, both as a direct exercise and, tangentially, via the establishment of European norms of contract law, product process regulation, competition policy and of representation facilitating procedural law.

Falling roughly into three periods of deregulatory judicial activism, executive re-regulation and a final 'political' period of the concretization of the character of the European consumer, the most immediate question to be asked of European legal engagement with matters of consumption is whether, in contrast to a national example, it has established a transparent, conscious and legally coherent construction of the consumer.

Historically, the EEC Treaty did not envisage a role for the European Court of Justice (ECJ) in the creation of a European market. Rather, the primary motor of integration was to be a political one, whereby the Council of Ministers would positively legislate to harmonize the market regulating provisions of the member states. Predictably, however, national resistance to specific instances of change, bolstered by the historic veto powers of individual nation-states and taken together with the sheer mass of national regulation requiring harmonization, determined that a strategy of positive integration would fail miserably to meet the target of the creation of a European market by 1969. Following a period of economic stagnation in the 1970s, however, a general political and economic recognition of the failure of post-war economic materialization, as well as of the need for liberalization,[31] combined to convince the ECJ to make use of its own considerable and powerful legal mechanisms to effect the European market through the 'deregulatory' setting aside of national regulatory provision. Accordingly, primary provisions of European law, deemed to be supreme over national law, were vigorously deployed to assert the dominance of the European internal market: 'the free movement of goods', establishing a principle of 'non-discrimination' (Article 28 European Treaty),[32] 'the four freedoms', establishing the character of the 'European market citizen' (Articles 39–49),[33] and European anti-trust policy (Articles 80 and 82).

Thus, the ECJ found in relation to German beer purity laws that member states must not crystallize given consumer habits so as to consolidate an advantage acquired by national industries concerned to comply with them (*Commission* v *Germany* [1987]).[34] All protests by the German government that provisions restricting the ingredients within beer to wheat, hops and water served a legitimate consumer protection aim fell on deaf judicial ears, as free movement of goods provisions were deployed to unpick the complex of national standards applied to production processes. Certainly, consumer 'protection' remained a legitimate legislative goal of the member states and would remain a guiding feature of internal market policy. Yet, the vital Community law principle of 'proportionality' would be wielded by the ECJ to review and set aside national standards: does national legislation really serve the aims it is designed to pursue or could less restrictive measures be applied to achieve the same goals?

Certainly, commentators on national consumer policy might argue that 'standards' are a vital element within notions of consumer protection, preserving 'culturally formed' expectations in relation to goods.[35] Nevertheless, in the pursuit of an integrationist interest, the German consumer was to be 'de-cultured': no one might claim that Belgian beer was more damaging to the health of the German consumer. Therefore, the German consumer would be relieved of cultural standards determining the nature of 'beer' and would be exposed to products labelled 'beer' by 'foreign' cultures. By the same token, however, 'labelling' and information on the ingredients of beer would not only be an adequate means to protect the German consumer, but would simultaneously serve consumer protection through the widening of 'consumer choice', as all beer-drinkers throughout the Community might decide for themselves which cultural form of beer was most palatable to them.[36]

Similarly, however, choice was to be extended to promote the figure of the active European consumer or, in terms of the 'bottom-up' integration of the European market, the roving 'entrepreneurial' European market citizen who could cross the Community in her efforts to find the best bargain amongst a range of products. Accordingly, in the insurance services cases of *Commission* v *France, Denmark, Germany* and *Ireland* [1986],[37] the ECJ began to encroach on matters of national competition policy, confirming a market right to the cross-border provision of insurance services within the Republic, at least in relation to 'large-scale' risks. Although the German government might be justified in its efforts to control the terms, conditions and price offers of insurance in relation to private consumers, large-scale consumers, such as large commercial enterprises (all suitably equipped with their own powerful teams of lawyers), would not require such protection and would be free to seek policies throughout a European market, where price and choice would become the sole regulatory factor.

The figure of the 'frontier' consumer, the active moulder of the European market, is likewise strikingly reconfirmed by judicial treatment of the free movement of goods: 'free movement of goods concerns not only traders but also individuals. It requires, particularly in frontier areas, that consumers resident in one member state may travel freely to the territory of another member state to shop under the same conditions as the local population' (*GB-INNO-BM* [1990]).[38] A distinctly upbeat European consumer was born. Consumer choice was extended beyond the narrow confines of the national market to be united with the concept of the European market citizen to give rise to a roving, entrepreneurial European consumer who would forge the European market.

If the insurance cases, with their emphasis upon the active consumer or market citizen, might indicate that the ECJ had established a scheme of 'regulatory competition' within the Community, whereby cross-border consumer dealings would be the main motor for the competitive dismantling of restrictive national regulation, the case of the *Sachverband der Deutschen Feuerversicherer* [1987][39] immediately confirmed that the ECJ had far greater ambitions and would itself also deploy competition provisions to review national competition policies having a direct impact upon the terms and conditions under which consumer goods and services would be sold.

With its decision that an exemption within German competition law could not be used to justify 'non-binding' price cartels within the fire insurance market in order, in the submission of the German government, to safeguard consumers by eliminating the danger of insurance failure in a volatile market by means of reduced competition, the ECJ signalled that it would add to the deregulatory pressure of a mass of active market citizens, reviewing for itself the application of measures of national competition policy. More strikingly, its assertion that it would not even consider the consumer protection arguments of the German government, since 'Ccommunity law does not make the implementation of [competition policy] dependent upon the manner in which the supervision of certain areas of economic activity is organized by national legislation',[40] heralded a return to classical interpretations of competition policy within Europe. Where the legal materialization efforts of the post-war years had seen various, often poorly coordinated, sections of national law engage in interventionist price control, European law would spare itself the effort of investigating the exact nature of supply and demand. European law would instead be (formally) dedicated to consumer protection through the pursuit of market transparency.

The impression that the Court had simply rolled back forty years of legal materialization efforts to resurrect the figure of the sovereign consumer, protected by a dual regime of competition law and transactional transparency, is further bolstered by the explicit and repeated emphasis placed by the ECJ on the notion of 'information' within its own perception of the European consumer: '[u]nder Community law concerning consumer protection, the provision of information to the consumer is considered one of the principal requirements'[41] (*GB-INNO-BM*). Alternatively, the Court is not convinced by, or simply does not make reference to, the raft of arguments that point out that consumer confidence may be induced in a variety of ways: since the consumer knows the producer, since the consumer trusts national legislation, or since consumers have a general belief in business morals.[42] Instead the paradigm returns to that of the sovereign consumer: armed with information, the consumer is made sovereign and confident, not within the production process but at the point of sale.

At one level, it might be tempting to review the actions of the activist ECJ and to designate it a 'formalist' court deaf to the cacophony of protest from a series of socially oriented lawyers who have consistently argued that consumers should be liberated from the sovereign consumer paradigm with its emphasis on information.[43] The story of ECJ engagement with the character of the consumer is, however, more complex. Certainly, it could be argued that the Court was never really concerned with the character of the consumer *per se*. Rather, its major interest lay in creating an integrated European market, to which the mass of inchoate national consumer protection legislation was a barrier. Equally, where the chosen means for pursuing the integrationist interest was 'liberalization', the consequent removal of 'barriers to business'[44] might be argued to demonstrate that the Court was concerned more with promoting an entrepreneurial market interest and less with a diffuse consumer interest. Who, after all, is more likely to give shape to a European market? Nevertheless, in the final analysis, it might also be suggested that the actions of the ECJ were never fully congruent with either a business or a consumer interest, however defined. Instead, a legal internal logic dictated and directed judicial deregulatory strategies, also setting limits to those strategies.

European law is a law *sui generis*. Its supremacy is a mere self-declaration of sovereignty by the ECJ. Given neither a firm constitutional basis nor a direct connection with any form of political legitimation, European law must perforce seek constant self-justification. Seen in this light, legal materialization, always also of doubtful legitimacy within a national setting (should lawyers or politicians give shape to social justice?), was an even more inappropriate approach at a European level: which national legal/economic system would support the imposition of unpalatable price control? Instead, European law was to seek its self-justifying legitimacy not only in formal analysis, but also in the mass of 'rational' and 'scientific' (seemingly neutral) literature re-establishing the concept of the 'confident' and 'informed' sovereign consumer, freeing it from its necessarily contentious political-philosophical context and placing it firmly within the analytically confirmed 'truths' of modern economic theory.[45] It is the marriage of law and modern economic 'science' (not 'theory') that furnishes the initial contours of the rationally sovereign European consumer and offers law a neutral hook on which to hang its liberalizing judgments. Ultimately, then, the definition of the legal consumer is once again prone to manipulation by legal external constructions of the consumer but is also very much a reflection of a legal internal battle to establish legal legitimacy.

In this final respect, the need to maintain the legitimacy of European law also explains various inconsistencies within the jurisprudence of the ECJ, most strikingly since European law must continue to coexist with the equally legitimate claims to sovereignty of the national legal orders. The member states still retain various competences in the matter of consumer protection, such as the right to continue to protect national 'health and safety' (Article 30). Accordingly, much of the ECJ's consumer-oriented jurisprudence has also been concerned with striking a balance between European and national legislation and it is at this interface of balance that various inconsistencies in the Court's jurisprudence arise: the continuing recognition that certain cultural factors may legitimately continue to determine patterns of consumption in the refusal to extend the reach of Article 28 to Sunday trading; somewhat incoherent efforts to prevent the abuse of free movement provisions by big business; and finally, the approval of UK measures demanding stricter tobacco labelling requirements than was the European norm.[46]

Condemned by some as incoherent and an 'example of result orientation' (legal metaphor for the notion of 'judge as headless chicken')[47] within ECJ jurisprudence, such cases are perhaps best explained not through legal reasoning but by a diffuse concern that the legitimacy of European law would be placed under threat, were it to stray too far into national sensitivities. Further, the recent case of the *Bayerische Hypotheken und Wechselbank* [1998],[48] in which the ECJ dismayed socially oriented legal commentators[49] by refusing to extend European consumer protection measures to bank guarantors with the formalist argument that they were not 'privy' to the primary binary contractual relationship, forcefully underlines its current unwillingness to encroach too far on national sensitivities. The ECJ is no longer in the business of creating a distinct European consumer. Instead, that consumer has now served its primary judicial purpose of acting as a vital motor of European integration and providing, at the same time, vital legitimacy for European law.

As the Court has withdrawn from its central role in creating the European consumer, the European Commission has readily filled the gap. Always highly aware of the legitimation potential of direct appeals to distinct (non-national) categories of the European citizen,[50] a long-standing Commission interest in consumer affairs was strengthened by the necessarily deregulatory tendencies of ECJ jurisprudence. In a final twist, then, whilst liberalization was necessary to effect market integration, the interests of the newly established European market were not necessarily wholly liberal, at least in matters of regulatory policy. The scheme of regulatory competition and mutual recognition established between national orders[51] may have broken the political deadlock that characterized the years of failed harmonization. Nonetheless, the newly established European market proved itself to be in need of regulatory inputs.

Not only did the member states retain a legitimate regulatory interest in the consumer's health and safety and consumer protection. Rather, the growing list of cases before the ECJ similarly attested that they were prepared to defend such interests. Accordingly, while mutual recognition remained the major regulating principle within the internal market, national obduracy increased the danger of inefficiency, as tortuous court proceedings were needed to confirm the liberalization of the market in ever more sectors. As a consequence, there was also a clear need for some degree and some form of harmonized re-regulation at the European level. Equally, regulatory 'standards' common to all the member states are not simply a matter of material intervention. Instead, they can be demanded by business itself to facilitate the growth of integrated markets and efficiencies of scale. Taken together with an undoubted consumer interest in the ability of harmonized standards to ensure the transparency of cross-border transactions, the benefits of harmonization within the newly founded market were thus highly convincing. Accordingly, new strategies were developed to afford a measure of harmonization within the new internal market.

Two particular elements of these strategies are of interest here. First, the Commission's Green Paper on the completion of the internal market, dating from 1985,[52] contained the seeds of a new approach to the 'executive' harmonization of the European market after the failure of traditional political harmonization measures. Mindful that a succession of Council of Ministers had singularly failed to agree on the provisions of directives regulating individual market sectors and interests, the Commission evolved the concept of framework directives, whereby the European Council would devolve to the Commission general regulatory powers for large economic areas. In turn, the Commission, together with committees of member state representatives, scientific experts and consumer interest groups, would concretize individual regulatory standards to combat individual dangers.

Second, the 'high level of protection' guaranteed consumers in the Single European Act heralded the first explicit development of a European competence in consumer affairs. The Commission, blessed with the sole European competence to make legislative proposals, was accordingly free to begin to suggest a series of direct legislative mechanisms 'in protection of the consumer'. The fruits of this effort to concretize the Commission's character as 'friend of the European consumer' are accordingly to be found in directives on Consumer Credit (87/102), Doorstop Selling (85/577), Package Travel (90/314), Unfair Terms in Consumer Contracts (93/13) and Distance Contracts (97/7).

Given this veritable avalanche of new regulatory standards, as well as corrective interventionist contract law provisions, a recent appraisal that 'European consumer law has come of age' may seem highly controversial if not counterintuitive. Coming as it does from an explicit belief that consumer policy should be informed by 'the needs of a rational information seeking consumer who can be adequately protected by the market and competition policy',[53] such a perspective seems strangely to overlook the extraordinary potential that exists within obscure executive structures for the reproduction of the same form of often incoherent, poorly coordinated and ineffective materialization debates that marked national consumer policy. The effects of the re-regulatory efforts of the European Commission have yet to be fully felt or assessed. Nonetheless, there is growing evidence that, the Commission's rhetoric of rational market regulation notwithstanding (a rhetoric supporting the dual informational and competition pillars upon which a modern rational consumer stands), various recent consumer measures have struck the same disturbing note within overall attempts to define European policy as did many national materialization measures.

The point at this juncture, however, is not whether the Commission is right or wrong to pursue particular consumer protection measures. Rather, the issue is the limited steering capacity of regulation and law in consumer affairs that is revealed when different parts of the same organization appear to be following disparate aims at uncoordinated moments. Thus, a powerful expressed sentiment within economic legal literature that European directives have gone far beyond what is necessary to ensure informational flow to the consumer and have instead begun to shape the product on offer to the consumer,[54] finds its echo in the ECJ's *Bayerische Hypotheken* judgment that the Unfair Contract Terms Directive represents too great an inroad into national private law autonomy. By the same token, some sections of the Commission may be dedicated to the formulation of a competition policy in line with the demands of the rationale for market transparency. Others, however, may be more concerned with industrial policies supporting vulnerable industries. Equally, a scientific presence within committees seeking to ensure the health and safety of consumers might ensure that 'rationality' is the guiding principle for production standards. However, a consumer or a Commission interest may also result in the erection of new European cultural production standards.

In short, the European debate is marked by the same dangers of conflict between rational (replacing formal) and material interests, lack of coordination and lack of legal steering capacity that were apparent at national level. Seen in this light, a major critique of legal literature on the nature and status of the European consumer might be its general disregard for the overall steering capacity of European law and its preparedness to take unreflective side with a particular nature and role of the European consumer.

The claim that we have now entered a third period, heralding the evolution of a political conception of the European consumer, may appear to be premature. Nonetheless, the current commitment of the Commission, expressed in its 2002–6 consumer strategy,[55] to a clear definition of 'consumer policy' that displaces considerations of the protection of health and safety to the general regulatory framework,[56] and locates the core of consumer policy in efforts to unite the forces of a diffuse consumer interest with the interests of the market, does herald a radical reformulation of the state-consumer-market triad. The state, once the primary champion of consumer interest, is (vitally) excluded from efforts to democratize the market.

A peculiar result of the supranational nature of the European Union and the lack of a European polity, the Commission's commitment to the 'privatization' of consumer affairs,[57] through both the strengthening of industry established European standardization bodies and the release of framework consumer policy directives, is an undoubted and radical intensification of efforts to establish the character of the citizen consumer through the direct democratization of the market. No longer should standards be imposed by political legislation. Instead, 'partnership' within the modes of production between industry, consumers and the executive (Commission oversight of the standardization procedure) will bring consumers into a direct relationship with the market.

With this, the political character of the Commission's new consumer policy strategy is readily apparent as the character of 'market-citizen-consumer' steps up to represent diffuse consumer interests and takes precedence over (national) political citizens. The character of the market-citizen consumer represents a revolution within the evolution of a consumer who is designed to integrate functionally distinct sectors of society. In the model of the citizen consumer, interaction between consumer groups and industry standardization should represent an advance beyond an informational model that places its regulatory faith in market transparency and provision of information to the consumer at the point of sale. Consumers will themselves be pivotal in the matter of creating products by virtue of their presence within standardization processes, thus democratizing the market. However, with the development of the market-citizen consumer any links to conventional paradigms of national citizenship or to the concept of the primacy of the national polity are severed. Direct consumer action and not politically motivated and traditionally formulated regulation will serve the aims of consumer protection and societal reintegration.

Law and the Consumer: A Constructive Summary

It is an underlying theme of this chapter that law cannot hope ever to furnish a fully coherent vision of the consumer: the political-philosophical context is too complex, the economic theory too contested and the number of legal fields impacted upon too diverse. Seen in this light, critiques of incomplete national and European efforts to secure the position of the consumer must be slightly tempered. To be sure, within legal science itself, an absence of reflection and/or a blind commitment to any one of a number of (extra-legal) constructions of the consumer might be considered to lack academic rigour. Nonetheless, in the practical field of the application of consumer policy within the law immediate harms *must* be combated and social demands *must* be met within a framework of law, which is severely constrained in its efforts by problems of coordination and coherence.

Although it is far too much to hope that law could ever give shape to a consistent concept of the consumer, a practice of what might be termed 'legal incrementalism' that seeks constructively to address the position of the consumer through its isolated interventions serves vital goals and must itself seek to retain a degree of overall legal and social legitimacy. In this regard, then, this chapter concludes by summarizing the forty-year legal debate on the consumer with a prospective outlook. If a 'modern' law is to retain integrity in its incremental dealings with consumer and consumption, it must take great care:

- To maintain *external integrity*, as, within a confusion of consumer policy goals and legal external constructions of the consumer, it keeps faith with a modern reality that law must in some way be 'a socially democratized law', serving an underlying structural aim of the maintenance of social integration and overall democratic steering capacity within complex societies.

● To maintain *internal integrity*, as, within a continuing battle between formal and material law, or between 'rational' and material law, demands for legal 'neutrality', or an ability to isolate law from particularist aims, can only grow as the primary consolidator of social and cultural values, the national polity, disintegrates under supranational and international demands for economic rationalization.

The 'sovereign consumer', the 'citizen consumer', the 'rational consumer' and the 'market-citizen consumer', with their concomitant satellites of the 'nationally embedded consumer', the 'culturally determined consumer', the 'informed consumer' and the 'confident consumer', all entail, often radically opposed, consumer policy aims and underlying political-philosophical or economic constructions of the consumer. Seen in this light, the law of consumer policy can find itself (often under a simple rubric of consumer protection) pursuing aims as diverse as the consolidation of the national polity and, in the highly ambivalent case of the European market-citizen consumer, the pursuit of a post-national polity, in which isolated groups of consumer interests become the major motor for reconnection between the addressees of production and modes of production and redistribution ('market democratization'). Nonetheless, if law is to combat harms such as BSE within this complex, it must find a neutral legitimacy. Here, however, Kennedy's 1962 speech gives us a hint of what role a modern law *should* be playing. The consumer debate, we are reminded, is not simply a matter of combating immediate harm, but rather a far deeper issue of re-establishing connections between markets, politics and society. Such reconnection has become ever more urgent, as various functionally differentiated sections of society have escaped the confines of nation-states and national economies (the market), whilst others (politics) seem unable to extend their steering capacities beyond national frontiers and yet others (consumers) have grown ever more diffuse and difficult to identify within a global arena.

Set against this background, law's function should always also be abstracted from its simple regulatory role and reframed within its constitutive function of the global regulation of society. Consumer policy and its pursuit by law, is also a constitutional task. The day-to-day acts of regulating the meat content within sausages, policing contract law terms, or of overseeing the presence of consumer interest groups within industry or regulatory standardization committees must thus be constantly reassessed in light of the law's vocational dedication to the maintenance of social integration and overall democratic steering capacity.

Whether called upon to support a diffuse consumer interest above a more general collective political interest, or whether seeking to give voice to notions of standard setting as opposed to measures supportive of consumer choice, a sensitive modern law must ultimately cease to work with any substantive vision of the consumer. Instead, a reflexive law must commit itself to the pursuit of the citizen consumer in its most abstract form. The issue is surely no longer one of whether law should seek to preserve its own formal rationality through the pursuit of paradigms of the sovereign consumer or should seek increased social validity through a materialization impulse which, say, privileges the nationally embedded consumer through the imposition of culturally produced standards. Nor is it one of whether law can shore up its own lacking social legitimacy through a marriage with 'science' and pursuit of the rational consumer. Rather, law's constitutive role requires it to review each and every simple operation of legal consumer policy from the criterion of whether it can be said, in the immediate context of application, to increase or decrease societal steering capacities.

Legal incrementalism, guided by constant constitutional prescription, can seem obscure and unsatisfactory from a logical viewpoint. At a practical level, however, it is probably already a guiding tenet of an ECJ that is no longer engaged in the activist creation of the integrated market. The inconsistencies in recent ECJ jurisprudence can thus be read not as an example of destructive result orientation within the Court, but rather as a sensitive effort, within a complex and disputed European polity, to ascertain which levels (national or European) and which forms of consumer policy (collective versus diffuse interest; standards versus choice) are best placed, and when, in order to maintain overall societal integration within Europe.

'Judge as headless chicken' may initially seem a strange character in which to place our faith that law might be able to maintain its own integrity within ongoing debate on consumer policy. Nonetheless, the currently highly incrementalist Justices of the European Court do seem to come closest to a model of legal thinking which locates the internal integrity of law not in formal or substantive paradigms but in the maintenance of the law's ability to ensure its own neutrality at a time of highly contested political, philosophical and economic thought and still serve, through the sensitive reflexive treatment of each individual case, a long-term constitutional goal of social consolidation. Considered constitutional reflection of a consumer interest by law, rather than legal pursuit of a substantive consumer interest, must be the guiding philosophy of modern legal consumer policy.

Notes

1. See Trentmann and Taylor in this volume.
2. D. Bollier and J. Claybrook, *Freedom from Harm* (Washington, 1986), p. 31.
3. Official Journal (OJ) 1975 C92/1.
4. See C. Offe, 'Ausdifferenzierung oder Integration', in G. Fleischmann (ed.), *Der Kritische Verbraucher* (Frankfurt, 1980), who (at this time implicitly) draws on the early writings of Niklas Luhmann to identify the defining characteristic of

post-war social and political organization: the increasing breakdown of society into individual functional spheres (society, market, economy, science, etc.), each with its own operating logic, and each wholly indifferent to the logics (ethics, regulatory goals) of other spheres.

5. In modern legal theory terms, talk of law's 'reintegrative function' is a common feature of legal analyses that draw on Luhmann's systems theory in order to explain the social environment within which law operates and to describe its modern goal of establishing communication between differentiated social spheres; see G. Teubner, 'Coincidentia oppositorum: das Recht der Netzwerke jenseits von Vertrag und Organisation', in Marc Amstutz (ed.), *Die vernetzte Wirtschaft: Netzwerke als Rechtsproblem* (Zürich, 2004) pp. 7–38 (an English version, 'Englische Fassung: Coincidentia oppositorum: Networks and the Law beyond Contract and Organization', is available within the series 'Storrs Lectures 2003/04' of the Yale Law School). Although earlier writings on the character and purpose of the citizen consumer are not as theoretically refined as modern systems theory approaches, they nonetheless represent their precursor as law struggled within the means then available to it to re-establish relations between increasingly differentiated social spheres.

6. See C. Joerges, *Verbraucherschutz als Rechtsproblem* (Heidelberg, 1981); U. Reifner, *Alternatives Wirtschaftsrecht am Beispiel Verbraucherverschuldung* (Neuwied, 1976).

7. For example, the European Commission, European Commission Consumer Policy Strategy 2002–6, (Com 2002) 208.

8. In other words, attempts by authors such as Bollier and Claybrook (*Freedom from Harm*) to highlight the dangers posed by modern production methods must also be understood as 'political' programmes dedicated to making law and regulation more receptive to prevailing social and economic conditions.

9. E. Kramer, 'Zur Konzeption des Konsumentenschutzes' *Kritische Vierteljahresschrift*, 270 (1986), 270–90: 286, 'Die Ablehnung eines Sondergesetzes für Kaufleute stehe mit den demokratischen Staatseinrichtungen in der Schweiz und mit der demokratischen Gesinnung des Schweizervolkes im Zusammenhang.'

10. See Kramer, 'Zur Konzeption des Konsumentenschutzes:' 'Die Einheitskonzeption (unity of contract law) rechfertige sich auch durch die wohl in keinem anderen Lande Europas in so hohem Grade durch alle Schichten der Gesellschaft gleichmässig verbreitete Schulbildung und geschäftliche Begabung des Volkes.'

11. See Kramer, 'Zur Konzeption des Konsumentenschutzes', p. 271. See also G. Kleinhenz, *Zur politischen Ökonomie des Konsums* (Berlin, 1978), p. 3; N. Reich and H. Micklitz, *Verbraucherschutzrecht in der Bundesrepublik Deutschland* (New York, 1980), p. 3.

12. See Joerges, *Verbraucherschutz als Rechtsproblem*, p. 46. A growing trend of differentiation within the law allowed a core of private law to maintain a myth

of legal isolation from politics, as interventionist impulses were seemingly isolated within new forms of regulatory law.

13. The historically high degree of intervention within the private insurance contract is perhaps the most striking indication of a lack of reflection within law about the nature of the consumer. Although the market was characterized by the direct regulation of terms and conditions, this challenge to the individuality of contracts never really resulted in an overall review of the underlying premises of a contract law that conceived of contractual partners as individuals.

14. By the same token, consumers themselves were beginning to shape the legal debate; see Trentmann and Taylor in this volume.

15. See Bollier and Claybrook, *Freedom from Harm*.

16. See Bollier and Claybrook, *Freedom from Harm*; Kleinhenz, *Zur politischen Ökonomie des Konsums*. See also F. Hirsch, *Die Sozialen Grenzen des Wachstums* (Hamburg, 1976); H. Schatz, *Verbraucherinteressen im politischen Entscheidungsprozess* (Frankfurt, 1981).

17. The debate and internal legal conflict on the materialization of law are not new. The existence of materialization tendencies form a major part of Max Weber's analysis of legal systems. However, the simmering long-term conflict between lawyers committed to an isolation of the law from all political or social direction (formalists) and lawyers concerned to adapt law to the demands for social justice prevalent within modern societies (materialization) burst into post-war life with the development of 'critical legal studies (CLS) movements', particularly within the US and Germany. Note, however, that continental and Anglo-American academic legal debate tended to caste the materialization effort in slightly different terms. In continental debate, Max Weber's notion of 'materialization', or the socialization of law, was developed to include legislative intervention within civil law codes of private law that aimed to give expression to politically expressed social demands for substantive justice within the general canon of legal interpretation. Within an Anglo-American setting, by contrast, socialization efforts within the law were provided within individual judicial alterations within the formal application of law. Exemplary for the US CLS movement, D. Kennedy, 'Freedom and Constraint in Adjudication: A Critical Phenomenology', *Journal of Legal Education*, 36 (1986).

18. Exemplary, Reich and Micklitz, *Verbraucherschutzrecht in der Bundesrepublik Deutschland*; see also H. Micklitz, *Der Reparatur Vertrag* (Munich, 1983).

19. Exemplary, E. von Hippel, *Verbraucherschutz*, 2nd edn (Tübingen, 1979).

20. See von Hippel, *Verbraucherschutz*.

21. See Reich and Micklitz, *Verbraucherschutzrecht in der Bundesrepublik Deutschland*.

22. See below, pages 110ff.

23. Insurance regulation again stands out.

24. An unparalleled exception offered by Kleinhenz, *Zur politischen Ökonomie des Konsums*.

25. See Joerges, *Verbraucherschutz als Rechtsproblem*, p. 40.
26. See Joerges, *Verbraucherschutz als Rechtsproblem*, pp. 40ff.; Reifner, *Alternatives Wirtschaftsrecht am Beispiel Verbraucherverschuldung*.
27. The definition of the 'consumer interest' lies at the core of regulatory debates on the consumer. As noted (Offe, 'Ausdifferenzierung oder Integration'), the consumer interest, even within a functionally differentiated society, is inherently diffuse: while industry and the market have a clear unitary interest in self-reproduction, consumers may have diverging interests; many consumers are also producers. Nonetheless, where the aim is to rise above the individualizing nature of the sovereign consumer, some form of 'collective consumer interest' must be found; N. Reich, *Europäisches Verbraucherrecht,* 3rd edn (Baden-Baden, 1996). Post-war, 'collectivity' was provided by the integrative cultural and social characteristics of the national polity and effected by national legislative action.
28. See Joerges, *Verbraucherschutz als Rechtsproblem*, pp. 49ff.
29. See above Kramer, 'Zur Konzeption des Konsumentenschutzes'; Micklitz, *Der Reparatur Vertrag*; Reich and Micklitz, *Verbraucherschutzrecht in der Bundesrepublik Deutschland*.
30. See S. Weatherhill, *EC Consumer Law and Policy* (London, 1997).
31. C. Joerges, 'Taking the Law Seriously: On Political Science and the Role of Law in the Process of European Integration', *European Law Journal*, 2(2) (1996), pp. 105–35; G. Majone, *Regulating Europe* (London, 1996).
32. That is, no discrimination against goods on grounds of national origin.
33. Giving the individual European rights to move across Europe in pursuit of work and business interests.
34. European Court Reports (ECR) 1227.
35. H.-C. von Heydebrand u.d. Lasa, 'Free Movement of Foodstuffs, Consumer Protection and Food Standards in the European Community: Has the Court of Justice Got it Wrong?', *European Law Review*, 16(5) (1991), pp. 391–415.
36. Weatherhill, *EC Consumer Law and Policy*, p. 37.
37. 2 Common Market Law Reports (CMLR) 69.
38. ECR I-667 [1991].
39. ECR 405 [1987].
40. ECR 405 [1987], p. 95.
41. ECR I-667 [1991], p. 1205.
42. V. Gessner, 'Europas holprige Rechtswege', in Krämer *et al.* (eds), *Law and Diffuse Interests in the European Legal Order* (Baden Baden, 1997), p. 163.
43. Exemplary, G. Howells and T. Wilhelmsson, 'EC Consumer Law: Has it Come of Age?', *European Law Review*, 28(3) (2003), pp. 370–88.
44. S. Weatherhill, 'Consumer Safety Legislation in the United Kingdom and Article 30 EEC', *European Law Review*, 13(2) (1988), pp. 87–105.

45. For a recent example of the methodology, S. Haupt, 'An Economic Analysis of Consumer Protection Law', *German Law Journal* (on-line), 4:11 (2003).

46. *Torfaen* [1989] (ECR 3851); *Keck* [1993] (1995) ECR I-6097; *Gallaher* [1993] (Case C-175/94) respectively.

47. S. Weatherhill, 'Regulating the Internal Market: Result Orientation in the Court of Justice', *European Law Review*, 19(1) (1994), pp. 55–67.

48. Not yet reported.

49. N. Bamforth, 'The Limits of European Union Consumer Contract Law', *European Law Review*, 24(4) (1999), pp. 410–18.

50. See Weatherhill, *EC Consumer Law and Policy*.

51. The basic tenet of ECJ jurisprudence was that all national standards and regulatory provisions should be recognized by other national authorities as being equivalent in nature.

52. Com (Commission White Paper) (85) 310.

53. See Howells and Wilhelmsson, 'EC Consumer Law.'

54. See Haupt, 'Economic Analysis of Consumer Protection Law.'

55. See the European Commission, European Commission Consumer Policy Strategy (Case C-5/96 [1998] All ER (EC) 332).

56. See Howells and Wilhelmsson, 'EC Consumer Law.'

57. See Howells and Wilhelmsson, 'EC Consumer Law.'

Part II
Commercial Relations: Retailers, Experts and the Contested Consumer

–6–

Packaging China

Foreign Articles and Dangerous Tastes in the Mid-Victorian Tea Party

Erika Rappaport

In 1826 the Quaker, abolitionist and parliamentary reformer John Horniman began selling tea in pre-weighed and sealed packages. Packet tea took some time to become established, but within a few decades this innovation secured Horniman's position as a leader in the trade. By the 1880s the practice became the norm when mass-market companies such as Lipton's began selling tea in this way. Packaged tea was thus a milestone in the history of mass retailing and the deskilling of the petty retailer, who had routinely blended tea in small batches. When it was first introduced, however, Horniman's innovation at once created and responded to the idea that the Chinese drink was not a luxury to be sought, but a poison to be avoided. John Horniman packaged his tea to distinguish it from the competition and as a reaction to widespread anxieties about the purity of Chinese productions.[1]

Between the 1820s and the 1870s merchants such as Horniman, scientists, journalists and politicians warned British consumers that Chinese manufacturing methods were dirty and fraudulent, the most dangerous practice being the colouring of tea, especially green tea, with unwholesome and even poisonous materials. This fear contributed to a sharp decline in the China trade in the second half of the nineteenth century, as consumers lost their taste for Chinese tea and developed an insatiable thirst for that produced under British-controlled and highly industrialized plantations in South Asia. New understandings of tea, its producers and its consumers were constituted within the volatile economic, political and cultural relations between China and Great Britain after the end of the East India Company's monopoly in 1833 and the forcible 'opening' of China in 1842.[2]

British food tastes were shaped in the Victorian period, as they are to a certain extent today, by consumers' fears about the nature of both manufacturing and retailing. The Victorian discussion of adulterated foods and drinks peaked between the 1850s and 1870s and was the product of wider concerns about public health, the growing authority of chemistry and food science, the mechanization of food production and the expansion of an international free trade in foodstuffs. It was also part of a moment in which the British were looking at things from a variety of new perspectives. The Great Exhibition of 1851, the rise of department stores, the periodical press and advertising led to a spectacular culture which allowed commodities to speak in new ways.[3] Like the exhibits on display at the Crystal Palace, the debate about adulteration raised the issue of the relationship between commodities and consumers and production and consumption. Anti-adulteration activists argued that consumers needed to know about where and how goods were produced since these facts were crucial to the taste, value and health of commodities.

Mid-Victorian reformers worked to expose and limit adulteration through the use of the microscope, chemical analysis, legislation, tax reform, consumer education, advertising and the establishment of new industries directly under British control, such as the Indian tea industry.[4] These early concerns about food safety fuelled the development of a highly fraught relationship between retailers, the State and consumers, and this in turn influenced food choices and tastes.[5] While debating the facts of adulteration, activists asserted truths about the value and costs of commodities. In doing so, a new culture of expertise took form, which was built upon its ability to draw boundaries between good and bad commodities, consumers and modes of production, distribution and consumption. Fears about dangerous foods thereby provided the terms through which the Victorians worked out the relationship between the individual and local and international markets. Rather than look at the anti-adulteration movement as public policy, however, I focus here on tea in particular to reveal how this movement was also animated by and stimulated anxieties about foreign substances entering British markets and bodies and how such concerns defined commodities and altered tastes.

The Victorians were worried about the quality of most manufactured foods, drinks and drugs, but in the middle decades of the century the anti-adulteration movement especially focused on Chinese green tea. Reformers cautioned consumers that drinking this favoured beverage brought them into close contact with unscrupulous British retailers and dangerous and filthy Chinese producers.[6] Though they rarely read lengthy reports in scientific and medical journals, consumers discovered that their tea was dangerous through reading periodicals, household guides and advertising, particularly that of John Horniman. Horniman's ads quoted scientists, China scholars and explorers to convey the truth about tea and its adulteration. This advertising cast the retailer as a benevolent patriarch who promoted the latest scientific findings and methods of food production and thereby watched over the nation's health.[7] The debate about adulteration aided retailers such as Horniman, produced knowledge about China and its productions and contributed to the growing authority of science, technology and advertising. Together 'modern' retailers and scientists promised to defend the British public from perilous Eastern pleasures and from the more unruly aspects of the marketplace.

During the nineteenth century, many of the products that lined grocers' and bakers' shelves were adulterated with a wide variety of spurious items. This situation was by no means new, but the meaning and extent of this activity shifted with the growth of mass consumption and intensified retail competition, the lifting of controls on international trade and the advancement of scientific methods for detecting additives in food.[8] Chemists were especially prominent in exposing the problem of food safety and in doing so helped their individual careers and aided in the establishment of chemistry as a profession. The topic was first thrust into public consciousness in 1820, when the chemist Friedrich Accum published a best seller which asserted that the 'unprincipled and nefarious practice ... is now applied to almost every commodity which can be classed among the necessaries or the luxuries of life and is carried on to a most alarming extent in every part of the United Kingdom'.[9] As Accum's work was reviewed in scientific and more popular journals, including those directed to a female audience such as *The Lady's Magazine*, consumers began to worry about the content of their foods.[10] Soon following upon Accum's success, popular books on chemistry, such as *The Domestic Chemist: Comprising Instructions for the Detection of Adulteration in Numerous Articles* (1831), promised to 'erect a barricade against the cupidity of fraudulent tradesmen and to put it into every man's power to ensure his health and wealth against the ravages of adulteration and disease'. This author sought to prove that chemistry had direct applications in 'common life' and was not the 'frivolous and fruitless pursuit which many consider it to be'.[11] Chemistry sought legitimacy by offering consumers knowledge about the goods they ingested; knowledge which acted as a 'barricade' between the consumer and the retailer. While popular chemistry primarily spoke to men and women of the educated middle classes, other reformers in this era focused on the working-class diet and identified adulteration as a class-specific crime.

Between the 1830s and 1850s social investigators concurred with chemists' basic conclusions and further stimulated consumer anxiety. Like chemists, these early social scientists believed that adulteration constituted a threat to consumers' health and to that of the marketplace. This sin was both a social and a commercial crime. Though addressing a primarily middle-class audience, mid-Victorian social investigations established the idea that the primary victims of adulteration were Britain's urban poor. In 1831, for example, William Rathbone Greg warned that inadequate, adulterated food was one of the factors leading to the great suffering of the manufacturing classes in England. The poor drank 'tea, diluted till it is little else than warm water, the materials of which never came from China, but are the production of one of those innumerable frauds which are practised upon the poor...'.[12] Though Greg did not spell it out, his work would have been understood as a condemnation of the petty retailers who were commonly thought to prey upon the labouring classes.

By the 1850s, however, scientists and explorers developed several new means of detecting this fraudulent activity. In doing so, they expanded the understanding of adulteration, defining it as a national problem, which could harm men and women from all classes and regions. The most important anti-adulteration activist during this period was the chemist Dr Arthur Hill Hassall, who would become known as the 'Apostle of Adulteration'.[13] Hassall is now remembered for his work on cholera, but while he was directing his microscope at the water supply, Hassall also looked at the nation's food. He argued that properly used the instrument could 'detect' adulteration better than the chemical tests that were the norm at that time. One of Hassall's admirers explained that, 'in Hassall's hands', the microscope could determine 'the ingredients hitherto described as "organic matter" '.[14] Even as late as 1851, this author claimed scientists had not been able to 'see' the difference between chicory and coffee, for example. Chemical tests were by no means abandoned, but the microscope became an increasingly important tool, which enabled scientists literally to see the constituent elements of substances more clearly.

In the early 1850s Hassall embarked upon an extensive and comprehensive investigation into the quality of the nation's food, conducted under the auspices of *The Lancet*. This work and the public outcry it inspired, led to the establishment of a parliamentary select committee and the passage in 1860 of the first law against the adulteration of food, drink and drugs. Using a combination of chemical tests and microscopic investigations, Hassall informed the public that the most common products of domestic consumption – among them sugar, honey, bread, milk, potted meats, tinned vegetables, spices, mustard, pickles and vinegar and every conceivable beverage – contained numerous, and in his estimation, unwholesome additives.[15] Some of the spurious elements were by-products of processing but most were deliberate attempts to defraud the consumer by manufacturing a heavier, stronger tasting, or more colourful product. Though he recognized that the working classes were often the victims of adulteration, Hassall deliberately characterized adulteration as a general and pervasive plague infecting the entire United Kingdom. In the spirit of much public health reform of the era, Hassall stridently argued that he had uncovered a national problem, one that could only be solved through the application of science and responsible government intervention.

During this period, the definition of adulteration was vague but it incorporated two somewhat distinct ideas, that of an inadvertent but nonetheless criminal act which could sicken its victims and that of a civil crime which defrauded the consumer through violating the basic contract implied when one purchased goods in a shop. The law incorporated both facets of this definition when it stated that an item was adulterated by 'the infusion of some foreign substance ... other than that which the article purports to be'. Food or drink was considered adulterated when it contained 'any ingredient which may render such article injurious to the health of the consumer' or if it was mixed with 'any substance that sensibly increases its weight, bulk, or strength, or gives it a fictitious value'.[16] Adulterated foods were essentially fictional commodities or at least products that contained elements that added a fictional value, which could financially and physically harm the consumer.

The debate over adulteration thereby articulated a central Victorian proble-matic, that of distinguishing the real from the artificial.[17] An 1871 poem, entitled *Poisoning and Pilfering: Wholesale and Retail* published to expose the prevalence of adulteration, fittingly began: '[s]carce an article bought – or so it seems to me – is the substance they'd have you believe it to be. There is hair sold as wool, there is cotton for flax. There is sugar for honey and tallow for wax... There is much that is noxious in the things that we eat'.[18] Indeed, anxieties about authenticity sparked the development of household guides professing to teach consumers how to detect the quality and substance of the items they ingested. *The Family Manual and Servants' Guide*, for example, advised housekeepers how to choose good tea and how to distinguish the genuine article from its counterfeit.[19] Lara Kriegel has noted in her study of copyright and Indian calicoes that manufacturers and politicians sought copyright protection to help define the original from the copy. As she has suggested, the mechanization of manufacturing and expansion of retailing and overseas trade gave rise to the 'cultural conundrum' of determining the nature of the real thing.[20]

Tea illuminated similar concerns about the real and the fake but also inspired worries about 'foreign' objects entering British bodies. As the author of a popular exposé on commercial quackery put it in the 1850s, '[t]here is scarcely any article of food more subject to adulteration than this now common necessary of life. Tea is not only taken advantage of by fraudulent dealers at home, but ... the Chinese are not behind us in roguish ingenuity'.[21] Of course, coffee, sugar, cocoa and spices were also foreign commodities, but they tended to be adulterated in Britain with relatively harmless and perhaps even healthy substances. Coffee, for example, was frequently mixed with chicory, roasted wheat, peas and parsnip.[22] Yet since chicory too was frequently adulterated, coffee drinkers were by no means safe. However, black and green teas were most often adulterated with dangerous chemicals introduced primarily, as one expert described it, 'in the Chinese ports'.[23] Though British retailers had been known to tamper with the public's tea, nearly all experts agreed that 'China' was the 'real hotbed of adulteration'.[24]

The tea plant had been an especially mysterious commodity, because, until their defeat in the Opium War, the Chinese had carefully guarded its cultivation and manufacture from European observation. In 1830, for example, food scientist Dr J. Stevenson angrily condemned the Chinese for preventing the development of Western science: 'While the present narrow and jealous policy of the Chinese continues, many interesting particulars respecting the natural history of this particular plant must remain unknown to Europeans'.[25] A few years later, a well-known botanist similarly complained that '[f]or a number of centuries the character, the manners, the customs and the institutions of the Chinese, from whom alone could be gathered any information upon the subject of the tea-plant, were veiled in the deepest curiosity'. He happily noted, however, that such 'obstacles which stood in the way of acquiring knowledge' had been removed.[26] Military defeat and developments in botany and chemistry meant that China and its goods were more available to European scrutiny in the 1840s and 1850s than ever before. Yet access did not dispel anxieties about Chinese products.

Although the British had begun to acquire more knowledge of the basic characteristics of the tea plant, a good deal of confusion remained. Debate persisted about whether black and green teas came from different plants or whether the variations in characteristics were due only to methods of cultivation and preparation.[27] In 1843 a Dr Pereira frustratingly concluded that there was still 'great discrepancy of opinion among writers as to whether the green or black teas of commerce are the produce of one or two species'.[28] The raging debates about the health merits or dangers of tea drinking itself had to a certain degree subsided in the Victorian period. Yet scientists and popular myth tended to conclude that black teas were healthier than green. The latter was thought to be the stronger of the two drinks and could therefore have 'severe effects' if drunk by, as Pereira put it, 'those popularly known as nervous'. For those with weak constitutions, green tea could give rise to 'tremor, anxiety, sleeplessness and most distressing feelings'.[29] Though generally in support of tea's benefits, Dr Sigmond, another tea expert, noted that, for some, green tea acted 'almost as a narcotic poison ... producing a distressing nausea, a sense of constriction of the chest and palpitation of the heart. The face becomes pale, the skin cold, the pulse altered ... [there may be] violent pains in the head, giddiness, dimness of sight, incapability of muscular action and a sensation of suffocation'.[30] Medical reports occasionally described the fate of individuals who suffered from their green tea habit. In one such case an 'English traveller who [after having] walked some distance during a hot summer's day under the stimulus of green tea' began feeling faint, had an irregular pulse, difficulty breathing and heart palpitations.[31] For most scientists, the health effects of this commodity thus depended on both the type of tea consumed and the physical and psychological condition of the particular consumer. In other words, what was good for one tea drinker could in effect be deadly to another. Though based on little evidence, the medical opinion of green tea played upon British fears by describing the injuries that the Chinese producers could inflict upon Western consumers.

In 1853, at the same time as Hassall's reports were appearing in the *Lancet*, Elizabeth Gaskell used the popular perception of green tea in her novel *Cranford* to establish the middle-class spinster Miss Matty's respectability after she embarked upon a tea-selling business. Though Miss Matty sold the morally questionable commodity, she sought to protect the most vulnerable of her customers against its pernicious effects. Miss Matty had the habit of entreating her customers not to buy green tea and 'of running it down as slow poison, sure to destroy the nerves and produce all manner of evil'. Rather than refusing to sell it altogether and thereby 'lose half her custom', she decided upon 'an occasional remonstrance, when she thought the customer was too young and innocent to be acquainted with the evil effects green tea produced on some constitutions'.[32] Gaskell, a friend of Charles Dickens, whose periodical *Household Words* also sought to convey the truth about this spurious production, was no doubt well aware that tea dealers who vended this beverage were on morally shaky ground. Much as John Horniman would do, Miss

Matty protected her reputation by claiming to protect her customers. Gaskell's readers would no doubt have found the reference to 'slow poison' quite entertaining since food reformers were also scolding consumers for desiring this treacherous commodity.

Both black and green teas had their dangers, however. In an article published in 1851, a chemist described a typical sample of Chinese tea as containing:

> A mixture of tea-dust with dirt and sand, agglutinated into a mass with a gummy matter, most probably manufactured from rice-flour, then formed into granules of the desired size and lastly, dried and coloured, according to the kind required by the manufacturer, either with black lead, if for black tea, or with Prussian blue, gypsum, or turmeric, if intended for green.[33]

Black teas, however, usually arrived in Britain free from adulterants, whereupon they might be 'sophisticated' with chemicals or spurious leaves from British-grown plants. In the early years of the century, it was quite common for British traders to add materials in order to 'revive' exhausted leaves. According to an Inland Revenue Office Report in 1843, at least eight manufacturers in London revived tea used by hotels, coffee houses and other public places. Once dried, used leaves were 'faced', that is mixed, with gum, rose-pink, black-lead or similar items and then resold as new.[34] These chemicals gave used leaves a deep colour and simulated the curled shape of new leaves.[35] A great deal of 'counterfeit' or 'British tea' was also grown and manufactured in the United Kingdom. In 1817 a prosecutor charging a grocer with manufacturing such tea explained to a jury that 'at the moment [the public] were supposing that they were drinking a pleasant and nutritious beverage, they were, in all probability, drinking the produce of the hedges round the metropolis'.[36] Both legal and scientific investigations revealed that 'tea' was being made from pigments added to beech, elm, oak, willow, poplar, hawthorn and sloe leaves and then mixed with either genuine tea or tea dust.[37] When they consumed tea, the working classes especially were likely drinking either an infusion of London's hedges or a more dangerous recycled version of the very leaves first drunk by the wealthier classes in places of public resort.

If black teas were only sometimes adulterated, virtually all green teas were enhanced. It was common, for example, for the Chinese to turn low-quality black into green tea with the help of colouring agents such as Prussian blue, an iron salt which, according to Hassall, was 'not absolutely poisonous' but was 'capable of exerting an injurious action'.[38] Pigments such as mineral green, verdigris and an arsenate of copper (a very dangerous poison) and chemicals such as chromate of potage and bichromate of potage were commonly used and known to produce inflammation of the bronchial and nasal mucous membranes, convulsions, paralyses and in the worst cases could be fatal.[39]

In the 1840s and 1850s explorers and botanists published accounts of Chinese manufacturing to aid the transfer of knowledge to the fledgling industry developing under British control in Assam. These travel narratives reinforced the findings of the chemists and food reformers. C.A. Bruce, the founder of the industry in Assam, described the colouring of teas as a regular and accepted part of the manufacture of green tea done 'to give it a uniform colour and appearance'.[40] When the botanist and explorer Robert Fortune published his description of his wanderings in China in 1847, he confidently claimed that all green tea was 'the result of a dye' and joked that 'the Chinese, I doubt not, could substitute for that colour either red or yellow, should our tastes change and lead us to prefer more glaring tints!'[41] A year later, Samuel Ball, a former employee of the East India Company, argued that 'factitious means are now generally or almost universally adopted to imitate or to increase the effect of the natural colour'.[42] On his return to China in the early 1850s, Robert Fortune reportedly disguised himself as a 'Chinaman' in order to 'obtain' tea seeds and a deeper knowledge of Chinese manufacturing. He claimed that the Chinese used so much pigment that the 'hands of the workmen were quite blue'. Fortune could not help but think 'that if any green-tea drinkers had been present during the operation, their taste would have corrected'.[43] Such descriptions of Eastern productions were common in travellers' accounts, but here they were attached to a product that most British quite literally craved. Chemists and botanist-explorers thus were all arguing that their inspection of the Chinese and of tea leaves had revealed a truth about the production of green tea, i.e. that its colour was the product of dangerous pigments added during the manufacturing and not something inherent in the plant.

Using a variety of methodologies, in the laboratory and in the field, mid-Victorian scientists believed that their observations of the tea plant and its production had proved that the Chinese were defrauding and possibly poisoning the British consumer. They focused upon and emphasized the difficulty of seeing, of tasting, of knowing the commodity and the potential ways in which the individual and nation could be cheated and fed something which was nothing, or worse, poison. Though these scientists looked at most domestically produced and imported foods, tea received the lion's share of attention because of its popularity in the British diet, its centrality to the government's revenues, and because it was produced in a far off land which resisted British control.

Throughout the Victorian period, novels, newspapers and the popular press translated scientific findings about food for consumers. However, during the mid-Victorian period consumers primarily learned about adulteration through advertising. Advertising also allowed the retailer to counter his ever-worsening reputation as defrauder of the poor and purveyor of poison. Advertising did not just quiet fears, however; often retailers found it profitable to stimulate these concerns. Nowhere was this more visible than in the advertising for John Horniman's packet tea. Horniman took advantage of the anxieties about the Celestial Empire and used them to brand his goods, cast himself as a food reformer looking after the public's health and thus set himself apart from the competition.

Throughout the early and middle years of the century, Horniman distributed shop cards, handbills, pamphlets, posters and circulars warning the British public about the Chinese threat and then proclaiming that his packet tea was imported 'free from the Usual Artificial Facing Powders'.[44] Advertising linked Horniman's brand with notions of 'purity' and 'wholesomeness' by repetitiously asserting that packet tea was 'Pure as Well as Fine'.[45] Horniman's beverage was healthy and, because of its packaging, it would stay that way. Packaging was thereby presented quite literally as a barrier standing between the British consumer, the fraudulent retailer and the 'unclean' Chinese producer. Technology thus contained the market and made the Orient safe and palatable.

Horniman also insured the 'purity' of his production by introducing a new method of retailing. His tea was distributed throughout Great Britain by agents who sold directly to chemists rather than grocers. Consumers who wanted to buy Horniman's brand thus had to go to their chemist's shop. Packet tea would be associated therefore in the public's mind with health and science. The same alliance was firmly established in Horniman's advertising, in which he quoted from many of the food authorities of the day, including French chemists, Robert Fortune, Board of Inland Revenue Reports, *The Times* and Hassall's *Sanitary Commission on Tea*.[46] Through the use of the testimonial, this advertising gave voice to a new culture of expertise. For example, in one widespread advertisement, Dr Hassall himself assures the public that when he personally visited London's docks, he found 'Tea, perfectly pure', in Horniman's stocks.[47] Horniman and Hassall were joined in the protection of the British consumer, united in advertising through juxtaposition and their progressive reliance on science, chemistry and technology. Of course, many manufacturers used similar marketing methods. Coleman's Mustard is just one example of a product claiming to be 'genuine' and 'warranted pure'. Others also cited Hassall's reports to bestow the label 'healthy' on a wide variety of foods, including Pooley's Patent Malt Bread, Hick's Baking Powder and Dr Ridge's Patent Cooked Food for Infants and Invalids.[48] However, Horniman uniquely used the debate about adulteration to inspire and then quell fears about free trade with China.

Horniman's ads made such fears explicit, many of which focused on the political economy of adulteration. For example, one handbill addressed to 'The Heads of Families and all Consumers of Tea' posited that since the 'retiring of the Honourable East India Company from commercial pursuits ... the Chinese commenced sending a counterfeit tea [which] is now extensively retailed in every Town and Village throughout the entire Kingdom'.[49] Most historians have likewise argued that adulteration worsened after the end of the East India Company's China monopoly. Prior to that time, the Company had paid inspectors in Canton to oversee the teas sent to Britain and had thereby established a reputation for importing an expensive but high-quality product.[50] The end of the Company's monopoly and higher taxation introduced in 1834 led to fewer controls, higher prices and the expansion of smuggling and adulteration. Free traders, arguing for the repeal of taxes on commodities, stridently contended that high taxes hurt the consumer by facilitating smuggling, adulteration and commercial fraud.[51] The duty on tea, particularly the lower quality teas drunk by the working class, was at its highest in history between 1834 and 1853.[52] Per capita consumption of tea did not expand during these years and may in fact have declined.[53] The problem of green tea was also aggravated because at the same time that the British were raising their duties on tea, the United States removed all taxes on the beverage. This created a surge in demand for green tea – the preferred beverage in the United States – and meant that demand outstripped supply. The Chinese solved this problem by turning black tea into green through the use of colouring agents and such tea made its way indiscriminately on to either British or American tea clippers.

Despite its prevalence in the British diet, tea's transformation into a commodity of mass consumption was by no means complete or secure in the mid-Victorian period. Horniman profited from this instability by warning the British public that '[t]ea no longer holds it own as the national beverage. It cannot be questioned that the consumption of ordinary tea does not increase in proportion to the population'.[54] The solution, posited by such advertising, was for consumers to transfer their allegiance to Horniman's brand and ensure that they were drinking an inexpensive yet healthy commodity. Within this debate, packet tea replaced the East India Company as guardian of tea's purity and the nation's health and branding seemed to assuage consumers' health concerns.

Although economic changes in the trade had led to adulteration, Horniman's ads emphasized that it was the Chinese, not the British, who primarily engaged in this nefarious crime.[55] A newspaper advertisement, for example, explicitly alerted consumers that the Chinese were cheating them and endangering their health. 'Anything of an injurious nature added to food or drink', it claimed, 'is a fraud on the stomach'. When 'the Chinese lace tea with poisonous colour', they defraud the British body and destroy the sanctity of the home. This advertisement, like many but by no means all, directly appealed to women, who were told that it was their 'first duty' as housewives 'to purchase good food and tea' and thereby ensure '[h]ealthy children and happy homes'.[56] Advertisements such as these thus built upon images of the East as Other. The important point, however, is that the Other was in Britain, inhabiting the tea table and being ingested by British bodies. Advertising thus alerted Britons of their intimate connections with and dependence upon other places for their comforts and pleasures. Postcards, booklets and trade cards made this point manifest when they detailed the travels of tea from a Shanghai tea farm, to the Port of London, to the British parlour.[57] Such ads reminded middle-class consumers in particular that domesticity was the product of an ongoing relationship between home and away, a relationship mediated by the tea trader.

Packet tea thus conveyed a materialist and gendered understanding of an empire which provided the raw material of English domesticity. 'Every land under the sun', the tea drinker was informed in one advertisement, 'is ransacked to provide the good things in life for Englishmen and Englishwomen and there is no other country in which the women have such chances of making a pleasant happy home'.[58] Tea and domesticity in general was to be enjoyed by both men and women, but by characterizing tea drinking as a female and private ritual Horniman's advertising domesticated a rather 'unruly' product. Especially in advertising that appeared in the 1870s and after, Horniman's consumer was frequently represented as a bourgeois woman or child playfully enjoying the domestic pleasure of tea drinking. Pictorial advertising in particular traded upon such images of female purity and childlike innocence. It thus merged common perceptions of classed and gendered consumers with those of the commodity, at a time when its production and distribution were going through rapid changes and competition was intense. These ads indirectly established the retailer as protector of the domestic and its pleasures, though he is visually absent from the scene. As we have seen, in political and scientific debate at this time, as well as some advertising, the image of the tea drinker was a broad one, sometimes identified as a working-class labourer but often simply as a British citizen in need of protection. Increasingly in advertising, however, the tea drinker epitomized the bourgeois ideal of domestic femininity. Yet advertising still acknowledged or, one might say, exposed the ways in which this class-based femininity was reliant upon Britain's imperial project.

In her recent ethnography of female tea pickers in India, Piya Chatterjee has argued that tea drinking illuminated the connectedness between Britain and its colonial project in which the 'desire to taste otherness' fuelled colonial expansion: 'teatime in the parlor and garden became the living metaphors of empire and the nation making it enabled'.[59] We should not assume, however, that the British understood that the products they ate, drank and wore were foreign goods or that they represented the empire. Rather, we must consider the precise ways in which these goods acquired such meanings and how these shifted over time. In the early and middle years of the century, tea was associated with imperialism but it was not an *imperial* good per se. Tea was produced *outside* the formal empire and during these years signified a particular problematic of control over the Chinese and their productions. There was no unitary or stable China being presented to English tea drinkers, precisely because the British were reliant upon a nation that still resisted colonial surveillance.

The partial 'opening' of the treaty ports stimulated desires and anxieties about China and its things. During and after the first Opium War, the popular press, exhibitions and Chinese art and artefacts produced a growing fascination to see, acquire and think about China.[60] Europeans had greatly admired Chinese civilization and culture, but in the nineteenth century they came increasingly to think of the Chinese as a lazy, dirty and dishonest people.[61] The adulteration of tea gave further evidence of such stereotypes. 'It is difficult to get the truth out of a Chinaman', concluded an author of an 1850 article on Chinese adulteration practices. Perhaps commenting on British immorality as well and the close ties between the opium and tea trades, this same author reported on a common Chinese belief that the British bought their teas in order to 'convert them into opium' and then resell them to the Chinese.[62] Though some may have had their qualms about the morality of the British tea trade, nearly all mid-Victorian Britons were agreed that the Chinese were a morally suspect people, whose once great civilization had stagnated and fallen far behind that of the progressive West. Though disheartened by the Chinese people and culture, Britons were, however, more excited than ever about the 'mighty empire' whose 'resources' were now 'open' to British consumers.[63] Packaged tea protected the British against Chinese dirt and dishonesty, allowing them to enjoy the Chinese good.

Public health reports and tea advertising were inextricably embedded within the larger debate about China and its things, which drew upon and produced a host of stereotypes about the Celestial Empire. As we have seen, worries about adulteration relied upon already common images of the dirty and deceitful Chinese. Yet advertising also sold enticing images of China and its goods. Horniman's promotions, like those of other tea traders at the time, also found it necessary to ignite British appetites for tea by constructing desirable representations of the Chinese landscape. This view of the Celestial Empire was similar to artistic representations of the day, but it departed from that being promoted by food reformers such as Hassall, or even that being produced in other Horniman advertisements.[64] In newspaper advertising and almanacs especially, Horniman reproduced a visually stunning, pastoral, picturesque and pre-modern China. Many advertisements featured a China of pagodas, villages, small-scale farming and hand production. Such images assured tea drinkers that if they bought packet tea, they could still enjoy this ancient beverage. These ads nearly always also referenced Horniman's intervention in this trade, highlighting his packaging techniques and thereby suggesting that the local 'ancient' mode of production now served and was subservient to world markets.[65] Thus, Horniman claimed to be harnessing the ancient to serve the modern.

Such stereotypical images of China could serve diverse interests. Those backing the new Indian plantations used anxieties about the Chinese good to present their industry as 'British', 'modern' and 'healthy' not 'foreign', 'backwards' and 'dangerous'. From the outset, tea produced on South Asian plantations gained a not altogether deserved reputation as entirely pure. As early as 1839 Dr Sigmond described the first batch of Assam tea as 'good, sound, [and] unadulterated'.[66] For Sigmond, who believed that tea was a gift from God and led to the particular British national characteristics of temperance and chastity, the expansion of control of South Asia became crucial to the health and morality of the British nation. This same theme was articulated by Robert Fortune in his 1860 report on tea prospects in the North-West Provinces and in the Punjab.[67] The most obvious uses of British anxieties about China appeared after the Indian industry was fully established in the 1880s, however.[68]

In his 1883 book *Tea: the Drink of Pleasure and Health*, Dr W. Gordon Stables elevated the Indian beverage at the expense of that of the Chinese. He, like many tea experts who would follow him, argued that after tea had been 'discovered' to grow indigenously in Assam in the 1830s, it became clear that it was originally from India not China and that it was therefore superior in taste and health properties. In comparing the two in a gendered language, Stables asserted that Indian tea is 'more racy, penetrating and possess[es] more backbone'.[69] He denigrated Chinese modes of production, which he noted had not advanced in anything 'unless it be in adulteration'. They were, he explained to British readers, 'carried on almost exclusively by natives ... in small batches [which] can deteriorate as they move from producer to buyer'. Moreover, the Chinese were 'careless' and not 'over cleanly, in the way they prepare tea for the English market'. Indeed, Stables reported one story of the Chinese using sacks of tea leaves as mattresses until they became 'putrid' before selling them.[70] Such 'filthy' practices were bad enough, but Stables also wrote extensively about how the Chinese manipulated 'the herb that finally finds its way into the dainty cups and saucers of England's fair daughters'.[71] Stables' commentary thus reinforced the story that Horniman's advertisements had told, that dirty Chinese producers could potentially sully the virtue and purity of English maidens. Stables was merely employing here a common trope by the 1880s, using the spectre of sullied womanhood to stand for the entire nation of consumers. His answer to this crime was not packaging or branding, however. Rather, he urged the British to place their faith in the Indian beverage. Quoting from *The Times of India*, Stables highlighted Indian tea's modern virtues, the most important of which was the fact that the British grower controlled the entire operation and thereby ensured that the herb was manufactured under what he and others repeatedly claimed were clean and orderly conditions. Thus, he concluded, the best way of 'steering clear of both filth and poisonous adulteration would be to use only pure Indian teas ... *the tea of the future*'.[72] Only after this new industry was extended, Stables argued, could tea truly become 'the national drink of England', with its civilizing and humanizing effects. 'Blessed tea ... may its influence extend', concluded this blatant promotion of South Asian teas.[73] In what became a standard formulation, most closely associated with Lipton's advertisements for his Ceylon teas, plantations under British supervision were deemed healthier, more moral and more modern than Chinese small-scale farming methods.[74] By the time that Stables and Lipton were highlighting the virtues of South Asia, however, the problem of tea adulteration had significantly diminished, as had the taste for green tea throughout Britain.

Though it is difficult to measure, green tea's reputation as slow poison did alter consumer tastes and consumption patterns, especially in particular regions of the United Kingdom. In general, black teas were more commonly drunk in southern England, while green was more popular in the Midlands and the North, though one expert claimed that by 1860 green tea was only consumed in England's eastern counties. Dr Charles Cameron, Professor of Political Medicine in the Royal College of Surgeons, Ireland, told a House of Commons Select Committee in 1874 that though they once drank a good deal of it, the adulteration scare meant that now 'the people of Dublin do not like the flavour of green tea ... [and thus] there is very little sold in Dublin'.[75] Many individuals and retailers liked to mix the two varieties, but by the second half of the century green tea had become much less popular overall, in part due to anxieties about adulteration.[76]

Tea dealers argued that the popular exposés, advertisements, parliamentary select committees and subsequent legislation, which targeted shopkeepers rather than importers, had led to a sharp decline in the British taste for green tea. While criticizing government interference in their trade, retailers and importers used liberal arguments to suggest that the first acts of legislation seeking to ensure pure foods in 1860 and 1872 had unduly contributed to public fears, damaged markets and altered tastes. They felt strongly that the 1872 Act had made it difficult to trade in green teas for fear of being accused as an adulterator and had put the public off its taste for green tea. Indeed, after the passage of the 1872 Adulteration of Food Act, tea merchants complained to the government that the law had damaged their reputations and magnified 'the evil of adulteration in the public mind'.[77] Augustus Thorne, a tea importer, told the parliamentary select committee investigating the 1872 Act that this piece of legislation had damaged the green tea trade. 'The public taste is going off green teas', he believed, 'simply owing to this Adulteration Act and that if they found that it was uncoloured they would not go back to it'.[78] Another merchant, who had worked as a tea inspector in China for many years, agreed with Thorne when he opined that the Act had led to a sharp depreciation in the value of both green and scented teas in England.[79] A London tea retailer perceptively noted that it was not just the legislation which was to blame for shifting tastes. It was also, he believed, the 'many paragraphs, taken from very popular journals, in which "death in the pot", "grocers", "poisoners", and all sorts of sensational headings appear, which we think must have had a very injurious effect upon the tea trade'. He then joked that such articles probably 'have been put in with the view the next day of inserting an advertisement in the same paper, that if people want a really good thing, they must come to their particular shop'.[80]

Retailers came before the 1874 select committee to defend their honour and to alter legislation that they felt unjustly prosecuted them. They also sought to redefine the terms of the debate and to argue that 'colouring' tea was not an adulteration at all but standard trade practice. In the midst of this discussion, they successfully pushed through the idea of adulteration as commercial fraud that posed little danger to the health of the consumer. The earlier wider definition, which had focused on the health effects of colouring agents, lost force in favour of the more limited notion of adulteration as a violation of contract. Throughout the proceedings, retailers argued that colouring green tea was almost never done in Britain, that it was not dangerous and that it was done to appeal to consumer tastes. An alderman and sheriff of the City of London who had worked in the grocery trade for thirty-seven years even joked about the ill effects of green tea. When asked by the committee's chairman whether it was injurious to health, he responded:

Certainly not; I remember a case 30 years ago; a gentleman came into my place of business and asked for two pounds of black tea; and my assistant asked him, 'Will you take any green tea;' he said, 'No green tea is slow poison'. An old lady, 80 years of age was sitting by in a chair and she said 'Yes, it must be very slow poison, indeed, for I have drunk nothing but green tea for 60 years and I'm not dead yet'.[81]

Nearly all the medical experts who appeared before the committee took a similar position, arguing that the colouring of green tea was not especially harmful. As one Scottish doctor explained, chemicals such as Prussian blue are 'not so nice ... but the proportion is so extremely small that it is not quite capable of proving injurious'.[82] Another quipped that not all disgusting things found in tea were bad for you, commenting that he once found a 'Chinaman's toe nail in some tea, but I do not call it an adulteration'.[83] The scientific community was far from unified on this point, however.

The most strident figure in the entire debate was the ageing Dr Hassall. When he appeared before the committee, Hassall explicitly challenged the neutral position of retailers and scientists and argued that colouring of green tea was indeed an adulteration. He maintained that it was a criminal and civil crime, fraudulent *and* physically harmful to consumers. Additives such as Prussian blue were especially dangerous, he noted, because they tended to accumulate in the body. Furthermore, he told the government that retailers should be knowledgeable and therefore held responsible for the goods they bought and sold. Hassall went further than any other witness when he called for an activist government that would 'teach people the component parts of everything' they ate and drank.[84] Here Hassall was rearticulating a vision of consumer rights he had first outlined in the 1850s. As he had explained twenty years earlier: 'The consumer entering a shop, asking for an article, has a right to expect that he will be supplied with that which he demands and for which he pays'.[85]

Hassall's comprehensive understanding of government intervention and consumer protection would have appealed to many consumer activists today. He was an early advocate of public health and market regulation at a time when such ideas were not popular. Like today's activists concerned about genetically modified foods and the host of recent food scares, Hassall believed that consumers, retailers and the government needed to maintain a sense of where and under what conditions food is produced and sold to consumers. Hassall and his contemporaries had great faith that a government which was responsive to science, and which promoted the expansion of the industrialization of food production, would be less appealing to today's activists, however. For many today have come to see science and industry as the source rather than the solution to the problem and have readily supported various alternatives to global trade, mass agriculture and retailing.

In mid-Victorian Britain the government's faith in liberal economics and the strength of the food lobby, which had pushed for a more limited definition of adulteration, meant that Hassall did not achieve his aims. In their report the select committee concluded that the colouring of green tea was not particularly harmful, though it could potentially disguise poor quality goods. They noted that consumers should be protected from frauds, but that they did not 'consider that Parliament desires needlessly to hamper or fetter trade'.[86] The 1875 Act that responded to the problems generated by earlier legislation did not create the kind of consumer protection that Hassall desired, narrowed the definition of adulteration and thus shifted the terms of the debate. Within a decade, however, South Asian black teas would gain the upper hand and become the norm in British households. Late-Victorian concerns about adulteration rarely discussed tea and were much more concerned with fraudulent domestic productions.[87]

Mid-Victorian debates about adulteration were thus one venue in which notions of consumers' rights, government responsibility and scientific efficacy were contested. It was also a site in which conceptions of the domestic and the foreign were produced, exchanged and consumed. Even as early as mid-century, consumer protection was discussed within a global context in which foreign trade had raised the issue of foreign substances entering British markets and being ingested by British bodies. A focus on tea adulteration allows us to see the ways in which botany, chemistry and retailing defined goods, consumers and healthy forms of production, distribution and consumption. It further illuminates the international concerns at the heart of domestic consumption. In early and mid-Victorian Britain tea gained new meanings through political, scientific and popular debates about fraudulent forms of Chinese production. Europeans did not regard all teas as equally healthy, nor did they regard all of Asia as a unitary site. They did, however, agree that Western science and industry could make the East profitable, safe and healthy for British consumption.

Notes

1. John Horniman's packet tea and its link to adulteration are discussed in most of the standard histories of the tea trade. See S.P. Day, *Tea: Its Mystery and History* (London, 1878), pp. 57–9; W.H. Ukers, *All About Tea*, Vol. II (New York, 1935), p. 132; D. Forrest, *Tea for the British: The Social and Economic History of a Famous Trade* (London: Chatto and Windus, 1973), pp. 130–4; J. Burnett, *Liquid Pleasures: A Social History of Drinks in Modern Britain* (London, 1999), pp. 60–2 and Burnett's 'The History of Food Adulteration in Great Britain in the Nineteenth Century, with Special Reference to Bread, Tea and Beer' (PhD thesis, London University, 1958), p. 201 and pp. 255–6. S. Strasser has developed the link between the progressive era food reform movement and the history of packaging and retailing in the US in *Satisfaction Guaranteed: The Making of the American Mass Market* (Washington, 1989), pp. 252–85.

2. The major studies of the China trade include Hoh-cheung and L.H. Mui, *The Management of Monopoly: A Study of the East India Company's Conduct of Its Tea Trade* (Vancouver, 1984); M. Greenberg, *British Trade and the Opening of China 1800–42* (Cambridge, 1951); R. Gardella, *Harvesting Mountains: Fujian and the China Tea Trade, 1757–1937* (Berkeley, 1994), and J.C. Evans, *Tea in China: The History of China's National Drink* (New York, 1992).

3. For a compelling discussion of this process, see L. Kriegel, 'The Pudding and the Palace: Labor, Print Culture, and Imperial Britain in 1851', in A. Burton (ed.), *After the Imperial Turn: Thinking with and through the Nation* (Durham, 2003), pp. 230–45. Kriegel builds on many of the insights of T. Richards, *The Commodity Culture of Victorian England: Advertising and Spectacle, 1851–1914* (Stanford, 1990).

4. Burnett, 'History of Food Adulteration'. Also see F.A. Filby, *A History of Food Adulteration and Analysis* (London, 1934). Filby makes the important argument that the adulteration debate aided the establishment of analytic chemistry as a discipline. See further I. Paulus, *The Search for Pure Food: A Sociology of Legislation in Britain* (London, 1974) and M. French and J. Phillips, *Cheated not Poisoned? Food Regulation in the United Kingdom, 1875–1938* (Manchester, 2000).

5. On the contemporary form of this relationship, see T. Marsden, A. Flynn and M. Harrison, *Consuming Interests: The Social Provision of Foods* (London, 2000), p. 2. See also H. Kamminga and A. Cunningham (eds), *The Science and Culture of Nutrition, 1840–1940* (Amsterdam, 1995); J. Burnett and D.J. Oddy (eds), *The Origins and Development of Food Policies in Europe* (London, 1994); A.P. den Hartog (ed.), *Food Technology, Science and Marketing: European Diet in the Twentieth Century* (East Lothian, 1995); and G. Jones and N.J. Morgan (eds), *Adding Value: Brands and Marketing in Food and Drink* (London, 1994).

6. They also challenged the health and morality claims being promoted at this time by the temperance movement. For an explicit discussion of tea's importance to British identities and health in these years, see 'Tea and Potatoes', *Chambers's Edinburgh Journal*, XV, no. 369 (25 January 1851), pp. 53–5. The temperance movement was an important site in which tea was being defined as key to British health and progress. However, the movement was divided over the issue of whether tea was healthy or harmful. For a voice of warning, see J. Bowes, *Temperance, as it is opposed to strong Drinks, Tobacco and Snuff, Tea and Coffee* (Aberdeen, 1836, reprinted from *The Christian Magazine and Herald of Union*).

7. Anandi Ramamurthy has persuasively argued that late Victorian tea advertising was central to shifting British tastes from Chinese to Indian tea. I argue, however, that this process began much earlier and was aided by the wider debate concerning adulteration. See A. Ramamurthy, *Imperial Persuaders: Images of Africa and Asia in British Advertising* (Manchester, 2003), pp. 93–130.

8. Even before many of these changes, the author of a tea-purchasing guide written in 1785 blamed consumers, arguing that the problem resulted from manufacturers

attempt merely to meet 'the amazing demand' that had developed in recent years. *The Tea Purchaser's Guide or the Lady and Gentleman's Tea Table and Useful Companion in the Knowledge and Choice of Teas* (London, 1785), p. 3.

9. F.C. Accum, *A Treatise on Adulterations of Food and Culinary Poisons* (Philadelphia, 1820), p. 14. Accum's work was widely reviewed and republished, but he had to leave England after having been indicted by the managers of the Royal Institution for mutilating books in their library. See Burnett, 'The History of Food Adulteration', pp. 11, 43.

10. Extract from the *Philosophical Journal* on 'Fabricated Tea', republished in *The Lady's Magazine*, no. 3, vol. 1 (March 1820), p. 156.

11. *The Domestic Chemist: Comprising Instructions for the Detection of Adulteration in Numerous Articles* (London, 1831), pp. vii–viii.

12. W.R. Greg, *An Enquiry into the State of the Manufacturing Population, and the Causes and the Cures of the Evils Therein Existing* (London, 1831), p. 10. This idea that the poor ate particularly fraudulent food persisted throughout the century. See Public Record Office (PRO), Home Office, 45/5338. *Frauds: Necessity for Taking Some Steps to Protect the Poor Against Short Weight, Short Measure and Adulteration*, 1854, and the Manchester and Salford Sanitary Association, *Report of the Sub-Committee upon the Adulteration of Food* (Manchester, 1863).

13. E.G. Clayton, *Arthur Hill Hassall: Physician and Sanitary Reformer* (London, 1908), p. xiii.

14. W. Alexander, MD, *The Adulteration of Food and Drinks* (London, 1856), p. 6.

15. A. Hill Hassall, MD, *Food and Its Adulterations; Comprising the Reports of the Analytical Sanitary Commission of 'The Lancet' for the years 1851 to 1854, revised and extended* (London, 1855). Also see his *Adulterations Detected; Or, Plain Instructions for the Discovery of Frauds in Food and Medicine* (London, 1857), and his significantly revised *Food: Its Adulterations, and the Methods for their Detection* (London, 1876).

16. Stroud, *Judicial Dictionary*, quoted in Filby, *A History of Food Adulteration*, p. 16.

17. H. Schwartz, *The Culture of the Copy: Striking Likenesses, Unreasonable Facsimiles* (New York, 1996).

18. *Poisoning and Pilfering; Wholesale and Retail.* Revised edition (London, 1871), p. 7.

19. *The Family Manual and Servants' Guide* (London, 1859), p. 32.

20. L. Kriegel, 'Culture and the Copy: Calico, Capitalism, and Copyright of Designs in Early Victorian Britain', *Journal of British Studies*, 43(2) (2004), pp. 233–65.

21. J.D. Burn, *The Language of the Walls: And a Voice from the Shop Windows. Or, the Mirror of Commercial Roguery* (Manchester, 1855), p. 231.

22. Hassall, *Food and Its Adulterations*, pp. iv–ix.

23. W.L. Scott, 'On Food: Its Adulterations, and the Methods of Detecting Them', *Journal of the Society of Arts*, IX(428) (1861), p. 159.

24. C. Estcourt, 'Adulteration of Food', in Manchester and Salford Sanitary Association, *Health Lectures for the People* (Manchester, 1878), p. 166.

25. J. Stevenson, *Advice Medical, and Economical, Relative to the Purchase and Consumption of Tea, Coffee, and Chocolate; Wines and Malt Liquors: Including Tests to Detect Adulteration* (London, 1830), p. 6.

26. G.G. Sigmond, *Tea: Its Effects Medicinal and Moral* (London, 1839), p. 7.

27. C.A. Bruce, the founder of the Indian tea industry, had asserted in 1840 that there was no doubt that the two came from the same plant. In 1847 Robert Fortune claimed that there were two varieties of tea, *Thea viridis* and *Thea Bohea*, and that in the north of China both green and black tea were produced from the former, while in Canton the latter was used. R. Fortune, *Three Years' Wandering in the Northern Provinces of China* (London, 1847), pp. 200 and 218. Also see C.A. Bruce, 'Report on the Manufacture of Tea, and on the Extent and Produce of the Tea Plantations in Assam', *Transactions of the Agricultural and Horticultural Society of India*, 7 (1840), p. 20. Consumers did not much worry about this problem, however, when they purchased their teas.

28. J. Pereira, MD, *A Treatise on Food and Diet with Observations on the Dietetical Regimen Suited for the Disordered States of the Digestive Organs* (New York, 1843), p. 189.

29. Pereira, *Treatise on Food and Diet*, p. 192. Also see E. Smith, MD, 'On the Uses of Tea in the Healthy System', *Journal of the Society of Arts*, IX (1861), p. 190.

30. Sigmond, *Tea: Its Effects* p. 124.

31. 'Green Tea', *The Monthly Religious Magazine* (Boston), 28 (1862), pp. 198–9.

32. E. Gaskell, *Cranford* (1853; Oxford, 1972), p. 146.

33. R. Warrington, 'Observations on the Teas of Commerce', *The Edinburgh New Philosophical Society*, LI (April–October 1851), p. 248.

34. Hassall, *Food and Its Adulterations*, p. 278. Rose pink was a dye made by infusing logwood in a carbonate of lime. Black lead, a product commonly used by Victorian domestic servants, contained both carbon and iron.

35. Hassall, *Food and Its Adulterations*, pp. 283–4.

36. Accum, *Treatise on Adulterations of Food*, p. 167.

37. Hassall, *Food and Its Adulterations*, p. 273.

38. Hassall, *Food and Its Adulterations*, p. 296.

39. Hassall, *Food and Its Adulterations*, p. 297.

40. Bruce, 'Report on the Manufacture of Tea', p. 20.

41. Fortune, *Three Years' Wandering*, p. 218.

42. S. Ball, *An Account of the Cultivation and Manufacture of Tea in China* (London, 1848), p. 243.

43. This passage from R. Fortune, *A Journey to the Tea Countries* (London, 1852), was much cited at the time. See, for example, 'The Tea Countries of China', *Chambers's Edinburgh Journal*, 27(442) (19 June1852), pp. 395–7.

44. Handbill, 10 March 1854. Tetley Group Archive, Acc#4364/01/001. London Metropolitan Archives (LMA).

45. Tea packets, c. 1850s and 1860s. Tetley Group Archive, Acc#4364/01/001. LMA.

46. Handbill, c. 1860. Tetley Group Archive, Acc#4364/01/001. LMA.

47. Advertisement, c. 1860. Tetley Group Archive, Acc#4364/01/001. LMA.

48. See, for example, the advertisements published in the back of Hassall's *Food: Its Adulterations, and the Methods for their Detection*. For other studies of health and advertising, see Richards, *Commodity Culture*, pp. 168–204, and L.A. Loeb, *Consuming Angels: Advertising and Victorian Women* (New York and Oxford, 1994), pp. 111–15. Other tea companies likewise advertised their tea as 'genuine' or particularly healthy. See, for example, *The Bristol Packet Tea Calendar for 1871* (Bristol, 1871) and an advertisement for Mazawattee Ceylon Tea Company published in the journal *Good Health: A Weekly Paper Devoted to Food, Drink, Medicine and Sanitation*, 3(67) (January 13, 1894), p. 249. Some retailers who sold Horniman's tea also used health claims to sell their product. See, for example, an ad from H. Ellis Jones, Family and Dispensing Chemist in Swansea, which explained the health benefits of tea drinking. Tetley Group Archive, Acc#4364/01/002. LMA.

49. Handbill, c. 1860. Tetley Group Archive, Acc#4364/01/001. LMA.

50. Burnett, 'History of Food Adulteration', p. 226. This link between the Company, high quality tea and the expansion of consumption was well known at the time. It had been developed during the political debates surrounding the ending of the Company's monopoly and protests against the introduction of new duties in the early 1830s. For example, in 1834 a critic of the government's new high duty on tea suggested: 'The East India Company ... certainly deserve praise for having used great care in the selection of their teas in the Chinese market; and to the general good quality of their teas the vast consumption of tea in this country is mainly to be attributed.' ('The Tea Trade: A full and accurate report of the extraordinary proceedings at the East India House, on the commencement of the March sale' (London, 1834), pp. 6–7). Also see E.E. Antrobus, *Observations on the 'Tea Duties Act'* (London, 1834), pp. 2, 17.

51. See, for example, J.R. McCulloch, 'Commutation of Taxes', *Edinburgh Review* (April 1833), p. 2.

52. Burnett, 'History of Food Adulteration', p. 210.

53. According to official statistics, per capita rates of tea consumption fell between 1810 and 1840. However, smuggling was pervasive during this period so that consumption may have been rising. See Burnett, 'History of Food Adulteration', p. 166.

54. Handbill, c. 1860. Tetley Group Archive, Acc#4364/01/001. LMA.

55. In doing so, these ads produced both visual and discursive representations of the dishonest Chinese. A frequently used illustration, for example, showed the 'Chinese at the Drying Pans Colouring Tea'. Handbill, c. 1860. Tetley Group Archive, Acc#4364/01/001. LMA.

56. Advertisement, c. 1875. Tetley Group Archive, Acc#4364/01/002. LMA.

57. See, for example, a booklet on how the Chinese prepare tea for export, c. 1860 (Tetley Group Archive, Acc#4364/01/001. LMA) and several almanacs from the 1870s and 1880s.

58. Advertisement, c. 1865. Tetley Group Archive, Acc#4364/01/002. LMA.

59. P. Chatterjee, *A Time for Tea: Women, Labor, and Post/Colonial Politics on an Indian Plantation* (Durham, NC, 2001), p. 49. Other scholars have similarly remarked that tea and other colonial products were some of the ways in which the British experienced their empire. See S.W. Mintz, *Sweetness and Power: The Place of Sugar in Modern History* (New York, 1985); J. Walvin, *Fruits of Empire: Exotic Produce and British Taste, 1660–1800* (New York, 1997); W.D. Smith, 'Complications of the Commonplace: Tea, Sugar, and Imperialism', *Journal of Interdisciplinary History*, 23(2) (1992), pp. 259–78; W. Schivelbusch, *Tastes of Paradise: A Social History of Spices, Stimulants and Intoxicants* (New York, 1992).

60. C. Pagani, 'Chinese Material Culture and British Perceptions of China in the Mid-Nineteenth Century', in T. Barringer and T. Flynn (ed.), *Colonialism and the Object: Empire, Material Culture and the Museum* (London, 1998), p. 28.

61. N.R. Clifford, *'A Truthful Impression of the Country': British and American Travel Writing in China, 1880–1949* (Ann Arbor, MI, 2001), pp. 46–59. Such images had existed before the war, however. See, for example, C. Mackerras, *Western Images of China* (Oxford, 1989).

62. 'Chinese Method of Colouring Tea', *Hogg's Instructor* (Edinburgh, 1850), p. 91.

63. *Illustrated London News*, 3 December 1842, 469, quoted in S. Shoenbauer Thurin, *Victorian Travelers and the Opening of China, 1842–1907* (Athens, Ohio, 1999), p. 28.

64. Pagani, 'Chinese Material Culture', p. 33.

65. Advertisement, c. 1875. Tetley Group Archive, Acc#4364/01/002. LMA.

66. Sigmond, *Tea: Its Effects*, p. 112.

67. R. Fortune, *Report Upon the Present Condition and Future Prospects of Tea Cultivation in the North-West Provinces and in the Punjab* (Calcutta, 1860), p. 93.

68. It was not until 1888 that the United Kingdom imported more teas from South Asia than from China. See CUST 44/11: *Board of Customs and Excise 34ᵗʰ Annual Report on the Customs, 1890*, p. 9.

69. W.G. Stables, *Tea: The Drink of Pleasure and Health* (London, 1883), p. 15. For a similar argument, see Lieut.-Colonel E. Money, *The Tea Controversy: Indian versus Chinese Teas: Which are Adulterated? Which are Better?*, second edition (London, 1884).

70. Stables, *Tea*, pp. 18–19.
71. Stables, *Tea*, p. 26.
72. Stables, *Tea*, p. 33.
73. Stables, *Tea*, pp. 106, 111.
74. See, for example, T.J. Lipton, *Views of Lipton's Ceylon Tea Estates* (New York, 1912). Also see Ramamurthy's discussion of Lipton's advertising in *Imperial Persuaders*, pp. 106–17.
75. Mr Charles Cameron, MD, evidence given, *Report from the Select Committee on Adulteration of Food Act (1872) Together with the Proceedings of the Committee, Minutes of Evidence and Appendix* (London, House of Commons, 1874), [C. 4641–4642], p. 230.
76. L. Wray, 'Tea and Its Production in Various Countries', *Journal of the Society of Arts*, IX (1861), p. 148. Also see Burnett, 'History of Food Adulterations', p. 172. Such concerns did not totally destroy the taste for green tea, however. Though American tea drinkers vastly preferred the green variety until well into the twentieth century, by the 1870s they primarily purchased unadulterated green tea from Japan not China. See 'Report on the Production of Tea in Japan', [C.740] LXVI (London, House of Commons, 1873). They also hoped to establish a domestic tea industry to avoid imported adulterated tea. For a discussion of adulteration in the US, see 'The Tea Culture', *The Merchant's Magazine and Commercial Review*, 33 (1855), pp. 759–60 and J.C. Draper, 'Tea and Its Adulterations', *The Galaxy*, 7 (1869), pp. 405–12.
77. *Select Committee on Adulteration of Food Act (1872)* [para. 67], p. 8.
78. *Select Committee on Adulteration of Food Act (1872)* [para. 384], p. 21.
79. *Select Committee on Adulteration of Food Act (1872)* [para. 5390], p. 27.
80. *Select Committee on Adulteration of Food Act (1872)* [para. 1531–3], p. 78.
81. *Select Committee on Adulteration of Food Act (1872)* [para. 1489], p. 77.
82. *Select Committee on Adulteration of Food Act (1872)* [para. 5068], p. 255.
83. *Select Committee on Adulteration of Food Act (1872)* [para. 3594], p. 177.
84. *Select Committee on Adulteration of Food Act (1872)* [para. 6304], p. 317.
85. Hassall, *Adulterations Detected*, p. 2.
86. *Select Committee on Adulteration of Food Act (1872) Report*, 1874 [para 262, 2a]. For a broader discussion of the history of food legislation and the adoption of the idea that consumers were cheated rather than poisoned, see French and Phillips, *Cheated not Poisoned?*.
87. CUST 44/5: *Report on the Commissioners of Inland Revenue on the Duties under Their Management, for the years 1856–1869 Inclusive*, 1870, notes that tea has improved. Foods such as milk and butter were of much greater concern in the 1890s. See, for example, PRO, Department of Science and Industrial Research, 26/247–49: Laboratory of the Government Chemist, *Food Adulteration Press Cuttings*.

–7–

From Neighbour to Consumer

The Transformation of Retailer–Consumer Relationships in Twentieth-Century Germany

Uwe Spiekermann

Modern mass consumer societies are organized around two principal actors. On the one hand, the consumer is often seen as the unchallenged sovereign, deciding what will be bought. On the other hand, retailers and retailing have established themselves as a central branch of the economy, deciding what people can buy and what will be sold. While it is debatable which of these two actors is more powerful, the changing relationship between them is clearly crucial to an understanding of modern consumer societies.

While studies of consumption have become a fashionable topic of historical and sociological research, the history of twentieth-century retailing in Germany remains largely unexplored.[1] This chapter will use the changing perspectives of retailers to provide new insights on the changing relationship between retailers and consumers in twentieth-century Germany. It will focus on retailers' awareness of consumers, their practices and behaviour within stores and, finally, on their changing understanding of their own strategic position for the consumer. Retailing has been and remains a fragmented economic sector. Rather than isolating the retailing sector, however, it is important to situate retailers and consumers within the broader socio-economic and political developments that helped shape their relationship.

Retailing and Shopping in Imperial Germany

The late nineteenth century was the formative phase of the modern consumer society in Germany. In contrast to other Western societies, especially Britain, France and the United States, however, consumer awareness was underdeveloped here.[2] In Germany there were no self-conscious consumers who expressed themselves in public politics and discourse before the turn of the twentieth century, when price increases and quality problems led to regional food riots, boycotts and political mobilization.[3] The relatively slow and incomplete evolution of consumer identity resulted not only from the relative weakness of the liberal bourgeoisie, but also from the strong position of academic and commercial experts, who regulated the broad fields of everyday consumption. For instance, the German food law of 1879 introduced fairly effective food control and, from 1885 on, was reinforced by official norms of the 'normal' composition of the most important foodstuffs. Quality standards were set by producers in different branches, such as the chocolate and cocoa industries from 1876. Chemists and lawyers, too, were experts, who moved a growing number of consumption-related problems on to the political agenda.

The most important consumption expert, however, was the retailer, in most cases the qualified owner of a small shop. Although their qualification might appear low in hindsight, for most shoppers retailers were *the* experts for new and seasonal consumer goods. In the late nineteenth century this expertise became more and more important, as increasing specialization of production led to a wider range of goods that had to be introduced and explained by retailers.

The number of these everyday experts of consumption increased rapidly in the late nineteenth century. In Germany the expansion of retailing far exceeded population growth. The number of businesses in 'trade with goods' rose from 483,300 in 1875 to 659,714 in 1895 and to 942,918 in 1907.[4] Expansion had significant implications for consumer–retailer relations. Competition increased, but in most cases it was not purely about price but service.[5] Shopping standards increased, thus changing the human relations between retailer and customer. In the German Empire, especially from the late 1880s, the shopper became increasingly recognized as the oft quoted 'king'. Increased purchasing power established a new, virtual hierarchy between retailer and customer.[6] Far from being fixed, the relationship between the two was fluid and contested in a kind of everyday theatre. The retailer became the link between a growing number of mass-produced consumer goods and a growing number of customers with expanding tastes and desires.[7] As experts of mass consumption, retailers had to adjust to individual customers in a distinct, personal fashion – a performance practiced in front of dozens of other shoppers.

On the eve of World War One, most German retailers were convinced that this cult of the individual had reached an unsurpassable height. The changing relationship between retailer and consumer reflected profound social changes in modern retailing.[8] Although the independent retailer remained the norm, the number of employees grew significantly in the late nineteenth century. Unlike the independent self-sufficient neighbourhood retailer, employees were trained in a new, professional way. For shop assistants, the shop was important but not the only site of work. In many cases, they had to visit and deliver goods to bourgeois customers at home. Home delivery and related services intensified during the 1880s. Working-class, like middle-class, customers now had their milk and bread delivered early in the morning. While retailers complained about the resulting increase in costs, male employees viewed such services as a challenge to their professional ethos and sense of duty.[9] They insisted their professional place was inside the shop, centring on personal contact with the customer – anything else was seen as a loss of status vis-à-vis clerical white-collar workers in wholesaling and administration. Consequently, the professional profile of sales personnel changed. Bourgeois manners and behaviour became a prerequisite. Likewise, the bourgeois consumer became the ideal customer for most German retailers. This socio-cultural transvaluation called, in turn, for new training methods, since most salesmen, and especially the quickly growing number of poorly paid saleswomen, came from the lower middle-classes and the working-classes.

The reform of behaviour and habitus led to a more differentiated type of business organization. Errands became the duty of apprentices and temporary workers, while salespersons and retailers remained in the shop, attending to regular customers. New forms of advertisement were used to attract new customers. Although the retailer was still a neighbour in many areas and although personal elements still dominated retailer–consumer relations in small and medium-sized shops, new reflexive forms of communication established themselves. Shopping was transformed into a ritual, where the process, aim and subject of commercial communication between retailer and consumer were increasingly regulated.[10]

The relationship between retailer and consumer, then, was situated in a normative discourse. The consumer should be respected as a generalizable subject, not as an individual with personal characteristics. A customer was entitled to high regard for being a customer, not for his or her particular personality. Salesmen and saleswomen, too, were not supposed to behave in a personalized, individuated fashion but to perform a general task. The standardization of products and salespersons was a parallel process.

The well-trained retailer was recast as a depersonalized facilitator of the sales transaction. Retailers were to attract the customer in an abstract not intimate fashion, guiding and instructing the consumer without obstructing the way to the product. This had two major emotional and psychological consequences for the consumer–retailer relationship. On the one hand, it required a new degree of self-discipline. Retailers and salespersons had to master and subordinate their own emotions to the imperatives of commercial success. Professional training and advice literature emphasized to retailers the need to control and analyse themselves in a self-critical way and to fight and eliminate personal preferences.[11] The relationship with consumers was determined by their solvency. On the other hand, 'knowledge of human nature' became the basis for a new style of customer management.[12] Retailers learnt how to profile the customer at first glance and abstract social background and even character. This knowledge enabled salespersons to act and serve in a differentiated and successful fashion. They were encouraged to lip-read a consumer's desires, but it was not their simple duty to fulfil existing tastes. Rather, retailers were trained to educate consumers and motivate them to buy goods of higher quality. A salesperson should present the requested goods but should also offer the customer better goods to choose from. At a basic material level, this upgrading practice reflected a commercial rationale of increasing turnovers and profits. In cultural terms, however, this new form of the service encounter also inscribed new habits and expectations into the relationship of retailer and consumer and their respective identities; it was a demonstration of the new ethos that the consumer was sovereign and free to choose.[13]

Compared to France or Britain, advice from salespersons was a normative expectation in Germany. Retailers' competence and trustworthiness became an ever more important, indeed central, feature of their role as experts of consumption. Of course, competence was an idealized discourse and conflict was a regular part of everyday life in a shop. Still, the communication of commercial expertise and skill were vital resources in the competition for the trust and custom of consumers. Knowledge of one's customers' life was considered essential to tie them to one's shop as faithful consumers: 'The customer must be turned into an acquaintance, otherwise the relationship will not endure'.[14]

The emotional and psychological reconfiguration of the interaction between consumers and retailers proceeded in tandem with the spatial transformation of shopping (see Figure 2). The space of shopping expanded, most prominently in the new department stores and the ambience of the shopping experience changed, especially in the larger stores. Shopping became a mass phenomenon.[15] Personal obligations and considerations retreated behind the new, more open and transparent, worlds of consumption.

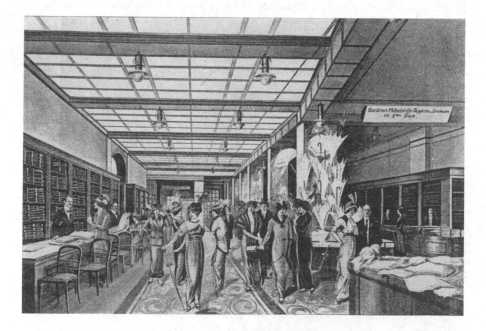

Figure 2 The Shop as a Stage: Rudolf Hertzog, Berlin, 1913

Source: P. Lindenberg, 'Berlin und das Haus Rudolph Hertzog seit 1839', in *Agenda Rudolph Hertzog Berlin 1914*, (Berlin: Rudolph Hertzog, 1913), p. 49.

Regular contact with the customer required skills that increasingly became associated with female qualities. At the turn of the twentieth century the growing number of low-paid female employees was concentrated primarily in shops selling goods directly to customers, while male employees occupied more attractive senior and managerial tasks.[16] One consequence of the intensified feminization of direct selling was that even medium-sized shops began to turn to cheap saleswomen. The shop became a differentiated and gendered workplace that mirrored the 'nature' of different genders.

These new forms of organizations allowed higher efficiency and became the basis of modern business management. Book-keeping became more common and indicators like turnover and profit rates more important. Especially 'new' business types, like the department stores and multiple shops, changed the way of selling to maximize profits.[17] Early marketing knowledge was rooted in commercial practice and became professionalized in newly established business schools.[18] At the same time, the practices and conventions of both retailers and customers were becoming regulated by an increasing number of governmental norms set by a range of academic experts. Hygiene regulations transformed the display and handling of groceries. Packaging became more important. The interiors and exteriors of shops were planned with the help of architects, psychologists and advertising experts. Retailer–consumer relations were one part of this broader framework of managing rationality and efficiency.

Middle-class and academic efforts to educate the consumer in the art of tasteful and morally upright consumption had limited success.[19] From the 1880s, especially, consumer cooperatives became an active force in the socialisation of the consumer.[20] They tried to improve the situation of the worker as a consumer by delivering high-quality products at non-profit costs. Their model of an egalitarian consumer society was based on the ideal of a rational consumer who knew his or her needs and who bought without being manipulated by commercial advertising.[21] Consumer and retailer here featured as allies in the development of a rational consumption that eventually would secure the coming of the cooperative commonwealth. While the behaviour of employees could be regulated with the help of instructions, the behaviour of the consumer was primarily understood as a problem of enlightenment and education. To reform capitalist society the consumer was instructed to buy as many goods as possible in the cooperative shop and to respond in a rational, flexible fashion to price rises or problems of supply. The consumer was seen as a vital link in a chain of social transformation: 'Inspired by a single wonderful vision, we, the army of consumers, are able to create paradise on earth'.[22] This vision, however, won over only a small number of consumers. Although consumer education remained a distinct branch of cooperative culture, competition with commercial retailers led the cooperatives to adopt retailer–consumer relations comparable to those of their profit-oriented rivals. For most consumers, cheap prices and standardized quality were more important than the idea of an egalitarian consumer society.

The First World War changed retailer–consumer relations dramatically. The established hierarchy of a buyer's market was transformed into a new hierarchy of a seller's market. The main focus of retailing was no longer to sell, but to obtain goods. Raw materials were increasingly controlled and regulated, while clothing and foodstuffs became part of an expanding rationing system. Retailers were integrated into the German war economy. They had to adopt the increasing number of regulations and communicate these to their customers. Tension between retailers and consumers grew rapidly. Retailers were blamed for scarcities, poor quality products and inflationary prices, resulting from the collapse of international trade and ineffective state controls. At the same time, many retailers tried to take advantage of wartime shortages and enhance their social standing by exploiting their superior position vis-à-vis consumers. Regular customers were favoured. Products were held back and prices raised excessively. As access to goods became a matter of life and death and prices spiralled from inflation to hyper-inflation in the war and immediate post-war years, the previously 'sovereign' consumer found itself at the mercy of the retailer. The retailer was now king, ruling over his small kingdom, his shop: 'Who doesn't honour the saleswoman isn't worth the merchandise',[23] as a typical saying put it during the war.

The economic crisis of the war had institutional consequences for consumer–retailer relations. At the end of 1914 consumer cooperatives, trade unions and housewife organizations founded the War Committee for Consumer Interests, whose main task was to represent consumers vis-à-vis local, military and governmental authorities. Although praised as 'a new factor of power', the Committee effectively became an arm of government planning during the war. Although it had some success in minimizing scarcities and price increases, its main function was to educate consumers, especially housewives, in the organized and economical consumption of food and clothing. Since it was unable to change the structural problem of a seller's market, however, the Committee's moral politics of consumption was largely ineffective.[24]

More important were changes in everyday supply, which undermined the central position of the retail trade. Customers made their own efforts to secure goods and to find alternative ways of supply. In the course of the First World War, the retail trade's share of consumer spending fell dramatically, as many customers bought directly from farmers and producers. In addition, many firms and local authorities began to purchase goods directly from producers, seeking to stabilize production and public order.[25]

Retailers found their commercial freedom increasingly circumscribed by the growing number of state regulations.[26] To protect consumers, maximum prices and supply rates were fixed. Retailers were obliged to start lists of their customers and adopt more transparent sales practices; for instance, prices had to be labelled openly. Price controls became routine, tax rates increased and a specialized bureaucracy took root. Meanwhile, the turnover of articles of everyday use decreased dramatically, inflation minimized real incomes and the state began to support bigger and more efficient forms of business. Although retailer–consumer relations therefore changed in retailers' favour, the First World War at the same time undermined their position in the supply chain and resulted in a drop in income and an increase in bankruptcies.[27]

A Late Consumer Society: Germany Between the Two World Wars

Peace in 1918 and the end of the Allied blockade and the rationing system in 1919 marked the beginning of the end of the seller's market. Retailer–customer relations in the immediate post-war years were characterized by widespread poverty, the disintegration of international and wholesale trade, inflation and political instability. The situation improved after the currency reform in 1923 and, after 1924, relations partly returned to their pre-war state: 'The hunt for consumer goods was replaced ... by the struggle for customers'.[28] Turnovers and ranges grew and contemporaries observed a new 'quality selection of the customer'.[29] For retailers this situation offered new opportunities, but in the first instance it meant new investment and increased fixed costs.[30] Weimar Germany witnessed a widespread debate about rationalization and its implications for retailers and consumer alike.

Although 'rationalization' was a topic in German retailing long before the First World War, the discussion of scientific management intensified in the 1920s, focusing on better business management.[31] Cost-benefit analysis, book-keeping and rational store management were propagated as the foundations of successful retailing.[32] The business school system was expanded. Rationalization also meant a new understanding of the customer. The idea of a uniform shopper was abandoned for the idea of segmented consumer types. This had different consequences for different branches of the retail sector.

Although department stores, consumer cooperatives and multiple shops enjoyed disproportionate growth between 1924 and 1932, small and medium-sized firms continued to dominate German retailing. In 1925 there were 768,618 retail establishments, in 1939 833,192. The number of employees per business rose from 2.14 in 1925 to 2.67 in 1939.[33] Personal relations with the customer seemed to stand a good chance of survival in the competition with larger, more impersonal stores.

As a consequence, shop owners tried to improve personal service. Retailers presented themselves as a 'competent partner and lively interested friend', who gives 'advice and help' and shows 'tact and discretion'.[34] Of course, this was a marketing strategy. Simultaneously, new index card systems were developed, which recorded customers' preferences and personal data. The training of apprentices was intensified.

Product quality became a prominent topic once again in the late 1920s. Next to the growing chain of one-price stores, there was also an expansion of the specialist store. This was promoted as a place where consumers could buy individual goods of high quality that, perhaps, were more expensive than mass-manufactured articles at the time of purchase but ultimately offered superior quality and durability. Specialist retailers positioned themselves as the champions of long-term use, quality and economy against consumerist mass production.[35] Choice and purchasing decisions were located in a moral discourse of social corporate responsibilities: consumers were urged to back small retailers because of their social function.[36]

The ghost that haunted the German debate about 'rationalization' was the 'Americanization' of German retail trade associated with department stores and cheap one-price stores (see Figure 3). Although their wealth was admired, the character of American consumers seemed very different from that of their German counterparts: 'The people are so uniform, their demands and all the articles produced to cover them so standardized, that one cannot believe that they are human beings. Customers are viewed as machines that instinctively buy what advertisements tell

Figure 3 Saleswomen as Objects of 'American' Advertising, Berlin, 1925

Source: *Warenhäuser. Ein Spiegelbild volkstümlicher Verkaufsstätten. Auf Grund einer Darstellung des grössten Warenhauskonzerns Europas im Eigenbesitz: Hermann Tietz,* (Berlin: Schröder, 1928).

them to'.[37] German visitors to the United States, by contrast, learnt to recognize new forms of service and recommended them to German retailers. Far from amounting to a paradigm shift, however, such recommendations were most influential where they reinforced established traditions and practices of service in German retail trade, such as an emphasis on kindness.[38] American retailing was embedded in a culture of competitiveness that was not comparable or applicable to the German situation. Large firms, which used service *and* price as elements of 'competition for the favour of the customer',[39] were successful because the importance of cheap goods increased especially during the world economic crisis. Still, the symbol of 'Americanization' of German retailing, the famous Karstadt department store on Alexanderplatz in Berlin, proved a commercial failure when turnover collapsed in 1930.

The consumer cooperatives, too, started to rationalize their organization in 1924. Although most managers rejected the cultural consequences of 'Americanization', they consistently applied scientific management. The education of their consumers remained one key element of rationalization. The consumer was regarded as a partner in the quest for global justice and equality. In the late 1920s the cooperatives even excluded more than one million so-called 'paper soldiers' from their membership, that is, dormant consumers who had ceased to buy in cooperative shops. Leading managers knew that education on its own was not enough: 'The struggle for sales is a struggle for the consumer's soul. In this fight the power of the cooperative idea stays at the side of the consumer cooperatives, but this non-material weapon is not enough to achieve far-reaching results in sales promotion'.[40] As a consequence, the cooperatives stressed the high quality of cooperative products.[41] Cooperative managers believed in the vision of Fordism, of perfect mass-produced goods. In social practice, the development of a 'rational' consumer remained a distant goal. Most members did not concentrate their purchase on cooperative products; fashion and brand articles especially were bought from capitalist competitors.

The relative failure of consumer cooperatives documents the dilemma of attempts to rationalize consumer behaviour. The consumer as 'king' required well-furnished shops, fast and competent service, a broad and well-packaged range of articles and low prices. To rationalize consumer behaviour was like trying to square a circle: 'If it were possible to educate the consumer to make his purchasing decisions only in a rational way, it would be possible to rationalize distribution, that is the different branches of distribution, too'.[42] In this view, rationalizing retailing failed because of the 'irrationality' of consumer behaviour. Consequently, at the beginning of the world economic crisis most experts still thought that consumers had to be educated and even regulated: retailing and consumption had to be rationalized simultaneously.

The new relationship between retailer and consumer in the 1920s developed in the context of limited competition. Even by the late 1920s large segments of the retail trade were regulated. Price competition was limited. The price of bread and bakery products was fixed in the whole country, meat prices in southern German towns. Fish supply was nearly monopolized, milk prices were set by local authorities. Brands with fixed prices made up more than half the turnover in the grocery trade. In food retailing, price competition existed only for so-called 'competitive articles' like salt, sugar or lard and even these were regularly sold below purchase price.[43] Between 1926 and 1932 the quickly growing market share of one-price shops showed that price competition could be a successful strategy. But, significantly, it did not become the general rule in retailing.

To educate consumers required hard empirical data. In this way, the attention given to consumer education facilitated the professionalization of market research and statistics. At the level of single firms, branches and business organizations, book-keeping and statistics had started long before the First World War.[44] Indicators like turnover, profit margins and turnover rates gave a first impression of consumer behaviour. This data was used as an empirical base for more detailed characterizations of consumers. Psychological research established differentiated consumer types. The consumer was no longer a person distinguished only by income and preferences, but was segmented further by cultural types, opinions and associations, such as 'the elegant lady, the practical housewife, the countryside shopper, the woman with a shawl, the old lady, the young girl, the child, the gentleman, the good lady-friend' or 'the demanding, the expert, the self-opinionated, the objective, the expensive one'.[45] It was hoped that such information would make the retailer–consumer encounter in single shops more productive. At the level of the retail trade in general statistics acquired new significance towards the end of the inflationary period. Retail trade associations collected and published data which was condensed by the new institutes researching economic cycles and commerce, such as the *Institut für Konjunkturforschung* in Berlin and the *Institut für Handelsforschung* in Cologne (see Figure 4). Rhythms and changes of consumption in different branches and businesses became the subject of systematic analysis. At the level of products and product groups, commercial market research began to be professionalized in the late 1920s, when journals like *Der Markt der Fertigware* and *Blätter für landwirtschaftliche Marktforschung* were published.[46] Founded in 1934, the institute of consumer research (*Gesellschaft für Konsumforschung*) combined quantitative data and psychological research to optimize the sales efforts of producers and retailers and to redirect consumer behaviour in line with Nazi policies.[47] As a result of this statistical transformation, retailers were able to reflect on consumption and consumers in a more abstract, scientific fashion.

In the 1930s retailer–consumer relations were more and more structured by state regulations. The national-conservative and then the National Socialist governments understood retailing as a necessary bridge between producer and consumer. Organic and corporate ideas of the economy now became dominant. On the one hand, this meant a rejection of the model of 'anonymous' distribution. 'The healthiest form of satisfying demand is when the retailer knows the customer and the customer knows the retailer', as one retailing advocate put it in 1934.[48] The retailer should 'ennoble'[49] commercial aspirations and educate the consumer as an active member of the racial

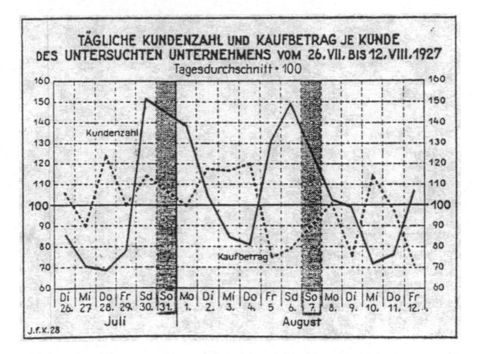

TÄGLICHE KUNDENZAHL UND KAUFBETRAG JE KUNDE
DES UNTERSUCHTEN UNTERNEHMENS VOM 26. VII. BIS 12. VIII. 1927
Tagesdurchschnitt • 100

Figure 4 A New View of the Consumer: Rhythms of Purchase 1927

Source: H. Grünbaum, *Die Umsatzschwankungen des Einzelhandels als Problem der Betriebs-politik* (Berlin: Hobbing, 1928), p. 34.

community, the *Volksgemeinschaft*. The relationship between retailer and consumer became a crucial element in the promotion of 'healthy' consumption and anti-Semitic behaviour. As two authors concluded in 1935: '"Public interest against self-interest" has been accepted in the sphere of the economy and has to create a new type of salesman... A salesman can and may only be someone who has the mental capacity to act from an economic and cultural point of view... The first duty, resulting from this, is to suppress the bad one to give the good one a breathing space. As the peasant continuously weeds the fields, to secure the yield, the healthy one will only push through on the field of culture, if the bad one is pushed back'.[50]

If retailer–consumer relations in the 1930s became dominated by the call for education, it was now officially propagated as a relation between partners with equal rights. The retailer was obliged to obtain the judgements of the consumers, to pass them on to the wholesale trade and industry. One result was the promotion of an efficient, but medium-sized retail trade as the economic norm. Large-scale enterprises, small shops and itinerant traders were suppressed, while new tax laws supported the establishment of a broad and decentralized network of independent and viable shops. Rationalization did not stop but was aimed at attracting the consumer.

Shops should be clean, tidy and beautiful. The interior of shops should express respect for employees and customers alike.[51] The design of products and packages should be simple but attractive. Consumption in Germany created communities that had to fulfil reciprocal duties. 'This sphere of a responsible satisfaction of demand can't be solely left to "her majesty, the customer".'[52]

After 1936, when the four-year plan intensified war preparations, retailer–consumer relations became ever more uneven. Personal relations always meant control of everyday activities: retailers knew who bought too much butter, coffee, alcohol, tobacco, sexy underwear or 'hygienic' articles. Customers had to register themselves to obtain scarce and popular products. Retailers became an integral part of directing consumption – a first sign of a re-emerging seller's market[53] – anticipating aspects of a rationing system already prior to the Second World War.

Germany entered the Second World War much better prepared than it had been for the previous war. Market research was one key element in Nazi consumption policy. By the mid-1930s the consumer was recognized as a 'risk factor'[54] for an imperial policy of expansion. Consequently, consumer research was intensified 'to control the unrestrained behaviour of the consumer somewhat and to direct it into reasonable directions', as one researcher put it in 1936.[55]

The rationing system once more established a seller's market, but the Nazi regime tried to contain conflicts between retailers and consumers. A price freeze and the rationing of raw materials and a growing number of consumer goods led to a 'directed freedom of consumption',[56] characterized by a 'comprehensive simplification of demand',[57] too. In the Second World War the function of the retailer changed dramatically in contrast with that in the First World War: the retailer now had moral authority and was responsible for 'just distribution'[58] and social morale. From 1942 on, the number of offences by retailers rose. Regular customers normally received privileged treatment from retailers. Until 1944, however, strict punishment limited practices of hoarding and corruption. Most German retailers and consumers behaved the way propaganda intended.[59]

Imagining Consumers in West German Society

The end of the Second World War did not lead to an immediate structural overhaul of the system of distribution. The Allied powers re-established the institutions of the German war economy to solve the most severe supply problems. As a result, the close relationship between retailer and customer continued during the subsistence crisis. The post-war years revealed the consequences of a seller's market. Although the strictly regulated official retail trade did not lose its main function in distributing basic supplies, new informal and unofficial systems, like black markets, expanded quickly. Many retailers profited from this situation and resulting suspicions and hostility eroded trust in retailer–consumer relations.[60]

The transition to a market economy in the western zones brought about by the currency reform and the foundation of the Federal Republic of Germany created new institutions and business organizations. These would gradually change the relations between retailers and consumers. Although shortages, black and grey markets did not disappear overnight, the introduction of the Deutschmark in 1948 amounted to a cultural paradigm shift for post-war society.

In the context of the new post-war market economy, debates about rationalization and the necessity of modernizing the retail trade led to significant changes in the management of distribution. Forms of retailing that had been suppressed by the Nazis, like the consumer cooperatives and multiple shops, developed new forward-looking standards. For example, they became pioneers of self-service in 1948, a decade before the general breakthrough of this new practice. Multiple shops started an aggressive price and advertisement policy to increase turnover.[61] Although medium-sized firms still dominated the retail trade, these new tendencies of commercialization left their imprint on the image of consumer and retailer alike. The sovereignty of consumers was the 'cornerstone of the new economic order',[62] the social market economy. Informed by neoclassical economics, the 'right to vote with money' would lead to an 'emancipation of the consumer'.[63] In this view, the role of the retailer was that of a dependent supplier. We have seen earlier that the idea of the sovereign consumer had been part of a long-standing fiction and had influenced the ritual of the commercial encounter between retailer and customer in medium-sized shops ever since the turn of the twentieth century. Developments after 1945, however, pushed notions of consumer sovereignty into new directions. On the one hand, the idea of sovereignty was challenged by new sociological perspectives. Attention to the complex realities of consumption was reinforced by a disillusionment with liberal ideals of the individual: 'The disoriented consumer, not the sovereign of the market, is the reality of the twentieth century'.[64] Like American consumers in the 1920s, German consumers in the 1950s were analysed as easily tempted dupes, in the grip of external, prearranged stimuli and at the mercy of modern advertising. The consumer was the product of 'economic degeneration': 'This is a picture of a human being who is empty and has degenerated to a materialist state'.[65] In this analysis, retailers regained a position of respect and importance as educators who could assist the consumer to regain a better life. On the other hand, economic experts began to stress the ongoing self-organization of the retail trade. Here, too, the sovereign consumer lost much of its liberal agency and was reduced to a mere economic function.

The main consequence of this debate was an intensified consumer protection policy, which set a modest regulatory framework for retailing. Consumer protection emphasized the need to provide consumers with better information and to institutionalize neutral advice. New consumption experts emerged who undermined retailers' traditional monopoly of expertise.[66] New forms of communication provided consumer information through journals, magazines and advice literature. Knowledge and expertise came to rely less on personal contact and more on general, statistical and abstract knowledge of goods and services. At the same time, consumer protection was also designed to allow for fair competition amongst retailers. To strengthen price competition, the Liberal–Conservative government cut down cooperative privileges. The cooperative and discount law (1954) thus limited the dividend of the consumer cooperatives to 3 per cent. The cooperatives consequently began to sell at current prices, forcing medium-sized retailers to join retailer-purchasing cooperatives (Edeka, Rewe) or the new voluntary chains run by international groups. Importantly, retail price maintenance began to unravel in the late 1950s and was officially forbidden in 1967.

The introduction of quality standards and safety regulations was a second policy initiative that challenged the retailer as expert. Consumers were greeted by an expanding number of quality signs and categories and an increasingly standardized set of consumer goods.[67] Norms and regulations were normally set in consultation with producers and retailers, but the German food law of 1958 shows that they were sometimes introduced against the organized resistance of the commercial sector. The quality of goods was no longer represented by the retailer but delegated to symbols and academic experts. The test of an article's quality no longer took place in the shop but was communicated through an expanding network of 'objective' scientific institutions, like the consumer research testing agency, *Stiftung Warentest*, in Berlin.

Consumer policy developed as a reaction to fundamental changes in West German retailing from the late 1950s. This was, first, a response to changes in industrial production. The increasing number of consumer goods and a rise in real income led to an intensive differentiation among retail types. The ideal of the shop as the normal place to shop was replaced by clear-cut images of different business models.[68] Second, it was the result of new business organizations themselves. In West Germany the first supermarkets opened in 1958, a response to increasing market segmentation. The range of goods increased, fresh products were integrated, self-service became the new convention (see Figure 5), and the size of shops grew exponentially, all of which encouraged very different ways of rationalizing consumers' shopping practices. Third, the transformation of German retailing was based on a more price-oriented commercialization of the sector, resulting in a new price awareness among consumers. The success of the discount shops after 1962 illustrates the growing commercialization of consumer behaviour. First denounced as a 'primitive sales' technique', which reminded contemporaries of the war economy, these new discount shops forced competitors to cut their own prices, to differentiate their business strategy, or to close shop altogether.[69] Branded goods started their long triumphant march to hegemony, although premium brands could still be valued for their higher quality, rather than price.[70] The expansion of retail firms led to tough price competition, with special offers dominating newspapers and shop windows. The focus on the regular customer was abandoned; those consumers retreated to the declining number

Figure 5 Self-Service Takes Command, 1956

Source: 'Selbstbedienung setzt sich durch. Hannover eröffnete seinen siebten Selbstbedienungsladen', *Der Verbraucher*, Vol. 10 (1956), p. 116.

of medium-sized shops. Price wars and commercial transformation focused attention on internal organization, the sourcing of goods, purchasing power, discounts from suppliers, turnover per square meter, or how to differentiate one's firm from competitors.[71] Intensified market research and a growing number of academic research institutes assisted these developments.

The commercial transformation of customer–retailer relations, then, resulted less from the alleged rise of the manipulated consumer than from complex socio-economic changes in the 1950s and 1960s. The individual retailer ceased to be the centre of the shop, marginalized by a new culture of self-service and standardized consumer goods. Instead of the personal encounter with customers, retailers now concentrated on administration and logistics.[72] Personal communication became a cost factor. From the middle of the 1960s the medium-sized retailer symbolized for most consumers expensive articles and old-fashioned business. The phrase 'Tante Emma Laden', Aunt Emma shop, the new nostalgic nickname for small shops in the 1960s, nicely captured the cultural recoding of the previously dominant small retailer as an old-fashioned vestige in the world of modern shopping.

This, of course, was not the end of personal relations between retailer and consumer. Rising turnovers and the advancing concentration of the retail trade did not mark the end of the evolving relationship between retailers and consumers. Advancing market saturation and the declining share of retailing in the consumption of private households since the late 1950s prompted fresh debates about the future place of retailing and the future role of consumers. The economic depression of 1973–4 amplified a sense of crisis for the model of concentration and cut-throat pricing.[73] There was a flourish of nostalgia that helped for a short time to re-establish smaller, mobile shops,[74] although many of these developments were far from traditional and drew on market research that had identified retail deserts in smaller towns and the countryside. Post-materialistic values promoted the new anti-hero of the 'new consumer', who consumes in a socially and environmentally responsible and reflective way.[75] Significantly, the niche market for ecological products started with small shops, thus re-establishing the figure of the honest, reliable and informed retailer, who favours consumers with advice and help.

In the early 1980s the concept of the 'new consumer' was appropriated by marketing experts in studies analysing differentiation and market segmentation. The consumer was increasingly sub-divided in efforts to specify the attraction of particular sales techniques in particular segments of the market. As a consequence, the personal characteristics of retail managers received renewed attention.[76] Leading retailers started to differentiate their shop ranges to attract different clientele. The assortments of supermarkets and early shopping malls were fused again. Regular promotions structured everyday shopping. In the late 1980s the model of polarized consumer behaviour introduced the microsegmentation of shop ranges. Today shops are planned on the basis of the socio-economic data of potential consumers. Trained salespersons are used to enforce a promotional event culture, to attract consumers' attention and to offer advice. In the 1980s segmentation and the renewed personalization of the shopping encounter thus came to coexist with the continuing emphasis on cut-throat price-oriented competition driven forward by discount stores.

Retailers and Consumers in a Planned Economy: a View from East Germany

The West German experience of commercialization, however, was not the only development after 1945. In the eastern zone, too, supplies were a central problem after the Second World War. The rationing system of the German war economy was perpetuated. The Soviet Military Administration and the newly established German Administration of Trade and Supply controlled the official part of retailing and organized the difficult task of procuring consumer goods.[77] Consumer cooperatives were re-established and became important suppliers. In general, though, the retail trade was still dominated by small or medium-sized, privately owned shops.[78] Things changed only slowly after 1947, when a planned economy was introduced to improve industrial production and supply.[79]

Although it took years to institutionalize a planned economy, this decision had far-reaching consequences for retailer–consumer relations. Relations were now framed by the socialist concept of demand.[80] Individuals were seen to have concrete needs, resulting from the state of productive forces. Consumers were normally also producers in this view. In capitalist society, where individual consumption and production were separated, the result was alienation and manipulation. In socialist society, by contrast, the collective ownership of the means of production would promote harmony between people's work and consumption. The people were sovereign, but as socialist consumers they would consume in a reflective and responsible way, aware of collective needs. A planned economy aimed at concentrating production and distribution to fulfil collective needs. Planning acknowledged the possibility of distinct tastes and habits of consumption – people had different skills and needs – but they had to be conditioned by the state of productive forces and the hierarchy of collective needs.

The logic of planning had far-reaching consequences for retailer–consumer relations. In a socialist society they were partners, working in different capacities for the same collective goal. Consumers had to be treated with respect and kindness, but retailers and salespersons were also expected to communicate collective needs. And collective needs were fixed through planning in the form of 'consumption funds'. Retailers and salespersons should help the consumer not to buy as much as possible, but to choose the right products. Their task was to rationalize consumption, to develop critical, responsible preferences. In short, socialist planning fused the egalitarian ideals of earlier consumer cooperatives with a technocratic vision of standardization and functionality. If the planned world of collective needs required an element of personal contact and instruction, relations between retailers and consumers were clearly depersonalized in socialist society, as aims and values were imposed from outside this relationship through the process of planning, leaving little space for the relative autonomy and individuality of either retailer or consumer.

When the first two-year plan began in 1949, it propagated an attractive vision: industrial development would focus on every-day supplies.[81] In reality, the reconstruction of the East German economy was dominated by investments in heavy and primary industries. The production of consumer goods was of subordinate concern. The retail sector was seen as little more than an economic necessity. Problems of supply were exacerbated by the slow but steady 'liquidation of futile and unhealthy elements' in the retail trade, that is, privately owned shops.[82] During the 1950s the face of the retail trade became more and more that of the female salesperson. Officially they were to provide service and convenience, but in everyday practice retailing was often reduced to little more than the handing out of goods or the explaining of supply problems.[83] Nevertheless, living in a seller's market meant consumers needed to develop special relationships with retailers to obtain scarce products and to maintain or improve their standard of living. Shops thus served as communication centres, where information was shared and where protest and spontaneous criticism could be articulated.[84]

The 1953 uprising demonstrated that this could be dangerous for the socialist regime. As a result, the regime not only adjusted its policy of consumption but reinforced the ideological education of salespersons. The retail body *Handelsorganisation* and consumer cooperatives were presented as an 'effective tool of our economic policy'[85] – the avant-garde of socialist consumer awareness. Their magazines were full of exemplary salespersons (see Figure 6). New symbols – like the Q sign (for quality) – were to symbolize to customers the benefits of consumer culture under socialism.[86] Socialist self-criticism revealed the gulf between ideal and practice. As one contemporary writer emphasized, salespersons were not normally 'polite, nimble, courteous and helpful'.[87] Many retailers were not motivated, behaved in an unfriendly way, or shut their shops before official closing times. The increasing amount of consumer goods led to untidy salesrooms. Inefficient shopkeeping and irregular supplies meant the loss or destruction of goods. By the early 1960s the retail trade was seen as a 'concentration point of negative influences arising from the private sphere, from production and private consumption'.[88] The critique of the retailer was complemented by a critique of the consumer. 'Bourgeois' expectations were criticized, as panic buying and hoarding became routine parts of everyday consumption.

The deep political and economic crisis had two main consequences for consumers and retailers. First, there was an expansion and professionalization of market research from the late 1950s. To fix production and consumption plans, the rationing system and the planned economy needed statistical information. In the late 1940s and 1950s socialist policy was able to draw on the principal categories of consumer research from the inter-war years, such as household budgets and market observation. The

VERKAUFSKULTUR

Darf es noch etwas sein?   Alles für den Kunden   Der Ton macht die Musike

Figure 6 Improving Selling Culture in East Germany with the Help of Self-Criticism, 1958

Source: *Handelswoche*, 3(40) (1958), p. 5.

problem was that planning experts and politicians failed to interpret this data in a satisfactory fashion. 'As long as a solid rationing system for consumer goods exists, the determination of the demand is a relatively simple thing', as one expert put the received wisdom crudely.[89] The end of the rationing system in 1958 demonstrated both that the coordination of supply was inefficient and that the standardization of consumer goods was underdeveloped. The image of an average consumer altogether underestimated regional differences in consumption and simultaneously caused scarcities and gluts of goods. As a result, the socialist regime began to professionalize research on economic demand. In 1961 the Institute of Demand Research was founded in Leipzig, which investigated the wholesale trade as well as the retail trade and consumer behaviour.[90] The decentralized retail trade had been unable to provide industry and planning bureaucrats with adequate data. This now became the function of experts.[91]

A second result was the transformation of the retail trade into a more modern, efficient sector, a process beginning in the late 1950s. Socialist policy in this area was partly a reaction to structural changes in consumption, such as the growing significance of consumer durables. Yet there was also an effort to put retailer–consumer relations on a new level. Efficient sales organizations were to rationalize distribution and consumption, to emancipate consumers from basic needs and to develop a modern socialist personality. Rationalization would free salespersons to concentrate on giving standardized personal advice to customers.[92] Self-service became an integral part of Eastern German retailing. A relatively late arrival from a Western perspective, self-service shops spread at an astonishing rate in the late 1950s and early 1960s. By 1956 only seven self-service shops existed; by 1966 the number had increased to 18,530. The gains from rationalization may have been limited and many shops may have been smaller than in the West, but the repercussions for retailer–consumer relations were nonetheless profound.[93] A more anonymous shopping encounter replaced personal interaction. Shop committees were established to offer customers a substitute arena for direct contact, advice and consultation.

In 1965 two department store combines (*Centrum* and *Konsument*) were founded, which centralized the shopping of durable consumer goods. Small shops lost their customers and faced closure. In addition, the privately owned segment of the retail trade was reduced to a handful of surviving shops. New forms of retailing, like mail order shopping, expanded in the 1960s; in 1965 the HO and the Konsument Mail Order House distributed one million catalogues. Centralized and depersonalized forms of retailing like mail order shopping further eroded the traditional role of the small retailer as expert and friend of the consumer.[94] Together, these developments amounted to intensified state influence and the decline of a '"bourgeois" sales culture'.[95] Government propaganda celebrated these changes as a manifestation of an increasingly mature socialistic consumer culture, but statist centralization merely made the discrepancies more apparent between town and countryside and highlighted the limits of production plans.[96]

The different function of prices in a planned economy made for very different developments in East Germany compared with those in West Germany. In Eastern Germany prices had to be set, but nobody 'knows how to set prices in a centrally planned economy'.[97] In a market economy prices reflect the relation between supply and demand, in a socialistic economy the division between basic and luxury needs. Prices of the latter were not designed to allocate investments, but to regulate consumer behaviour. Though reflecting costs of production and distribution, prices had a mainly political function. This divide between basic and luxury price systems was mirrored in a divide between retail systems, when the 'free shops' of the nationally owned *Handelsorganisation* were founded in 1948 to sell products of better quality and 'luxury' products for higher prices and without rationing stamps.[98] This decision created different types of customers: those who were able to buy in more exclusive shops and those who had to buy rationed goods in the basic retail trade. Although the price differences between the *Handelsorganisation* and the other retail trade were gradually minimized with the help of growing subsidies, new forms of retailing perpetuated the segmentation of Eastern German consumers. In 1955 the Intershop was established, where foreigners could shop with foreign currency. From the middle of the 1960s these shops became open to select groups of East German customers and in the course of the 1970s to more and more ordinary consumers purchasing quality products for (West) German marks.[99] Even earlier, socialist consumers had the opportunity to buy fashionable and 'luxury' products in the *Exquisit* and *Delikat* shops, founded in 1961 and 1966.[100]

This segmentation of the retail trade was a result of changing demand structures, which were not mirrored adequately by a change in retail prices and subsidies. The cautious reform of the price system during the 1960s did not change the misallocation of resources. While in West Germany intensified price competition led to a fundamental change in retailing and unprecedented price awareness among consumers, this structural turn was never possible in East Germany. The end of the New Economic System and the intensification of politically motivated subsidies after 1972 led to a structural crisis, which was a crucial turning point for the eventual collapse of the German Democratic Republic.[101]

The lagging transformation and rationalisation of East German retailing – between 1971 and 1977 the number of shops decreased by a mere 16 per cent[102] – perpetuated a system of distribution with a high number of relatively small and inefficient outlets. The intended mechanization of consumption failed; the number of salespersons stayed relatively high. When changing demands and post-material values found their way into East Germany in the early 1980s, personal elements and the expertise of salespersons were promoted once again.[103] But this renaissance of human resources was accompanied by insufficient investment in the design and interior of shops. Plans to promote a distinct socialist shopping culture were limited to the most important urban centres, while ordinary shops lacked the resources to integrate new elements of the promotional-event culture, like 'tasting corners, special sales or test sales'.[104]

Limited product ranges, the relative dependence of consumers and the dynamics of a seller's market continued to be the bottleneck of consumption in the GDR. The often romanticized ingenuity of East Germans, with their ability to overcome supply problems, came to a quick end when the two German states were reunified in 1989/1990. The East German retail trade collapsed and consumers had to learn the hard lessons of rationalization, commercialization and price competition.

Everywhere and Nowhere: Retailer–Consumer Relations in Segmented Markets

At the beginning of the twenty-first century, relations between retailers and consumers retain elements of ritual, but the rules of the game have changed substantially in the last hundred years. Today the framework of retailing is normally determined by managers and executives, who reduce consumers and retailers to economic indicators in a battle for profitability and shareholder approval. The cash-nexus rules.[105] Discounters represent the ongoing economization of the retail trade and of retailer–consumer relations. Market imperatives have transformed social relationships. The role of the salesperson is reduced to that of a cashier or shelf-stacker, who is poorly paid and lacks professional education. Nevertheless, the success of such bargain-shopping concepts should not be entirely reduced to cheap prices. Today discount stores offer reliability without any frills. As one commentator has observed, shops like Aldi perform the function of a hyper-community, offering consumers a sense of shared identity: 'To shop at ALDI connects people, because everybody is part of a popular and collective movement, united by the belief that at ALDI all human beings become "brothers in greed". Stepping into an ALDI market is a liberating process of de-individualization. Here noone has to bother about etiquette or put on airs. Instead, they become part of a greedy mass that – backed by the rational mask of thrift, quality and the cult of modernity – plunders shelves and boxes and brings them to the checkout'.[106]

The identity and perception of consumers have acquired a growing repertoire of performative and emotional characteristics. The cultivation of 'personal' relations between shop and consumer and between brand and consumer have become a vital part of marketing and retailing. Drawing on psychological and economic research, some marketing has substituted 'real' with constructed, imagined 'personal' relations. The fate of small-sized, traditional, ecological retailers shows that most consumers will not pay for the personal integrity of the retailer. By contrast, high-quality ecological supermarkets have been successful: shopping here is part of social representation and distinction. Consumers do not mind paying more in cases where they enjoy participating in more expensive rituals of consumption. In affluent societies, consumers may be selfish, but also selfish enough to demand they play their own part in the consumption experience. Retailers are often little more than part of the stage set. This may be functional for the smooth working of modern consumer society, but there are also costs:

> We live in a culture where the primacy of the self and its satisfaction is everything. We are bombarded with messages telling us that we should have what we want because we're worth it. As consumers, we are kings. We know that we have rights, that brands seek our favour; that as long as we can pay, we feel powerful. We like that sensation. It is seductive because it is so at odds with the reality of the rest of our lives.[107]

Notes

1. H.-G. Haupt, *Konsum und Handel: Europa im 19. und 20. Jahrhundert* (Göttingen, 2003).
2. See the chapters by Chessel and by Trentmann and Taylor in this volume for further discussion and literature.
3. C. Nonn, *Verbraucherprotest und Parteiensystem im wilhelminischen Deutschland* (Düsseldorf, 1996). For a comparative view, P. Maclachlan and F. Trentmann, 'Civilizing Markets: Traditions of Consumer Politics in Twentieth-Century Britain, Japan and the United States' in M. Bevir and F. Trentmann (eds), *Markets in Historical Contexts* (Cambridge, 2004), pp. 170–201.
4. U. Spiekermann, *Basis der Konsumgesellschaft: Entstehung und Entwicklung des modernen Kleinhandels in Deutschland 1850–1914* (Munich, 1999), p. 83.
5. See Spiekermann, *Basis der Konsumgesellschaft*, pp. 596–602.
6. 'Höflichkeit des Verkaufspersonals', *Der Manufacturist*, 30(38) (1907), p. 12.
7. See R. Albrecht, *Konsumentenmoral und Käufervereine* (Düsseldorf, 1909), p. 3.
8. For further discussion and references see Spiekermann, *Basis der Konsumgesellschaft*, pp. 599–602.
9. See 'Stiefkinder Merkurs', *Deutsche Handels-Warte* (*DHW*), 3 (1896), pp. 35–7.
10. See R. Seyffert, *Der Mensch als Betriebsfaktor* (Stuttgart, 1922).
11. See H. Krüer, *Geschäftskunde für den Kleinhandelsstand*, vol. 1 (Leipzig, 1924), pp. 1–2.
12. See H. Pobbig, 'Wie eine Verkäuferin sein sollte', *Konsumgenossenschaftliche Rundschau* (*KR*), 5 (1908), p. 212; 'Höflichkeit und Aufdringlichkeit des Verkäufers', *Zeitschrift für Waren-und Kaufhäuser*, 13(2) (1914), pp. 8–9.
13. See 'Der Verkäufer', *DHW*, 11 (1904), pp. 177–8; A. Neumann-Hofer, 'Shopping in Berlin und Paris', *Die Woche*, 1 (1899), pp. 316–17.

14. L. Goldberg, 'Kaufmännische Aphorismen', *Der Materialist*, 25(2) (1914), p. 1

15. See U. Spiekermann, 'Display Windows and Window Displays in German Cities of the Nineteenth Century: Towards the History of a Commercial Breakthrough' in C. Wischermann and E. Shore (eds), *Advertising and the European City: Historical Perspectives* (Aldershot, 2000), pp. 139–71, esp. pp. 158–65.

16. See S. Fischer, *Der Verkäufer: Praktisches Handbuch für Verkäufer und Verkäuferinnen in allen Branchen* (Berlin, 1899), pp. 53–74.

17. One example was the standardization of the clothes of the salesperson. See P. Höhner, 'Die Anforderungen an die Verkäufer und Verkäuferinnen in den Konsumvereinen', *KR*, 9 (1912), pp. 4–6.

18. V. Böhmert, 'Die Handelshochschulen und die Arbeiterfrage', *Der Arbeiterfreund*, 35 (1897), pp. 79–92; Λ. Roth, *Das kaufmännische Fortbildungsschulwesen in Deutschland, sein gegenwärtiger Stand und seine fernere Ausgestaltung* (Hamburg, 1903).

19. See 'Eine Liga der Konsumenten', *Blätter für Genossenschaftswesen*, 45 (1898), pp. 101–2.

20. M. Prinz, *Brot und Dividende: Konsumvereine in Deutschland und England vor 1914* (Göttingen, 1996); Spiekermann 'Basis der Konsumgesellschaft', pp. 238–77.

21. See U. Spiekermann, 'Medium der Solidarität. Die Werbung der Konsumgenossenschaften 1903–1933' in P. Borscheid and C. Wischermann (eds), *Bilderwelt des Alltags: Werbung in der Konsumgesellschaft des 19. und 20. Jahrhunderts* (Stuttgart, 1995), pp. 150–89, esp. pp. 153–5.

22. 'Plauderei eines Konsumenten', *Der Konsumverein*, 16 (1924), p. 35.

23. Moderne Sprichworte, *Kladderadatsch*, 71, 1918, No. 30 v. 28.07.

24. See R. Schloesser, *Die Kriegsorganisation der Konsumenten: 'Kriegsausschuß für Konsumenteninteressen' – K.f.K.* (Eßlingen, 1917).

25. W. Rudolff, *Die Wohlfahrtsstadt: Kommunale Ernährungs-, Fürsorge- und Wohnungspolitik am Beispiel Münchens 1910–1933*, vol. 1 (Göttingen, 1998).

26. See W. Wiskott, 'Die Rolle des Handels bei der Zwischen- und Unterverteilung', *Beiträge zur Kommunalen Kriegswirtschaft*, 1(38) (1916/17), pp. 7–9; 'Der Lebensmittel-Kleinhandel im Zeichen der Kriegswirtschaft', *Deutsche Handels-Rundschau (DHR)*, 11 (1918), pp. 259–61.

27. See H. Geithe, *Wirkungen der Lebensmittelzwangswirtschaft der Kriegs- und Nachkriegszeit auf den Lebensmittelhandel* (unpublished dissertation: Halle a.d.s, 1925).

28. 'Tätigkeitsbericht der Industrie- und Handelskammer zu Osnabrück für das Jahr 1924', p. 42, Niedersächsisches Staatsarchiv Osnabrück Dep. 3b IV Stadt Osnabrück, no. 1514.

29. H.L. Schmitt, *Gutachten über die Entwicklung des Milchabsatzes in Deutschland an Hand des Fragebogens des Ausschusses zur Untersuchung der Erzeugungs-*

und Absatzbedingungen der deutschen Wirtschaft (Enquete-Ausschuß), (n.d. [1926]), p. 11.

30. A. Lampe, 'Einzelhandel' in *Handwörterbuch der Staatswissenschaften*, 4th edn, vol. 3 (Jena, 1926), pp. 496–543, here p. 533.

31. W. Woynack, 'Wissenschaftliche Betriebsführung und Warenverteilung', *KR*, 17 (1920), pp. 120–21.

32. R. Seyffert, *Der Mensch als Betriebsfaktor: Eine Kleinhandelsstudie* (Stuttgart, 1922).

33. U. Spiekermann, 'Rationalisation as a Permanent Task: The German Food Retail Trade in the Twentieth Century' in A.P. den Hartog (ed.), *Food Technology, Science and Marketing: European Diet in the Twentieth Century* (East Linton, 1995), pp. 200–20, here p. 205.

34. 'Der Umgang mit Kunden', *Edeka DHR*, 27 (1934), p. 855.

35. Frhr. v. Pechmann, 'Der Qualitätsgedanke bei Kaufmann und Verbraucher', *Edeka DHR*, 28 (1935), p. 541.

36. See F.W. Schulze, 'Die Hausfrau und der Einzelhandel', *Der Materialist*, 50(17) (1929), p. 6; J. Jessen, *Der Handel als volkswirtschaftliche Aufgabe* (Berlin, 1940).

37. W. Grotkopp, 'Abgepackt', *KR*, 25 (1928), pp. 269–70, here p. 270.

38. W. Grotkopp, 'Service', *KR*, 25 (1928), pp. 458–60; H. Springorum, 'Amerikanische Erinnerungen. II.', *DHW*, 23 (1935), pp. 459–64, here pp. 462–64.

39. [W.] Pelletier, *Anwendbarkeit amerikanischer Wirtschaftsmethoden im deutschen Einzelhandel* (Berlin, 1927), p. 10.

40. V. Klepzig, 'Die Rationalisierung der Konsumgenossenschaften', *KR*, 24 (1927), pp. 673–5, 693–5, here p. 694.

41. V. Totomianz, 'Vom Preis zum Qualitätsgedanken', *KR*, 26 (1929), pp. 93–5; E. Bieberitz, 'Der Verbraucher in der Wirtschaft', *KR*, 29 (1932), pp. 789–90.

42. W. Vershofen, 'Moderne Absatzformen', in B. Harms (ed.), *Strukturwandlungen der Deutschen Volkswirtschaft*, 2nd edn, vol. 2 (Berlin, 1929), pp. 116–24, here p. 123.

43. 'Das Erwachen des Konsumenten', *Magazin der Wirtschaft*, 6 (1930), pp. 2139–43, here p. 2141.

44. See A. Calmes, *Die Statistik im Fabrik und Warenhandelsbetrieb*, 6th edn (Leipzig, 1921).

45. Foerster, 'Verkaufskunst und Organisation im Einzelhandelsbetrieb', *Industrielle Psychotechnik*, 5 (1928), pp. 127–8, 147–58, here pp. 151–2.

46. See W.L. Spängler, 'Zur geschichtlichen Entwicklung der Marktanalyse', *Zeitschrift für Handelswissenschaft und Handelspraxis*, 22 (1929), pp. 221–3.

47. See H. Berghoff, 'Enticement and Deprivation: The Regulation of Consumption in Pre-War Nazi Germany', in M. Daunton and M. Hilton (eds), *The Politics of Consumption* (Oxford and New York, 2001), pp. 165–84, here p. 179; C. Conrad, 'Observateur les consommateurs. Études de marché et histoire

de la consommation en Allemagne, des années 1930 aux années 1960', *Le Mouvement Social*, 206 (2004), pp. 17–39.

48. M. Kammerbauer, 'Mittelständische Wirtschaftspolitik', *DHW*, 22 (1934), pp. 55–61, here p. 61; C. Witt, *Handel und Kaufmann in der gelenkten Wirtschaft* (Stuttgart, 1938).

49. 'Kundgebung des Westdeutschen Handels', *Edeka DHR*, 28 (1935), p. 271.

50. H. Gretsch and G. Sieber, 'Schulung der Verkaufskräfte', *DHW*, 23 (1935), pp. 496–503.

51. See 'Das vorbildliche Einzelhandelsgeschäft', *DHR*, 32 (1939), p. 310.

52. Hartmuth, 'Kaufmann mitten im Volk', *DHW*, 24 (1936), pp. 178–9, here p. 179.

53. T. Wieseler, 'Qualität und Geschmack im Blickfeld des Einzelhandels', *DHW*, 26 (1938), pp. 394–7.

54. H. Stürmer, 'Verbrauchslenkung durch Absatzforschung', *DHW*, 23 (1935), pp. 399–402, 455–9, here p. 400.

55. A. Fritz, 'Praktische Verbrauchslenkung. Neue Wege deutscher Wirtschaftspolitik', *DHW*, 24 (1936), pp. 24–30, here p. 26.

56. R. Schaeder, 'Um die Zukunft des deutschen Handels. Eine Klarstellung', *Jahrbuch für Gesetzgebung, Verwaltung und Volkswirtschaft*, 66 (1942), pp. 159–88, here p. 162.

57. O. Ohlendorf, 'Handel als Berufsstand und Leistungsraum. Eine Entgegnung', *Jahrbuch für Gesetzgebung, Verwaltung und Volkswirtschaft*, 65 (1941), pp. 385–413, here p. 397.

58. 'Gedanken am Ladentisch', *DHR*, 33 (1940), p. 360.

59. See U. Spiekermann, 'L'approvisionnement dans la Communauté du peuple. Approches du commerce «allemand» pendant la période nationale-socialiste', *Le Mouvement Social*, 206 (2004), pp. 79–114, esp. pp. 108–13.

60. See W. Bauer, 'Der gegenwärtige und künftige Lebensstandard in Deutschland' in *Die deutsche Wirtschaft zwei Jahre nach dem Zusammenbruch* (Berlin, 1947), pp. 159–94.

61. See U. Spiekermann, 'Rationalisierung als Daueraufgabe. Der deutsche Lebensmittelhandel im 20. Jahrhundert', *Scripta Mercaturae*, 31 (1997), pp. 69–129, here pp. 99–103.

62. W. Donner, 'Mythos und Möglichkeit einer Konsumentensouveränität', *Gewerkschaftliche Monatshefte*, 4 (1953), pp. 655–61, here p. 655.

63. U. Zoch, 'Verbraucher und Handel', in J. Bock and K.G. Specht (eds), *Verbraucherpolitik* (Cologne, 1958), pp. 116–41, here p. 117.

64. E. Egner, 'Die Marktstellung des Konsumenten', *Jahrbücher für Nationalökonomie und Statistik*, 165 (1953), pp. 21–49, here p. 37.

65. Egner, 'Die Marktstellung des Konsumenten', pp. 40, 42.

66. See I. Landgrebe-Wolff, *Mehr Käuferbewußtsein! Verbrauchererziehung und Ernährungsberatung in den USA mit Anregungen für Deutschland* (Frankfurt,

1957); C.V. Braunschweig, *Der Konsument und seine Vertretung: Eine Studie über Verbraucherverbände* (Heidelberg, 1965).

67. See E.D. Herzog, 'Aufgaben und Möglichkeiten der Verbraucheraufklärung' in Bock and Specht, *Verbraucherpolitik*, pp. 217–42.

68. 'Einstellung der Verbraucher im Saarland zu ausgewählten Betriebstypen im Einzelhandel', *Der Markenartikel*, 26 (1964), pp. 475–8.

69. 'Gegen Konzentration und primitive Verkaufsformen. Eine Stellungnahme der REWE', *Der Markenartikel*, 24 (1962), pp. 779–780, 783.

70. E. Noelle-Neumann and G. Schmidtchen, *Verbraucher beim Einkauf: Eine wirtschaftssoziologische Studie über die Rolle des Markenartikels* (Allensbach, 1968).

71. G. Redwitz, 'Handelsentwicklung: Wertewandel-Perspektiven für die Handelslandschaft', in R. Szallies and G. Wiswede (eds), *Wertewandel und Konsum* (Landsberg am Lech, 1990), pp. 257–80, here p. 264.

72. See K. Ditt, 'Rationalisierung im Einzelhandel: Die Einführung und Entwicklung der Selbstbedienung in der Bundesrepublik Deutschland 1949–2000' in M. Prinz (ed.), *Der lange Weg in den Überfluss: Anfänge und Entwicklung der Konsumgesellschaft seit der Vormoderne* (Paderborn, 2003), pp. 315–56.

73. *Die Konzentration im Lebensmittelhandel. Sondergutachten der Monopolkommission [...]* (Baden-Baden, 1985); *Konzentration im Zwielicht: Binnenhandel auf Konzentrationskurs*, ed. Deutscher Industrie- und Handelstag (Bonn, 1987).

74. 'Rollende Lebensmittelläden: Tante Emma wird mobil', *Test*, 10 (1974), pp. 503–4; F.W. Fertsch, 'Zurück von der grünen Wiese', *Die Ernährungswirtschaft*, 22 (1975), pp. A224–A227.

75. *Der neue Konsument: Der Abschied von der Verschwendung – die Wiederentdeckung des täglichen Bedarfs* (Frankfurt, 1979).

76. E. Buß, 'Referat aus der Sicht der Soziologie', in *Der neue Konsument*, (n.p. 1983), pp. 3–27, here p. 8.

77. See 'Versorgung mit Lebensmitteln. Das Kartensystem in der sowjetischen Besatzungszone', *Die Versorgung*, 1 (1946/47), pp. 71–2.

78. P. Friedländer, 'Die neue Rolle der Konsumgenossenschaften', *Die Versorgung*, 3 (1948/49), pp. 12–14.

79. K. Ritter, 'Planung. Zur Problematik der Versorgungspläne', *Die Versorgung*, 1 (1946/47), pp. 161–4; K. Gay, 'Schwarzmarktbekämpfung durch verbesserte Planungsarbeit', *Die Versorgung*, 3 (1948/49), pp. 29–30; H. Wolf and F. Sattler, 'Entwicklung und Struktur der Planwirtschaft der DDR', in *Machtstrukturen und Entscheidungsmechanismen im SED-Staat und die Frage der Verantwortung* (Baden-Baden, 1995), pp. 2889–940.

80. J. Backhaus, 'Der Konsument im ökonomischen System der DDR' (unpublished dissertation: Cologne, 1971).

81. H.-P. Ganter-Gilmans, 'Der Zweijahresplan und die Versorgungswirtschaft', *Die Versorgung*, 3 (1948/49), pp. 1–2.

82. R. Gruner, 'Versorgungshandel im Zweijahresplan', *Die Versorgung*, 3 (1948/49), pp. 35–6. See H. Schlenk, *Der Binnenhandel in der Sowjetischen Besatzungszone Deutschlands* (Berlin (W), 1960); H. Schlenk, *Der Binnenhandel der DDR* (Cologne, 1970).

83. E. Freund, 'Mehr Aufmerksamkeit dem Handel', *Die Versorgung*, 3 (1948/49), pp. 134–5.

84. I. Merkel, 'Konsumkultur in der DDR: Über das Scheitern der Gegenmoderne auf dem Schlachtfeld des Konsums', *Mitteilungen aus der kulturwissenschaftlichen Forschung der Universität Berlin*, 37 (1996), pp. 314–30, esp. pp. 324–5.

85. W. Ulbricht, 'Aufgaben und Probleme des sozialistischen Handels' in *Durch sozialistische Gemeinschaftsarbeit im Handel zur mustergültigen Versorgung der Bevölkerung* (Berlin, 1959), pp. 6–44, here p. 12.

86. See C. Jeschke, 'Ihr Lächeln hat tieferen Sinn', *Handelswoche*, 6(11) (1961), p. 3.

87. 'Wo Händler Kunden sind', *Handelswoche*, 25(2) (1980), p. 10.

88. W. Cramer and G. Fabiunke, *Verbrauchen wir richtig? Unser Lebensstandard und die Verkäuferin* (Berlin, 1964), p. 47.

89. G. Last, 'Marktbeobachtung und Bedarfsanalyse', *Die Versorgung*, 4 (1949/50), pp. 1–2, here p. 1.

90. See 'Die Aufgaben und die Arbeitsweise des Instituts für Bedarfsforschung', *Mitteilungen des Instituts für Bedarfsforschung*, 1 (1962), pp. 1–6; A. Kaminsky, 'Warenproduktion und Bedürfnisse in Übereinstimmung bringen. Markt- und Bedarfsforschung als Quelle der DDR-Sozialgeschichte', *Deutschland-Archiv*, 31 (1998), pp. 579–93.

91. P.F. Donat, 'Die Entwicklung des Genußmittelbedarfs in der DDR und die Möglichkeiten seiner aktiven Beeinflussung zur Durchsetzung eines der sozialistischen Lebensweise adäquaten Konsumentenverhaltens', *Marktforschung*, 27(4) (1988), pp. 7–13, esp. p. 13.

92. W. Jarowinsky, 'Die Anwendung des neuen ökonomischen Systems im Handel und die Auswirkungen auf die Konsumgüterindustrie', *Handelswoche*, 9(6) (1964), pp. 3–9.

93. Schlenk, *Binnenhandel der DDR*, pp. 82–3; S. Rothkirch, 'Moderne Menschen kaufen modern' in *Wunderwirtschaft: DDR-Konsumkultur in den 60er Jahren* (Cologne, 1996), pp. 112–19.

94. A. Kaminsky, *Wohlstand, Schönheit, Glück: Kleine Konsumgeschichte der DDR* (Munich, 2001), pp. 41–8.

95. I. Merkel, *Utopie und Bedürfnis: Die Geschichte der Konsumkultur in der DDR* (Cologne, 1999), p. 169.

96. W. Noack, 'Ein Festtag für Hoyerswerda', *Handelswoche*, 13(29) (1968), p. 3; R. Taeschner, 'Hoher Besuch am Brühl. Walter Ulbricht besichtigte neueröffnetes "konsument"-Warenhaus in Leipzig', *Handelswoche*, 13(37) (1968), pp. 4–5.

97. P. Heldmann, 'Negotiating Consumption in a Dictatorship: Consumption Politics in the GDR in the 1950s and 1960s', in Daunton and Hilton, *The Politics of*

Consumption, pp. 185–202, here p. 196; A. Steiner, 'Preispolitik im Vergleich: Nationalsozialismus, DDR und Bundesrepublik', Potsdamer Bulletin für Zeithistorische Studien 26/27 (2002), pp. 20–33.

98. K. Pence, 'Building Socialist Worker-Consumers: The Paradoxical Construction of the Handelsorganisation – HO, 1948', in P. Hübner and K. Tenfelde (eds), *Arbeiter in der SBZ-DDR* (Essen, 1999), pp. 497–526.

99. J.R. Zatlin, 'Consuming Ideology: Socialist Consumerism and the Intershop 1970–1989', in Hübner and Tenfelde, *Arbeiter in der SBZ-DDR*, pp. 555–72.

100. Merkel, *Utopie und Bedürfnis*, pp. 248–77; P. Knötzsch, 'Gedanken zur Entwicklung des Angebots an hochwertigen Nahrungs- und Genußmitteln', *Marktforschung*, 20(1) (1981), pp. 13–15.

101. C. Boyer, 'Grundlinien der Sozial- und Konsumpolitik der DDR in den siebziger und achtziger Jahren in theoretischer Perspektive' in R. Hürtgen and T. Reichel (eds), *Der Schein der Stabilität: Betriebsalltag der DDR in den siebziger und achtziger Jahren* (Berlin, 2001), pp. 69–84.

102. S. Günther, 'Handelsnetz, Öffnungszeiten und Bedienungsniveau im Urteil der Bevölkerung', *Marktforschung*, 21(2) (1982), pp. 30–34, here p. 31.

103. See G. Briska, 'Bestlösungen Sache aller', *Handelswoche*, 25(10) (1980), pp. 6–8.

104. P. Knötzsch, 'Zu einigen Aspekten der weiteren Entwicklung des Angebots an hochwertigen Nahrungs- und Genußmitteln', *Marktforschung*, 21(3/4) (1985), pp. 20–22, here p. 21.

105. C. Rivinius, 'Authentizität ist oberstes Gebot', *Lebensmittelzeitung*, (20) (2001), p. 49.

106. N. Hanisch, S. Wiesmann, J. Lönneker and S. Grünewald, 'ALDI als Überheimat', *Rheingold Newsletter*, no. 2 (2002), p. 5.

107. J. Russell, 'The Selfish Generation', *The Guardian*, no. 48907 f., 6 December 2003, p. 25.

–8–

Consumers with Chinese Characteristics?

Local Customers in British and Japanese Multinational Stores in Contemporary China*

Jos Gamble

During the Cultural Revolution a man in his fifties entered a department store in Shanghai. Browsing the goods he asked for the store assistant's help. She treated him brusquely and in an off-hand way. He pointed to the slogan above the counter: '*wei renmin fuwu*' (serve the people), a mantra omnipresent at that time and indicated that her behaviour fell short of this revolutionary ideal. Unabashed she retorted, 'how do I know that you're "the people"?'

(Interview with Shanghai citizen)[1]

Introduction: in Favour of Plurality

In early anthropological texts it was *de rigueur* to write of 'the native'. Similarly, orientalist accounts presented, for instance, 'the Chinaman'.[2] Today, it seems, only one category of beings can be reduced, ad absurdum, to the singular: the consumer, undefined, yet reified; depthless yet all-powerful. Several studies explore discourses on 'the consumer' and 'the customer'.[3] Gabriel and Lang, for instance, delineate representations of 'the consumer' as chooser, communicator, explorer, identity-seeker, hedonist or artist, victim, rebel, activist or citizen.[4] They observe the way in which '[t]oday's Western consumer is often treated as the terminus of a historical process, which will be duplicated in other parts of the world'.[5] Similarly, Trentmann argues that policymakers, business people and academics deal 'almost exclusively with the abstract figure of the consumer as a rational utility-maximising individual'.[6] Such an essentialist abstraction tells us little about consumers as active, socially embedded and meaning-creating agents. As soon as one leaves behind the mythic, de-contextualized, one-dimensional consumer of economics textbooks and begins to explore consumers as socially embedded in cultural and institutional contexts, the complexities become manifold.

Numerous studies explore the use of goods and their communicative potential, including the ways in which, through the consumption of goods, we may communicate with others or ourselves and reinforce social categories and classifications.[7] All too often, however, any account of actual consumers is lacking.[8] Scant attention, for instance, has been paid to the communication that takes place between store assistants and customers at the point of sale and to the nature of the relationships involved in these interactions from employees' perspectives.[9] Rather than attempt to read off identities from human relations with objects, store interactions provide the opportunity to observe them in practice.

Even in otherwise illuminating accounts of retail workplaces customers are surprisingly absent or muted voices.[10] However, several studies conducted on front-line workplaces indicate that customers often have a central role as active participants in service environments.[11] It is not possible to make sense of the labour process in the retail sector, for instance, without exploring the nature of customers and of the interactions between employees and customers. It is vital to explore the nature of consumers in socially and historically defined contexts. As the world's largest and most rapidly developing market, China is the most important of what Gabriel and Lang term 'the new terrains of consumerism'.[12] This chapter, then, explores the nature of interactive service workers' encounters with actual embodied customers in the Chinese context. Adopting an ethnographically orientated approach, the focus is upon workers' own accounts and constructions of their experiences with customers.

In recent years many retail firms have sought to extend their presence overseas,[13] and there has been a globalization of 'the consumer apparatus'.[14] There are compelling reasons to explore developments in China; this country is the world's largest developing market and has become a magnet for multinational retail firms. In addition to interrogating the processes involved in this transitional period, we can also explore the extent to which notions of 'consumer sovereignty' have been diffused to non-Western environments and with what consequences.[15] Du Gay and Salaman argue that the customer is increasingly used as a key source of legitimacy within organizations, with management actions justified in terms of following the dictates of the sovereign consumer.[16]

Globalizing Firms: Local Customers

In contrast to the view that globalization eliminates national and regional differences and homogenizes, anthropological accounts are replete with descriptions of how indigenous peoples make their own sense of imported 'global' products.[17] Studies of MacDonald's in the Asia Pacific, for instance, indicate how consumers across the region make and remake their own differing meanings of the *bête noire* of globalization.[18] Similarly, when management practices developed in one cultural and institutional environment are transferred to alien environments, they do not enter a void. Local employees' consumption of the transferred practices will be coloured by unique configurations of experiences, norms and expectations. The process of consumption is inherently dialectical; transferred practices may both mean and become something rather different in novel contexts.[19] This discussion should also alert us to the probability that the nature of interactive service workers' encounters with customers will vary in different cultural and institutional contexts.

In the retail firms studied for this research the phrase 'the customer is God' (*guke shi shangdi*) was repeated widely by Chinese employees, a sentiment they took to be axiomatic of the situation in Western contexts.[20] Yet, most Chinese people are atheist. Moreover, neither Buddhism nor Confucian philosophy has a god, while Daoism has a bewildering panoply of spirits and immortals (God, which god?). If the consumer is 'god', how then do Chinese people conceive of 'god'? What kinds of relationship do they have with god? Occasionally, employees indigenized the expression, stating that 'the customer is the emperor' (*guke shi huangdi*). Clearly, the implication is of a figure with great power, yet it is worth recalling that China's last emperor was overthrown in 1911.

Retailing in China

In the late 1970s China's state planners identified foreign direct investment (FDI) as a key means to update the nation's economy. Since that time China has been enormously successful in attracting FDI. Between 1978 and the end of 2002,China approved a total of 427,720 FDI projects.[21] The economy has shifted from being uncompetitive and autarkic to one that is open to commercial pressures, with intense competition between private, state, collective and multinational firms. In 1978, for instance, the individual sector accounted for just 0.1 per cent of retail sales: by 1998 37.1 per cent of retail sales of consumer goods were generated by the private sector.[22]

The liberalisation of controls over the retail sector has matched changes in other industrial sectors. China's retail sector has opened gradually to FDI; foreign companies have been allowed to participate in this sector since 1992. In that year the State Council approved the first foreign joint venture retail project, a $100 million scheme by the Japanese company *Yaohan* to build a 120,000 square metre shopping centre in Shanghai's Pudong district.[23] By 1997 there were 500 to 600 retail joint ventures in China.[24] In Shanghai alone, by late 1999, over forty foreign chain stores had been set up with investments by companies such as Carrefour, Isetan, Ikea and B&Q.[25] Before the reform era, customer choice was severely restricted; customers could shop only in state-owned stores. These stores offered poor customer service and sold the same limited range of products at the same prices; there was little incentive for customers to compare stores.[26] Nowadays, retailers must compete to attract and retain customers.

The opening of China's retail sector to domestic competitors and foreign investment has been paralleled by the emergence of a vigorous and re-energized consumerism. During the Maoist era (1949–76), China pursued economic and ideological policies that precluded the emergence of consumerism.[27] Since that time China's social fabric has undergone substantial changes, processes in which the inflow of foreign companies, products and people has been both imbricated with and hastened.[28] The state's legitimacy has become deeply entwined with the ability to deliver improving living standards and there has been a marked shift from deferred gratification to a stress upon consumption and material rewards in the present. Income levels generally have risen, and a 'new wealthy stratum' (*xinfu jieceng*) has emerged.[29] A far greater range of consumer products is available, ration coupons are a thing of the past and there is fierce competition amongst both producers and retailers. In 1993, a year after Deng Xiaoping re-energized economic reforms, local newspapers described a 'consuming passion' and a 'shopping craze' in China's major cities.[30] Between 1992 and 1997 sales of consumer goods rose in value from 46 billion *yuan* to over 132 billion *yuan*.[31] There is ample evidence that China has undergone a revolution in consumption.[32]

In recent years a substantial body of research has focused on service sector employment relations in Western contexts.[33] However, little attention has focused on service sector human resource management in China. This neglect overlooks the rapid rise of the service sector and retailing in particular. Similarly, although there is a developing body of work on China's retail sector,[34] most studies focus on strategy or the technology of retailing rather than employment relations or customer service.[35]

The Research Sites

The data for this chapter are derived from research undertaken in China between 1999 and 2003 at four stores owned by the British multinational retailer, UKStore.[36] Over 120 semi-structured interviews were conducted with a cross-section of local employees and expatriate staff. These stores were located in two different cities; shorter visits were made to three other stores owned by the firm. Research at JStore was carried out between 2001 and 2003 in Japan and 2002 and 2003 in China. Research in Japan focused primarily upon company policy and strategy; in China fifty semi-structured interviews were conducted with local employees and expatriate managers at three stores in two different cities. The author's facility in Chinese permitted interviews with employees to be conducted on a one-to-one basis without the necessity for a translator. The firms shared an explicit strategy to replicate as closely as possible their parent-country approach to customer service. This approach was facilitated by operating on 'greenfield' sites with no established workforce.

UK-invested Stores: UKStore

> When you first come over, you think England and how they shop. You need to understand why they shop the way they do here, then you can start to compromise and use things

from the UK and put in the good points from Chinese culture. (Expatriate project manager)

In June 1999 StoreCo became the first major UK retailer to enter mainland China, when it opened a purpose-built decorative materials warehouse store, UKStore, in Shanghai. Up to September 2003 a further twelve stores had opened in various cities, with the intention to open a total of 60 stores by the end of 2007. For the first year of operations two expatriate managers filled the assistant store manager and store manager roles. Since 2000 responsibility for day-to-day store management has been transferred to locally recruited managers. The market is increasingly competitive, with competition from state and private stores as well as other foreign-invested firms.

The company sought to replicate its UK format, for instance in terms of racking, displays and store appearance. In the Chinese context, some aspects transferred from the UK were relatively novel. Examples were 'touch and feel' displays that allowed customers to feel the products. In pre-reform China, as in America until the Second World War,[37] most stores did not permit customers to touch products. However, UKStore had to make some adaptations to meet the expectations of local customers. For instance, displays were more elaborate than their UK equivalents. Similarly, Chinese customers were more brand-orientated and the company moved to group displays by brand rather than purely by function.

The Chinese stores had more employees than UK stores of a comparable size. This partly reflected lower labour costs in China, but additionally customers had higher expectations of customer service. The notion of self-service was new to China and customers had to learn how to shop in a new way. An expatriate manager explained that 'people aren't used to just picking up the product, putting it in a basket and taking it to the checkout. Customers have asked us how to buy things'. In addition to expecting staff to help them reach down products from the shelves and carry goods to the checkout, customers also asked sales staff more questions about the products than in the UK.

UKStore's Attraction to Consumers

Shanghai people are very conscious of getting value for money. Customers here are very demanding, much more so than in Taiwan,[38] and even more so than in the UK. For example, if people buy a stack of timber in the UK, they'll buy it if there are no visible marks, but here people carefully check each sheet of fifteen for the quality. (Expatriate operations director)

Employees suggested a range of motives for customers to shop at UKStore. These rested partly upon visible, objective features such as the large range of merchandise at reasonable prices and the attractive store environment. The importance of trust was also a recurring theme; customers' need for trust reflected the fact that these purchases were amongst the most substantial in their lives. Typically, new apartments were empty shells; the purchaser received only a concrete box. In Shanghai, for example, homebuyers had to spend an average of 150,000 to 180,000 yuan (£11,540 to £13,850) on decoration and the work would take around six weeks. Even though UKStore's prices were approximately half their UK equivalent and average incomes about one-tenth of those in the UK, the average sale per customer was higher. As a consequence of the importance of the purchase, customers took great care in selecting products.

Ironically, after half a century of propaganda denigrating the role of foreigners and foreign firms in China and 'long-standing ambivalence toward foreign involvement in the Chinese economy',[39] the store's foreign ownership was a source of attraction. A marketing executive at UKStore believed that, 'in terms of it being a foreign company, it doesn't matter if it's the government or the ordinary people; they all have a sense of reassurance (*fangxingan*), even a feeling of infatuation (*miliangan*) towards a large multinational company'. To promote this image, the company made extensive use of the senior British expatriate's image in its advertising campaigns.

The attraction of foreign companies derived in part from a general sense that things foreign were 'modern' and of better quality. A showroom customer assistant had found that 'customers have a trusting attitude (*xinren taidu*) towards UKStore as it's a UK-invested enterprise'. Some practical considerations lay behind this trust in a foreign multinational. Before investing, all foreign firms are vetted by the Chinese authorities and retailers must demonstrate their secure financial status before they are granted a business licence. Additionally, local customers know that multinationals are concerned about their brand image and are susceptible to having this image tarnished by adverse publicity.

Customers' fear of buying inferior quality or fake products encouraged them to shop at UKStore. Under the command economy products were frequently of low quality. In the reform era, this problem has been compounded by rampant copyright infringement and markets awash with fake products, everything from Viagra and cosmetics to aircraft parts, DVDs and computer software. A hardware department deputy supervisor remarked that 'Shanghai's ordinary people buy goods here as they feel the price is okay, but especially as they feel reassured about the quality'.

Although being a foreign-invested store was a source of competitive advantage, it also raised customers' expectations. For instance, it was assumed that prices would be higher than in local stores. Additionally, a checkout department supervisor had noticed that 'customers are very severe to UKStore as it's a foreign firm. With a local store they'd be more lenient. You have a different feeling; if I go to a foreign store, I feel that I have more power'. Similarly, a store manager observed: 'if we do something wrong, as a foreign firm it will get shown on TV, but this won't happen with a Chinese-owned store'.

Customer service was perceived as another key factor that attracted customers. Some employees had previously worked in other retail stores and could compare UKStore's approach to customer service. Former employees of state-owned stores considered UKStore's approach to be different; whereas it was 'customer-orientated', their former workplaces were 'employee-orientated'. A customer assistant in the receiving section, for example, remarked that 'the special order system here is better than at other stores, a state store wouldn't bother to order specially for people'. Similarly, a building materials department customer assistant, formerly employed in a state department store, commented that it had been 'the old style, eating from the big pot (*chi daguofan* – a synonym for a poor work ethic), not going out of your way to help customers. We didn't stress customer service like we do here'. Attracting customers to the store was considered by employees to depend heavily upon particularistic bases of trust. A supervisor in the receiving section believed that, 'if we have good service, news about this will get spread by word-of-mouth very quickly, much faster than by thousands of yuan spent on advertising'.

Many retailers in China operate with large numbers of vendors' representatives in their stores. In the case of faulty goods and returns it can be difficult to gain satisfaction from these outlets. An attraction of UKStore was that the company itself engaged with vendors on customers' behalf. The firm had also transferred from the UK its one-month no quibble returns policy. This was an innovative feature that helped secure customers' trust, since local stores operated more restrictive policies on returns. UKStore's employees contrasted their firm with the situation at outlets operated by *getihu*, small-scale private entrepreneurs, which were said to ignore customer complaints. A showroom supervisor explained:

> There are many *getihu* that sell products more cheaply, but customers come here as they feel reassured and have our promise (*chengnuo*). *Getihu* may be here today gone tomorrow and cannot be found when there's a quality problem. Customers feel that just once in this life they spend this much, so they come here even if it costs more as they feel assured.

Customers' expectations with regard to customer service were rising steeply. A store manager observed that 'in terms of their buying behaviour Chinese customers used to be concerned only about price. Now they want customer service and respect; they want it to be, "I'm your owner, you do something for me"'. A receiving section supervisor remarked astringently 'in China, if somebody spends one *yuan*, they want one thousand *yuan* worth of service'.

As mentioned above, producing sales and thereby assuring the firm's success was seen to depend heavily upon creating a basis of trust. In part, the creation of trust depended upon systemic features such as the returns policy; however, it was also grounded in and dependent upon the customer service provided by individual staff members.

The Shopping Process in China: Reports from the 'Front Line'

From interviews with sales staff it was evident that much customer behaviour could be construed as culturally constructed and as reflecting differing modes of human interaction in the Chinese context. Most customers did not visit the store alone, especially on their first visit. Many were married couples. Often they brought their child and/or grandparents, a reflection of the fact that frequently three generations live under one roof or, at least, in close proximity. Typically, customers also brought the labour contractor who would lead the work team that would undertake the decoration work.

The ways in which customers reached buying decisions were said by store employees to differ in accordance with their age and gender. Where older people asked more questions and exercised caution in buying products, younger customers decided quickly and were attracted by products' aesthetic attributes rather than their pure functionality. Similarly, female customers were perceived as concerned with detail in the buying process, while male customers made faster purchasing decisions. Sales staff also remarked upon differences that they attributed to customers' regional origins, income and educational levels.

As in Western contexts, managers sought to recruit those who held customer-orientated values. Those responsible for recruitment at UKStore emphasized that while educational qualifications and experience were important, personality was crucial. The desired values were reinforced and refined through induction and post-induction training, performance appraisals and general socialization. As in the call-centres studied by Korczynski in Australia, Japan and the USA,[40] workers were regularly exhorted to 'stand in the customer's viewpoint'. A training video shown to new recruits during induction reminded them to ask themselves in all situations, 'am I doing this for the customer?'

The basic elements of customer service training were taught, often using role-play exercises in which employees took the part of customers, in induction training and post-induction training, the latter often occurring during the daily morning briefing sessions. The form of customer service style inculcated at UKStore matched contemporary UK norms and preferences.[41] Thus employees were instructed to approach customers only when they looked directly at a product and appeared to require help; they should then maintain a distance of one metre from the customer. It was apparent that training messages had reached home. A hardware section deputy supervisor recalled how, at his former state store, 'some employees ignored customers, here you should go up to them if they fix their gaze on a product'. Moreover, whether learnt from their training or picked up from the prevailing *Zeitgeist* in China since the 1990s when this phrase was widely disseminated, employees made frequent reference to the customer as God. For instance, a decorative materials deputy supervisor stated: 'we're patient with customers as the customer is God. Even if the customer is unreasonable, we're still patient'. Similarly, a flooring and tiles deputy supervisor remarked that, 'some employees get upset by customers. I tell them not to argue with customers as, after all, the customer is God (*guke bijing shi shangdi*)'.

In some instances, customers appropriated for themselves the role of God or master and sought to exert direct control over sales staff. A showroom deputy supervisor observed that 'customers are unreasonable because there are lots of competitors, some treat us like servants'. Similarly, a service desk supervisor encountered several unreasonable customers each week. As she expressed it, 'sometimes the customer feels that s/he is God and goes beyond the bounds of what we can do. They feel, "I'm God; you're just here to serve me"'.

As some of these quotes suggest, there was a world of difference between treating the customer as if he or she were God and actually believing this to be the case. While the customer might be encouraged to consume the myth of sovereignty, they were to be carefully controlled and regulated. It was recognized that customers could make unreasonable demands; they were people who, literally, 'do not speak with reason' (*bu jiang daoli*). The returns desk witnessed the largest proportion of unreasonable customers. Perhaps emboldened by the lenient returns policy, customers could seek to gain advantage from this. Every employee had their favourite story of unreasonableness, such as the customer who returned a defective light bulb and sought compensation for the long taxi journey they had made to return the product. Because they were buying products, customers saw themselves as having a right to control their encounters with cashiers. Meanwhile, cashiers sought to exert control over encounters in order to carry out their role effectively and efficiently. In supermarkets in Israel, Rafaeli reports a similar 'struggle for control' between cashiers and customers.[42] In UKStore, as in these Israeli supermarkets, employees needed to retain control not least since they were held responsible for errors in stocktaking and excessive shrinkage. The inherent ambiguity of the interaction emerged clearly in a showroom sales expert's explanation that, in seeking to make a sale, 'it's vital to have persuasion for customers'. Moments later he remarked that, 'you have to do what customers say'.

Employees as Experts, Customers as Students

> If you explain well, people will feel that you're an expert (*neihang*) and will do business with you. (Showroom, sales expert)

> You persuade customers to buy by introducing the products well. (Decorative materials and lighting, customer assistant)

In the same way as Bin Zhao distinguishes 'Confucian consumers', so too there were distinctively Chinese dimensions to the interactions between customers and store employees.[43] A recurring feature of sales staff–customer interactions was the degree to which both parties sought to establish particularistic style bases of trust. In these encounters sales staff described two morally positive ideal type relationships for themselves: that of expert and that of friend. These depictions mesh with the extensive research in China that has focused on the nature of *guanxi*, 'connections'.[44] The term *guanxi* refers to 'dyadic, personal relations between people who can make demands on each other'.[45]

The first of the ideal roles was that of expert. The term used most often by sales staff was *neihang* – literally someone who knows the inner workings of a trade. Occasionally this was replaced by the rather more formal term *zhuanjia*, specialist or expert. In this role sales staff were a source of knowledge and expertise, while customers were students or apprentices to be trained in aspects such as the variety, nature and use of products and the mode of shopping at the store. The need to interact and find common ground with customers and the importance of product knowledge were all evident in the following explanation from an electrical and lighting department deputy supervisor:

> Customers ask lots of questions even though they bring the decoration work team boss with them. They ask because they still want to understand the product's composition, use and quality, etc. They still want to have an interaction (*jiaoliu*). Also they may not entirely trust (*fangxin*) the work team boss and fear that he wants to cheat them. We don't have a conflict of interest with the customers, we just do the sale.

A notable aspect of this comment is that the employee considers himself to be in a neutral and impartial role with respect to the customer. He appropriates the role of expert in a rational bureaucracy rather than active agent of a profit-maximizing enterprise.

At times, customers were portrayed as blank sheets or empty vessels, ready and willing to be led by sales staff provided that they possessed the requisite skill.[46] As the deputy supervisor just quoted remarked, 'few people know much about the products as they often just decorate once. Customers are a blank sheet (*kongbai*) when they come in and have to ask you everything'. In offering guidance on products' price, quality, variety, use and maintenance, employees acted as teachers or experts. This role could extend into that of advisor or consultant as they suggested the best match between products in terms of style and aesthetic quality. A flooring and tiles department deputy supervisor linked this role with his own motive for joining UKStore: 'it's part of the company culture to give the customer inspiration (*linggan*). I learnt this during training; it is showing respect for people. These aspects attracted me'. In some instances the teacher–student relationship could verge on a paedocratisation of the customer. A returns desk customer assistant explained how she dealt with difficult customers: 'if they're angry, you say a couple of words to soothe them, then they'll quietly wait there just like children. First you listen to the customer; then you tell them that you'll help to solve the problem'.

In early twentieth-century American department stores, '[s]aleswomen were convinced of their customers' ignorance about merchandise and often made no secret of it; they were the professionals, their customers the amateurs'.[47] In UKStore, sales staff were not always so convinced of their abilities and the student–expert role could, occasionally, be reversed. A paint and decoration department customer assistant, for instance, explained how his product knowledge had developed. This had accumulated not only from training by the company and vendors but also from learning, 'from customers who are experts (*neihang*)'.

These examples indicate how foreign-invested retail outlets can play a part in educating consumers. Watson found similar evidence when the first McDonald's restaurant in China provided consumer education on how to eat its hamburgers.[48] This role also had a potential downside, evident in the comment of an administration department supervisor that 'customers ask lots of questions, they treat you as an expert (*zhuanjia*). If you say something wrong, they'll make a complaint, this can be very difficult to deal with'.

Customers as Friends

> Most customers come here about ten times in the decorating process, so it's like seeing an old friend. (Decorative materials, customer assistant)

> My sales are very high. When customers return, they look for me, many customers see me as a friend and call for me if I'm on a break. (Receiving section, sales expert)

Employees often characterized the relationship between themselves and customers as akin to that between friends. A newly appointed store manager had noticed that returns were a recurring problem at her former store. Her solution was to give complainants her business card and mobile phone number. They phone her 'and then become friends and introduce their friends. In this way they trust me'. Employees could also find a shared base with customers. A checkout supervisor had discovered that a customer came from the area where she lived, 'now she always seeks me out for help with any problems. We have a shared point (*gongtong dian*) as we're neighbours, so she trusts me'. In some instances, the roles of friend and expert overlapped. A timber department deputy supervisor commented: 'customers need to come three or four times and we train (*peixun*) the customers. When they come again, they feel that you're a friend'.

Creating an actual or a surrogate friendship not only provided a basis of trust, it also bound both parties into the norms and expectations of this relationship in Chinese society. A showroom sales expert pointed this out, when he reflected on the way 'customers have feelings, so when they return they'll feel embarrassed if they don't buy something'. This observation illustrates the reciprocal obligation that is often implicit in particularistic relations in China. Friendship involves affect or feeling (*ganqing*), which brings an obligation to reciprocate; not to do so would risk losing face.[49]

Customers as Enemies

Sales staff sometimes referred to themselves as being on the 'front line'. They used this term in the sense of being the employees who engaged directly with customers. However, there were occasions when the potentially confrontational connotations of this metaphor had real resonance. In these encounters, customers could be negotiators, opponents or parasites, categories that sometimes overlapped. During his first year in China an expatriate manager had found that 'selling here one is much more used to negotiating'. In some local stores it was possible to bargain over prices, and UKStore had altered this local practice with its regime of fixed prices.

Customers could view the firm with suspicion and as a potential opponent. A hardware department customer assistant explained that 'customers ask very detailed questions since for many people this is the first time they decorate and they fear to get ripped-off'. Meanwhile, staff could perceive customers as opponents to be outwitted in terms of preventing theft, although levels of theft were lower than in the UK. At an extreme level, customers could become opponents in court cases. However, the main area where customers became opponents was with respect to returns. When acting as store manager in the first UKStore, a UK expatriate had discovered that:

> Customers really get on their high horse over refunds; we can easily get a crowd of fifty people. The UK idea of customer service is higher; we want to avoid a scene. When I come down, I always say that I won't talk to people who shout. The staff are very protective of me. They know that I'll be very lenient; they prefer to have the battle themselves and may tell the customer that I'm away. The UK view is to give the customer the benefit of the doubt, but customers are so much more demanding here.

In some instances, customers appropriated store space in ways that could verge on the parasitical. A decorative materials and lighting department customer assistant had noticed that, 'as UKStore is large, some people bring their children here just to play'. An assistant store manager could cite instances where customers had tried to return defective products purchased in other stores. In another store, the store manager motioned to a group of customers relaxing on the store's display of garden chairs. It was, he complained, a common occurrence for customers to convert this zone into private space and to relax in this way for two or three hours.

Japanese-Invested Stores: JStore

> In Japan they put the customer first, but in China to put the customer first is a new concept. The Japanese stress customer service, standing in the customers' viewpoint.

Before, at Chinese stores, staff ignored customers. Each time we get paid, they tell us the customers pay this salary. (Personnel manager)

JStore is a major retail firm in Japan and has three stores in China. The first store opened in 1997 and further stores were planned. JStore is categorized as a general merchandise store; it comprises a mixture of a department store and a supermarket. Food sales accounted for about 50 per cent of turnover. A store manager remarked that, 'the aim is to make the store become local residents' refrigerator'. Surveys showed that many customers visited the store three or four times per week.

Like UKStore, JStore sought to implement its parent company retail format, including not only store layout and procedures but also employment relations and customer service.[50] JStore shared some characteristics with UKStore but there were also significant differences. Although both firms had relatively flat organisational hierarchies, JStore made greater use of expatriates, with most senior positions held by Japanese staff, including all store manager roles. As with UKStore, the number of employees per store was higher than in the parent country. For example, one JStore had 640 full-time and 300 temporary staff. A store in Japan of comparable size would have about 100 regular staff, 100 part-time 'arbeito' and 100 temporary staff. However, this JStore also had two to three times more customers than a comparably sized store in Japan, with an average of 35,000 to 40,000 per day making purchases at the weekend and 25,000 on weekdays. Up to three times this number might pass through the store. This compared with around 1,000 customers per weekday and 1,500 at weekends at one of the UKStores.

Expatriate Japanese managers, like their British counterparts, noticed that Chinese customers had rising expectations of customer service. Similarly, the demands of this foreign firm were higher than those upon local stores. The firm's senior expatriate recalled that when the first store opened, it had easily provided the best customer service in the city, but that it now had to struggle hard to retain this status. He added that whereas 'at first customers had rarely seen such good service, now they take this for granted and expect more and more'. A store manager concluded that 'China has gone from a time when stores selected customers, to an era where customers select the store'. Another store manager considered that customers' demands had been boosted following the SARs outbreak in 2003, as consumers' desire for quality products had increased.

In her study of supermarket cashiers in Jerusalem, Rafaeli quotes a cashier: 'The customer is paying for the merchandise. But he is not paying my salary. Why does he think he can tell me what to do?'[51] Rafaeli explores the way in which cashiers and customers had different perceptions of who had the right to control the process of the interaction between them. Cashiers, who considered the checkout process a part of their job, were observed to develop strategies to maintain control of their encounters with customers. In JStore, employees received a rather different message. In a distinct step towards the cult of the consumer, during a store-wide morning briefing session I attended, the Japanese store manager told the assembled staff that, 'the customers are our parents, they give us our salary'.

JStore's emphasis on customer service as a source of differentiation was even more marked than at UKStore. The firm's chief executive in China described politeness to customers (*daike de limao*) as the key feature that would attract and retain customers. Despite the large volume of customers, for example, employees were expected to bow and welcome each one. The approach to customer service interactions was more prescriptive and detailed than UKStore's. Correspondingly, training was more intensive and extensive and also more likely to be provided by expatriates than by local staff. Recruits appointed before store openings underwent three months' training, with attention to company history, product knowledge, job content, dress and appearance, use of the 'six polite phrases' (such as 'please wait a moment', 'I'm sorry', 'thank you'), appropriate gestures and behaviour and bowing.[52] Training stressed the necessity for employees to abide by strict dress and behavioural codes and to show faultless, high levels of enthusiasm and politeness to customers. A checkout assistant who had previously worked in a state store remarked that 'people there were lazy, we often ignored customers. The atmosphere was not good, because of the poor management style. The supervisors and managers stayed in their offices reading the newspaper and didn't come out, not like the bosses here'. Another checkout assistant recalled: 'during induction training we're told two rules. Rule one, the customer is always right. Rule two, when the customer is wrong please refer to rule one'; an echo across time and space from Philadelphia, via Tokyo, to, in this case, western China of John Wanamaker's slogan 'the customer is always right'.[53]

JStore sought to codify and stipulate the behaviour required in detailed training manuals and the employee handbook, with fines imposed for transgressions. The employee handbook contained approximately three times more rules than that used in Japan. Store managers attributed the need for extensive and detailed rules to different behaviour standards in Japan and China. For example, rules such as those instructing employees not to spit and to pick up rubbish were seen as unnecessary in Japan, since employees would observe this behaviour without being instructed.

Correct customer service was reinforced in post-induction training. A personnel officer remarked that 'we're a training school (*peixun xuexiao*) since we need to keep training and to check constantly that employees are doing what they're supposed to do'. For instance, bowing and polite phrases were practised and repeated every morning at store-wide and departmental briefing sessions (see Figure 7).

As at UKStore, role plays were a common means of conveying customer-orientated values. Following these sessions, the general manager, his deputy and three other Japanese managers, along with six local staff acting as 'greeters', assembled by the store's main door. Forming two phalanxes, they waited for the door to open and bowed and repeated 'Good morning, welcome to the store!' to the day's first customers (see Figure 8). Initially, it appears, Chinese customers had been rather startled by this welcome but had now become accustomed to it.[54]

Figure 7 Early Morning Bowing Practice at a Japanese-Invested Store in China, 2003

Source: Jos Gamble.

Figure 8 The Store Doors Open at a Japanese-Invested Store in China and the Day's First Customers Enter, 2003

Source: Jos Gamble.

Even with constant reinforcement, though, it was not always possible to maintain the high level of customer service that was required. A store manager observed that 'after a while employees sometimes leave the customers' viewpoint and stand in the store's viewpoint. They need to stay in the customers' viewpoint. We educate employees to stand in the customers' viewpoint and not be somebody who does business (*zuo shengyi*)'.

Customer Service Interactions at JStore

To an extent the forms of customer–sales staff interactions at JStore overlapped with those at UKStore. The rhetoric of the customer as God was similar and, although it appeared weaker, the perception of customers as friends was also present. For instance, a customer assistant in the men's clothing section explained: 'I treat customers like friends and then introduce the products. In this way, you reduce the distance between yourself and the customers'. Sales staff remarked that some customers liked to visit the store every day and have a chat. A meat section customer assistant was proud of the frequent customers (*lao guke*) who asked for him by name, who sought his recommendations and had him cut and prepare their meat. The perception of employees as 'experts' was less evident. This difference can be attributed to the reduced contact time per customer compared to UKStore and the fact that the products were usually familiar to customers and required less explanation, although this depended on the section involved. A women's clothing section customer assistant, for instance, reported that customers asked many questions about products and added: 'when the customer comes to your area, you should introduce the products and then their desire to purchase (*goumai yuwang*) will be aroused'.

Two categories that appeared more common at JStore were those of customer as guest and as family member. A housewares section customer assistant explained that if you showed politeness and warmth to customers, including smiling, this would give them 'a feeling of closeness (*qinqiegan*) as if they're at home, like you're their closest relatives'. A checkout assistant remarked that, 'some customers are prejudiced, they feel, "By coming here, I'm giving money to the Japanese." But they also feel that customer service is very good, so they feel very happy. It gives customers a feeling as if they're returning home (*huijia de ganjue*)'. As a children's clothing section customer assistant described it, their customer service ensured that customers felt like 'a guest who feels as if they are at home (*binzhi rugui de ganjue*)'.

Sales staff found provision of this emotional labour exhausting. However, although such labour was demanding and stressful, they took pride in providing what they considered the best customer service available. Convinced of this superiority, they were aware of both locally owned and other foreign stores' attempts to mimic their company's customer service and astute critics of their failure to live up to JStore's high standards.

Work on the checkout was particularly stressful; a situation exacerbated by high staff turnover that frequently left the section understaffed. One checkout assistant, for instance, recalled that of fifty new recruits who had joined with him five years before in 1998, just two were left. Another assistant explained how seventeen new checkout staff had recently been recruited. Of these, seven left during training and, of those who actually started, 'some left before you even knew their name, you just see their face once and that's it, you never see them again'. Significantly, these roles were amongst the most Taylorized in the store and also allowed the least space for meaningful interactions with customers or other employees. These factors undoubtedly contributed to the high labour turnover. As at UKStore, returns were a particular source of stress. A returns section deputy supervisor remarked that some products could not be returned, such as underwear. She explained that 'if you stand in the other customers' viewpoint, you cannot return them'. This view indicates the elasticity and flexibility of the rhetoric of the customer; here it serves to differentiate one customer from another.

Conclusion

Both the Japanese and UK-invested stores sought to transfer and implement their parent country's visions of the consumer and of customer service. These notions were underpinned by an array of human resource management practices, including selection and recruitment of those with customer-orientated values, as well as training, discipline and incentive strategies. If anything, the rhetoric of the sovereign consumer was most pronounced at JStore, where the customer was said even to pay the salary. Company strategies extended to schemes to train customers in the appropriate means to consume in these new consumption venues. However, both customers and sales staff remain embedded in complex institutional and cultural contexts that defy such hegemonic projects. The imported practices were understood and interpreted in accordance with local norms and patterns of behaviour.

In the scale of things, the rhetoric of the sovereign customer appeared quite positive for sales staff. Chinese retail store employees, like their counterparts around the world,[55] were often attracted by the opportunities to interact with other people. Additionally, firms sought to recruit those with such personalities and to develop further the skills involved. As in other service work contexts,[56] interaction with customers and playing an active part in ensuring customers' satisfaction were key elements that brought employees both pride and pleasure. A typical comment was one made by a deputy supervisor in UKStore's decorative materials and lighting department: 'the greatest sense of achievement comes from when a customer arrives knowing nothing and through my explanation they buy something and are happy'. Indeed a key frustration for front-line workers was when their job was structured in such a way that they were unable to deliver the form of emotional labour they would like to.[57] Such a disjuncture was evident among cashiers at JStore, where the time and space available for interaction with both colleagues and customers was most attenuated. Their high turnover rate may be closely related to the lack of potential for engaging in meaningful social interaction and indicates limits to the proliferation of deskilled McJobs predicted by George Ritzer.[58]

If we return to the comments on 'God' in Chinese society, it is tempting to note that traditionally in China the spirit world is perceived as a parallel universe replete with familiar figures of the earthly world, for instance officials that need bribing.[59] In the same way, relations with customers are a microcosm of human relations outside the workplace; trust, for instance, must be built in similar ways. Retail employees' encounters with customers were socially embedded and there was much evidence of the ways in which both parties sought to create or at least replicate generally understood, valued and accepted categories of interaction. The relationships developed or imputed at UKStore appeared generally to have more 'depth' than those at JStore. However, in both firms the creation of meaningful relationships was common and significant. Differences between the relationships with customers in UKStore and JStore were dependent upon a range of factors, such as differences in job roles, extent of consumers' existing knowledge about products, the cost of products and their relative importance to the customer's life project, the time available per sale and duration of customer contact, company policy with regard to transactions, nationality of the store's ownership and the gender, age and social status of customers *vis-à-vis* employees.

Gabriel and Lang remark on the way both Marx and Simmel perceived the cash nexus to dissolve social bonds.[60] This chapter has indicated the extent to which customers and sales staff sought to re-embed these exchanges in social relations and to reinsert at least a weak or surrogate version of meaningful social bonds. The need for reassurance based upon particularistic trust was especially important when consumers were making purchases that were important to their life project, as in home decoration. In part, at least, customers' urge to develop a relationship with interactive service workers appears to reflect insufficient trust in systems. In the context of weak institutional environments, where the ground rules of economic interaction could be opaque,[61] individuals sought reassurance in particularistic relationships. This absence of trust was also reflected in employees' frequent refrain on the efficacy of word-of-mouth in attracting customers to the stores.

This chapter has led us far from the abstract, one-dimensional and atomized figure of 'the consumer' and presented a diverse array of embodied customers engaged in interactions with sales staff. The findings highlight the productive capacity inherent in the interaction between global capitalism and local contexts; these encounters might 'bring new homogeneity, but equally spawn new heterogeneity'.[62] The comparative study of UK-invested and Japanese-invested firms has demonstrated how shopping might be 'divided into a series of "genres", each of which lends itself to distinct forms of social relations and symbolic systems'.[63] Indeed, one could produce a richly nuanced ethnographic account of different styles of shopping, modes of customer service interaction and diverse labour processes even within a single store.

Consumers have occasionally been portrayed as victims.[64] From this perspective, consumers in the developing world are perceived to be particularly vulnerable. This approach seems precariously lodged between humanistic concern and a nouveau orientalism. To portray the consumers explored in this chapter as victims of a rampant multinational capitalist hegemony would be a gross distortion. Customers in these foreign-owned retail stores readily, sometimes aggressively, asserted their rights as consumers. In China, at least, the consumer citizen appears increasingly distant from the 'timid figure at the borders of contemporary consumption' depicted by Gabriel and Lang.[65] Local consumers' higher expectations of foreign-invested stores provided a fertile basis to strengthen notions of the consumer as citizen. The assertion of the right to consume goods and customer service of increasingly improved quality, to be able to reject defective or unwanted products and to demand accountability from firms might have analogies in the political sphere. It is, perhaps, from just such quotidian encounters that deep-rooted social changes might develop.

Notes

*I would like to acknowledge the support of the ESRC/AHRB Cultures of Consumption programme award number RES-143-25-0028 for the project 'Multinational Retailers in the Asia Pacific', and a British Council China Studies Grant. I would also like to thank Frank Trentmann for his valuable advice and comments on this chapter.

1. J. Gamble, *Shanghai in Transition: Changing Perspectives and Social Contours of a Chinese Metropolis* (London, 2003), p. *215, note 4*.
2. See, for instance, E.J. Hardy, *John Chinaman at Home: Sketches of Men, Manners and Things in China* (London, 1907).
3. See, for example, Y. Gabriel and T. Lang, *The Unmanageable Consumer: Contemporary Consumption and Its Fragmentations* (London, 1995); P. Rosenthal, R. Peccei and S. Hill, 'Academic Discourses of the Customer: "Sovereign Beings", "Management Accomplices" or "People Like Us"?' in A. Sturdy, I. Grugulis and H. Willmott (eds), *Customer Service: Empowerment and Entrapment* (London, 2001) and M. Korczynski, *Human Resource Management in Service Work* (New York, 2002).
4. Gabriel and Lang, *Unmanageable Consumer*.

5. Gabriel and Lang, *Unmanageable Consumer*, p. 5.
6. F. Trentmann, 'The Modern Genealogy of the Consumer: Meanings, Identities and Political Synapses before Affluence' in J. Brewer and F. Trentmann (eds), *Consuming Cultures, Global Perspectives* (Oxford and New York, forthcoming), ch. 2.
7. See, for example, M. Douglas and B. Isherwood, *The World of Goods: Towards an Anthropology of Consumption* (Harmondsworth, 1978) and Gabriel and Lang, *Unmanageable Consumer*, pp. 47–67.
8. For a valuable exception which investigates customers' perspectives on everyday shopping in a Western context, see D. Miller, P. Jackson, N. Thrift, B. Holbrook and M. Rowlands, *Shopping, Place and Identity* (London, 1998).
9. For an excellent exception see R. Leidner, *Fast Food, Fast Talk: Service Work and the Routinization of Everyday Life* (Berkeley, CA, 1993).
10. See H.W. Wong, *Japanese Bosses, Chinese Workers: Power and Control in a Hong Kong Megastore* (Richmond, 1999); L. Matsunaga, *The Changing Face of Japanese Retail: Working in a Chain Store* (London, 2000); K. Broadbent, *Women's Employment in Japan: The Experience of Part-time Workers* (London, 2003).
11. See, for example, A. Rafaeli, 'When Cashiers Meet Customers: An Analysis of the Role of Supermarket Cashiers', *Academy of Management Journal*, 32(2) (1989), pp. 245–73 and Leidner, *Fast Food, Fast Talk*.
12. Gabriel and Lang, *Unmanageable Consumer*, p. 20.
13. See K. Davies and F. Ferguson, 'The International Activities of Japanese Retailers', *The Service Industries Journal*, 15(4) (1995), pp. 97–117; G. Akehurst and N. Alexander, *The Internationalisation of Retailing* (London, 1996); R. Shackleton, 'Exploring Corporate Culture and Strategy: Sainsbury at Home and Abroad during the Early to Mid 1990s', *Environment and Planning A*, 30 (1998), pp. 921–40.
14. P.N. Stearns, *Consumerism in World History: The Global Transformation of Desire* (London, 2001), p. 16.
15. These ideas have been explored in a Western context by P. Du Gay and G. Salaman, 'The Cult[ure] of the Customer', *Journal of Management Studies*, 29(5) (1992), pp. 615–33, and P. Du Gay, *Consumption and Identity at Work* (London, 1996).
16. For an exploration of the way organisations seek to reify the sovereign consumer and imbricate and utilize customer feedback in the labour process, see L. Fuller and V. Smith, 'Consumers' Reports: Management by Customers in a Changing Economy', *Work, Employment & Society*, 5(1) (1991), pp. 1–16.
17. See A. Gell, 'Newcomers to the World of Goods: Consumption among Muria Gonds' in A. Appadurai (ed.), *The Social Life of Things: Commodities in Cultural Perspective* (Cambridge, 1986) and J.L. Watson (ed.), *Golden Arches East: McDonald's in East Asia* (Stanford, CA, 1997).

18. Watson, *Golden Arches East.*
19. For an exploration of the way in which a UK retail firm's introduction of its flat organizational hierarchy to China was transformed in subtle and unexpected ways, see J. Gamble, 'Transferring Human Resource Practices from the United Kingdom to China: The Limits and Potential for Convergence', *International Journal of Human Resource Management*, 14(3) (2003), pp. 369–87.
20. For reference to the consumer as 'king' in 1880s Germany, see U. Spiekermann's chapter in this volume.
21. Hong Kong Trade Development Council website, www.tdc.org.hk.
22. Figures from S. Young, 'Wealth but not Security: Attitudes towards Private Business in China in the 1980s', *Australian Journal of Chinese Affairs*, 25 (1991), p. 120, and Hong Kong Trade Development Council website, www.tdc.org.hk.
23. D. Ho and N. Leigh, 'A Retail Revolution', *The China Business Review*, 21(1) (1994), pp. 22–8.
24. A. Goldman, 'The Transfer of Retail Formats into Developing Economies: The Example of China', *Journal of Retailing*, 77(2) (2001), p. 239, note 1.
25. 'Good Opportunity for Retail Sector', *Shanghai Star*, 23 November 1999, p. 7.
26. For the portrayal of a similar scenario in the GDR, see Spiekermann in this volume.
27. See W.L. Parish and M.K. Whyte, *Urban Life in Contemporary China* (Chicago, 1984).
28. These processes are explored in detail in Gamble, *Shanghai in Transition.*
29. For studies on China's new social differentiation, see D.S.G. Goodman, 'The People's Republic of China: The Party-State, Capitalist Revolution and New Entrepreneurs' in R. Robison and D.S.G. Goodman (eds), *The New Rich in Asia: Mobile Phones, McDonald's and Middle Class Revolution* (London, 1996); J. Gamble, 'Stir Fried Stocks: Share Dealers, Trading Places, and New Options in Contemporary Shanghai', *Modern China*, 23(2) (1997), pp. 181–215; C. Buckley, 'How a Revolution Becomes a Dinner Party: Stratification, Mobility and the New Rich in Urban China' in M. Pinches (ed.), *Culture and Privilege in Capitalist Asia* (London, 1999).
30. *China Daily Business Weekly*, 14–20 February 1993, p. 8, and *China Daily*, 22 February 1993, p. 6.
31. *Financial Times Survey*, 19 May 1998, p. 19.
32. See R. Taylor, 'The Emergence of a Consumer Market in China', *Asia Pacific Business Review*, 2(1) (1995), pp. 37–49; *Far Eastern Economic Review*, 'China: Rising Consumer Superpower', 26 November (1998), pp. 37–77; L. Chao and R.H. Myers, 'China's Consumer Revolution: The 1990s and Beyond', *Journal of Contemporary China*, 7(18) (1998), pp. 351–68; D.S. Davis (ed.), *The Consumer Revolution in Urban China* (Berkeley, CA, 2000) and J. Gamble, 'Consumerism with Shanghainese Characteristics: Local Perspectives on China's Consumer Revolution', *Asia Pacific Business Review*, 7(3) (2001), pp. 88–110.

33. See, for example, S.P. Benson, *Counter Cultures: Saleswomen, Managers, and Customers in American Department Stores, 1890–1940*, (Urbanna IL, 1986); Leidner, *Fast Food, Fast Talk*; H.C. Philips and R.P. Bradshaw, 'How Customers Actually Shop: Customer Interaction with the Point of Sale', *Journal of the Market Research Society*, 35 (1993), pp. 51–62; K.F. Winsted, 'The Service Experience in Two Cultures: A Behavioral Perspective', *Journal of Retailing*, 73(3) (1997), pp. 337–60; P. Rosenthal, S. Hill and R. Peccei, 'Checking Out Service: Evaluating Excellence, HRM and TQM in Retailing', *Work, Employment and Society*, 11(3) (1997), pp. 481–503; A. Sturdy, I. Grugulis and H. Willmott (eds) *Customer Service: Empowerment and Entrapment* (London, 2001) and Korczynski, *Human Resource Management*.

34. See K. Davies, 'Foreign Investment in the Retail Sector of the People's Republic of China', *Columbia Journal of World Business*, 29(3) (1994), pp. 56–69; W.-K. Chan, J. Perez, A. Perkins and M. Shu, 'China's Retail Markets Are Evolving More Quickly Than Many Companies Anticipate', *The McKinsey Quarterly*, 2 (1997), pp. 206–11; R. Letovsky, D.M. Murphy and R.P. Kenny, 'Entry Opportunities and Environmental Constraints for Foreign Retailers in China's Secondary Cities', *Multinational Business Review*, 5(2) (1997), pp. 28–40; A. Goldman, 'Supermarkets in China: The Case of Shanghai', *International Review of Retail, Distribution and Consumer Research*, 10(1) (2000), pp. 1–21, and Goldman, 'The Transfer of Retail Formats into Developing Economies', pp. 221–42.

35. But see now Gamble, 'Transferring Human Resource Practices from the United Kingdom to China'; J. Gamble, 'Working for *Laowai*: Chinese Shopfloor Workers' Perceptions of Employment in a Western Multinational', presented at Asia Pacific Researchers in Organisation Studies conference, Universidad Autonoma Metropolitana, Iztapalapa, Mexico, 7–10 December 2003; J. Gamble, 'Skills and Training in Multinational Firms: The Perspective from British and Japanese Retailers in China', presented at IIRA 5th Asian Regional Congress Dynamics and Diversity: Employment Relations in the Asia-Pacific Region, Seoul, 23–6 June 2004; J. Gamble, 'Turning Japanese? Chinese Workers in Multinational Retail Firms from Japan', presented at 'Multinationals and the International Diffusion of Organizational Forms and Practices' conference, IESE Barcelona, 15–17 July 2004.

36. Pseudonyms are used for the firms included in this research.

37. Benson, *Counter Cultures*, p. 290.

38. The company began operations in Taiwan in 1995, and this expatriate had worked there for several months.

39. K. Gerth, *China Made: Consumer Culture and the Creation of the Nation* (Cambridge, MA, 2003), p. 357.

40. Korczynski, *Human Resource Management*, p. 93.

41. See Miller *et al.*, *Shopping, Place and Identity*, pp. 118–19.

42. Rafaeli, 'When Cashiers Meet Customers', pp. 259–62. See also K.A. Weatherly and D.A. Tansik, 'Tactics Used by Customer-Contact Workers: Effects of Role Stress, Boundary Spanning and Control', *International Journal of Service Industry Management*, 4(3) (1992), pp. 4–17.
43. B. Zhao, 'Consumerism, Confucianism, Communism: Making Sense of China Today', *New Left Review*, 222 (1997), pp. 43–59.
44. See J.B. Jacobs, 'The Concept of *Guanxi* and Local Politics in a Rural Chinese Cultural Setting', in S.L. Greenblatt, R.W. Wilson and A.A. Wilson (eds), *Social Interaction in Chinese Society* (New York, 1982); M.M. Yang, *Gifts, Favors and Banquets: The Art of Social Relationships in China* (Ithaca, 1994); T. Gold, D. Guthrie and D. Wank (eds), *Social Connections in China: Institutions, Culture, and the Changing Nature of Guanxi* (Cambridge, 2002).
45. R.L. Tung and V. Worm, 'Network Capitalism: The Role of Human Resources in Penetrating the China Market', *International Journal of Human Resource Management*, 12(4) (2001), p. 521.
46. The topic of skills in multinational retail firms is explored in more detail in Gamble, 'Skills and Training in Multinational Firms'.
47. Benson, *Counter Cultures*, p. 261.
48. J.L. Watson, 'Transnationalism, Localization, and Fast Foods in East Asia' in Watson (ed.), *Golden Arches East*, p. 28.
49. For the classic study on reciprocity in Chinese society, see L.-S. Yang, 'The Concept of *Pao* as a Basis for Social Relations in China' in J.K. Fairbank (ed.), *Chinese Thought and Institutions* (Chicago, 1957).
50. See Gamble, 'Turning Japanese?'.
51. Rafaeli, 'When Cashiers Meet Customers', p. 245.
52. Recruits who joined after store openings usually received one week's training.
53. Benson, *Counter Cultures*, p. 93.
54. This practice is examined in more detail in Gamble, 'Turning Japanese?'
55. See, for example, Benson, *Counter Cultures*, p. 216, and Rafaeli, 'When Cashiers Meet Customers', p. 259.
56. See, for example, M.B. Tolich, 'Alienating and Liberating Emotions at Work: Supermarket Clerks' Performance of Customer Service', *Journal of Contemporary Ethnography*, 22(3) (1993), p. 368, and Korczynski, *Human Resource Management*, pp. 76–7, 94–5.
57. Korczynski, *Human Resource Management*, p. 155.
58. G. Ritzer, *The McDonaldization of Society* (London, 1993).
59. See A.P. Wolf, 'Gods, Ghosts, and Ancestors' in A.P. Wolf (ed.), *Religion and Ritual in Chinese Society* (Stanford, CA, 1974).
60. Gabriel and Lang, *Unmanageable Consumer*, p. 174.
61. A topic explored in D. Guthrie, 'Information Asymmetries and the Problem of Perception: The Significance of Structural Position in Assessing the Importance of Guanxi in China', in Gold *et al.*, *Social Connections in China*.

62. D. Miller, *Capitalism: An Ethnographic Approach* (Oxford, 1997), p. 15.
63. Miller, *Capitalism*, p. 301.
64. This dimension is discussed, for example, in Gabriel and Lang, *Unmanageable Consumer*, pp. 117–36.
65. Gabriel and Lang, *Unmanageable Consumer*, pp. 173–84.

–9–

A Becoming Subject
Consumer Socialization in the Mediated Marketplace
Stephen Kline

I hope that every-day readers will excuse my paradoxes; you cannot avoid paradox if you think for yourself and whatever you may say I would rather fall into paradox than into prejudice.

Rousseau, *Emile*

Faced with a rising tide of youth vandalism and violence, on 7 June 2004 the council of the small Quebec border town of Huntington passed a bylaw that placed a 10:30 p.m. curfew on teenagers under the age of 16. The council felt that the curfew would prevent young people who were hanging out in town from being unduly tempted into crime and vandalism. The controversial bylaw immediately became a national *cause célèbre*, condemned as an indiscriminate and ineffective restriction on teen leisure, not only by local teens but by a member of the provincial legislature Andre Chenail, who referred the bylaw to the Quebec human rights commission as an unfair restriction on children's rights. On 14 July 2004 the commission stated that, in its opinion, this legislation might infringe the Provincial Charter of Human Rights and Freedoms by unfairly restricting the freedom of movement and peaceful assembly of law-abiding young people. So the town council decided to fine the teenagers' parents instead.[1] Ironically, Quebec youth are now guaranteed the freedom to hang out with friends in public places, but deprived of the most basic democratic right – the vote – revealing the paradoxical status they have acquired because of their developmental inadequacy.

Another example of this paradox of immaturity recently burst on to front pages around the world in the wake of the World Health Organization's announcement of the globesity epidemic. The medical establishment declared that children were getting fat because their diets were energy dense and their lives were sedentary.[2] Popular writers pilloried the fast-food industries which knowingly preyed on unwitting consumers with constant advertisements and super-sized promotions.[3] The emerging crisis of obesity highlighted the fact that current advertising regulations were unable to protect very young children from 3.2 billion dollars of fast-food promotions every year. A law suit launched against McDonald's in the USA on behalf of three overweight teens was intended to highlight the fact that young people are inadequately informed of the dangers they experience growing up in a fast-food culture.[4]

Weary from guarding the home front against the pervasive influence of expanding commercialization, in Britain food advocates took a different tack, mobilizing around the health and safety risks associated with children's marketing.[5] The evidence they gathered showed that fast-food advertisers subjected children to an overwhelming barrage of advertising for salty, sugary and fattening foodstuffs. They complained that lax regulation of fast-food advertising was the equivalent of handing socialization over to the corporate sector.[6] The National Family and Parenting Institute held a seminar on marketing to children, where Shotbolt reported a study which showed that fast-food 'pester power' fans the flames of conflict in the family, making it ever harder for parents to ensure their children had healthy diets.[7] Supported by the Food Standards Agency's review of the advertising literature, which concluded that food marketing can influence children's preferences,[8] this coalition of advocates have called for a ban on fast-food advertising directed at children.[9]

Opposing these calls to regulate its marketing efforts, the food industry challenged the scientific evidence linking fast-food advertising to rising obesity rates.[10] They argued that, rather than being victims of marketing, young people were becoming increasingly media literate: one proponent pointed to a six year old who was able to tell adults about the benefits of different laundry products. An occasional hamburger or chocolate bar will not make a child fat. Because advertising to kids has such a marginal role in family lifestyle choices, banning it would have little effect. Besides, was it not the parents' responsibility to provide children with healthy food? In the absence of school programmes in nutrition, advertising served a positive educational function, providing vital information to kids about the things they could buy and aspire to with their growing spending power. If the affluent world had an obesity epidemic, it was because bad parents and failed health education were to blame. The head of Kid Smart even suggested that given the advertising industry's familiarity with children, it could play a useful role promoting advertising literacy in schools.[11]

The obesity epidemic brought to a head the long-simmering debate about children's consumer competences and vulnerabilities. The emerging battle between parents and fast-food marketers thus exposed the underlying tensions emerging within the mass-mediated marketplace that set schools, parents and merchandisers in a struggle over children's consumption.[12] On one side are the child protectionists arguing that children's immaturity demands greater regulation of children's cultural industries – especially marketing. On the other stand the child liberationists, arguing that children's media competence merits greater 'freedom of choice' in the marketplace and therefore greater protection from their parents. And in the centre are government policymakers worried about the rising costs of lifestyle risks, who must adjudicate between parents and corporate interests by figuring out how to both protect and prepare young consumers. Viewing the long-standing debates about socialization through a cultural historical lens, this chapter sets out to trace why youthful leisure and lifestyles have become a site of constant struggle over consumer subjectivities in market democracies.[13]

Fathers of the Enlightenment

In all societies, social reproduction depends on childrearing traditions which ensure that knowledge, values and social practices are transmitted between generations. Although the means are diverse, each culture must prepare its young by communicating the beliefs, roles and precepts that enable the young to become self-regulating and productive members of the community. And every community must also ensure that adults accommodate to the task of caring for their young by developing discursive strategies for childrearing that cultivate normative 'subjectivities' and 'competences', including the knowledge, identities and skills that enable the young to participate as full members of their community. In short, every society must construct itself through its children.

Philippe Ariès' 're-discovery of childhood' awakened among cultural historians who had long ignored children a profound desire to reassess modern constructions of childhood.[14] Pointing to the changing representations of children within early modern European paintings, he finds evidence of a widening gap between conceptions of the adult and the child and an expanding reflection on children's growth from innocence to citizenship. Ariès suggests that the modern world's emerging interest in the transformation of the vulnerable child into the rational adult became one of the intellectual pillars of the reformation which eventually overturned the Catholic church's declaration that seven years was the age of moral reason. Tracing the evolving ideas surrounding childrearing, Ariès illustrates both a revival of the classical ideals of formal education and a genuine intrigue with childrearing practices and children's maturational experiences.

The contradictory roots of this modernist rethinking of childhood can be seen in the philosophical reflections of two key 'fathers' of the Enlightenment, Locke and Rousseau. Both were political writers preoccupied with the coexistence of individual freedoms and state power. And like many other liberal thinkers, both held that this issue was only resolved when rational individuals freely agree to be governed in the interests of a general good. It is only through consent that the individual *becomes subject* to the will of the majority. Since they both also rejected the doctrine of original sin, it is hardly surprising that each also wrote thoughtfully on the civilizing process through which rational individuals were able to understand and give their consent to be governed – if from radically opposing paternalistic perspectives.

For Locke, education – the preparation of the young for adult life through appropriate parenting and tutoring – was an urgent mission for a civilized society: 'great care is to be had of the forming children's minds and giving them that seasoning early, which shall influence their lives always after'. Throughout his treatise on education Locke speaks as both a doctor and father, of how failing to feed, clothe and respond to the child appropriately can lead to their ill health, disrespect and indulgence. Responding to the moral panics of his time he states:

> I wish that those who complain of the great decay of Christian piety and virtue ... of this generation, would consider how to retrieve them in the next. This I am sure, that if the foundation of it be not laid in the education and principling of the youth, all other endeavours will be in vain. And if the innocence, sobriety and industry of those who are coming up, be not taken care of and preserv'd, 'twill be ridiculous to expect, that those who are to succeed next on the stage, should abound in that virtue, ability and learning, which has hitherto made England considerable in the world.

For Locke, the young child's unrestrained biological demands implied the careful application of a guiding hand in the long-term interests of the child – and parents. His formula for preparing rational subjects dwells on the ways in which children learn to make their impulses, desires and actions 'subject to the rules and restraints of reason'.[15]

Rousseau agrees with Locke that from the parent's point of view 'the most dangerous period in human life lies between birth and the age of twelve. It is the time when errors and vices spring up, while as yet there is no means to destroy them; when the means of destruction are ready, the roots have gone too deep to be pulled up'. But he refuses Locke's claim that education is achieved by the active instruction of the rational subject through moral guidance, exposure to knowledge and self-discipline, chiding 'You torment the poor thing for his good':

> If the infant sprang at one bound from its mother's breast to the age of reason, the present type of education would be quite suitable, but its natural growth calls for quite a different training. The mind should be left undisturbed till its faculties have developed; for while it is blind it cannot see the torch you offer it, nor can it follow through the vast expanse of ideas a path so faintly traced by reason that the best eyes can scarcely follow it.[16]

Rousseau's belief in the 'natural innocence' of the child is foundational for his approach to the education of the authentically rational subject. 'The mind, bound up within imperfect and half grown organs, is not even aware of its own existence. The movements and cries of the new-born child are purely reflex, without knowledge or will'. But rather than imprinting this *tabula rasa* with adult rationality, he advocates trusting the child's natural instincts: 'Nature provides for the child's growth in her own fashion and this should never be thwarted. Do not make him sit still when he wants to run about, nor run when he wants to be quiet... If we did not spoil our children's wills by our blunders, their desires would be free from caprice'.

Education, then, consists of supporting the child in their natural interests, including pleasure and leisure. Children must be protected from corrupting influences and artificial contrivances of civilization that would alienate their natural being and make them into 'slaves' or 'victims to the excessive care of their fathers and mothers':

> May I venture at this point to state the greatest, the most important, the most useful rule of education? Education of the earliest years should be merely negative. It consists, not in teaching virtue or truth, but in preserving the heart from vice and from the spirit of error.

What he means by this is to refrain from hastening children's ascent to mannered civility, particularly when they are young.

For a long time Locke seemed to be winning the debate about how to educate rational subjects in democratic society. As scholars have emphasized, the history of democracy is deeply entwined with the changing media of communication.[17] Neil Postman has argued that the 'new communication environment' which began to take form in the sixteenth century as a result of printing and social literacy started to have a profound impact on the conception of childhood in the seventeenth and eighteenth centuries. 'Because reading makes it possible to enter a non-observed and abstract world of knowledge, it creates a split between those who cannot read and those who can'.[18] Print culture fostered 'a new definition of adulthood based on reading competence and correspondingly, a new conception of childhood based on reading incompetence'.[19] Thus literacy came to be a key competence separating the status of child and adult. And so it was not just moral reasoning but the ability to read and write that now defined the gulf between child and adult. Without literacy the young were ill prepared to participate in political life. Moreover, 'great books' were morally and ideologically instructive, passing on the thoughts and expectations of society in an uplifting form. This new literacy agenda became the basis of the expanding school system during the nineteenth century that came to see reading, writing and numeracy as the core competences of future citizen-workers. Investment in universal schooling was the sign of the modern state's growing interest in childhood.

The Age of Socialization: Literacy Ascendant

Ariès' work began a quest which has restored the missing child of history. Building on Ariès' observations, psycho-historian Lloyd de Mause draws particular attention to the Victorians' mounting fascination with childhood experience, witnessed in the popular parenting advisories and novels of the eighteenth and nineteenth centuries.[20] De Mause calls this moment in the construction of childhood 'socialization', reflecting the expanding public investment in the control of children in schools and public places which brought the child within the rational administration of state control. As the law of paterfamilias broke down, children came under the scrutiny of professionals – educators, psychologists, judges and social workers whose role it was to civilize, train, assess and study them.

Increasingly, the public debates about protecting and preparing the young citizen for the modernizing world became institutionalised, making the child's mental development a matter of professional judgement. Physicians, educators and psychologists contributed to the public discourses of the twentieth century, offering advice on social deviance and control, measuring intelligence, diagnosing the childhood roots of psychosis and generally assessing children's capacity to learn. What they found was that there was no age of moral reason. Rather children were in a state of perpetual transition. The developmentalist accounts of Freud, Winnicott, Klein, Erikson and Piaget describing children as 'becoming subjects' circulated widely through professional institutions, which now had to adjust the guidance, learning and discipline of the child to their 'stage of mental development' – an idea that became central to schooling.

Historians have noted that throughout the last two hundred years the state played an ever greater role in protecting and preparing the child, as public concern about child labour, family brutality, universal literacy, temperance, public recreation, children's rights, media and marketing grew.[21] Socialization became a site of conflict, as the public desire to protect the 'innocent child' from social brutality, labour and disease vied with public anxieties about the failure to curb children's anti-social impulses, idleness and moral laxity.[22] On the one hand, the child was now constructed as an innocent precursor to the civilized and responsible self, whose vulnerability implies the state's obligation to protect them in their own interest – even from the abuses of their own parents. On the other hand, valorized as future citizen-workers, they were provided with a literate education and health care at state expense, provided with leisure, self-expression and recreational facilities and gained special rights and privileges until the age of majority. For this reason, Chris Jenks suggests that the social construction of modern childhood exists not as a sharp conceptual divide between adult and child but as a constant ideological struggle over the future of society within the modern matrix of socialization.[23] The social mobilization around children has resulted in the state both constructing a legal cordon sanitaire around them and investing heavily in the cultivation of their civility.

The Matrix of Socialization

Lloyd de Mause notes that educators, psychologists and sociologists had a profound impact on public discourses on childrearing.[24] Their 'developmentalist approach' privileged a style of parenting seeking to 'help' the immature child grow rather than constrain their natural instincts. After all, it was 'just a stage kids were going through'. These tolerant ideals are exemplified in the fatherly advice offered in Dr Benjamin Spock's best-selling book, which became the bible of American childrearing.[25] Spock advocated a less controlling approach to childrearing, which he thought befitted a generation that could claim the windfall of affluence and comfort.

This return of innocence was manifested in the acknowledgement of the young child's needs for unrestricted leisure and self-regulating consumption. Freedom to explore and to assess for themselves, was essential to the child's healthy maturation. By granting the child a secure environment and supporting them in establishing their own peer relations and cultural tastes, parents were encouraging the child's development according to their own needs and timing. This 'helping' strategy was widely discussed in health magazines, promoted in parenting manuals and also expressed regularly in advertising directed at the fledgling baby boom parent, where the child's struggles for autonomy and their perpetual needs for self-discovery and self-expression were celebrated from birth. Marketers of children's products, like baby foods, clothes and toys, joined a growing chorus of health professionals proclaiming the importance of the twinned deities of love and permissive leisure in children's lives. Toys, stories, peers and most of all patience were becoming the new tools for a healthy upbringing.

As the war economy gave way to a rapidly expanding commercial culture, the Spock psychology of supportive parenting was woven into public discourses about leisure and consumption for the baby-boom generation.[26] As sociologists Berger and Kellner suggested, 'these new modern worlds of childhood' could be easily grasped by comparing the fundamental values with those of the pre-war years: the 'gentle revolution' sought to cultivate 'individuals' who were 'used to being treated as uniquely valuable persons, accustomed to having their opinions respected by all significant persons around them and generally unaccustomed to harshness, suffering or, for that matter, any kind of intense frustration'.[27] But the moral dangers to the liberated child were also becoming apparent, because, when left to choose for themselves, children did not always do so wisely. In the United States, the first skirmish over the implications of *laissez-faire* parenting erupted over the comic book.[28] Precipitated by Dr Wertham's infamous *Seduction of the Innocent*,[29] educators and parents began to fear that children's fascination with the comic's simplistic crime and war tales were undermining the moral instruction provided by a literate education in schools. Without the guiding hand of parents and teachers, would the immature child have the knowledge and perspective necessary to discriminate between the banal and the civilized in popular culture?

This first 'media panic' portended the politicization of children's culture in the post-war era, where the civilizing agenda of the schools pushed children in one direction while the *laissez-faire* parenting and affluent lifestyles enjoyed at home pulled in the other. Daniel Bell saw in the growing discontents of the American family a reflection of the deeper 'cultural contradiction' in post-industrial capitalism caught between the opposing poles of its economic and cultural dynamics: 'The social structure today is ruled by an economic principle of rationality defined in terms of efficiency in the allocation of resources; the culture, in contrast, is prodigal, promiscuous, dominated by an anti-rational, anti-intellectual temper'.[30] We had entered the post-modern age in which parents, schools and the media as agencies of socialization were drawn into a perpetual tug of war over affluence, leisure and domesticated consumerism.[31]

The Mediatization of Childhood

The introduction of television into American households was initially heralded as the next way-station on the march to democratic civility. Its broad reach into every home prophesied a powerful tool of mass education. Television, liberals believed, held great potential because it could replace boring books and incompetent teachers with visually engaging knowledge about the modern world. Optimism was especially strong among progressives, who imagined that television's 'window unto the world' would provide the post-war generation with universal access to the Western legacy of cultural and scientific knowledge. Paul Porter, the chairman of the Federal Communication Commission, envisaged in his 1945 inaugural speech an American television system that would be an instrument of mass enlightenment:

> television's illuminating light will go far, we hope, to drive out the ghosts that haunt the dark corners of our minds – ignorance, bigotry, fear. It will be able to inform, educate and entertain an entire nation with a magical speed and vividness... It can be democracy's handmaiden by bringing the whole picture of our political, social, economic and cultural life to the eyes as well as the ears.[32]

Watch TV children did. Children were abandoning the streets and parks and sitting in front of the television. They even stopped reading comics. But in the commercialized media system it was becoming apparent that programmes for children were being designed with the size of the audience rather than children's uplift in mind. The networks prospered by giving kids what they most wanted – cartoons and sundry dramas sponsored by fast-food, cereal snacks and, increasingly, toy manufacturers. The optimistic vision of children gaining access to the best and brightest the world had to offer was quickly obliterated by that of a child alone with its snacks or toys watching cartoons punctuated by messages from paying sponsors selling Coon Skin Hats, Burp Guns and Barbies. The invisible hand of children's marketing was leaving fingerprints on the screen.

However visually attractive, it was hard for parents steeped in the values of progressive education to see endless cartoons and crime dramas as intellectually engaging or morally uplifting to the degree that literature was. As Spigel notes, early enthusiasm for TV was increasingly contested, as parents and educators began to ask whether commercial TV was a magic kingdom of delightful folk tales or a vast commercialized spectacle cultivating a spoiled, aggressive and uncivilized generation of young couch potatoes? Parents worried not only about their children's exposure to mature contents, but alsdo about their diminishing control over their children's moral and psychological maturation:

Worse still, parents may not even know how and where their children have acquired this information. With the mass commercial dissemination of ideas, the parent is so to speak left out of the mediation loop and the child becomes the direct addressee of the message. Perhaps for this reason, the history of children's involvement with mass media has been marked by a deep concern on the part of adult groups to monitor their entertainment and survey their pleasures.[33]

In the 1970s, the violent cartoons that punctuated Saturday morning TV brought the ideological tensions within the post-war matrix of socialization to boiling point, as the affluent boomer generation ignored parental restraints on their leisure and entertainment choices.[34] What was happening to children's commercial media seemed to symbolize the general issues facing the global mass-mediated market-place, as the 'new forms of electronic media together with the flow and forces of capital converged in the last quarter century fomenting a post-modern childhood inseparable from media use and media surveillance'.[35] Alarmist voices everywhere proclaimed a generational 'crisis' pointing to moral decline, the rise of violence and degradation of popular entertainment. What could children possibly learn from the commercialized drivel that now masqueraded as popular culture? Post-modern childhood was seen as 'a potentially disintegrative threat to sociological worlds' that 'emerges almost as a struggle between old orders and new orders'.[36] It seemed as if the long investment in civilizing the child through literacy, numeracy and high culture was escalating generational conflicts in the mass-mediated world.

The rhetoric of generational struggle infiltrated the debates about 'socialization' in home and schools. Journalists like Mary Winn mobilized American parents, raising fears that, by granting children excessive leisure time in front of the television, families were endangering their children's educational attainment, promoting aggressive attitudes and fostering a sedentary lifestyle. Cultural historians like Neil Postman, too, warned that the media's intrusion into the sacred realms of socialization foreshadowed the end of literate childhood: 'I believe the epistemology created by television not only is inferior to print based epistemology but is dangerous and absurdist'.[37] The media's refusal to respect the distinction between child and adult ways of knowing was overturning two hundred years of attempts to protect children from the brutalizing forces of industrialization. Echoing Rousseau, he argued that, in our mass-mediated society, children were being asked to grow up too quickly. By exposing the young to war, sex and politics before they had the maturity to fully understand these complex issues, we had unwittingly disturbed the graduated development of moral and critical understanding. Postman's lamentations for the dissolution of 'literate civility' struck a responsive chord. Many felt it was time for governments to insist that, as agents of socialization, media industries had responsibilities to ensure that the Enlightenment mission of civilized protection and preparation of children did not disappear.

Towards Media Literacies

Because professional educators set the curriculum of mass education, the ability to read and write was considered inherently unproblematic and empowering for children. But in a mass-mediated society, where TV both displaced reading and exposed children to knowledge beyond the control of both schools and parents, educators were forced to reconsider the relationship between mass media and the literacy agenda.[38] Optimistic about television's potency as a learning tool, schools experimented with the idea of using audio-visual media in the classroom to enhance the literacy agenda. Teachers, failing to get classes to read Shakespeare, showed their classes film versions because they made high culture more accessible and engaging for their students. Others showed news and specially made educational films to enliven the history, maths and science curriculum. And so media gradually, but warily, became an accepted tool within schools. Precipitated by media panic, the US government reluctantly mandated PBS – the US public broadcast network – to fulfil the public education mission originally assigned to the commercial networks (leaving them free to entertain). Sesame Street, launched in the 1960s, reinvigorated the hopes of American liberals that it was still possible to harness television's communicative powers to give the TV generation a head start with their literacy skills.[39]

The invention of personal computers during the late 1970s was to hasten the acceptance of media technologies into the curriculum. Computers were celebrated by leading educationalists like Seymour Papert as 'smart' technologies that would help customize learning to the needs of the individual child.[40] Echoing arguments mustered forty years prior about television, they suggested children's love affair with computers would ensure they were motivated to learn for themselves. Schools would no longer be teacher driven but student centred. Computers, like books, were thought to be a constructionist technology eliciting active rather than passive engagement. Even while playing computer games, children were learning to solve problems, gaining control over their lives and feeling good about themselves – all the while acquiring operational skills that they would need in automated and computerized workplaces. In 1994 Al Gore sketched the US government's plans to computerize public education, making 'computer literacy' a national goal.[41] Since then, schools throughout the developed world have become wired into the now commercialized and unregulated Net in the name of providing children with 'the skills and competencies needed to function meaningfully in the current media environment'.[42]

The presence of electronic media within the classroom provoked a lively debate among educators about the competences that children required as future citizens in a media-saturated world. Since children spent as much time consuming TV and computers at home as in formal learning at school, some radical educators argued that being an avid user was not the same as literacy because teachers had not approved the curriculum. Instead, they proposed a critical media literacy training which 'encourages a reflective questioning stance towards the forms and contents of print and electronic media'.[43] To become rational consumers of popular culture required 'empowering' children with critical ideas so that they could resist the media's influence over them. In many countries – Canada, Australia, Britain – such critical media and computer literacy programmes found their way into schools. Students were asked to deconstruct popular culture using the tools of ideological, literary and film analysis to make sense of cartoons, soap operas and video games. In this way comics, advertising, sports programmes – and even *The Simpsons* – became debated within a media literacy curriculum.

To prepare children to make informed choices in the multi-media marketplace would require a prophylactic education which told them about the dangers that lurked in the networked society. Digital media educators argued that, rather than computer 'programming' skills, what children needed to survive in the new media environments were ways of protecting themselves against viral marketing, cyberstalkers, hackers and pornographers.[44] Fusing the goals of preparation and protection, these new media literacy advocates have argued that the competences and knowledge that make children rational cultural consumers in a networked marketplace require a critical reflection on consumerism. A recent review of media education remarks on the growing view that 'protection no longer is viewed exclusively in terms of keeping children away from certain content, or vice versa, but is also a question of strengthening children in their role as critical consumers (and producers) of the media'.[45] This prophylactic conception of media literacy has been challenged by media educators who have rubbished the 'protectionist ideology' of media literacy, arguing that 'such an approach was implicitly premised on the notion of media as an enormously powerful (and almost entirely negative) influence and that children were vulnerable to manipulation'. Arguing that the 'missionary rhetoric of public schooling – its claim to "emancipate" students from power and transform them into autonomous social agents' – has not worked, Buckingham advocates instead a constructionist approach which stresses the acquisition of operational 'competences'. Rather than critical understanding, media educators should honour children's pleasures of media consumption and help them express themselves through media production: 'the identity politics of contemporary media education, with their emphasis on rationality and "realist" conceptions of representation, need to be questioned, as does the rhetoric of "democratic citizenship" upon which they are often based'.[46]

Consumer Literacy in a Media-Saturated World

During the 1980s Postman's nostalgic pleas for literacy were drowned in the global wave of market expansionism which saturated households with commercial media and granted new freedom to children's marketers.[47] Targeting children as future consumers rather than citizens, food, toy and media companies exponentially escalated their investments in marketing directed at children. Commercial television – the visible tip of the children's merchandising iceberg – became the focal point for critics of children's overly rapid socialization as consumers. Deriding the banality of TV programming and the Manichean growth of children's advertising, marketing critics claimed that children's immaturity was being violated by the depredations of the dark lords of marketing – Hasbro, McDonald's, Disney and Sony – hell bent on turning our children into impulsive consumers.[48] To them, children's love of Big Macs, Barbie make-up sets and *Grand Theft Auto* video games revealed the promotional forces that were weakening corporations' restraints in marketing to children.[49]

Direct-to-children marketing, according to these critics, had transformed the traditional child worlds of construction toys, social games and sports into an empty consumerist spectacle of murder, fashion and chaos in the quest for global sales. The idea of childhood immaturity, which had once separated adult and child consumers, was under assault. The promotional force exerted through media made it ever harder for parents to negotiate with their children about their consumption practices and preferences.[50] The problem of media saturation of the home was now associated less with the content of programming than with its de-regulation, which left children – especially those under the age of twelve – vulnerable to constant advertising and defenceless against marketing's sophisticated promotional strategies.[51] Surely, argue these critics, the state has a responsibility to protect children under twelve from excessive persuasion by regulating children's TV advertising and teaching critical consumer literacy.[52]

Opposing regulation, the media industries argued that children's fascinations with commercial media, fashion and food were a positive indication that the modern child is being 'liberated' from the dictatorship of taste imposed by their moralizing parents and nanny-state educators whose constraints on children's choices exemplified a misunderstanding of children's media consumption. Children's culture scholars argued that children growing up with media had developed a sophisticated understanding of programming and advertising. Moralizing parents' fears reflected a failure to comprehend how competent their children had become in watching and surfing the media.[53] Rather than passive viewers lost in a promotional vortex, the new generation of media-savvy kids were actively interpreting and even critically 'resisting' commercialized media.[54] By the time they reach school, children have acquired a fairly sophisticated understanding of media genres and production techniques. Moreover, they know what they like and make thoughtful choices about their favourite programmes and criticize ads.[55]

To these celebrants of popular leisure, the very idea of childhood innocence is a counter-productive bit of protectionist propaganda wrapping modern childhood in an anxiety-ridden sense of vulnerability in the name of constraining their pleasures and denying their rights as consumers. Dismissing parental anxieties about children's exposure to sex, violence and consumerism, they snigger at the cordon sanitaire protectionist parents and educators cast around children.[56] Rather than censoring children's media, or filling the screen with sanitized pleasantries, we should support children as active consumers in the pursuit of freedom, identity and self-expression in this commercialized world.[57] The central mistake is to see children as exploited by media marketers and therefore to protect them from our media saturated world by censoring it. It may be true that kids grow up faster today. But is it a bad thing that kids learn about mature themes and issues, because over-controlling parents wish to deny them? How can we have sex and drug education programmes in schools and not allow them to be discussed on TV? This approach, then, parallels that of the cultural industries and marketers: media consumption prepares children for adult life by granting them a domain of freedom in which they become informed and choose pleasures for themselves.

The blurring of boundaries between socialization and consumerism has made it especially hard for parents and educators to protect children. Nor has the cordon sanitaire constructed by public education been of much use, as underfunded schools have become increasingly commercialized.[58] As Cook points out, in the post-modern era 'children and childhood cannot be insulated and protected from the outside because inside and outside no longer exist'.[59] How could children be prepared as rational consumers when school boards in the US, in exchange for free televisions in every classroom, allowed Channel One to beam eight minutes of dumbed down CNN 'news' and two minutes of commercials to captive audiences of students in 12,000 schools, in the name of media education? Was the media-savvy generation enjoying the freedom to express itself through consumption or being abandoned to the addictive and time-wasting distractions of global mass marketing?

Especially in the deregulated American media, where marketers penetrated deeply into family life and schools, the protectionist ethos that had buffered children from cruelty, premature sexuality and corporate manipulation was discarded. Children had become consuming subjects whose rights to choose for themselves had to be respected. But child consumers, left to follow their instincts, were also becoming lazy, selfish, fat and spoiled. Their favourite toys and games were violent and sexist. Their grades were declining, their fitness in question and their rude and anti-social behaviour rampant. Parents reared in the glow of the television might empathize with their children's desire for consumer distraction and popular culture, yet found it hard to ignore the risks associated with children's consumer lifestyles. As they became aware that their children's incessant demands at Christmas and in supermarkets were a result of 'pester power', they resented marketers growing control over their children's health and intellectual development. So progressive hopes for a generation of consumer citizens dissolved into an anxious fretting about the post-modern child running down virtual pedestrians, drinking litre-sized Coke and eating 'supersized' fries.

Debating Children's Consumer Socialization

Given the calls to protect children from marketing, a few social scientists began to examine the developmental processes underlying children's competences as consumers in the mediated marketplace. Scott Ward first defined consumer socialization as the acquisition of the various competences required for functioning in the consumer marketplace[60] – that is, the developmental sequence through which children acquire the knowledge, understanding and skills which enable them to perform rational market transactions. His approach has been taken as the gold standard in marketing research ever since, focusing researchers' attention on the mental prerequisites for rational consumer decision-making.[61]

Over the last thirty years a few social scientists have attempted to assess children's economic competences and consumer decision-making abilities.[62] Marketers like to claim that advertising plays an educational role, helping to create general consumer knowledge. Young people are sophisticated 'readers' of promotional messages, they argue and are enthusiastic about having more say in lifestyle choices – and, in the process, gaining more power in family provisioning of food, clothes, toys and entertainment. As consumer researchers confirm, even young children can be avid consumers and devoted media watchers.[63] They form preferences for programmes and characters they like quite early, organizing their leisure time around their media consumption. Children are interested in advertising and actively choose to watch some, not only because they are fun, but because ads provide them with one of the few sources of information about products they aspire to or buy (snacks, treats, cereals, movies, toys and games). They can identify an advertisement as a distinct genre, are more or less aware of its selling intent and are competently deciphering the selling points and persuasion techniques.[64] Certainly by the age of twelve, children have acquired the basic cognitive skills and information-processing abilities thought essential for functioning as competent consumer decision-makers in conditions of mass-mediated consumption: children understand the role of TV advertising and seem able to formulate their preferences for particular brands based on it.[65]

Hardly surprising, then, that by the age of five many children are brand conscious and discriminate between ads they like and do not like.[66] Their brand awareness can breed loyalty – a loyalty which can last a lifetime.[67] Their knowledge of and preferences for specific brands enter into their negotiations with their parents over family provisioning.[68] By age eight most have become strategically effective in supermarket and toy stores so that they obtain the things they request most often.[69] By age eight they not only exhibit knowledge of many children's goods, but also media, cars and foods. Moreover, they have become strategically successful in using their knowledge of brands as cultural capital among peers to achieve standing and acceptance.

Many young people do become competent customers. The majority have money skills which allow them to manage their increasingly large allowances, save for a future purchase and count their change after making it. Most have also become active shoppers in their own right, window shopping, chatting with sales personnel and carefully choosing their favourite products (or influencing their parents to buy these).[70] But as Brian Young recently noted, this account of children's successful consumer socialization has not ended the debate about their vulnerability to persuasion.[71] The debate has been most vocal about children's daily exposure to ads which are often not intended for them, like tobacco and alcohol, or products like fast-food which have some risks associated with them. Reviewing the legal issues in the case of tobacco advertising and children, Wong concludes that:

> while older children may in fact be able to 'read' commercials, children at earlier stages of development cannot. Furthermore, even older children may lack the capabilities for intelligent consumer decision making. Thus, an outright ban on advertisements of tobacco products to children would appear to be morally justifiable and capable of being upheld by the Court in the event of a constitutional challenge.[72]

In this view, a protective interest of the state in the marketing of risky products to children is fully justified.

To say that children have been empowered to define themselves and their lifestyles in the market, relative to earlier generations, does not imply that they are fully rational economic subjects.[73] And to say that children understand the fundamental role of advertising in the marketplace and recognize its intent to persuade them does not necessarily mean that children are fully informed consumers.[74] Moreover, since marketers target brand attitudes and affect, the formation of preferences is no indication that rational or fully formed choices are being made.[75] As Paine points out, 'comprehending persuasive intent is less complex than making consumer judgments'.[76] While we can recognize young children as 'media savvy', developmental psychologists legitimately ask: do young consumers have the mental capacity or access to all the information they need to make rational comparative choices in the marketplace?

The answer to this question depends on the criteria used for judging young people's consumer competences.[77] Although it appears self-evident that children have acquired a degree of financial power and brand knowledge, by far the most controversial skill is children's information search and processing abilities – particularly their capacity to make consumer lifestyle decisions for themselves or critically 'resist' direct-to-child advertising campaigns. For example, Paine has argued that children cannot be regarded as sovereign consumers because they still lack 'understanding of time, self and money',[78] implied by the idea of consumer citizenship in a market democracy. Economic psychologists would argue therefore that rational consumerism implies a pro-active shopping strategy which evaluates the risk–price benefits of a product. To fulfil this definition children must be able to search out information in order to compare various goods available to them for price; second, they must be able to critically evaluate the advertising claims about utility, cognitively weighing up the various benefits offered by the whole range of products; and, finally, they must be able to assess product utility and performance before they can be considered competent.[79] Few researchers have found that adults, let alone children, meet these criteria. The sparse literature suggests that children under six probably lack the mathematical knowledge and developmental skills implied by the benefit–price calculus. Even nine year olds may not possess the numerical ability to calculate interest rates or the conceptual dexterity to rationally compare products on multiple attributes.

Although they can judge whether they 'like' an ad or a product, the evidence is limited concerning when children become cognitively able to compare different products on multiple attributes.[80] Children as young as five can recall advertising messages and recognize techniques such as overstatement in ads directed at them, but when researchers investigate the processes of interpretation, it is found that not even adolescents fully comprehend the complexly layered irony of many ads.[81] Moreover, because children can rarely explain how advertising costs affect the pricing of products, or demonstrate information search strategies necessary for comparative shopping, how capable can young consumers be? With current synergistic cross-marketing strategies, product placements and programme-length commercials, it is hardly surprising that some children are confused by the lines between programming and advertising content. And even if they become aware of it, it does not mean they accept it as justified. As an eleven-year-old informant told me recently:

> when I watched Spiderman, when Spiderman just gets his powers, he is shooting his webs and he gets a Doctor Pepper ™ back. I don't think this is right because if I was watching a movie I really liked and then found out it was trying to get me to buy stuff I would feel cheated ... in conclusion, the leaders of big companies are morons.[82]

When it comes to the Internet, it is far from clear that the majority of children can avoid the pop ups and pornography, distinguish the commercial intent of sites such as Neopets, avoid cyber-lurkers or understand how the information they enter is being used by marketers.[83] Although some children are computer-literate comparison shoppers, using shopbots and their parents' credit cards to download their favourite games, there is growing evidence in Canada at least that children, like adults, do not appreciate the Internet's all-encompassing commercialization.[84]

The obesity crisis has identified two additional questions that can be raised concerning children's abilities to make informed consumer decisions in a risk society. The first concerns whether information about the risks associated with their lifestyle choices have been fully disclosed. Given the highly skewed weight of promotional communication towards the pleasures of fast-food or the excitement of violent games – where billions of dollars are spent promoting the fun and enjoyment of consumption without any mention of lifestyle risks – is it reasonable to expect young consumers to fully appreciate the long-term health risks of their unhealthy diets or the long-term desensitization of repeated exposure to violence? The second concerns the inadvertent exposure of child audiences to adult marketing campaigns for risk products like tobacco, alcohol and fast-food.[85]

Conclusion

> You can't control us in our homes with our parents. You know some day kids will RULE, RULE I tell you and when it happens you will be banished. (ten-year-old male)[86]

The modern mediated marketplace confronts children with its diverse ideologies, tastes and aesthetics, tempting them to explore the pleasures, lifestyles and identities that it offers. To the degree that media marketing expands lifestyle choices and brings benefits to young consumers, it seems largely unproblematic. But to the degree that it promotes risky products and anti-social behaviours, disturbs the negotiation between parents and children about lifestyles and values or undermines the literacy agenda, it has been a site of escalating public controversy over how both to protect and to prepare the young for consumer citizenship. Children's marketers have responded by suggesting that any regulation of children's advertising infringes on merchants' commercial speech and children's rights as autonomous consumers. The contemporary state is caught in the vice grip in this paradox of immaturity with little clear idea about how it can be resolved.

This chapter has argued that the politics of childhood revolve around two key consumer competences that children need in the mass-mediated marketplace: the first, *media literacy*, refers to children's ability to access and interpret the information about product attributes and benefits circulating in the mediated marketplace – particularly their understanding of the claims made in television advertising and their ability to critically interpret them. The second, *economic literacy*, concerns children's ability to be rational economic subjects – that is, to have the financial power and cognitive capacity to shop effectively by comparing the relative benefits of competing goods along a standard yardstick of monetary value. Research suggests that although children under twelve are able to distinguish ads from programming, recognize the intent of advertisers and save money towards purchases, their understanding of the mediated marketplace remains incomplete. They are hazy on who pays for cross-promotion and websites and they lack some of the skills and knowledge that are required for rational decision-making about long-term risks.

Granted children's growing freedom to manage their own lifestyles, the obesity crisis has highlighted another form of consumer literacy associated with unintended, systemic consequences of mass marketing in children's media. Even if it can be said that most children know what they want, there is little evidence that children can perform the cost–risk benefit analysis necessary to be considered fully competent consumers of cigarettes, alcohol or pharmaceuticals. Parenting advocates therefore argue that the state has an obligation to protect young consumer citizens from commercial persuasion in our risk society until they are fully capable of making informed decisions about the long-term consequences of consumerism. To the degree that consumer education can lessen the tension between parents and merchandisers, it might be worth trying.

Notes

1. Ha, Tu Thanh, 'Quebec Teens Fight for Right to Stay out at Night', *Globe and Mail*, 26 July 2004, p. 1.
2. World Health Organization, 'Health and Health Behaviour Among Young People', *WHO Policy Series: Health Policy for Children and Adolescents*, Issue 1: International Report, (Geneva, 2001).
3. E. Schlosser, *Fast Food Nation: The Dark Side of the All-American Meal* (New York, 2001); G. Critser, *Fatland: How Americans Became the Fattest People in the World* (Boston, 2003); M. Wootan, *Pestering Parents: How Food Companies Market Obesity to Children* (Center for Science in the Public Interest, 2003), p. 62.
4. S. Kline, 'Countering Children's Sedentary Lifestyles', paper presented at 'The Pluridisciplinary Perspectives on Child and Teen Consumption', University of Poitiers, Angoulême, France, 23 March 2004.
5. S. Kline, 'Fast Food, Sluggish Kids: Moral Panics and Risky Lifestyles', *Cultures of Consumption Working Paper no. 9* (2004), www.consume.bbk.ac.uk.
6. Sustain, *TV Dinners: What's Being Served up by the Advertisers* (London, 2001).
7. V. Shotbolt, 'The Parents', Marketing to Children Seminar, National Family and Parenting Institute, London, 25 November 2003.
8. G.B. Hastings, M. Stead, L. McDermott, A. Forsyth, A.M. MacKintosh, M. Rayer, C. Godfrey, M. Caraher and K. Angus, 'Review of Research on the Effects of Food Promotion to Children', report for the Food Standards Agency, Glasgow, UK, 22 September 2003.
9. Sustain, 'For Better Food and a Healthier Future', *Children's Food Bill*, (2004), http://www.sustainweb.org/child_index.asp.

10. H. Pringle, 'Why Banning Advertising to Children Would Be Naïve', *Media Week*, 14 January 2004, www.ipa.co.uk; J. Preston, 'The Way Forward, Choices and Challenges', Marketing to Children Seminar, National Family and Parenting Institute, London, 2003; I. Blair, 'The Regulators', Marketing to Children Seminar, National Family and Parenting Institute, London, 2003.

11. P. Jackson, 'The Way Forward, Choices and Challenges', Marketing to Children Seminar, National Family and Parenting Institute, London, 2003.

12. Kline, 'Countering Children's Sedentary Lifestyles'.

13. D. Cook, 'Beyond Either Or', *Journal of Consumer Culture*, 4(2) (2004), pp. 147–52.

14. P. Ariès, *Centuries of Childhood: A Social History of Family Life* (New York, 1962).

15. J. Locke, *Some Thoughts Concerning Education* (14th edn) (London, 1773).

16. J.J. Rousseau, *Émile, ou L'éducation* (Columbia, 2004).

17. M. McLuhan, *The Gutenburg Galaxy* (London, 1962); H.A. Innis, *The Bias of Communication* (Toronto, 1964); R. Williams, *The Long Revolution* (New York, 1961); R. Hoggart, *The Uses of Literacy* (London, 1958).

18. N. Postman, *The Disappearance of Childhood* (New York, 1982), p. 13.

19. N. Postman, *Amusing Ourselves to Death: Public Discourse in the Age of Show Business* (New York, 1985), p. 18.

20. L. de Mause, *The History of Childhood* (New York, 1974).

21. L.A. Pollock, *Forgotten Children: Parent–Child Relations from 1500 to 1900* (New York, 1983); N. Field, 'The Child as Laborer and Consumer: The Disappearance of Childhood in Contemporary Japan' in S. Stephens (ed.), *Children and the Politics of Culture* (Princeton, NJ, 1995), pp. 51–78; N. Sutherland, *Growing Up: Childhood in English Canada from the Great War to the Age of Television* (Toronto, ON, 1997); K. Hultqvist and G. Dahlberg (eds), *Governing the Child in the New Millennium* (New York, 2001); N. Jankovicek and J. Parr (eds), *Histories of Canadian Children and Youth* (Oxford, 2003).

22. S. Kline, *Out of the Garden: TV and Toys in the Age of Marketing* (London, 1993).

23. C. Jenks, *Childhood* (London, 1996).

24. De Mause, *History of Childhood*.

25. B. Spock, *Baby and Child Care* (New York, 1964).

26. D. Riesman, *The Lonely Crowd: A Study of the Changing American Character* (New Haven, 1950).

27. P. Berger, B. Berger and H. Kellner, *The Homeless Mind* (London, 1974), p. 173.

28. B.W. Wright, 'Turning Point: Comic Books in Crisis, 1954–1955' in *Comic Book Nation: The Transformation of Youth Culture in America* (Baltimore, MY, 2001), pp. 154–79.

29. F. Wertham, *The Seduction of the Innocent* (New York, 1954).

30. D. Bell, *The Cultural Contradictions of Capitalism*, cited in P. Murray, *Reflections on Commercial Life* (New York, 1977), pp. 429–46 (p. 432).

31. Kline, *Out of the Garden*.

32. N. Minnow and C.L. Lamay, *Abandoned in the Wasteland* (New York, 1995), p. 83.

33. L. Spigel, 'Seducing the Innocents' in H. Jenkins, *The Children's Culture Reader* (New York, 1998), p. 114.

34. S. Kline, 'Toys, Socialization and the Commodification of Play' in S. Strasser and C. McGovern (eds), *Getting and Spending* (Cambridge, 1998).

35. D. Cook, 'Exchange Value as Pedagogy in Children's Leisure: Moral Panics in Children's Culture at Century's End', *Leisure Sciences*, 23 (2000), pp. 81–98, p. 82.

36. Jenks, *Childhood*.

37. Postman, *Amusing Ourselves to Death*, p. xiii.

38. D.E.H. Alvermann and M.C. Hagood, 'Critical Media Literacy: Research, Theory, and Practice in "New Times"', *Journal of Educational Research*, 93(3) (2000), pp. 193–205; W.J. Potter, *Media Literacy* (Thousand Oaks, CA, 2001).

39. H. Hendershot, *Saturday Morning Censors* (Durham, 1998).

40. S. Papert, *Mindstorms: Children, Computers and Powerful Ideas* (New York, 1998).

41. D. Tapscott, *Growing Up Digital: The Rise of the Net Generation* (New York, 1998).

42. H. Jenkins, 'Media Literacy Goes to School: Digital Renaissance' (2004), http://www.med.sc.edu:1081/jenkins2.htm.

43. B. Warnick, *Critical Literacy in a Digital Era: Technology, Rhetoric and Public Interest* (London, 2002).

44. K.C. Montgomery, 'Government Must Take Lead in Protecting Children', *Advertising Age*, 69(25) (1998), p. 40; S. Livingstone, 'Children Online – Consumers or Citizens?', *Cultures of Consumption Working Paper no. 8* (2004), www.consume.bbk.ac.uk.

45. U. Carlsson, 'Introduction' in C. Feilitzen and U. Carlsson, *Promote or Protect: Perspectives on Media Literacy and Media Regulations* (Goteborg University, 2003).

46. D. Buckingham, *Media Education: Literacy, Learning and Contemporary Culture* (London, 2003), p. 171.

47. Kline, *Out of the Garden*.

48. Critser, *Fatland;* J.L. Kincheloe, *The Sign of the Burger: McDonald's and the Culture Of Power* (Philadelphia, PA, 2002); J. Kapur, 'Out of Control: Television and the Transformation of Childhood' in M. Kinder, *Late Capitalism: Kids, Media, Culture* (Durham, 1999), pp. 122–36; S. Linn, *Consuming Kids: The Hostile Takeover of Childhood* (New York, 2004).

49. J. Kincheloe, 'The Complex Politics of McDonald's and the New Childhood: Colonizing Kidworld' in G. Cannella and J. Kincheloe (eds), *Kidworld: Childhood Studies, Global Perspective and Education* (New York, 2002); B. Langer, 'The Business of Branded Enchantment: Ambivalence and Disjuncture in the Global Children's Culture Industry', *Journal of Consumer Culture*, 4(2) (2004), pp. 251–77; G. Ritzer, *The McDonaldization Thesis: Explorations and Extensions* (London, 1998).

50. S. Kline and K. Steward, 'Family Life and Media Violence: A Qualitative Study of Canadian Mothers of Boys' in Van den Bergh and Van den Bulck (eds), *Children and Media: Multidisciplinary Perspectives* (Garant, 2001), pp. 89–110; P.B.K. Stratton, 'Families' Accounts of the Causal Processes in Food Choice', *Appetite*, 33(1) (1999), pp. 89–108.

51. B. Wilcox, J. Cantor, P. Dowrick, D. Kunkel, S. Linn and E. Palmer, *Report of the Task Force on Advertising and Children* (Washington, 2004); H.J. Kaiser, *Foundation: The Role of the Media in Childhood Obesity* (Menlo Park, California, 2004), p. 13.

52. P.M. Valkenburg and J. Cantor, 'The Development of a Child into a Consumer' in S.L. Calvert, A.B. Jordan and R.R. Cocking (eds), *Children in the Digital Age: Influences of Electronic Media on Development* (Westport, CO, 2002), pp. 201–14.

53. R. Hobbs, 'The Seven Great Debates in the Literacy Movement', *Journal of Communication*, 48(1) (1998), pp. 16–32.

54. M. Nava, *Changing Cultures: Feminism, Youth and Consumerism* (London, 1992); D. Buckingham, *Children Talking Television: The Making of Television Literacy* (London, 1993).

55. Buckingham, *Media Education*.

56. H. Jenkins, 'Professor Jenkins Goes to Washington' (2003), http://web.mit.edu/21fms/www/faculty/henry3/profjenkins.html.

57. D. Buckingham, 'Media Education and the End of the Critical Consumer', *Harvard Educational Review*, 73(3) (2003) pp. 309–27.

58. K. Ervin, 'Schools Expel Channel One; New Policy Also Limits Ads, Logos', *Seattle Times* (2001), http://www.asu.edu/educ/epsl/CERU/Articles/Schools.expel.channelone.htm, http://www.channelone.com/common/about/ 15 August 2004.

59. D. Cook, 'Exchange Value as Pedagogy in Children's Leisure', p. 89.

60. S. Ward, *Children and Promotion: New Consumer Battleground?* (Cambridge, MA, 1972).

61. D.R. John, 'Consumer Socialization of Children: A Retrospective Look at Twenty-Five Years of Research', *Consumer Research*, 26 (1999), pp. 183–213.

62. P. Lunt and A. Furnham (eds), *Economic Socialization* (Cheltenham, 1996).

63. R. Duff, 'What Advertising Means to Children', *Advertising and Marketing to Children*, 5(2) (2004), pp. 41–50.

64. M. Nava, *Changing Cultures*; D. Buckingham, *Moving Images: Understanding Children's Emotional Responses to Television* (Manchester, 1996); M.E.R. Ritson, 'A Model of Advertising Literacy: The Praxiology and Co-creation of Advertising Media', European Marketing Academy Conference, Paris: ESSEC, 1995; G. MacDonald, *Is the Way We Understand Advertising Changing?* (WARC, 1999), http://www.warc.com/Content/Content/Admap.asp.

65. John, 'Consumer Socialization of Children'; B. Young, 'Does Food Advertising Influence Children's Food Choices? A Critical Review of Some of the Recent Literature', *International Journal of Advertising*, 22 (2003), pp. 441–59; B. Young, 'Does Food Advertising Make Children Obese?', *Advertising and Marketing to Children*, 4(3) (2003), pp. 19–26.

66. J. McNeal, *The Kids' Market: Myths and Realities* (Ithaca, NY, 1999); G. del Vecchio, *Creating Evercool* (New York, 1997).

67. S. Thomson and G. Woodham, 'Myths and Realities of the Global Young Consumer', (ESOMAR seminar on youth research, 1997), available http://www.warc.com.

68. Wootan, *Pestering Parents*, p. 62; B. Sutherland and A.T. Thompson, *Kidfluence: Why Kids Today Mean Business* (Toronto, 2002).

69. J.U. McNeal, *Kids as Customers: A Handbook of Marketing to Children* (Don Mills, ON, 1993).

70. McNeal, *The Kids' Market*.

71. B. Young, 'Does Advertising to Children Make them Fat? A Sceptical Gaze at Irreconcilable Differences', paper for seminar 'Children as Consumers: Public Policies, Moral Dilemmas, Academic Perspectives', The Royal Society, London, 20 February 2004. Available at http://www.consume.bbk.ac.uk/childconsumer. html.

72. K.L. Wong, 'Tobacco Advertising and Children: The Limits of First Amendment Protection', *Journal of Business Ethics*, 15(10) (1996), pp. 1051–64.

73. A. Furnham, 'The Economic Socialization of Children' and A.S. Bombi, 'Social Factors of Economic Socialization' in Lunt and Furnham (eds), *Economic Socialization*, pp. 11–34 and pp. 183–201.

74. J. Lannon, 'Asking the Right Questions – What Do People Do with Advertising?', *Admap*, June, (1992), pp. 17–22; P. Lunt, 'Introduction: Social Aspects of Young People's Understanding of the Economy', in Lunt and Furnham, *Economic Socialization*, pp. 1–10; E. Hitchings and P.J. Moynihan, 'The Relationship between Television Food Advertisements Recalled and Actual Foods Consumed by Children', *Journal of Human Nutrition and Dietetics*, 11 (1998), pp. 511–17.

75. D.L. Borzekowski and T.N. Robinson, 'The 30-Second Effect: An Experiment Revealing the Impact of Television Commercials on Food Preferences of Preschoolers', *Journal of American Diet Association*, 101(1) (2001), pp. 42–6; V. Kraak and D.L. Pelletier, 'The Influence of Commercialism on the Food

Purchasing Behavior of Children and Teenage Youth', *Family Economics and Nutrition Review*, 11(3) (1998), pp. 15–24.

76. L. Sharp Paine, 'Children as Consumers: An Ethical Evaluation of Children's Advertising', *Business and Professional Ethics Journal*, 3(3 and 4) (1983), pp. 119–46.

77. S. O'Donahue and C.T. Tynan, 'Beyond Sophistication: Dimensions of Advertising Literacy', *International Journal of Advertising*, 17(4) (1998), p. 467.

78. Paine, 'Children as Consumers'.

79. P. Pliner, J. Freedman, R. Abramovitch and P. Darke, 'Children as Consumers: In the Laboratory and Beyond', in Lunt and Furnham, *Economic Socialization*, pp. 35–46.

80. MacDonald, 'Is the Way We Understand Advertising Changing?'.

81. K. Drotner, 'Youth, Media and Cultural Identities', *The Nordicom Review*, 2 (1995), pp. 37–44.

82. Quotes cited are from focus groups undertaken in Vancouver in April 2004.

83. Montgomery, 'Government Must Take Lead in Protecting Children'; Livingstone, 'Children Online – Consumers or Citizens?'.

84. Media Awareness Network, 2001, 'Young Canadians in a Wired World' at http://www.media-awareness.ca/.

85. S. Kline, 'Countering Children's Sedentary Lifestyles: An Evaluative Study of a Media Risk Education Approach', *Childhood*, forthcoming.

86. From research interviews conducted in Simon Fraser School, Vancouver, April 2004.

Part III
Reframing Consumers and Consumption

Contemporary Culture and Political Economy

−10−

Competing Domains

Democratic Subjects and Consuming Subjects in Britain and the United States since 1945

Frank Mort

Every quarter the Henley Centre for Forecasting, a prestige marketing organization specializing in long-term planning for the consumer industries, publishes its survey of leisure in the United Kingdom. One of its survey findings makes particularly depressing if familiar reading. Since the late 1980s sample profiles of the British population have been monitored for their main leisure patterns. What came out on top in survey after survey was a list of contemporary pleasures that were principally made available through market-based forms of provision: personal shopping, eating out, DIY and video watching. Right at the bottom of the list came politics; going to a political meeting ranked on a par with a visit to the circus as one of the British public's least likely things to do![1] Politics understood as something pleasurable, as something to do with one's disposable leisure time, it seems, was a definite non-starter. Mounting a grandiose argument on the back of these quarterly findings, the Centre concluded that British society was in the process of undergoing a major shift in its 'structures of authority'. The highest authorities these days, Henley emphasized, were reserved for those people, institutions and forms of intellectual and cultural capital most closely associated with our own sense of personal well-being. Deference to traditional structures of authority, especially political authority, has hit an all-time low, while the values of the consumption side of life have risen enormously.[2]

The Henley Centre's findings on the subordination of political culture to consumer culture are of course in one sense entirely predictable, given that the organization is dedicated to the promotion of commercial goals. But similar findings have been registered repeatedly by political analysts and by sociologists who have sought to map recent shifts in cultural and political behaviour. Voter turnout in British and European elections, which was in steady decline for decades, has fallen rapidly in recent years, precipitating an atmosphere of crisis surrounding the structures of political representation. For Zygmunt Bauman, 'Britain's exit from politics', manifested as apathy, a profound distrust of politicians and alienation from public institutions, has been fostered by successive governments that have encouraged the electorate to 'buy oneself out of politics'. According to Bauman, politics is now seen only as a nuisance, a barrier to real life, which lies elsewhere, in the world of personal freedoms, the market, human relationships and so on.[3] Such a shift has been fostered by the combined effects of neoliberal economic policies, the politics of globalization and by the successes of the new right. In Britain one of the long-term achievements of the Thatcher government in the 1980s lay in its ability to reconstruct political discourse as a minimalist endeavour, but one in which the consumer and consumerism replaced many of the more established understandings of public culture. Efforts by the subsequent Labour administration, under Tony Blair's direction, to actively reconnect with the electorate have repeatedly evoked models of consumer empowerment in an attempt to revitalize the languages of representative democracy. Market democracy, as Ross McKibbin recently termed the programmes of Third Way governments, has at its core a strategic attempt to reconfigure the discourse of domestic politics as one where the relationship of the citizen to the market becomes the defining feature of public provision and political relationships.[4]

This chapter is not about a direct evaluation of these transformations in British politics, rather it aims to show how the agendas and rhetorics of democracy and consumerism have a more complex and inter-related history than is usually understood. Shifts in democratic political culture and in the sphere of consumer behaviour are not discrete developments, they are intimately related features of British society from at least the mid-twentieth century onwards. My aim, therefore, is to trace the recent genealogy of two competing but interconnected domains of knowledge and social action. First, I examine a set of post-war political discourses defining the character and progress of liberal democracy in Britain and in the USA. Second, I turn to a set of studies, mainly produced by sociologists and by social researchers, which privileged cultural practices and habits, especially those shaped by commercial cultures, as their central object of concern. Taken together, this body of research made explicit connections between perceptions of a weakening in the structures of representative democracy and shifts in the sphere of leisure and private-sector consumption. In other words, the citizen subjects of democratic politics and the subjects of commercially driven consumer culture were understood to be intimately connected. Brought together in this account are two sets of debates that have conventionally been separated by the boundaries of political science, on the one hand and the various traditions of cultural analysis, on the other. I explore these reciprocal relationships in the organization of politics and cultural life principally via a focus on the 1950s to the 1970s, though I emphasize that these developments are also part of a longer *durée* relating to broader shifts in social knowledge and in patterns of mass leisure.

Recent historical and cultural studies of modern forms of consumer activity have tended to bifurcate around understandings of the socially motivated consumer, participating in significant activities in the public sphere and consuming subjects who are shaped by retailing, advertising and all of the other commercially organized technologies associated with the world of goods.[5] Social consumers tend to be located in the world of politics and civic life, where their activities are seen to be governed by various forms of collective or voluntary association. Cultural consumers, in contrast, are seen to be motivated by the whole panoply of pleasures, possibilities and projections of identity and fantasy associated with the consumer marketplace. Lizabeth Cohen's exemplary study of the politics of mass consumption in post-war America provides important insights into the ways in which this dualism separating the social subjects from the cultural subjects of modern consumption has been shaped by specific historical processes. Cohen identifies the ideal types of the 'citizen consumer' and the 'purchasing consumer' as two competing models of activity that were promoted by the US government and by commercial agencies from the late 1930s onwards. She notes, however, that such identities were not fixed but were 'ever shifting categories' that often overlapped or existed in tension, reflecting 'the permeability' of different domains of consumption.[6]

My own study amplifies and develops Cohen's arguments about the potential liminality of these fields of consumer activity and their attendant forms of identity. I explore the ways in which distinctive but inter-related conceptions of the consumer were mapped in Britain and to a lesser extent in the USA, after the Second World War. A central part of my argument here is directed against understandings of post-war consumption, including some of my own earlier work, which tended to privilege the more spectacular forms of commercial culture associated with modern urban life.[7] This focus on the most visible consumers has often been at the expense of the quotidian and mundane rituals of cultural participation. Focusing on the interdependencies between political subjects and consuming subjects can deliver fresh insights into the character of participatory democracy and mass affluence during the high-point of post-war consumer expansion.

Civic Culture

Charting connections between political participation and cultural life involves dusting down a research tradition that was prominent in the USA and in Britain in the 1950s and 1960s but has since been conspicuously neglected. In America this project centred on the work of liberal political scientists who explored the conditions generating stable, participatory democracy and 'mature' political development. Across the Atlantic it was the renewed scrutiny of the British working class, conducted by post-war sociologists, ethnographers and the founders of an indigenous tradition of cultural studies, that made visible working people's perceptions of politics and democracy, in the context of work, community and family life. The relationship of both American and British researchers to the historical conditions that sustained their projects – long-term economic growth, liberal and social democratic values and mass culture – have frequently been commented on.[8] What have remained relatively under-explored are the connections between political and public discourses and cultural networks in this body of research.

American studies, especially Gabriel Almond and Sidney Verba's *The Civic Culture* (1963) and Seymour Lipset's *Political Man* (1960), celebrated the democratic structures of Britain and the USA, as opposed to the more precarious political cultures of Germany and Italy. They concluded that democratic stability rested not simply on the maturity of political elites or mass parties, but on the formation of an active and responsible civic culture that guaranteed ordinary citizens participation in the political process.[9] The significance of these texts for our argument lies in the questions their authors posed about the relationship between political participation and cultural life, or what Almond and Verba termed political culture and civic culture. In this respect, for Lipset and for Almond and Verba one issue was pre-eminent: how to maintain the values of liberal democracy? As Verba explained in his retrospective on the civic culture paradigm in the late 1980s: 'The survival of the democracies in the developed world was problematic … our dependent variable was the likelihood of survival'.[10] This genre of political science was driven by a desire to revitalize the idea of citizenship in the face of recent European history, notably the collapse of confidence in conceptions of democratic government and their replacement by totalitarian regimes, both before and after the Second World War. 'Democratic revisionism' has often been characterized as exhibiting a high degree of intellectual coherence corresponding to its own Cold War championing of democracy. In fact it was a much looser and often eclectic amalgam of different research traditions. There was the influence of political theories of social elites, derived from Pareto and Schumpeter, together with contemporary systems theory. Positivist forms of political science, driven by the search for normative laws of development, also jostled for space alongside the functionalist sociological tradition of Talcott Parsons. But it was the influence of empirical sociology, almost for the first time within the traditions of political research, that enabled these liberal theorists to explore the cultural field and to investigate its possible impact on political behaviour.

As Lipset insisted, political science could not be compartmentalized; it could only be properly studied as part of 'more general sociological and psychological relationships'.[11] Lipset's dedicated aim was to trace empirically the social underpinnings of political motivation. Almond and Verba noted that the day-to-day reality of the ordinary British or American voter was rarely that contained within the idealized political universe of civic textbooks, where the citizen was forever rational, reasonable and well-informed. Their aim was to map some of the social and cultural determinants that equipped 'ordinary men' to develop high levels of civic competence.[12] Previous studies of the impact of culture on politics had usually dealt in much more impressionistic evidence, mobilizing notions of national character and the variable atmosphere of civic life in European and American societies. In the 1940s and early 1950s social anthropologists such as Margaret Mead, for the

USA and Geoffrey Gorer, for Britain, claimed to have identified the ways in which national characteristics shaped political and cultural participation.[13] Post-war political scientists claimed to be more quantitatively grounded in their research, aiming to understand how family networks, community organizations, education and leisure either stimulated or inhibited active political involvement. Lipset cautioned against reading even the limited act of voting as 'just a matter of spending an hour going to the polls', for behind it, he argued, lay social and cultural rituals that were crucial in developing political awareness.[14]

It was liberal theorists' scrutiny of those social actors who failed the test of active citizenship, quite as much as their prioritization of those who took their democratic responsibilities seriously, that drew attention to the importance of cultural and psychological factors in shaping political response. Here preoccupations centred on two principal groups: workers in low-status occupations, one of the classic strata for sociological anxieties about undemocratic manifestations of the so-called 'authoritarian personality', and married women. For the former group, it was not only the continual pressure of economic worries, but also rigid family patterns and 'ego insecurities' that predisposed unskilled male workers to adopt authoritarian programmes rather than assenting to a vision of gradualist political change.[15] For married women, it was the 'sheer demands on a housewife and mother' that militated against their gaining 'politically relevant experience'.[16] According to Lipset, the social position of working-class wives was doubly complex. Caught between pressure from their husbands, who were often energetic political activists and what Lipset defined in quasi-essentialist terms as their own feminine desire for conservative status emulation of a middle-class domestic ideal, the irreconcilability of these competing value systems forced many women to withdraw from political discussion and debate.[17]

It has now become almost *de rigueur* for writers on democratic theory to open with an exposure of the limitations of this post-war paradigm. Recent commentators have highlighted the historically and culturally specific notions of 'stability' embedded in the research agenda, together with liberal theorists' failure to reflect on the tightly circumscribed idea of political participation and active citizenship that formed the centrepiece of their arguments.[18] Yet these difficulties notwithstanding, what was noteworthy about their arguments was precisely issues about the relationship between political participation and cultural life that were brought into alignment. It was the empirical research embedded within their discussions that raised broader questions about the way political culture was understood and participated in, not from the vantage point of the most prominent social actors and the political elites, but at the level of the ordinary, the mundane and the everyday.[19]

British sociology and community studies in the 1950s and early 1960s posed a related set of questions about political involvement and cultural activity, though they were shaped by different intellectual traditions in response to the social changes taking place within British society. Here the concern was less obviously with political stability than with shifting patterns of urban working-class life, under the combined impact of economic growth, increased geographical mobility and changes to community and family networks.[20] The intellectual traditions that informed these investigations were again enormously varied: they covered ethnographic research, with their origins in the 'blue-book' traditions of Victorian social investigation, the post-war genre of community studies with its hermeneutic commitment to empathetic *Verstehen* on the part of the observer, as well as techniques of presentation derived from literary studies and the more pragmatic demands of social policy. What these varied methodologies shared was an emphasis on the 'experiential' – or what Richard Johnson has defined as the inwardness of experience – as against sociologies that were functionalist, reductive or deterministic.[21] This commitment to the touchstone of experience was as true for the attempts to understand working-class political involvement as it was for the more characteristic focus on community and culture.

The classic British study in this genre was the volume on the sociology of the affluent worker which dealt with political behaviour. The project on working-class affluence, funded by the Human Sciences Committee of the Department of Scientific and Industrial Research (forerunner of the Science Research Council) and led by John Goldthorpe and David Lockwood from the Department of Applied Economics at Cambridge University, produced various monographs and articles throughout the 1960s. In *The Affluent Worker: Political Attitudes and Behaviour* (1968) the overriding concern was to discover if the combined effects of relative economic prosperity and post-war cultural change had precipitated a destabilization of 'traditional' voting patterns within sections of the skilled working class.[22] Because the scope and the methodology of Goldthorpe and Lockwood's research were cast much more widely than in the stricter psephological studies of voting behaviour favoured by the Nuffield Institute at Oxford University, the factors shaping political affiliation were understood to be correspondingly broad. Like Lipset, the Cambridge affluent-worker team insisted on the need to 'know something about the people in our sample not only as voters but also as industrial employees, as neighbours and friends with certain life histories and objectives'.[23] The questionnaires that underpinned their study probed some of the informal circuits that fed into local political culture, such as male workplace associations and female friendship networks.

Private-sector consumption loomed large in Goldthorpe and Lockwood's efforts to map the cultural influences that informed the political decision-making of the affluent worker. This was largely because the importance of consumer goods had emerged as a central point of reference in those sections of the research dealing with changes in leisure, community and domesticity, such as the new patterns of suburbanization and potential shifts in the gendered dynamics of working-class family life. But consumption also figured prominently in the Cambridge study because it pointed to possible connections with political behaviour. Goldthorpe and Lockwood claimed to have identified a sea-change in working-class political attitudes that had been strongly influenced by post-war prosperity. In accordance with their much quoted theory of *embourgeoisement*, the affluent worker's participation in electoral politics was seen to be increasingly based on 'economic self-interest' rather than on traditional class loyalties – what the researchers famously termed an 'instrumental collectivism' as opposed to a 'solidaristic collectivism'.[24] However, when Goldthorpe and his team turned to examine the actual levels of political participation among their affluent workers, the picture they projected was not one of an energetic civic culture at all. Rather, the project registered how politics was not a salient topic of conversation among the majority of men in their sample. It was a relative disinterest in political activity, rather than any conception of active citizenship, that was understood to be on the increase among the skilled working class.[25] A similar argument was presented in a more psychological form in Ferdynand Zweig's *The Worker in an Affluent Society* (1961). Political issues became increasingly insignificant, Zweig claimed, for via consumer activity social relations had been transformed into an increasingly person-centred view of the world.[26]

Ghosting both the projects of British sociologists and American liberal theorists was an understated debate about gender and especially about how the core concepts of democracy, leisure and culture were differently inflected by masculine and feminine access to the structures of modern political and social power. Awareness of gender difference in the writings on political democracy and working-class culture was *sotto voce* rather than explicit. Conclusions to the various studies almost always vindicated either the 'wisdom' and 'maturity' of distinctive cadres of British and American professional men, or the political centrality of skilled male workers to the operation of mass democracy. Nonetheless, this body of research did raise questions about the different ways that men and women participated in civic culture, popular leisure and consumerism. Gender was empirically present but structurally absent in much of the work. Most of the key reference points in this vocabulary and most crucially the distinction between the public and private spheres, were conceived without any systematic conception of the gendered dimensions of these forms of political and social activity. As a result, this post-war generation of political scientists and sociologists was unable to integrate its specific findings about sexual difference into its more general hypotheses about democratic stability or cultural change.

Some of the most significant absences on this score were revealed in the civic culture debate itself. Lipset marshalled considerable evidence to show that, along with workers in the lower socio-economic groups, women in all of the Western democracies displayed low levels of civic confidence.[27] Yet as Carol Pateman has demonstrated, the question of why such a sexual division was recurrent within so many political cultures was never seriously posed.[28] Almond and Verba's assumption appeared to be that women's demonstrably low level of active political participation was accidental and contingent, rather than structural. Ultimately, this gender blindness was related to the whole conception of democracy that underpinned their arguments, not simply in its post-war manifestations but in terms of the longer historical legacy derived from Locke, Mill and other classic theorists of representative government.

Almond and Verba's professed aim was to uncover the informal underpinnings of liberal democratic systems, what they described as 'a particular distribution of political attitudes, feelings, information and skills'.[29] Yet this professed desire to move the analysis of political participation beyond a theory of elites or functional systems analysis balked at any attempt to cross the public/private divide, as such a conception of the separation of spheres had been defined historically within theories of representative government. This, quite literally, marked the limits of liberal democracy.

A related set of cultural refusals was at work in the British studies. The debate over the condition of the affluent worker and his family pointed to the changing dynamics of post-war domestic life and associated patterns of leisure. A central theme here was the growth of a more home-centred culture, fostered by migration from the old working-class communities, with their extended and semi-public kinship and friendship networks, to the privatized suburbs and the new council housing estates. Working from their London-based Institute of Community Studies, Peter Willmott and Michael Young noted how a sense of domestic privatization defined the experience of wives and mothers who moved out from the old urban environments, in Bethnal Green in the East End, to the new settlements on the East London perimeter and to the new towns beyond.[30] The affluent worker team also observed how a post-war generation of skilled working-class men placed in these new settings played an increasing if secondary role in parenting, domestic labour and home-centred leisure.[31] This expansion of the working-class family's private universe was cited as an important factor in accelerating the decline of the worker's traditional involvement in trade unionism and Labour Party politics. Despite these efforts to grasp the inter-relationship between the world of home and the spheres of work and political action, it was overwhelmingly a masculinist understanding of the growth of privatized leisure that predominated in the research. Though the sociologists of working-class affluence did acknowledge the family as a site of labour and one in which women as housewives and mothers played the major part, it was home and family as a place for the pleasurable consumption of goods and services and for the servicing of personal and emotional needs, that shaped their accounts. The reproductive and labour-related features of household consumption, together with women's gender-specific relationship to consumer activity, tended to be subsumed under the rubric of an expanding conception of post-war leisure.

Political Culture Under Stress

The collapse of confidence in American and British theories of liberal democracy did not follow the same timescale. A major difference between the two national perspectives on the democratic process, at least until the late 1960s, lay in their respective expressions of optimism about the state of civic culture. American liberals remained convinced that a viable political culture was sustained not by any grandiose political philosophy but by local, pragmatic and frequently mundane networks of association and they remained relatively confident about the performance of this system for longer than their British counterparts. It was not until the 1970s that the pressures of economic stagnation, a divisive war in Vietnam and major social dislocations at home, focused around the civil rights movement and student protest, fuelled a crisis in American democratic theory and its value systems.[32] British perceptions of decline came somewhat earlier and were driven by Britain's specific domestic conditions.

The decline of consensus politics is a well-charted theme in British post-war political and social history.[33] What I want to examine here is a more specific strand of that argument: the ways in which perceptions of democratic instability, as they were understood from within mainstream politics, were related to a specific reading of mass consumer culture and its relationship to the political process. Debates about democratic decline and cultural transformation, though largely contemporaneous, were shaped by different research frameworks and social actors. What was notable was the sharpness with which the boundaries were drawn between different approaches and problematics. If this in reality was an interdisciplinary story about the relationship between political discourse and cultural activity, it was one in which the different players in the field rarely entered into a sustained conversation.

British studies of the post-war working class had already sounded warning noises about the relative disinterest of a substantial section of the population in the institutions of national democratic politics. From the mid-1960s onwards, concern about the decline of political culture took on a much higher public profile. A plethora of government commissions and reports, books and opinion poll surveys, as well as a series of extensive public debates, testified not to a vision of active and energetic citizenship, but to a picture of a democratic system that was in urgent need of reform. Within the space of a decade, politicians, political scientists and psephologists were contrasting the immediate post-war period as a high-point of active and stable democracy, as against the 1960s and 1970s, which were characterized as unstable and politically disaffected.[34]

The collective anxiety under which so many of the British worries about democracy were grouped was the issue of parliamentary reform. In one respect this debate identified very particular problems and grievances, but in another sense such discussions were much broader. There were arguments expressed by political sociologists, the most prominent being Bernard Crick in *The Reform of Parliament* (1964), together with a study of the role of MPs under the auspices of Political and Economic Planning and the Study of Parliament group.[35] The aggressively populist stance on parliamentary decline was nicely captured in the celebrated remarks by Humphrey Berkeley, the Conservative MP for Lancaster, who denounced Parliament from the floor of the House of Commons in 1964 with the comment: 'Well, it's dead! Nobody attends debates and this gives a general atmosphere of lifelessness about the whole place'.[36] Berkeley's sweeping condemnation was broadcast as the opening caption in a BBC television programme on Parliament in 1964, while the alleged weaknesses and failures of democratic institutions were rapidly becoming a favourite topic for the press, broadcasters and satirists by the early 1960s. The infamous BBC programme *That Was The Week That Was*, hosted by David Frost and other young Oxbridge graduates, was among the sharpest examples of a satire boom that became the scourge of Harold Macmillan's Conservative government, at a time of various high-profile security leaks and the raucous sexual scandal of the Profumo affair.[37]

The demand for some form of overhaul of the democratic process was seen as sufficiently urgent for Harold Wilson, as leader of the Opposition, to announce in 1963 that a future Labour government would introduce an immediate programme of parliamentary reform if elected to office.[38] Within the House of Commons itself, discontent became focused on the issue of constitutional change, a cause that was championed by the well-publicized activities of the Labour Members' Reform Group.[39] Despite initial vacillations, the new Labour administration did establish a number of substantial inquiries into the machinery of government and the working of democracy: the Royal Commission on Local Government in England, 1966–9 (dealing with the proposed re-organization of local authorities), the Fulton Committee on the Civil Service, 1966–8 (addressing civil service reform) and the Royal Commission on the Constitution, 1969–73 (set up in response to demands for Scottish and Welsh devolution).[40] While these inquiries were driven by quite specific political and administrative pressures, their reports were wide ranging and included lengthy discussions of the workings of democracy.

How were these expressions of anxiety and discontent focused? Was there a distinctive language or discourse of grievance? Crick listed a myriad of problems including state secrecy, political and civil service recruitment, ministerial irresponsibility and media coverage of politics, but he also acknowledged that the prevailing sense of dissatisfaction went even wider and deeper.[41] Some of the strongest observations on the democratic malaise were caught in the dissenting memorandum from Lord Crowther-Hunt and Professor Alan Peacock in the *Report of the Royal Commission on the Constitution* (1973):

> The combined evidence of our witnesses and various surveys of public opinion reveals a widespread and grave disquiet about our system of government today. What is particularly distressing is the pervading sense of powerlessness in the face of government and the attendant indications of a growing alienation from the governmental system.[42]

This diffuse atmosphere of unease with the political process was captured more concretely in recurrent opinion poll surveys throughout the 1960s and 1970s. Probing public attitudes to democracy, these surveys prefigured the later findings of the Henley Centre. All of the polling began by noting that voting turnout at British general elections had been falling consistently since the early 1950s, a trend that ran counter to almost all other western European democracies.[43] Surveys also revealed how specific sections of the electorate were unrepentantly 'non-active citizens'. A National Opinion Poll Survey, sponsored by Granada Television for a series on Parliament in July 1973 and published in *New Society*, noted that there was a 'substantial proportion of the public who expressed dissatisfaction or cynicism about Parliament', seeing it as merely an arena for 'petty squabbling', 'like schoolchildren bickering in a school playground'.[44] Attitudinal polling reinforced a perception of political and social powerlessness by many of the electorate. The Royal Commission on the Constitution characterized this as a 'We' and 'Them' situation, whereby 'ordinary people' felt that those who assumed government responsibilities were a totally different breed from the general public. Such perceptions echoed Richard Hoggart's earlier 'Us' and 'Them' picture of working-class people's attitudes to social and political authority in *The Uses of Literacy* (1958).[45] The Royal Commission's *Report* concluded that in the space of less than a decade Almond and Verba's celebration of Britain's vibrant civic culture was now seriously in question.

Taken together, these findings raised as many questions as they claimed to answer about the perceived loss of confidence in formal democracy. Though young, educated voters displayed the strongest feelings of disaffection, this was also the group who were confident that the democratic deficit could be plugged – predictably by their own public participation. In contrast, there was a core of the electorate clustered in the lower socio-economic groups, who, while registering profound dissatisfaction with the political status quo, displayed 'a completely passive and uninterested' attitude towards public life.[46] Confidence in democracy very much depended on where individuals and social groups were placed in the system and how they viewed it. Moreover, the idea of a spiralling decline in political authority, with the 1950s implicitly constructed as the moment of stable equilibrium, rested on persistent if unspoken assumptions about the immediate post-war years as the high-point of democratic consensus. Against this coherent image of the 1950s, the political developments and culture of later decades were invariably judged to be lacking. Such accounts of the consensus years have been challenged both by contemporary commentators and by recent historians. Dissenting voices have argued that this period produced equally strong feelings of political and cultural disassociation, notably the rise of a variety of spectacular male youth cultures, the emergence of the Campaign for Nuclear Disarmament, social protest in the media and the arts and the revitalization of feminist politics.[47]

Mainstream arguments about the state of British democracy in the 1960s and 1970s were usually narrowly political in form and character. Despite a strongly populist tone and a take-up of many of the issues well beyond the parliamentary arena, this was a debate in which the boundaries and meanings of the political were relatively fixed and taken for granted. Consequently, when commentators turned to examine the factors shaping the perceived decline of civic culture, the majority tabled broadly political and economic explanations. British political scientists and social democratic politicians and commentators displayed a general reluctance to examine the cultural factors influencing contemporary politics. This neglect or disinterest in culture as an issue that could potentially influence political perceptions, decisions and outcomes was the result of a tightly bounded conception of politics advanced both by academic analysts, anxious to advance the claims of their own nascent discipline and by many post-war politicians, who increasingly defined their own role in quasi-professional terms. Perspectives of this sort were not necessarily hostile to cultural discussion and analysis; rather they tended to see culture as distinct, as uninvolved with the business of politics, taking place in a separate sphere beyond the boundaries of parties, programmes and elections.

It was the New Left of the early 1960s that threw down the most coherent intellectual challenge to this restricted political vision.[48] The championing of culture and more particularly a debate about the significance of leisure by New Left intellectuals such as Stuart Hall and Raymond Williams, were important initiatives extending analysis of the way market-based forms of popular entertainment shaped political aspirations.[49] From within mainstream social democracy, the most prominent efforts to engage with consumer culture emerged from the group of Labour MPs who were committed to the economic and political modernization of Britain, thereby challenging the shibboleths of unionism and Bevanism. For these self-styled Labour Party revisionists, notably Tony Crosland and Roy Jenkins, culture loomed large in their political agendas because it was understood to be synonymous with affluence and with the expansion of consumption. These latter issues, they argued, needed to focus the collective mind of Labour politicians and party activists because what informed them was a cluster of cultural images and aspirations affecting electoral choice that were missed by the obsessive labourist focus on production and social welfare.[50] Revisionists demanded that Labour should foster a process of 'cultural reform' that was broadly in keeping with the precepts of social and economic modernization. Both Crosland and Jenkins privileged patterns of taste and styles of living that had much in common with their own progressive middle-class or *haute bourgeois* lifestyles. Culture in their language had a distinctly Parisian or Scandinavian feel. Crosland and Jenkins regularly espoused an enlightened 'continentalism' which centred on the reform of English puritanism and its replacement by a more relaxed style of living and a progressive code of social manners. Consumption featured in their world-view as part of the iconography of modern taste – as good design, food and drink connoisseurship and as an enlightened attitude towards the reform of outdated moral legislation.[51] Revisionists also argued vigorously for an expanded idea of private freedoms that should include greater scope for cultural appreciation and personal decision-making. This enlarged private sphere was to be governed by educated individual choice, thereby reinforcing a definition of culture as discrete and shaped by personal tastes and preferences.

The Social Survey

The cultural focus of the dominant political groups remained relatively restricted. However, a series of adjacent studies produced in the 1960s and 1970s did identify the way in which transformations in contemporary mass culture were reshaping political imagery and aspirations. The British social survey was a project dedicated to commercial and cultural mapping and it was set within an expanded framework of social democracy and a commitment to the mixed economy. The origins of survey techniques have been conventionally located in the nineteenth and early twentieth-century investigations into poverty, unemployment and the social conditions of urban working-class life.[52] David Glass, a key figure in the demographic surveys produced after 1945, defined this tradition as 'a scientific study of social conditions and social problems within a limited geographical setting, the objects of ... study being implicitly or explicitly related to social policy'.[53] During the inter-war period much of the empirical research that was loosely grouped under the category of the social survey was undertaken outside or on the margins of British universities.[54] This enforced isolation from academic institutions reflected the ambivalence of many traditional intellectuals to a type of knowledge that was explicitly concerned with investigating social attitudes (with its potential connotations of propaganda or 'brainwashing') and with the dubious effects of commercial culture. The early techniques of psephology, pioneered under the auspices of the British Institute of Public Opinion from 1936, the growing impact of the survey questionnaire on commercially driven market research, together with the grander projects espoused by Charles Madge and Tom Harrison at Mass-Observation, were among the most visible examples of survey work.[55]

In contrast, survey research in the USA was already integrated into the work of some leading academic institutions by the 1930s. The development of influential schools of empirical sociology and social policy at the University of Chicago, under Robert Park and Ezra Burgess and at Paul Lazarsfeld's Bureau for Applied Social Research at Columbia University in New York, testified to a well-developed tradition of quantitative and qualitative social science that deliberately mixed academic studies of policy with commercially oriented projects.[56] Lazarsfeld's professed aim was to endow consumer research with a greater intellectual complexity, understanding consumer purchasing as 'a special case of human decision behaviour'.[57] While much of the commercial survey work was a practical expedient for keeping his Columbia research centre afloat, Lazarsfeld also polemicized for an intellectual agenda that integrated consumer research into the more traditional orbit of public policy.[58] In the American presidential elections of 1940 and 1948 Lazarsfeld began to address the relationship between mass communications, especially radio and print media and American voting habits. His conclusion was that the national media had only a secondary effect on shaping political beliefs. Echoing the civic-culture debate,

Lazarsfeld insisted that it was family, friends, co-workers and primary groups that were much more influential agents in determining political responsiveness.[59]

The Anglo-American origins of the survey produced an expanded definition of social policy, deliberately mixing heterogeneous methodologies and research themes in a focus on public and private-sector provision. Recent work on the genesis of 'the social' and its relationship to nineteenth and twentieth-century forms of urban modernity has tended to associate such techniques of measurement and information-gathering with government operations, or state programmes and techniques of rule.[60] What was significant about the social survey was its deliberately eclectic character, combining knowledge about the commercially driven consumer with a broader understanding of public provision and political citizenship. This breadth of scope opened the space for a new approach to domestic and personal consumption, which drew on the vocabulary of market research while integrating this work into more established programmes addressing social policy.

In Britain Mark Abrams was one of the key figures in the transatlantic networks that produced an expanded blueprint for the social survey. Trained in sociology at the London School of Economics, where he studied under R.H. Tawney in the late 1920s, he joined one of Britain's leading advertising agencies, the London Press Exchange (LPA), after spending time at the Brookings Institution in Washington. His first post at the LPA was in the Research Department, where he embarked on one of the first major readership surveys. During the war Abrams undertook work for the Ministry of Food on the effects of rationing on nutrition, together with a project on the impact of German bombing on civilian morale.[61] Abrams founded his own company, Research Services Ltd., in 1946, an organization dedicated to studies of public policy and political research, as well as undertaking commercial work on advertising, print media and product usage. Under Abrams' leadership, staff at his company received a wide training in political and social survey techniques that were framed in an Anglo-American intellectual context. Abrams was in close touch with Lipset and Lazarsfeld, engaging their services for seminars and research training whenever they were in London.[62]

Abrams' most frequently cited contribution to consumer research was his fore-casting of the new forms of demand by young people, published as *The Teenage Consumer* (1959). This was the manual that prepared the ground for an expanded conception of the youth market and with it an argument about the commercial significance of post-war generational change. However, behind the specific study lay a much more expansive project on the social analysis of contemporary consumption. As early as 1945, at the height of wartime austerity, Abrams was already polemic-izing for a national assessment of the British population that would divide the nation into consumer units. This was with a view to providing information about consumer demand for government and industry.[63] In practical terms Abrams' arguments influenced the expanded categories covering consumption that were included in the national population censuses between 1951and 1971 and in other government research such as the Family Expenditure Surveys started in the 1950s.[64] In the 1970s Abrams directed the General Household Survey, a project that was conceived as a large-scale sampling of selected households, covering not only traditional aspects of social measurement, such as employment, housing, demography and health, but also leisure and consumption patterns.[65] The Survey Unit of the newly created Social Science Research Council, co-directed by Abrams during the 1970s, championed similar work.[66] It was at this point that his ambitions for the social survey began to draw together research on the markets for leisure and consumer goods with the activities of political and social citizens.

Abrams began his political involvement by assisting the Labour Party with their research strategy in the 1950s, but his ideas did not find immediate favour with some sections of the political leadership. The criticisms that Abrams' polling work provoked, with its notion of the electorate as a political market and his emphasis on effective media communications, anticipated more recent debates about 'spin'. Defending an organic and romanticized view of the politician, Aneurin Bevan reputedly accused Abrams of 'wanting to take the poetry out of politics'. Confronted with Abrams' opinion surveys, Bevan argued that they were superfluous since 'it was the role of the politician to know instinctively what the electorate needs and wants'.[67] Abrams received a warmer reception among the party's modernizers. As leader, Hugh Gaitskell recognized the value of using Abrams' research in his battle to change the political culture of labourism in the late 1950s, while Abrams' quantitative methods found favour with Wilson, himself a former government statistician.

Abrams' commitment to political polling, though partisan, claimed to gauge the opinions of the mass electorate. Attitudinal research reinforced social democratic values, Abrams believed, because it captured the concerns that preoccupied 'ordinary people' and represented them in the raw to professional politicians. But in the 1970s his work in this field registered a growing conflict between political values and what he sensed to be the quite different preoccupations of the majority of the population. Here Abrams returned to the theme of the relationship of politics to contemporary culture. In 1974 he published the results of his national survey, 'Changing Values: a Report on Britain Today', in the journal *Encounter*. His research claimed to provide evidence of the relative levels of satisfaction evidenced by a sample of Britain's adult population with various aspects of their lives. For Abrams, the precise measurement of what he had already termed 'subjective social indicators' provided a way of exploring some of the broader-based value systems held by consumers and citizens.[68] Measurement of the 'objective' yardsticks of income, housing and other levels of social provision, Abrams insisted, was only one side of the equation underpinning perceptions of quality of life. What was also needed was some way of registering subjective satisfactions.

The context of the *Encounter* survey was largely set by the debate about the state of democracy. Abrams was concerned to identify a set of values that he claimed was in serious competition with public and political institutions. He had already made a similar intervention in the post-mortem on the Labour Party's general election defeat in 1959, arguing for greater knowledge of what he termed the electorate's personal imagery and claiming that this exercised an important informal influence on political choices.[69] The findings published in *Encounter* suggested that it was 'personal well-being', in both a 'material' and an 'emotional' sense, that was now the most important focus for positive perceptions of quality of life. The state of political parties and public institutions came a poor second to this individualizing emphasis.[70] Abrams had undertaken a more detailed analysis using similar categories in the early 1970s under the auspices of the newly created Social Science Council's Survey Unit. While the various survey returns recorded the usual low levels of satisfaction with politicians and with democratic institutions, these factors appeared to have little bearing on perceptions of quality of life. What the majority of respondents prioritized were issues that were much closer to home: marriage, family life and crucially leisure, rather than traditional public institutions, in their evaluation of personal well-being.[71] Summing up his findings, Abrams announced that his research confirmed a fundamental change in the values held by large sections of the British public, namely the greater centrality of personal and material well-being and particularly the emphasis on 'a comfortable life', in shaping political response.[72]

Abrams' social-survey findings bring our story about the perceived decline of representative democracy and the accelerated rise in personal consumption back to the point where we began, with the Henley Centre. What has this excursion into the dual history of liberal democracy and social research revealed about the relationship between political citizenship and the subjects of consumption during the post-war years? I have attempted to establish the outlines of an intellectual history that brought politics into alignment with consumer culture during a period of major economic expansion and cultural change. This was not, of course, the first time that intellectuals and politicians had debated such a relationship and its consequences. The late-nineteenth and early-twentieth centuries witnessed related discussions about the connections between the new political subjects of mass democracy and the impact of popular leisure and entertainment across Europe and the USA. During the period after the Second World War projects dedicated to understanding this relationship were prioritized by a group of intellectuals who were central to both social democratic politics and commercial culture. One of their most striking features was that unlike so many from the English cultural elite, the values that this group championed were neither inward-looking, nor defensive, nor paternalistic. Figures like Abrams were self-consciously eclectic in the conceptual resources that they drew on and in the hybrid nature of their institutional location. Mixing statistical research with qualitative methods, which ranged across the social sciences and the humanities, they frequently crossed the boundaries separating business and entrepreneurship from traditional public institutions. Much of the social research they championed was conceived as a transatlantic project, rather than as an affirmation of one specific national culture, because liberal political values and consumerism were understood to have a broad Anglo-American reach. This was a story played out in an international context that was increasingly shaped by transnational flows of personnel and knowledge about consumer demand and social democracy.

English and American liberals displayed an increasing sense of anxiety about the state of their respective political cultures, but they remained optimistic about private-sector consumption and about its ability to shape the social values of contemporary society. Their version of secular materialism was confident and unapologetic; as such it was grounded in a belief in the culture of abundance and the release from scarcity that characterized so much mainstream political and cultural commentary in the 1950s and 1960s. In this respect their championing of post-war affluence and with it a vision of progressive social transformation, was sharply differentiated from the critiques of consumer capitalism that were emerging in Europe and the USA at broadly the same period, under the combined auspices of a revived tradition of western Marxism and the new social movements. Equally, liberal intellectuals also distanced themselves from later versions of market supremacy espoused by the political right, because the ameliorative vision projected by social research was always dependent on a mixture of public and private-sector provision, in ways that combined consumer choice with civic responsibility. The consumer market could not serve as the blueprint for all types of social and political relationships; it was the interdependencies and obligations between different groups of subjects – voters, social citizens, consumers – that ideally characterized the working of a mature and responsible democracy. Such a vision enshrined a highly selective reading of the social actors who were understood to be central to these processes. Yet the relationships posed by this liberal intellectual tradition between democratic forms of government and the expansion of consumer society point to an important set of connections between formal politics and commercial culture that demands more sustained attention. Political and cultural historians would do well to explore in greater depth these liminal features of modern commercial society and the ways in which citizen subjects and consuming subjects are very often mutually dependent on each other.

Notes

* I should like to thank Frank Trentmann, Peter Thompson and Chris Waters for their helpful comments on this piece.

1. The Henley Centre for Forecasting, *Planning for Social Change*, Vol. 1 (London, 1986), p. 119. See also the Henley Centre's *Consumer and Leisure Futures*

(London, Spring 1997) and *Planning for Consumer Change 11/99* (London, 1999).

2. Henley Centre, *Planning for Social Change*, p. 119.

3. Z. Bauman, 'Britain's Exit from Politics', *New Statesman and Society*, 29 July 1988, p. 37. See also Z. Bauman, *The Individualized Society* (Cambridge, 2001); Z. Bauman, *Legislators and Interpreters* (Cambridge, 1987). See also A. Gorz, *Farewell to the Working Class* (London, 1982), p. 91.

4. R. McKibbin, 'How to Put the Politics back into Labour', *London Review of Books*, 25(1) (7 August 2003) pp. 3, 5.

5. For work on the citizen consumer see M. Daunton and M. Hilton (eds), *The Politics of Consumption: Material Culture and Citizenship* (Oxford and New York, 2001); M. Hilton, *Consumerism in Twentieth-Century Britain* (Cambridge, 2003); P. Maclachlan and F. Trentmann, 'Civilizing Markets: Traditions of Consumer Politics in Twentieth-Century Britain, Japan and the United States' in M. Bevir and F. Trentmann (eds), *Markets in Historical Contexts* (Cambridge, 2004), pp. 170–201. For work on the cultural consumer see D. Hebdige, *Subculture: The Meaning of Style* (London, 1979); T. Modleski, *Loving with a Vengeance: Mass-Produced Fantasies for Women* (Hamden, CT, 1982); M. Nava, *Changing Cultures: Feminism, Youth and Consumerism* (London, 1992). For the connections between these spheres see also the chapters by Merkel, Rappaport, Trentmann and Taylor, and Kline in this volume.

6. Lizabeth Cohen, *A Consumer's Republic: The Politics of Mass Consumption in Postwar America* (New York, 2003), p. 8.

7. See especially F. Mort, *Cultures of Consumption: Masculinities and Social Space in Late Twentieth-Century Britain* (London, 1996); F. Mort, 'Archaeologies of City Life: Commercial Culture, Masculinity and Spatial Relations in 1980s London', *Environment and Planning D: Society and Space*, 13 (1995), pp. 573–90. See also E. Wilson, *Adorned in Dreams: Fashion and Modernity* (London, Virago, 1985); V. Steele, *Paris Fashion: A Cultural History* (Oxford and New York, 1998); C. Breward, *Fashioning London: Clothing and the Modern Metropolis* (Oxford and New York, 2004).

8. See S. Verba, 'On Revisiting the Civic Culture: A Personal Postscript' in G. Almond and S. Verba (eds), *The Civic Culture Revisited* (Boston, 1989), pp. 394–410; L. Joseph, 'Democratic Revisionism Revisited', *American Journal of Political Science*, 25(1) (February 1981), pp. 160–87; B. Crick, *The American Science of Politics: Its Origins and Conditions* (London, 1998). For the deep scepticism about liberal political democracy in inter-war Europe see W. Rappard, *The Crisis of Democracy* (Chicago, IL, 1938); C. Schmitt, trans. E. Kennedy, *The Crisis of Parliamentary Democracy* (Cambridge, MA, 1985); M. Mazower, *Dark Continent: Europe's Twentieth Century* (London, 1998), chapter 1.

9. G. Almond and S. Verba, *The Civic Culture: Political Attitudes and Democracy in Five Nations* (Princeton, NJ, 1963), pp. 473–505; S. Lipset, *Political Man: The Social Bases of Politics* (London, 1960), Parts I and II.

10. Verba, 'Revisiting the Civic Culture', p. 407.
11. Lipset, *Political Man*, p. 9.
12. Almond and Verba, *Civic Culture*, p. 29, also pp. 117, 206.
13. The early civic culture debate acknowledged a significant debt to 'historians, social philosophers, anthropologists, sociologists, psychologists, and psychiatrists who have been concerned with the relations between the psychological and political characteristics of nations', Almond and Verba, *Civic Culture*, p. 13. For examples of these studies see: R. Bricker, *Is Germany Incurable?* (Philadelphia, 1943); M. Mead, *And Keep Your Powder Dry: An Anthropologist Looks at America* (New York, 1943); G. Gorer, *Exploring English Character* (London, 1955).
14. Lipset, *Political Man*, p. 197. See also S. Lipset and R. Bendix, *Social Mobility in Industrial Society* (London, 1959), pp. 68–9.
15. Lipset, *Political Man*, p. 115. See also T. Adorno, E. Frenkel-Brunswick, D. Levinson, R. Nevitt Sanford *et al.*, *The Authoritarian Personality* (New York, 1950). For debates about the relationship between economic status and civic participation see Mass Observation, *Puzzled People: A Study in Popular Attitudes to Religion, Ethics, Progress and Politics in a London Borough* (London, 1947), p. 119; T. Bottomore, 'Social Stratification in Voluntary Organizations' in D. Glass (ed.), *Social Mobility in Britain* (London, 1954), pp. 349–82; H. Maccoby, 'The Differential Political Activity of Participants in a Voluntary Organization', *American Sociological Review*, 23(5) (October 1958), pp. 524–32.
16. Lipset, *Political Man*, p. 199. See also R. Milne and H. Mackenzie, *Marginal Seat 1955: A Study of Voting Behaviour in the Constituency of Bristol North East at the General Election of 1955* (London, 1958), p. 69; J. Narbonne and M. Dogan, 'L'Abstentionnisme Electoral en France', *Revue Française Science Politique*, 4(1) (January-March 1954), pp. 5–26. For critiques of gender blindness see C. Pateman, *The Sexual Contract* (Cambridge, 1988); M. Shanley and C. Pateman (eds), *Feminist Interpretations and Political Theory* (Cambridge, 1991); N. Fraser, *Unruly Practices: Power, Discourse, and Gender in Contemporary Social Theory* (Minneapolis, 1989).
17. Lipset, *Political Man*, p. 207. Lipset based his arguments on R. Lynd and H. Lynd, *Middletown: A Study in Contemporary American Culture* (London, 1929); R. Lynd and H. Lynd, *Middletown in Transition: A Study in Cultural Conflicts* (London, 1937).
18. For critiques of post-war liberal democratic theory see S. Brittan, *The Economic Contradictions of Democracy* (London, 1977); R. Ingelhart, *The Silent Revolution: Changing Values and Political Styles among Western Publics* (Princeton, NJ, 1977); D. Kavanagh, 'Political Culture in Great Britain: The Decline of the Civic Culture' in Almond and Verba, *Civic Culture Revisited*, pp. 124–76; C. Pateman, *The Disorder of Women: Democracy, Feminism and Political Theory* (Cambridge, 1989), chapter 7; J. Gibbins, 'Contemporary

Political Culture: An Introduction' in J. Gibbins (ed.), *Contemporary Political Culture* (London, 1989), pp. 1–30.

19. To its adherents, political culture was defined as 'a particular distribution of political attitudes, feelings, information and skills', G. Almond and G. Powell, *Comparative Politics Today: A World View* (Boston, 1984), p. 37, or as 'political orientations – attitudes towards the political system', Almond and Verba, *Civic Culture*, p. 13. For commentary see Gibbins, *Contemporary Political Culture*, p. 7.

20. For some of the varied methodological approaches defining this culturalist tradition see: R. Hoggart, *The Uses of Literacy* (London, 1957); R. Williams, *Culture and Society 1780–1950* (London, 1958); E.P. Thompson, *The Making of the English Working Class* (London, 1963). For analysis see C. Critcher, 'Sociology, Cultural Studies and the Post-War Working Class' in J. Clarke, C. Critcher and R. Johnson (eds), *Working Class Culture* (London, 1979), pp. 13–40; S. Hall, 'Cultural Studies and the Centre' in S. Hall, *et al.* (eds), *Culture, Media, Language* (London, 1980), pp. 15–47; D. Dworkin, *Cultural Marxism in Postwar Britain* (Durham, NC, 1997).

21. Richard Johnson, 'Three Problematics: Elements of a Theory of Working-Class Culture' in Clarke *et al.*, *Working Class Culture*, pp. 201–37.

22. J. Goldthorpe, D. Lockwood, F. Bechhofer and J. Platt, *The Affluent Worker: Political Attitudes and Behaviour* (London, 1968). See also their *The Affluent Worker: Industrial Attitudes and Behaviour* (London, 1968) and *The Affluent Worker in the Class Structure* (London, 1969). For commentary see J. Platt, *Realities of Social Research: An Empirical Study of British Sociologists* (London, 1976).

23. Goldthorpe *et al.*, *Affluent Worker: Political Attitudes*, p. 8.

24. Ibid., p. 75. See also J. Goldthorpe and D. Lockwood, 'Affluence and the British Class Structure', *Sociological Review*, 11(2) (July 1963), pp. 133–63.

25. Goldthorpe, *Affluent Worker: Political Attitudes*, p. 75.

26. F. Zweig, *The Worker in an Affluent Society* (London, 1961), p. 209. See also his *The New Acquisitive Society* (Chichester, 1976).

27. Lipset, *Political Man*, p. 207.

28. Pateman, *Disorder of Women*, p. 143.

29. Almond and Verba, *Civic Culture*, p. 53.

30. M. Young and P. Willmott, *Family and Kinship in East London* (London, 1957); P. Willmott and M. Young, *Family and Class in a London Suburb* (London, 1960); Elizabeth Bott, *Family and Social Network: Roles, Norms and External Relationships in Ordinary Families* (London, 1964).

31. Goldthorpe, *et al.*, *Affluent Worker in the Class Structure*.

32. A. Abramowitz, 'The United States: Political Culture under Stress' in Almond and Verba, *Civic Culture Revisited*, pp. 177–211; D. Bell, *The Coming of Post-Industrial Society* (New York, 1973); D. Bell, *The Cultural Contradictions of Capitalism* (New York, 1976).

33. D. Marquand, 'The Decline of the Post-War Consensus' in A. Gorst and W.S. Lucas (eds), *Post-War Britain* (London, 1989), pp. 1–21; D. Kavanagh and P. Morris, *Consensus Politics from Atlee to Major*, second edition (Oxford, 1994), and their 'Controversy: Is the "Postwar Consensus" a Myth?', *Contemporary Record*, 2(6) (1989), pp. 12–15. For critiques of consensus from the right see C. Barnett, *The Audit of War* (London, 1989); C. Barnett, *The Lost Victory: British Dreams, British Realities 1945–1950* (London, 1995); A. Roberts, *Eminent Churchillians* (London, 1994), p. 3.

34. S. Beer, *Britain against Itself: The Political Contradictions of Collectivism* (London, 1982), pp. 144–6; J. Alt, *The Politics of Economic Decline: Economic Management and Political Behaviour in Britain since 1964* (Cambridge, 1979), p. 200; V. Hart, *Distrust and Democracy: Political Distrust in Britain and America* (Cambridge, 1978).

35. See B. Crick, *The Reform of Parliament* (London, 1964). Crick pointed out that his study had earlier and more overtly political origins in a Fabian pamphlet, *Reform of the Commons* (London: Fabian Tract No. 319, 1959), and in his personal contribution to Lord Chorley, B. Crick and D. Chapman, *Reform of the Lords* (London, Fabian Research Series No. 169, 1954). For a contemporary overview of this debate see A. Barker, 'Parliamentary Studies, 1961–65: A Bibliography and Comment', *Political Quarterly*, 36(3) (July–September 1965), pp. 347–59; A. Barker and M. Rush and Political and Economic Planning, *The Member of Parliament and His Information* (London, 1970).

36. Quoted in A. Sampson, *Anatomy of Britain Today* (London, 1965), p. 38. For further commentary see Barker and Rush, *Member of Parliament*, pp. 131–2.

37. D. Frost, *An Autobiography: Part 1 From Congregations to Audiences* (London, 1993), chapter 3; C. Booker, *The Neophiliacs: A Study of the Revolution in English Life in the Fifties and Sixties* (London, 1969), chapters 7 and 8.

38. See 'Labour Will Repeal Rent Act, says Mr. Wilson', *The Times*, 23 February 1963, p. 8, also H. Wilson, 'The Role of the Commons I', *Listener*, 14 November 1963, pp. 775–6; H. Wilson, 'The Role of the Commons II', *Listener*, 21 November 1963, pp. 815–16, 833. See also B. Pimlott, *Harold Wilson* (London, 1992), chapter 13.

39. Barker and Rush, *Member of Parliament*, p. 379.

40. See Royal Commission on Local Government in England, 1966–9, *Report*, Vol. 1, Cmnd. 4040, 1968–9, XXXVIII; Civil Service Commission, *The Civil Service*, 1968, Vol. 1, Cmnd. 3638, 1967–8, XVIII; Royal Commission on the Constitution 1969–73, *Report*, Vol. 1, Cmnd. 5460, 1973–4, XI.

41. Crick, *Reform of Parliament*, pp. x, 2.

42. Royal Commission on the Constitution, *Memorandum of Dissent by Lord Crowther-Hunt and Professor A.T. Peacock*, Vol. 2, Cmnd. 5460–I, 1973–4, XI, p. 34.

43. Royal Commission on the Constitution, *Report*, Vol. 1, p. 124. The Commission noted that the percentage turnouts at British general elections had fallen steadily

from 84 per cent in 1950 to 72 per cent in 1971, with the exception of 1959 when there had been a slight rise. It also noted that voting figures for other European democracies were mostly higher than in the United Kingdom, and while allowances needed to be made for differences in the voting system, 'no country comparable to the United Kingdom shows a similar downward trend' (p. 124).

44. I. Crewe and J. Spence, 'Parliament and Public', *New Society*, 12 July 1973, pp. 78–80.

45. Royal Commission on the Constitution, *Devolution and Other Aspects of Government: An Attitudes Survey Prepared for the Office of Population, Census and Surveys by Social and Community Planning Research*, Research Papers No. 7 (London, 1973), pp. xi, 14. The findings of the Royal Commission on Local Government in England reinforced this sense of the electorate's belief that politicians were a separate class or caste, see *Report*, Vol. 1.

46. For political distrust among the young see R. Inglehart, 'The Silent Revolution in Europe: Intergenerational Change in Post-Industrial Societies', *American Political Science Review*, LXV(4) (December 1971), pp. 991–1017; Hart, *Distrust and Democracy*, p. 38. For evidence that political distrust tended to be greater among the less formally educated and among sections of the working-class see Royal Commission on the Constitution, *Report*, Vol. 1, p. 21; Hart, *Distrust and Democracy*, pp. 58, 61–2.

47. For evidence of political disaffection in Britain during the 1950s see Mass Observation, *Puzzled People*, p. 151. For the questioning of consensus see S. Hall and T. Jefferson (eds), *Resistance Through Rituals: Youth Subcultures in Post-War Britain* (London, 1976); S. Hall, C. Critcher, T. Jefferson and B. Roberts, *Policing the Crisis: Mugging, the State, and Law and Order* (London, 1978); E. Wilson, *Only Halfway to Paradise: Women in Postwar Britain* (London, 1980); P. Gilroy, *There Ain't No Black in the Union Jack: The Cultural Politics of Race and Nation* (London, 1987); A. Sinfield, *Literature, Politics and Culture in Postwar Britain* (Oxford, 1989); B. Conekin, F. Mort and C. Waters (eds), *Moments of Modernity: Reconstructing Britain 1945–1964* (London and New York, 1999).

48. For the cultural politics of the New Left see R. Archer *et al.*, *Out of Apathy: Voices of the New Left Thirty Years on* (London, 1989); M. Kenny, *The First New Left: British Intellectuals after Stalin* (London, 1995); Dworkin, *Cultural Marxism*.

49. R. Williams, *The Long Revolution* (London, 1961); S. Hall and P. Whannel, *The Popular Arts* (London, 1964). For a more pessimistic position see Hoggart, *The Uses of Literacy*.

50. C. Crosland, *The Future of Socialism* (London, 1956); C. Crosland, *The Conservative Enemy: A Programme of Radical Reform for the 1960s* (London, 1963); R. Jenkins, *The Labour Case* (Harmondsworth, 1959).

51. For Roy Jenkins' own curiously understated analysis of this reforming agenda see his autobiography, *A Life at the Centre* (London, 1991), chapters 9 and 10. On Crosland see S. Crosland, *Tony Crosland* (London, 1983); K. Jefferys, *Anthony Crosland* (London, 1999); S. Hall, 'Reformism and the Legislation of Consent' in National Deviancy Conference (eds), *Permissiveness and Control: The Fate of the Sixties Legislation* (London, 1980), pp. 1–43.

52. See C. Booth, *Life and Labour of the People of London*, 17 vols, 1892–7 (New York, 1970); H. Llewellyn Smith, *The New Survey of London Life and Labour*, 9 vols (London, 1930–5).

53. D. Glass, quoted in M. Bulmer, K. Bales and K. Kish Sklar (eds), *The Social Survey in Historical Perspective* (Cambridge, 1991), p. 3. See also M. Abrams, *Social Surveys and Social Action* (London, 1951).

54. Queenie Leavis, a member of the Cambridge Scrutiny movement with her husband F.R. Leavis, conducted her own survey of contemporary reading habits, using these findings to reinforce arguments about popular culture and moral decline, see Q. Leavis, *Fiction and the Reading Public* (London, 1932).

55. For earlier examples of the social survey questionnaire see P. Redmayne and H. Weeks, *Market Research*, Library of Advertising No. 2 (London, 1931); Mass-Observation, *First Year's Work* (London, 1938); Mass-Observation Archive, *Papers from the Mass-Observation Archive at the University of Sussex, Part 3, The Worktown Collection, 1937–40* (London, 2001).

56. P. Lazarsfeld, 'An Episode in the History of Social Research: A Memoir' in D. Fleming and B. Bailyn (eds), *The Intellectual Migration: Europe and America 1930–1960* (Cambridge, MA, 1969), pp. 270–337.

57. Quoted in J. Converse, *Survey Research in the United States: Roots and Emergence 1890–1960* (Berkeley, CA, 1987), p. 137. For Lazarsfeld's commitment to consumer research, especially audience research, see E. Katz and P. Lazarsfeld, *Personal Influence* (New York, 1955).

58. J. Converse, *Survey Research*, p. 271. For other examples of Lazarsfeld's commercially commissioned work see P. Lazarsfeld, B. Berelson and H. Gaudet, *The People's Choice* (New York, 1944); P. Lazarsfeld and P. Kendall, *Radio Listening in America* (New York, 1948).

59. See W. Severin and J. Tankard, *Communication Theories* (New York, 1997), pp. 222–3, 361–6.

60. For treatments of the social as part of modern governmentality see D. Levin (ed.), *Modernity and the Hegemony of Vision* (Berkeley, CA, 1993); J. Law, *Organising Modernity* (Oxford, 1994); N. Rose, *Governing the Soul: The Shaping of the Private Self* (London, 1999); P. Joyce, *The Rule of Freedom: Liberalism and the Modern City* (London, 2003).

61. D. Mitchell, 'Research for the Truth; Obituary Mark Abrams', *Guardian*, 27 September 1994, p. 17. See also 'Mark Abrams: Obituary', *The Times*, 29 September 1994, p. 21.

62. Mitchell, 'Research for the Truth'.
63. M. Abrams, *The Population of Great Britain* (London, 1945).
64. Ministry of Labour, *Family Expenditure Survey: Report for 1957–59* (London, 1961); Central Office of Information, Social Survey, *Family Expenditure Survey: Handbook on the Sampling, Fieldwork and Coding Procedures* (London, 1969).
65. See, for example, Office of Population Censuses and Surveys: Social Survey Division, *The General Household Survey: Introductory Report* (London, 1973); Office of Population Censuses and Surveys, *Women in Britain 1971–76* (London, 1978). For analysis see M. Bulmer, *Essays on the History of British Sociological Research 1880–1914* (Cambridge, 1985); Bulmer *et al.*, *Social Survey*.
66. See M. Abrams, *A Review of Work on Subjective Social Indicators*, Occasional Papers in Survey Research 8 (London, 1976), p. 16.
67. Quoted in 'Mark Abrams: Obituary', *The Times*, p. 21. For this emotive and instinctual view of British politics and politicians during the 1950s see M. Francis, 'Tears, Tantrums, and Bared Teeth: The Emotional Economy of Three Conservative Prime Ministers, 1951–1963', *Journal of British Studies*, 41 (July 2002), pp. 354–87.
68. M. Abrams, 'Changing Values: A Report on Britain Today', *Encounter*, October 1974, p. 29. See also Abrams, *A Review of Work on Subjective Social Indicators;* M. Abrams, 'Subjective Social Indicators', *Social Trends*, 4 (1973), pp. 35–50.
69. See M. Abrams and R. Rose, with a commentary by Rita Hinden, *Must Labour Lose?* (Harmondsworth, 1960), pp. 7–11.
70. Abrams' arguments in *Encounter* were the results of a national sample of one thousand interviewees. They measured the levels of satisfaction and dissatisfaction of Britain's urban adult population with the quality of their lives. Respondents were asked to rank four value statements in terms of which appeared the most desirable. These were: 1. Maintain law and order in the nation. 2. Give the people more say in important political decisions. 3. Achieve a higher standard of living for everyone. 4. Protect freedom of speech. Forty-three per cent gave first or second preference to higher living standards, while only 4 per cent gave first or second preference to greater political participation and freedom of speech, and 53 per cent gave other combinations of values (Abrams, 'Changing Values', pp. 30–1).
71. Abrams, *Subjective Social Indicators*, p. 41.
72. Abrams, 'Changing Values', p. 38.

–11–

From Stigma to Cult

Changing Meanings in East German Consumer Culture

Ina Merkel

It is astonishing: an enraptured outcry travelled through East Germany when the hazelnut-filled chocolate bar Bambina (thought to be lost) appeared again on supermarket shelves. Shortly thereafter a prominent actor wistfully remembered the Trabant: 'It smelled terrible, was loud and uncomfortable, but one loved it, what else could one have loved'.[1] The company Rondo (the only coffee production company in the GDR) is in profit again, the cigarette brands F6 and Cabinet have gained cult status and in East German bars and kiosks one can buy Club-Cola, which leaves a furry residue in one's mouth. The symbols of a ridiculed, meagre, easily disposable culture of consumption have today become the starting point of happy remembrance. And as if this were not enough, young girls buy blue T-shirts with the socialist emblem of the Ernst-Thälmann-Pioneers, and on the streets young men walk about with the script Interflug (a GDR-airline) emblazoned on their chests. The ice-skating star Katarina Witt poses in a blouse of the socialist youth organization FDJ for the magazine *Super-Illu*, and next to her a colleague from the West is dressed in a brown tracksuit of the former army sports team.

Company logos and advertising slogans, even the symbols of political culture, are wantonly incorporated into fashion and everyday aesthetics. The GDR – which became defunct as a 'society of shortage',[2] failing in the competition of social systems – celebrates its resurrection as, of all things, a brand (see Figure 9). The commercialisation of the GDR past reached a new peak in the summer of 2003 in nostalgic retro-shows in public as well as commercial television programmes. In public discourse this phenomenon has become known as *Ostalgie* (Ostalgia*).*[3]

Ostalgia takes its pictures, images and symbols, its signs of remembrance, mainly from the field of consumption – as is customary in every wave of nostalgia – but also from political culture. The everyday world of the GDR and the objects people lived with more or less casually received their symbolic character retrospectively. This happened in such a way that people today are able to gain a belated distinction and new admiration. Ostalgia is, in the first instance, a politics of identity.

Ostalgia is embedded in a discursive field. On the surface it concerns the negotiation of cultural hegemony between West and East Germans. The change in political

> ▶NEUE DEUTSCHE WELLE
>
> ▣ Kultige Wiedervereinigung Mit flotten Wende-Sprüchen und alten DDR-Emblemen bedruckt sind T-Shirts aus Berlin bei Jugendlichen der Renner

Hoppla, jetzt kommen wir!

OSTALGIEWELLE Seit »Sonnenallee« und »Good bye, Lenin!« entdeckt auch der Westen flippige Mode, flotte Musik, freche Sprüche und Kultstars des Ostens

Figure 9 Young Girls Wearing GDR Symbols, 2003

Note: From left: 'Mondos' = condom, 'Held der Arbeit' = hero of labour, JP = Junge Pioniere (youth organization), GDR emblem, 'Interflug' = GDR airline.

Source: Andre Kowalski, *Super-Illu + RTL Sonderheft*, No. 1 (2003), p. 6.

systems, which involved a transfer of institutions and elites from West to East Germany as well as a Western-dominated process of economic transformation, has been publicly discussed in ethnic terms: 'The West Germans vs. the East Germans'.[4] Consumer culture is especially suited for this discursive negotiation, since it had always been a highly politicized sphere in the competition between systems – which the GDR lost. Hence the label a 'society of scarcity' or *Mangelgesellschaft*.

The comparison with the Western world of consumption offered a decisive opportunity for the voting out of the system, both in the exodus and the elections of 1990. After 1989 the whole world of Eastern objects was thrown away and treated as waste. There has never been a more radical devaluation of everyday life in history and to a great extent it was driven by people living in the GDR. Why is it that now the GDR is fondly, even euphorically remembered with regard to consumption? How can we explain that the symbols of the system – initially associated with terms like a state of injustice, (welfare) dictatorship and command economy – came to be reabsorbed so easily? Why do new generations use the design, brands and slogans of the product culture of the GDR in the expression of their everyday aesthetics? How can this change of interpretation from stigma to cult, or what Wolfgang Engler has called the shift from the notion of scandal to the notion of festivity,[5] be explained?

Objects of consumption are energized with meanings that lie beyond the immediate process of consumption (purchase, use, design). A polysemic repertoire of consuming signs emerges that is used in different contexts of interpretation. The same objects can be invoked as representations of a political system as well as signs of everyday life. Such signs and symbols are principal forms for negotiating fundamental questions about the value systems of the two parts of Germany, that is questions about repression and freedom, individuality and community, distinction and equality. The discourse of consumption therefore functions as proxy for debates surrounding the problems of reunification, the transformation of East German society and the rapprochement or polarisation of the two German cultures. Like no other, consumption is a particularly rich sphere for this symbolic discourse, because it is immediately connected to the experience of individuals and issues of maintaining one's life as well as designing one's lifestyle.

This chapter explores the transformation of people's relationships to material objects since the collapse of the GDR at three discursive levels. At first desired and loved, objects were later hated, rejected, hidden or forgotten. Or they were ridiculed and scorned, but then rediscovered in the trash bin, pitied, exoticized and raised to the level of cult object. The cycle from purchase, use, disposal and reappropriation has been energized and accelerated in a previously unknown fashion since the collapse of the socialist system. It has resulted in a simultaneity of conflicting practices. These reflect individual experiences with East German cultures of consumption, biographical ruptures after reunification, new opportunities and the first encounters with a foreign land.

At a second level, this chapter concerns the public speaking and handling of GDR cultures of consumption, their consumers, practices and objects. The dominant discourse has seen a significant interpretative change from scandalizing or stigmatizing objects to that of incorporating them into museums and festivals. Ethnic representations, the use of irony and commercialisation can be identified as three discursive counter-movements in this process. The different politics of identity that have emerged, however, cannot be reduced to clearly defined social positions such as class, generation or milieu. There are discursive alliances between West German Christian Democracy and East German dissidents in the dominant discourse, while cultural counter-movements bring together Western participants in Ostalgia with youth subcultures, East German pensioners, artists and entrepreneurs. We are therefore dealing with situational forms of behaviour. East Germans share a collective experience of the collapse of the socialist regime and reunification, but they occupy a range of different positions and interpretations. A third level concerns the re-establishment of old GDR brands after reunification in a market setting. Depending on target groups and their positioning in regional or European contexts, marketing strategies appealed to modern lifestyles or to a sense of solidarity and patriotism.

These three discursive levels stand in dialogue with each other, sometimes addressing each other, sometimes moving in opposite directions. What they share is a pejorative view of Ostalgia whenever strategies of remembrance carry a positive sense of the GDR. The label Ostalgia is reserved for the strategic mobilisation of the East German past designed to add positive cultural value to East German life. Within these politics of identity it is not possible to see any clear positive reflection on the political system of the GDR. Rather, distinct aspects of East German life, cultural particularities, social structures and even political practices are remembered and represented in distance, opposition or resistance to the former political system. Ostalgia, in other words, is not nostalgia in the literal sense. Instead of a nostalgic culture of remembrance, it is about East Germans insisting on their specific identity. Thus they declare themselves implicitly as an oppressed, even 'colonial', part of German culture. Ostalgia is ascriptive and serves the labelling of the identity politics of East Germans. It is a term that classifies certain strategies by East Germans in the lifeworld as backward looking and inadequate,[6] ranging from the cultural critique of the process of transformation to West German hegemony in all aspects of economics and political and academic life.

Metamorphoses of Relations to Objects: The Trabant[7]

The Trabant has been particularly suited for the symbolic appropriation of East German objects and offers a case study of the multiple changes of meanings attached to the GDR in general,[8] and to consumer culture in particular. After the worst shortages of the post-war era had passed, the dream of the average East German centred on a car of one's own. Resulting from a mixture of enthusiasm for technology, the fantasy of wealth and the wish to service the needs of the population, the GDR aimed at the production of a small car. Because of a lack of raw materials, Duraplass was invented for the chassis – the origin of the nickname 'Rennpappe'[9] (racing cardboard).

In GDR times the range of cars was very limited. There was the home-produced Wartburg, also a two-stroke engine and various cars from other socialist countries, such as the Skoda, Dacia, Polski-Fiat and Lada in even more limited numbers. The Trabant was and remained the most prominent car on the streets, its design staying the same over a long period of time. It was a typical, small car with simple technological functions. It was robust, easily repaired by the owners themselves, easy to care for and in the pale colours typical of the time. As the waiting time for a car increased – between the 1960s and the end of the 1980s it had increased to 14 years – the car had to be constantly cared for. On the used-car market, five-year-old cars were still selling for the original price and even more.

This may have been acceptable in the 1950s and 1960s, because for many people a car only then became affordable, but owing to the expansion of wealth in the 1970s the status of the car was downgraded from luxury to that of an object of everyday life. Demand now heavily exceeded supply. Under these circumstances one was happy to be able to have a car at all. Dissatisfaction with the old-fashioned, not very efficient, slow, loud and uncomfortable car was reflected in loving, ironic comments: *Kugelporsche* (ball Porsche), *Hutschachtel* (hatbox), *Karton de Blamage* (embarrassment box). In short, people had little choice. Use value exceeded the value of social distinction. When the Wall came down, masses of GDR citizens drove across the border in Trabants, where West Germans laughed at the cars, viewed them as curiosities and were annoyed because of the smell they made. The masses of single identical cars, full of people in faded jeans, queuing in front of banks to collect their welcome money and then rushing to the discount supermarket Aldi, caused negative associations in the West: here they come, the poor brothers and sisters.

The Trabant became the symbol for the ambivalence of the fall of the Wall. At the same time as the peaceful revolution was being celebrated, the devaluation of the GDR continued, a process partly driven by GDR citizens themselves. The Trabant became a stigma, the people who drove them an enigma, an amazing race of drivers: what, you waited for years just to get a car like this? No sooner was the West German mark there than Trabants were abandoned by the roadside in large numbers, given away or sold for a symbolic mark. Many had only one thing on their minds, to get rid of the Trabant as quickly as possible and never to have to drive one again. This process of devaluation, from everyday object to waste and worthlessness, was fast and steady. After only a few years Trabants had almost completely disappeared from the streets.

Interestingly, already by 1991 the Trabant had become the subject for a successful movie. A Trabant by the name of Schorsch was the main character in *Go, Trabi, go!*,[10] a road movie in which a family drives all the way from Saxony to Rome after the fall of the Wall. The car of the simple man, with the possibility of erecting a tent for three people on the roof, cheap, often broken, slow but practical, was looked upon with astonishment – a phenomenon. All the characteristics of reunification are there in the movie, though in a rather atypical fashion for the time. It allowed East Germans a liberating, rehabilitating but also a valedictory laugh. The very short time, only one month, between abandoning Trabis in droves and its symbolic revaluation in a movie is symptomatic for the process of reunification; things happened abruptly and simultaneously and people behaved in seemingly contradictory manners.

Only three years after reunification a huge advertisement at Tegel (Berlin) airport proclaimed 'Rent a Trabant!' in English. The sign signalled a change in interpretation. The company was marketing a 'lost' feeling. Rarity made the Trabant again desirable, but not for everybody. The English slogan is not only funny; it points to the target audience, foreigners, West Germans and the young, people who had never had to drive it. Distinction stemmed from rarity. Nowadays there are Trabant-safaris through the Märkische Schweiz and Ostalgia tours through Mecklenburg in a Trabant. Driving through the streets in one is as sensational as a veteran car show.

Figure 10 Trabi as Advertising Medium, 2004

Source: Ina Merkel, Berlin, 2004.

In the following years the Trabant was used for art and advertisements (see Figure 10). People changed it into a convertible or just kept it in a shed, to forget it or hoping for its resurrection as a valuable oldie. Almost simultaneously with its disappearance, it became a cult object (in the private sphere) and museum piece (in the public sphere).

From rubbish to exhibition piece to cult status – this is the normal metamorphosis of objects in modern consumer societies, when they are no longer used in everyday life. Normally there are decades between these phases. The uniqueness of the collapse of the GDR is that this process happened at an unbelievable pace and all at once. While the last hardy Trabant drivers were still fighting for their next MOT, they could already see the car in a museum. Such objects did not lose their value slowly and steadily; they became rubbish and immediately reached the museum stage.[11] A current part of life was suddenly consigned to the past. This is, however, a prerequisite to qualify as 'old' and thus to gain 'nostalgic beauty', that is, to stimulate a historical conscience.[12] Those who conserved objects thus afterwards appeared as 'saviours' – not only of a lost product culture but of their identity.

These saved objects offer continuity in the process of transformation. They convey identity and familiarity. In this context the notion of something being East

German serves as a counter-identity, acting against the characteristics claimed by the outside; that is, they are put forth instrumentally. After the aestheticizing of the object, one can see a new, more performative revaluation. The Trabant is assigned a modern experience value. Youngsters from East as well as from West Germany now use it again, not for reasons of distinction but to experience a retrospective sense of collectiveness and common interest.

When the Trabant is invoked in Ostalgia shows as a sign of remembrance, it is not about past and present usage but about the way of life of East Germans in Germany today. The Trabant is transformed into a symbol of the collapse of the GDR and the subsequent process of transformation. Fifteen years after reunification East Germany has no car production of its own. In the Wartburg town of Eisenach, Opel has an assembly plant, and in Leipzig BMW is building a new production site. However, these are essentially extended workbenches from the West, which are often the only jobs available in the region. When viewers are then reminded in TV shows of the long wait to acquire a Trabant, it is in the first place not an association with shortage but with social security and continuity. In GDR times not only could one be certain of getting a car in twelve to fourteen years time and that it would probably look exactly like that of one's parents, but one was also certain of still having a job and probably the same one at that.

The Trabant became a symbol for social security and state care, creating a picture of a community of solidarity; people were there for each other because they had the same social interests and they all lived under similar social conditions. From a Western point of view it was a state-regulated life, an ordered collectivity. At the same time, the Trabant is a symbol for the liberation from those conditions that were perceived as restrictive. At the East-side gallery (a piece of the remaining Wall with pictures painted on the East Berlin side) a Trabant is shown breaking through the Wall (see Figure 11).

For some it is a symbol of self-liberation, for others the path to Western democracy and freedom. As a symbol, the Trabant thus stands in the midst of a cultural contestation between rival interpretations of an ambivalent past and a problematic present. It stands for the devaluation of East Germans within German society, as well as for the fight against this. The Trabant may have had a particularly pronounced symbolic polyvalence, but much of the changing engagement with it can be found elsewhere. Especially for high-quality industrial commodities, use value exceeded that of a value of social distinction. This was partly the result of a utopian socialist project; objects were made to last, not to serve social distinction. In a society aiming at social equality, little consideration was given to status distinction. Except for a small number of well-designed commodities that today can be admired in design museums, industrial products often looked cheap, pragmatic, raw and unsophisticated. Early on, the desires of East German consumers turned West.

In the GDR the benchmark of desire was the product world of the West. Western products were more colourful, more modern and cheaper. One did not have to queue

Figure 11 Graffiti Painted at the Berlin Wall, the So-Called East-Side Gallery, 2004

Source: Ina Merkel, Berlin, 2004.

for these things but could decide in freedom according to one's wallet (GDR citizens were pulled into the West in large numbers).[13] Desire did not stem from shortage or need – there was enough to eat and drink and enough clothing in the GDR – but from a cultural yearning for affluence. It was a question of taste, of everyday aesthetics and an altered interpretation of value, which has been aptly described by Gerhard Schulze as a change to an *Erlebnisgesellschaft*, a society of adventure and emotional experience. 'If the mark doesn't come to us, we shall go to it' was one of the sayings of the legendary Monday demonstrations in Leipzig. The self-deprecation was logical, but it was not necessarily promoted in the West. West Germans found East Germans uncomfortable. They mocked their unruly consumerism, their need to catch up and their lack of restraint. East Germans appeared to West Germans as lower class and as having very little distinction. Interestingly, the picture of the ubiquitous desire for bananas demonstrated this better than the picture of the car.[14]

With the onset of the currency union in 1990, a complete change of material culture began, East against West. Overnight the stores were completely restacked with West products, GDR products disappearing from the shelves. Private households got rid of their clothing, furniture and everyday objects and swapped them for products of Western provenance. Cars were given away or simply left at the roadside. GDR objects had lost their value. This meant the end for many companies whose markets collapsed overnight. As one commentator observed:

> Sometimes happily, sometimes with sadness, almost everything was thrown away, those things which the people had lived with for years and which carried their memories. Attached to the new world of objects were no intelligible life signs. The institutions and their rules inherent in these objects held nothing familiar for them and they carried no memories either good or bad. Everything that was new in the East came from another world. Invisible for the East Germans, it was primed with the world of experiences of other generations, who lived in another country.[15]

It was not until years later that GDR citizens realized that when they discarded their belongings, they had also rid themselves of their memories and biographies.

Counter-movements

The self-deprecation of East Germans as well as their stigmatization by West Germans created counter-movements early on. The older generations especially refused to be part of consigning their lifeworld to the rubbish bin. They practised restraint; after all, these objects had cost a lot of money (industrial products were very expensive), a lot of energy and time (the waiting, looking for these things or making them yourself). Preserving and collecting, however, are inconspicuous, private forms of consumption.

Alongside those who threw things away appeared the first collectors, who picked up the things that had just been thrown away or who consciously bought typical GDR products. They were not concerned with the value of the objects but wanted the pale packaging that remained from the 1960s, or the funny names that these objects carried, such as *Tempolinsen*. These collectors (especially young West Germans but also East Germans) who fished out these curiosities and strange objects with an unwavering instinct were the protagonists of a counter-movement, which could be described as original Ostalgia. The saviours of a lost culture, they formed the basis for the real nostalgia: the wallowing in the disappeared.

As soon as everything had been thrown away, the remaining objects acquired rarity value. The saving of poor packaging or old-fashioned designs after the products had been devalued had something touching. The corpse had been robbed, now one could grieve over it. Particularly because of the seriousness with which many products promised useful value, they were seen as friendly ironic representatives of a different, admittedly rather strange world. The purity of Tempolinsen, Mitropa-cutlery or ATA brought the alternative social concept of socialism more to the fore than any political rhetoric had ever been able to. Suddenly, GDR products reincorporated the utopia from a different (better) world; since it had just fallen apart, it was now only possible to approach this utopia in an ironic way. At the first private East parties, little private altars were created in apartments with strange combinations of Lenin sculptures, a coffee cup from the Palace of the Republic, children's soap and medals. A distanced and mocking but caring affinity to the products of the East was nourished, a form of intellectual Ostalgia.

This ironic reinterpretation rehabilitated objects. They were ritually removed from everyday life and accorded cult status. It became fashionable to wander through flea markets looking for curiosities. The GDR now represented a collectors' terrain with rarity value. Objects increased in value quickly, particularly for those who had never lived in the GDR. They were easily incorporated into distinctive civilian and youth-oriented lifestyles. Suddenly it was cool to drive through the streets on a Schwalbe moped.[16] In a private context the cult association served the stylized development of individuality. Old objects have become such rarities that their possession provides distinction.

Table 1 Metamorphoses of Relations to GDR Consumer Goods

Time	Dominant practices	Counter-movements
GDR period	Use value	Distinction value
	Waiting, searching, procuring	Unloved, profane, desire for Western goods
Reunification, 1989–1991	Devaluation, disposal/waste	Conservation, biographical value
Transformation, since 1992	Indifference, rot, forgetting	Preserving, collecting, rediscovering, exoticizing, cult, Western Ostalgia, irony, performative qualities

The metamorphoses of meanings are not yet complete. The GDR's world of consumption appears in ever-new varieties to the eyes of the astonished public. But are these possibilities of interpretation really that new and original? Notwithstanding the speed and simultaneity of the interpretive process, why define it with a specific term, such as Ostalgia?

Struggle for Recognition: The Invention of a Community for all East Germans

The term Ostalgia carries an ethnic undertone that points to the continuing existence of a separate East German culture. Initially its continuation was noted with astonishment; now it has become accepted. It was assumed that socialism had not left a deep mental and cultural imprint, but rather that the nation had established long-lasting legacies. If viewed in a strictly political context, this initial expectation is understandable. Once the perspective shifts to everyday culture, however, significant differences emerge that transcend a simple contrast between regimes of plenty and scarcity. In consumption, in particular, different cultural value systems come into contact and conflict concerning different expectations of leading a life and organizing everyday practices. If the West is associated with choice, fashion, comfort and convenience, positive values in the East are associated with social security, equality and social justice. The latter concerns not only a secure job, but also informed consumption: expectations of low rents and low costs of transport and childcare, holiday provision, culture and education as well as subsidized utilities, food and children's clothing.

In the course of economic transformation in the 1990s, unemployment jumped to almost 25 per cent. Savings were mostly exhausted and it had been difficult to build up equity in the East. The recent debate about 'shrinking cities' reflects not only declining birth rates and rising migration to the West, but also the rapid impoverishment of large sections of Eastern communities. One outlet for this enormous potential for conflict is the battle over meanings and recognition attached to the East German past.

The contestation of the place and meanings of East German consumer culture has been characterized by several cultural developments:

1. *Stigmatization*: The product culture of the GDR is devalued as cheap, old-fashioned and profane. A mockingly sarcastic book that appeared in 1990, *SED-Schönes Einheits Design* by Georg C. Bertsch and Ernst Hedler, gives such examples as 'scratchy razors', the 'worker in his broken and stinking Trabant', 'porous and softened dustbin liners', 'fossils' that were 'good and cheap' twenty to thirty years earlier in West Germany. The authors wanted to create an 'archaeology of world brands'.[17] They photographed abnormal window displays of old flowers, piled up cans and political solutions, packaging, plasticine eggcups, razors and hair rollers. 'We are bewildered by these objects; we do not know really how to handle them. We find them shabby ... if one touches them the bewilderment grows'.[18] The repulsiveness could hardly be hidden. 'The products that developed "over there" have a banal identity, not really developed, rather improvised, but at the same time they have a humane identity precisely because they are not perfect'.[19] The GDR is exposed as ridiculous.

2. *Museum Representation and Scandalization*: In the immediate wake of reunification the first exhibitions of the GDR started. The posters of the legendary demonstration of 4 November 1989 in Berlin were collected by eager co-workers and only days later exhibited in the foyer of the historical museum. Through their exhibition, objects acquired new meanings well beyond their use value. In the case of the GDR these meanings emanated from a political East–West discourse. The exhibition of objects 'from above' through state-supported museums, such as the German Historical Museum, takes its patterns of meaning mostly from the

political system.[20] Wolfgang Engler has noted a 'scandalization of the GDR', that is, a political interpretation of everyday life in terms of Stasi, command economy and repression. This meaning pervaded the exhibition of GDR objects as 'rubbish'. In early exhibits of GDR history, objects were shown just as they had been pulled out from the rubbish: dirty, damaged, worn and wrinkled.[21]

3. *Denial, Indignation*: Scandalisation triggered a protective instinct among those who themselves had just thrown objects away. This was not the way that the act of disposal had been meant. The 'battle of pictures' (*Bilderstreit*) in Weimar in 1999 captured the sense of public indignation. Here a mass of pictures had been hung along trucking tarpaulin in a multi-purpose hall. West German politicians, civil servants and businessmen were attacked as 'colonizers'.

4. *Museum Representation from below/an Ironic Turn:* Since the middle of the 1990s there have been some attempts to describe the GDR from the perspective of everyday life.[22] In particular the Documentation Centre of Everyday Culture of the GDR in Eisenhüttenstadt has contributed cultural-historical exhibitions that seek to connect lifeworld and system via personal biographies. The exhibition 'Wunderwirtschaft' (miracle economy) in Berlin in 1996 played with Western as well as Eastern clichés of GDR consumer culture. A 'room of 1,000 little things', for example, showed hundreds of aluminium household goods hanging from the ceiling. Here was an irony of scarcity as well as of the production policy of the GDR, where big industries like shipbuilding were obliged to produce meat mincers. An Intershop was represented as a dark room, where blinking light chains led the visitor into the Holy of Holies: a small carousel of goods behind glass, showing brandy, cigarettes and nylon stockings. The room carried the scent of the West, a combination of coffee, washing powder and orange peel that was replaced on a weekly basis.

5. *Aesthetic Appropriation*: At the time of writing [2004] a new trend can be observed: the GDR product world is being aestheticized in select design exhibitions. In a new wave of collecting and representation the objects are carefully cleaned, placed behind glass and illuminated with spotlights. They are rescued from anonymity, from the namelessness and the mass product and instead placed in the biographical context of their inventors and designers. Visitors learn about the conflicts of the period, about production figures and the use of objects. They press their faces close to the exhibits, and one can overhear how they proudly tell their grandchildren that once they possessed an identical object.

6. *Commercialisation*: Once the remembrance of objects had become popular, marketing strategies became linked to the museum-representation of the GDR. Objects first appeared fleetingly in second-hand markets, then in bars and restaurants and finally on the T-shirt. By now, signs and symbols of political as well as consumer culture have become a regular part of modern experience. Games appeared in which participants had to run away from the Stasi, queue for a flat or collect stickers for best performance. Personal ID cards and boxes with survival kit appeared for sale, all with an ironic touch.

The label Ostalgia not only provides a distinct East German culture with sentiment-ality or irony against the interpretive power of West German culture, it is also an aggressively used market niche, a tough commercial process. Most significantly, Ostalgia is a post-modern game with changing identities on offer. The phenomenon of Ostalgia is no longer about a regime of shortage but about the logic of superfluity, that is, about consumers who assemble their worlds of consumption from the many different objects and styles on offer, creating styles and aesthetics in different ways, in which the objects, stars and even political symbols of the lost GDR can be placed without any problems.

7. *Becoming a Festival*: If the above discursive developments point to a gradually more differentiated engagement with the GDR, the so-called Ostalgia television shows move in the opposite direction. Different strands and meanings are mixed together: a little bit of scandal (Stasi or doping), a spoonful of indignation by the little man, a dose of resistance, rounded off with a pinch of state welfare. Thrown together, the effect is that of suggesting a shared sense of community amongst all East Germans. The East shows represent the provisional climax of the new wave of Ostalgia, as public and commercial television achieved unexpectedly high viewing figures in 2003. Ostalgia shows follow the same pattern as any other retro-show of the 1950s, 1960s or 1970s; past times are remembered fondly, sometimes with self-irony, sometimes with melancholy. Objects of everyday life function as prompts for remembrance, objects that today come across as ludicrous, poor or unexpectedly trendy; or forgotten stars are brought back from oblivion, most of them now fat and old but still hopping around merrily. The props, the music and the clothing of the presenters are chosen to match the occasion. For older viewers the pleasure of seeing former stars again dominates (along with a little malicious delight that the years have not passed unnoticed). For younger viewers there is the surprise that one wore such ugly things in those days, or that one already had such trendy stuff then. Producers and viewers have come to an agreement to see the past from its funny side. After all, it is the period of one's youth that is remembered – celebrated as innocent, free and beautiful.

Retro and Ostalgia shows give a similar kind of pleasure – with one crucial difference – and it was about this that the press wrote with such fulsome and hasty indignation: the contested past of the GDR could not simply be transfigured in such a way. As a result of heated debate, political events began to be incorporated in Ostalgia shows. A victim of Stasi persecution, who was forced into prostitution, told the story of her recruitment from behind an opaque glass wall using a distorted voice. A refugee showed the audience her pullover, which got caught on the wall when she was trying to flee. Camp prisoners, election forgers and dissenters appeared. Doping, the young pioneers and censorship were some of the topics talked about and these were really not funny. Whilst it is relatively easy to incorporate a sentimental touch into a programme, it is considerably more complicated to incorporate political indignation. Viewers, however, understood that it was necessary to show an act of political correctness. They listened as intently to Berghofer, the former mayor of Dresden, who disputed his involvement with the Stasi in a credible way, while admitting to having taken part in the forgeries at the community elections in 1989, as they did to Rainer Eppelmann, the dissident pastor, who was instrumental in exposing them. In the mutual applause that followed, a strange unanimity developed amongst the audience.

In the shows created by West German producers with the help of East German editors and presenters, a number of typical thought patterns appeared that have become rooted in the memories of East and West Germans since reunification. In the six episodes alone of the mdr show 'Ein Kessel GDR', the following objects became triggers for elaborate chains of association. The triangular bathing trunks for men, small, tight and with white stripes, became the symbolic means to discuss the subject of nudism or FKK, a form of popular culture and alternative holiday. In another sequence a highly polished white Wartburg convertible gave way to the comparatively humble Trabant. In that particular episode the general topic was waiting times, bartering and the problem of getting hold of spare parts. A stall with southern fruits, grown by an amateur gardener in a self-built greenhouse, displayed the slogan: 'Necessity is the mother of invention'. Piles of parcels from the West illustrated the topic of relatives living in the West, status distinctions and Intershop. The display of a pram led from the topic of support for families with many children, to community care of children and, finally, to the pioneer organizations.

Embedded in all these topics was an underlying reference to austerity and shortage. Previously a matter of scandal, it was now about a display of cultural practices, their evolution, of inventiveness, improvisation and bartering, which illustrated the principles of solidarity. The message was: people learnt to get by with very little. In hindsight this regime of shortage is now even positively compared to the West and its culture of superfluity. Money, apparently, was not a consideration. The people of the GDR present themselves as consumers who had their own, if peculiar and often resistant, ways of coping with organized shortage. The difficult business of everyday life was mastered with humour. In this new media narrative it was from this position that the citizens of the GDR were able to distance themselves from the political system, and that gave them the strength to eventually disempower the system in a peaceful way. Consumer culture, then, is assigned a political interpretation: a slowly erupting volcano, ready to destroy the government of the GDR.

This narrative serves a basic pattern of nostalgia. It was not necessarily better then – it is not about making pictures of a perfect world – but it was more exciting. It was a world full of challenges; people may have been poor, but they were happy. It is a reconstruction that aims at recognition, from West Germans as much as from one's own children – recognition for being disciplined and hard working and at the same time resistant, able to cope with shortages and being creative. These are qualities which, according to this view, are missing from the later generation. It is also claimed that a distinct form of individuation took place in the context of a fate-ridden community. Emphasis is placed on the great joy people experienced when receiving something for which they had waited for a long time – a satisfaction felt to be missing since the collapse of the Wall.

The ability to enjoy at a time of shortage has been the second topic of the Ostalgia shows. People remember the well-known but long-lost taste of coffee and chocolate, of tasty sausages and hot mustard, of sweet wines and gherkins – a taste that mattered little at that time of scarcity. Then people were keen to pursue the taste of the big wide world. Even Western yoghurt was bought at an Intershop when extra foreign currency was available. A bar of Western chocolate beat the peculiar cocoa-biscuit-mix by miles. By contrast, in the Ostalgia shows celebrities now happily eat Nudossi, the Nutella of the East, by the spoonful. In these shows, taste creates a collective identity for all East Germans.

Through the continuing cultural contestation of the GDR, a peculiar national character is invented, marked by genuineness, equality and justice: the noble savage. Unspoilt by any commercialisation, the East German here maintains a pure, original hedonism (the poor man can still be happy), genuine morality and free sexuality, social solidarity and the ability to improvise. It echoes the myth of the noble savage with patterns of infantilism.[23]

To reinforce this sentimental representation, old East German pop songs are played again, with the audience humming along enthusiastically. Sometimes the mood resembles that of older folklore programmes; members of the audience discreetly wipe a tear from the corner of their eye or clap along with the music. There is growing pride in regional stars, even though they never succeeded in conquering the big wide world and still only possess a certain provincial charm. In 'Kessel Buntes' – the original GDR show – the highlight had always been a Western star, a memory repressed in the recent Ostalgia shows.

Sporting celebrities, singers, actors and even politicians are presented as typical people in the GDR. They present themselves as if they shared everyday life with their audience (irrespective of their minor or considerable privileges). We learn that even actors had to wait fourteen years for a car, had to change West German marks at the Intershop, had problems with their children's teachers and even had to queue to buy oranges.

What is this cultural representation and repackaging all about, what does it have to do with life in the GDR? Images from the past are always projections of the present. Beyond good and evil, a community of East Germans is invented that transcends social and generational and above all political differences. Yet this picture of everyday life is not apolitical, far from it. Presenting oneself as a consumer in relation to the socialist regime is a new positioning act that provides people with a favourable or at least a sceptical and resistant image of their past. This works because protagonists, like viewers, practise a great deal of self-victimisation throughout an Ostalgia show – being spied upon, controlled and restricted in their perspectives and possibilities. In this way, recognition is called in from the West, the main addressee

Table 2 Public Discourses about the GDR

Time	Dominant discourse	Counter-discourses
Reunification	Euphoria: heroes of the velvet revolution	Astonishment, outrage: greedy masses
1990s	Stigmatization, scandalization (cheap, poor, Stasi, doping)	Resistance and indignation ('It was not so bad, after all')
	Incorporation into museums (from above); living under dictatorship, between resistance and adaptation	Incorporation into exhibitions (from below); biographies, irony
Post-2000	Commercialization: flea markets, antiquities, T-Shirts	Aesthetic appropriation; design, art, literature
	Becoming a festival: (East parties, East TV shows)	

of these shows and the target of countless jokes below the belt.[24] The people of the East present themselves as a marginalized group fighting for recognition from society, that is the West German population. Ostalgia shows reflect a ten-year-old politics of recognition centring on an appreciation of personal life stories and the achievements inscribed in these.

Marketing Strategies

Since reunification the industrial sector of the GDR has been more or less dissolved or closed down. De-industrialisation particularly concerns the East German consumer goods industry. Thanks to the shift towards Western brands, the East German market for consumer goods broke down rapidly, even without the help of the *Treuhand*. Before the currency reform GDR products were simply discarded. Only a few products survived; one of these is Florena (modelled on Nivea). Few products survived from the textile, fashion and furniture industries or household durable sector. It is rare to find today a new refrigerator or cooker, bicycle or camera produced in the GDR. It has almost been forgotten that the GDR was once a highly developed industrial country. What is left are mostly processed foods and spirits, cigarettes, chocolate, coffee and alcoholic drinks. The spectrum of products might suggest we are looking at an underdeveloped country. If cars and stereos, fridges and furniture disappeared silently, the return of food products and spirits was greeted with euphoria. Suddenly GDR coffee (Rondo) was bought again, and East German consumers began to speak highly of 'Spreewälder Gurken' and 'Hallorenkugeln'. When Bambina was sold again, former young Pioneers sobbed in each other's arms. Resurrection came with a new outfit; packaging was restyled, glowing in brilliant new colours. Nevertheless, most products failed to find their way into supermarkets in West Germany.

The marketing of Eastern products has adopted two opposed strategies: a regional versus a European route. The first is explicitly targeting the East German regional market and advertises an East German spirit of life that appeals to ideas of solidarity, patriotism and community. Here the principal signs are landscape, history and culture, almost eternal values that bracket any reference to the former GDR. For years, for example, representation and advertising avoided the image of the East Berlin telecom tower; only its rediscovery by a rock band has made it culturally acceptable once more. Yet, only certain products lend themselves to this form of regionalisation. If aiming to capture the broader German or European market, an appeal to specific aspects of East German culture is less successful. In this case, consumer goods that have been produced in East Germany pursue a strategy of silence about their origin; to be seen as an East German product would amount to self-stigmatisation. Hence, advertising strategies have opted here for conventional images of modernity, adventure and youth. Significantly, East German consumers do not mind this act of self-denial. On the contrary, the establishment of Eastern products in Western markets is celebrated as a form of shared success.

East German Culture in the Contested Zone of Identity and Difference

In times when entire lifeworlds are being aestheticized, consumption becomes a principal site of cultural identity politics. Bought objects are covered with images and marks that go far beyond their use value. Thus it is not only about personal distinction, the pursuit of status or the creation of an individual lifestyle. Commodities are also expressions of belonging to or exclusion from a community. The choice of clothing and furniture, for or against the newest technology, a visit to the cinema, the pub or the opera, these are part of a search for a certain lifestyle, for a community of interpretation, a milieu or a subculture. Normally the positions are clear and confirmed through the aesthetics of everyday life. In modern societies the milieus are rarely any longer hierarchical, but rather develop along a horizontal mode. Occasionally, subcultural groups provoke disruptions, but these are short lived, and the established system quickly reasserts itself.[25]

The reunification of Germany produced an altogether novel constellation for modern societies. Suddenly, an entire alien culture had to be integrated into a pre-existing structure. Inevitably, positions within society had to be rearranged. Significantly, the integration of GDR citizens did not proceed on a horizontal plane but on a vertical scale. West German society, where milieus had arranged themselves next to each other, now became preoccupied with devaluation and exclusion. The new East German arrival worked according to a different social logic. It was alien, an unfamiliarity that was not recognized as an alternative rationality but as representing lesser value.

Social structures, for example, were different. After decades of dispossession, migration and ideological discrimination, bourgeois culture was hardly present any longer in the GDR. Wolfgang Engler has coined the concept 'arbeiterliche Gesellschaft' to capture this new populist, working-class habitus. A different scale of values existed, where success, career and wealth carried negative connotations. Moreover, East German society was in an inner state of turmoil that defied simple categories of analysis. The East Germany now joining the rest of Germany was one of change, transitory, limited and ambivalent.

When signs and meanings are constantly changing, instant, accurate recognition becomes ever more difficult. This is especially the case for individuals who change from one culture to another. Their state of not belonging is obvious and can quickly become a stigma. What applies to migration generally had distinct implications for East Germans. Rather than leaving for a foreign society, this society came to them. In addition, the encounter revealed an unexpected degree of unfamiliarity. In spite of the same roots and the same language, more than forty years of separate development had led to enormous cultural differences that, against all expectations, could not be overcome without difficulty. The resulting culture shock was something that was not supposed to happen. It became a taboo for both sides.

Alongside the experience of reunification with its emancipating effects ('Helden-stadt' Leipzig), then, an experience of transformation developed, marked by an extensive devaluation of the lived past under the weight of West German cultural and institutional superiority. Feelings of superiority and strategies of devaluation, the mechanics of exclusion and the development of stigma found cultural expression. In the cynical jokes of satirical journals and in political discourse, East Germans were presented as poor brothers and sisters – underdeveloped, hopelessly old fashioned and uncivilized. Theories of modernization provided the blueprint for categories of difference. The developmental paradigm of 'catching up' appeared valid for East Germany in a model where Western industrial society was the universal norm of modernity.

This is not something that was exclusively imposed upon the East Germans from the outside. One of the most important triggers of reunification was the desire of GDR citizens to join modern global developments. Here was the start of the journey into the Western world. Even before reunification it was attractive to identify with a Western modernity and its encouragement to be mobile and flexible, the imperative of individuation and the plurality of ideas and values. Such cultural identification was facilitated partly by the GDR's own self-representation as a modern society where social structures had been transformed, partly through a shared imagined world made possible through film and kinship.

In everyday life the attraction of modernity was mediated through its associ-ated values: freedom of choice of consumer goods, entertainment and lifestyles.

Throughout the process of reunification, GDR citizens showed a clear commitment to Western modernity. The simultaneous erosion of social security and full employment was not always anticipated. However, the paradigms of modern life in the West with its sentiment and situational arrangements cannot be located regionally or locally. Their attraction resulted from a lack of obligation, their fragmentary nature and a community created in a moment that might disappear just as fast as it had appeared.

The people of the GDR were and in part still are, engaged in a conflict of values which, we know today, they were not able to resolve. The socialist utopia promised equality, distributional justice, social security and strong community ties. Real existing capitalism promised freedom of election and opportunities of self-development. To put it simply, it was impossible to have both. Ostalgia is the mirror image of this conflict of values.

Alongside the encounter with bourgeois modernity, a fundamental structural transformation of the economy unfolded abruptly and at breakneck speed. A change of system and globalisation had to be mastered simultaneously. Entire phases of development and adjustment were jumped or taken in express mode. Some developments that were already visible in the East had not even started properly in the West. A social laboratory situation emerged, where one could observe reactions, try out new strategies and constantly change the order of testing – an open situation in which there were more questions than answers. East Germans had to integrate themselves into Western modernity under the disadvantageous conditions of de-industrialisation and migration. East German culture became shaped by the simultaneous experience of having to leave and of being left behind, of beginning a journey to a strange world and of staying, to be the last one remaining to turn off the light.

In their simultaneous longing for acceptance and for retaining difference, in their fight for recognition in a modern, self-confident, autonomous system, East Germans have followed very diverse strategies depending on income, age, educational level, sex, job situation and family status. Alongside unobtrusive adaptation or catching up with modernity, they developed strategies of distinction which found expression in regional identity and stubbornness. Some ignored the past and opted for a quick embrace of a Western European way of life, making themselves invisible as East Germans; others re-emphasized and valorized their East German identity.

In this way, fourteen years after reunification, a lively East German culture has developed within Germany that, on the one hand, shares basic values and possibilities of action with the whole of German society, but that, on the other hand, clearly differentiates itself from that society because of specific biographical experiences and mentalities, requiring its own patterns of reflection. It would be simplistic to speak of a GDR succession society. Rather it is a society in transition, living in a liminal phase of not-anymore but not-yet. The experience of reunification alone, that is the implosion of a system that until then had seemed omnipotent and the empowering experience of making politics (although it only lasted for a few weeks) must have created distinct ways of coping with such fundamental changes. For those actively involved in this moment of empowerment, authority lost much of its former, permanent status and power. East Germans interpreted and responded in vastly different ways to the radical rearrangement of all social structures which called for a new positioning of the individual in a quickly changing social landscape and to the transvaluation of previously valid ideas and values attached to property, money, wealth, security, continuity, work and family. As an experience, however, it was obviously substantially different to that of continuity for West Germans.

Even in this East German part of German culture, East Germans are no longer among themselves. West Germans who moved East belong to it just as much as naturalized resident foreign workers from Vietnam, Poland or Mozambique, or students and experts from Europe, Turkish, Italian or Greek entrepreneurs, Russian Germans and returning refugees, a complex mix of people with no assigned space in the original construction of this East German partial identity. East Germans do not exist as a homogeneous group, but during the pursuit of recognition they inevitably appeared homogenized. The Ostalgia phenomenon is the cultural expression of such endeavours towards homogeneity, where the complex forms of assimilation and identity formation are reduced to a barely understandable obstinacy.

Ostalgia is part of a politics of recognition. It is directed firstly at the process of transformation and the hegemony of West German norms and values. Secondly, it responds to the process of globalisation that reinforced the marginalisation of a once-industrialized region. In the course of constructing an East German culture, former GDR citizens became conscious of how they had walked out on their own history, becoming spiritually homeless. Remembering the society left behind provides a point of orientation for the present. These patterns of remembrance provide a key for ongoing problems of communication. They simultaneously create distance and an emotional reconnection. The personal past is read in such a way that it allows individuals to orientate themselves in the world according to their specific way of life. It reflects a yearning for a collective identity, for *Heimat*, a home and community. East Germans have not lost *Heimat* as a place but as a secure orientation.

Notes

1. Jaeckie Schwarz in the mdr TV programme 'Ein Kessel GDR', September 2003.
2. There was not shortage as such; shortage and scarcity are relative terms. What is perceived as shortage differs from culture to culture, across class and time. The label 'society of shortage' acts as a combative term in East–West discourse; the cultural critique of consumerism or a society of abundance is simply ignored.

The West becomes a coloured layer, the GDR appears in black and white. The term 'society of shortage' also carries a misreading, that is, that shortage leads to frustration, greed, envy, parsimony and stinginess. But, arguably, it is at times of shortage that consumer behaviour reveals a potential for improvisation and enjoyment. The cultural practices in handling shortage are ambivalent and not solely concerned with restriction and moderation or the wise handling of resources.

3. The term Ostalgia was coined by a cabaret artist at the beginning of the 1990s.

4. Obviously, 'the West Germans' and 'the East Germans' do not exist. These are ascriptive categories. They are used in public discourse as signs of affirmation and to draw boundaries for inclusion and exclusion. Whereas East Germans, however, adopt or act out a collective identity in various contexts – as audience in Ostalgia shows, for example – West Germans emphasize instead the heterogeneity of social positions and the plurality of political opinions. In this chapter, therefore, 'East German' and 'West German' refer to commonly used discursive ascriptions.

5. So quoted in C. Dieckmann, 'Honnis heitere Welt. Das Unterhaltungsfernsehen verklärt die DDR', *Die Zeit*, 28 August 2003, No. 36.

6. T. Ahbe speaks of 'Laienpraxis' in 'Ostalgie als Selbstermächtigung: Zur produktiven Selbststabilisierung ostdeutscher Identität', *Deutschland Archiv*, 4 (1997), pp. 614–19.

7. The name for the GDR car. Most probably the name stemmed from the meaning of satellite (the moon as trabant of the earth), in connection with the socialist space exploration euphoria (1957 Sputnik). The basic meaning of 'Wahrig' is a warrior on foot, bodyguard, or someone dependent on someone else, a companion held in tutelage.

8. This case study is based mainly on systematic field observation since 1983, discourse analysis and interviews with about fifty East Germans from 1993 to 1997.

9. In 1954 the GDR council of ministers agreed to develop a car with the following properties: a small car with two main and two back seats, weighing no more than 600 kg, an average petrol consumption of 5.5 l/100 km, yearly production of 12,000 at a price of 4,000 marks. The development plan was set for 18 months. GDR citizens later said ironically that the instructions for building a *Trabant* were to build a roof over two spark plugs.

10. Unlike most other cars, *Trabants* received names – ours was called Charlie – perhaps because it was often the first car and turned into something like a member of the family, not so different from a pet.

11. This transition happened so smoothly partly because the designs of many commodities were from the 1950s and 1960s. While in West Germany there were retro-exhibitions of kidney-shaped tables, similar objects lived on in everyday life in East Germany.

12. H. Lübbe, *Der Fortschritt und das Museum: Über den Grund unseres Vergnügens an historischen Gegenständen* (London, 1982), p. 8.
13. Of course it was also about freedom (of travel), democracy and whatever else may be Western values, but consumption was definitely a strong motivation.
14. The unforgettable caricature in the satirical magazine *Titanic*: a dolled-up young East German girl is peeling a cucumber next to the text 'Gabi from the East in happiness – her first banana'.
15. D. Mühlberg, 'Vom langsamen Wandel der Erinnerung an die GDR', *Kultur-nation* (online journal), 1 (2003).
16. A moped built until 1989 following the same design as in the 1950s.
17. G.C. Bertsch and E. Hedler, *SED, Schönes Einheits Design* (Cologne, 1990), p. 7.
18. Bertsch and Hedler, *SED*, p. 9.
19. Bertsch and Hedler, *SED*, p. 12.
20. The exhibitions 'Auftragskunst', 1995, and 'Parteiauftrag: ein neues Deutschland. Bilder, Rituale und Symbole der früheren GDR', 1996/7.
21. The GDR section of a modern art exhibition in Weimar in 1999 developed into a genuine scandal. Masses of pictures were hung in a crowded fashion in a multi-functional hall crudely decorated in grey tarpaulin.
22. Partly in the DHM exhibition 'aufbau west und aufbau ost. Die Planstädte Wolfsburg und Eisenhüttenstadt', 1997; as a starting point in the exhibition of the documentation centre in Eisenhüttenstadt 'Tempolinsen und P2', 1995/6; and in the exhibition of the NGBK 'Wunderwirtschaft: GDR-Konsumkultur in den 60er Jahren', 1996, which was developed under my guidance by a student group at the Institute for European Ethnology.
23. An appeal to childhood tastes, like Schlagersüßtafel, Hallorenkugeln, Bambina, Negerküsse (the 'disgustingly' sweet GDR, as Katarina Witt put it), affirms the political innocence of everyday life. Diminutive terms such as *Ampelmännchen* or *Trabi*, or even a term like *Ossi*, invoke the innocence of childhood. With a childish naive belief in communist promises, the political sense of belonging then becomes acceptable.
24. The showmaster Gunther Emmerlich made a joke in the third episode of 'Ein Kessel GDR' on the 5 September 2003 on mdr. 'To say that all "wessis" are arrogant is the same as saying all Negroes are black', a comment that earned him wild applause and laughter.
25. See G. Schulze's discussion of the milieu in West Germany in the late 1980s, *Die Erlebnisgesellschaft: Kultursoziologie der Gegenwart* (Frankfurt, 1992).

–12–

The Limits of Culture

Political Economy and the Anthropology of Consumption*

James G. Carrier

The past two decades have seen growing interest in the study of consumption in anthropology. The resulting work reflects a culturalist orientation, apparent in the classic texts that helped spur that growth and that have to some degree defined what counts as anthropology of consumption. This orientation construes people, objects and consumption in particular ways and has led to interesting and worthwhile work. However, the spread of this orientation has meant forgoing other ways of seeing the place of consumption in social life. This chapter draws on selected anthropological work that deals with consumption but that does not adhere to this culturalist orientation, to try to point to some of the approaches and issues that were forgone and to raise questions about the status of that culturalist orientation.

Studying Consumption

A recent article by Frank Trentmann discusses different approaches to consumption.[1] His focus is on approaches among historians, but what he describes seems common to consumption studies generally. This is because his historians tend to approach consumption in terms of its links to other issues and processes, whether as indicators, facilitators, cause or effect. This chapter is about anthropologists and it seems that they are no different. Perhaps this is to be expected, for this is a discipline which advertises itself as being concerned with contextualizing what it studies, to show how it is linked to other things. Anthropologists, then, appear to run in parallel with Trentmann's historians. Both may spend some time trying to identify consumption as a social or historical thing, event or process, but they seem to spend much more time looking beyond it, to see what light it sheds on other issues.

That expansive view shapes this chapter, which is concerned not with how consumers see themselves but with how anthropologists see consumers. My goal here is not the impossible one of reviewing and synthesizing anthropological work on consumption. Rather, it is to use some of this work to raise questions about how anthropologists have thought about consumption and particularly questions about the larger contexts in which they place consumption and consumers. So, like an anthropologist, I will use work on the processes and mechanisms and practices of consuming to look beyond consumption.

The first, brief section of this chapter sketches some of the formative works on consumption by anthropologists and the writers who have influenced them. The purpose of this sketch is to raise questions about the approaches to social life those works contain. The next and much longer section contains three case studies based on anthropological works that engage with consumption in Mexico, in the English-speaking Caribbean and in Papua New Guinea. These cases deserve attention because they locate consumption, consumers and what might be called innocent bystanders in terms of approaches and issues that seem to have slipped from view at the time that consumption rose to prominence as a topic within the discipline.[2] Before beginning, however, it is worth reflecting a bit on the rise of the study of consumption.

In anthropology and elsewhere, consumption became an important topic in the 1980s. Some observations about that decade will help to make problematic the sort of world constructed in the important works I will describe. While the academic study of consumption boomed, the activity itself became more uncertain for many people. In the United States, Great Britain and many other parts of the world this was, after all, the decade that saw the marked onset of neoliberal policies that shifted a lot of economic power from workers and states to the owners of capital. The consequences were striking. Media attention was focused on the consumption boom amongst a small body of the newly enriched, the 'yuppies' (young upwardly mobile professionals) and the 'dinks' (dual-income no kids) and the industry that catered to them.[3] However, the less visible statistical reality was disheartening for more ordinary people. In the United States, for instance, the decade saw a continuation of the decline in hourly workers' purchasing power; adjusted for inflation, the average weekly earnings of production workers in manufacturing industries were lower in 1990 than in 1965.[4] Households coped with this threat to their consumption by working harder: an average of 245 additional hours per year since 1973.[5] In more peripheral countries things could be worse. For instance, in Mexico between 1982 and 1986, real income dropped by 40 to 50 per cent.[6] In some countries, then, the 1980s was a decade of declining consumption; in many others, consumption became more uncertain for significant sections of the population.

The fervour with which anthropologists and others embraced the study of consumption in that decade would have been understandable, if it had reflected this problematic state of affairs, or at least taken cognizance of it. However, this was not the case. The big names and the big ideas that motivated a lot of anthropological work on the topic construed a world of choice among a world of goods by a world of people constrained only by the need to decide which object, among all those available, they wanted. I find this unsettling and what I present here is a way of expressing my unease.

Key Works

For those who are not anthropologists, the anthropology of consumption is probably defined by the influential thread within the work described here. Focusing on this thread necessarily means ignoring other work, but this was the dominant approach at the time and remains influential. Presenting this thread in a few paragraphs necessarily means simplifying it, locating an analytical core that was increasingly overlaid, elaborated and qualified as the 1980s turned into the 1990s and into the 2000s. The works that laid the foundation for this thread are Baudrillard's *For a Critique of the Political Economy of the Sign*, Sahlins's *Culture and Practical Reason*, Douglas and Isherwood's *The World of Goods* and Bourdieu's *Distinction*.[7] These works use a culturalist frame, focusing on the meanings that objects bear, meanings that are taken to explain why people consume those objects rather than others. I want to discuss these briefly.

Baudrillard's notion of 'sign value' exemplifies this frame. He says that objects of a certain type have meaning because they are different from objects of another type. Those types and their meanings define an overall structure of objects that maps on to a structure of society, made up of various types of people defined by their differences from other types of people. Sahlins illustrates this structural, semiological approach nicely, which is not surprising given his extensive invocation of Baudrillard. For instance, his discussion of American clothing revolves around 'basic notions of time, place and person as constituted in the cultural order' and he argues that the classification of clothing in the United States produces and reproduces 'the meaningful differences between' social units.[8]

Baudrillard's and Sahlins's are the most structural and semiological of these culturalist texts. Douglas and Isherwood are more concerned with the social processes that give objects their meanings and significances, as when they point out that certain items have value because they allow households an increased flexibility in their routine and hence a greater ability to maintain desired social relationships. However, this aspect of their work tended to attract less attention than their discussion of the ways in which patterns of consumption reflect and recreate the structures of social life, as in their analysis of the ways that the structure of meals maps on to the structure of time.

Bourdieu's work is the one that aspires to the most comprehensive account of consumption preferences and hence sits more uneasily in this set of formative culturalist works. *Distinction* rests on a model of society, of social resources or capitals and of predispositions or habituses and is as much about French society as it is about taste. Within this complex model of capitals and habituses, however, is a consideration of why different sets of French people prefer some things rather than others (the 'judgement of taste' of his subtitle) and the ways that these sets of preferences visibly differentiate one set of people from another (the 'distinction' of his main title). A key aspect of this is the contrast between the sensuous orientation of those driven by necessity, particularly unskilled manual workers, and the aesthetic orientation of those who are relatively free of necessity, elites of various sorts.[9]

These classic works exhibit some important common themes that appear more broadly in anthropological and related work on consumption. The first is the construction of objects as bearers of meaning generated by advertisers[10] and by ordinary people, whether in their mundane decisions about what to wear today (of the sort Sahlins describes) or more consciously as consumers.[11] This has led analysts to focus mostly on items like toiletries, clothes, beverages, foodstuffs and television programmes. These are fairly cheap, so that the differences between them can be treated as almost nothing but symbolic. Also, they are inconsequential, so that the purchase on Tuesday afternoon of one soft drink rather than another, like the decision on Saturday morning to cook eggs benedict rather than pea soup or porridge, or the decision on Sunday afternoon to go to an exhibit of modern art rather than a popular movie, makes no difference that anyone can detect. Another common feature of these models is their distinctive use of time. This is the evanescent time of wanting and choosing, most visible in the more structuralist works, with their attention to meaning and taste, but less salient in Douglas and Isherwood, with their (relatively neglected) concern with people's practical strategies.[12] The third common element in these works is their broadly psycho-cultural orientation to consumption. This orientation implies that all that we really need to know in order to understand consumption is the framework of meaning that is in each individual's head (psychological), itself a manifestation of the collective (cultural) construction of a structure of the identity of objects of consumption and a parallel structure of the identity of people, places and times.

In its restricted time frame and its psycho-cultural orientation, these works portray the same sort of world as that in neoclassical economics, for both are interested in the same issue, people's consumption choices in a world of goods. And those consuming people are representative bearers of taste or interpreters of meaning. Indeed, for some people they are nothing but bearers of taste or interpreters of meaning: 'The old, rigid barriers are disappearing – class and rank; blue collar and white collar; council tenant and home owner; employee and housewife. More and more we are simply consumers'.[13] These similarities are provocative, for they point out that both economists and anthropologists concerned with consumption focused on the moment of choice, whether the market choice of the shopper who confronts shelves piled high in a store or the domestic choice of which meal to cook or which clothes to wear. In this focus, these writers generally (Bourdieu is an exception) tend to ignore what lies outside that moment, the fact that people's perceptions and their consumption are shaped by and shape the material, social and cultural constraints of their situations,[14] just as they tend to ignore the fact that these choices have consequences not just for the consumers who make them, but for others as well.[15]

This influential thread in anthropological work on consumption does not, of course, define the whole of the anthropology of consumption. Most especially, it excludes work by anthropologists that relates the emergence of or changes in consumption to changes in the broader political-economic order, such as the evolution of capitalism,[16] the expansion of the British capitalist empire[17] and the emergence of the nation state.[18] However, this thread continues to be influential within the discipline, where much work remains concerned with people's choices among meaningful objects and it continues to help define for those outside the discipline just what it is that anthropologists have to say on the topic. This predominance tends to obscure other interesting work that, precisely because it takes different approaches and situates consumption in different frames and addresses different issues, appears to be less obviously about consumption and more about other things. For instance, the contributors to a volume edited by Daniel Miller have much to say about consumption, but on the face of it the volume is concerned with modernity and the distinction between the local and the global.[19]

I turn now to three cases that make use of this sort of work, each of which sees consumption less as an individual choice framed by meaning and more as a collective consequence, itself consequential, of political-economic forces. In seeing consumption this way, these cases view consumers less as choosers to be understood in terms of structures of meaning and more as people whose acts can constrain them to choose in certain ways and whose choices can constrain those innocent bystanders and their actions.

Capitalist Consumption in Mexico

The first case is directly concerned with consumers, but it focuses on people who are on the margins of capitalist society. These are people in the highlands of Sonora, in northwest Mexico adjacent to the United States border. The anthropologist who has described these people is Joe Heyman, who has used fieldwork, oral histories and archives to study these people's consumption patterns as they have changed over the course of the twentieth century.[20] This was a momentous century for Sonora's people, for it saw the industrialization of the border region, first with copper mines at the start of that century and then with the assembly plants, *maquiladoras*, that emerged in the 1960s to serve US markets.

Heyman's work has been concerned with changes in people's consumption as this industrialization and their involvement with it have changed. He provides intriguing discussions of changes in the items that people consumed (e.g. beds, shoes, radios, cowboy hats, denim clothing), and some of those discussions approximate the culturalist approach that I have described. However, his main concern is the relationship between people's patterns or strategies of consumption and their position in the economic order. He summarizes his treatment of these strategies as a distinction between two ideal types, which he calls 'flow-through' and 'flow-conserving' strategies.[21]

While Heyman presents these as consumption strategies and particularly household consumption strategies, he relates them to people's resources, though what is important is not so much the sheer volume of their resources as the pattern. In relating patterns and strategies of consumption to patterns of resources, Heyman is rooting consumption in the realms of economy and political economy, rather than in the realms of culture and sign that have been the most visible anthropological approaches to the topic.

Put briefly, the flow-conserving strategy is one in which the consumption of purchased items tends to be discontinuous and the ratio of purchase to self-provision varies markedly over time. On the other hand, the flow-through strategy is characterized by a steadier level of consumption of purchased items and, except in times of extraordinary hardship or prosperity, a more constant ratio of purchases to self-provision.

Heyman relates consumption strategies to resource patterns when he says that the flow-conserving strategy characterizes households where income is discontinuous, perhaps most obviously farming households. For them, income is tied to the agricultural cycle; the income they receive from this harvest has to last them until the next one. In contrast to flow-conserving households, flow-through households have continuous income flows, perhaps most obviously households reliant on wage labour. Because of their continuous income, such households have much less need to restrict their expenditures to specific times of the year. Indeed, they tend to avoid the uneven expenditure pattern of the flow-conserving households, preferring instead to have relatively continuous and predictable expenditures, balanced against their relatively continuous and predictable incomes.

These differences in strategies have a number of corollaries. One concerns the pattern of household debt. The flow-conserving households tend to accumulate debt gradually over the course of the year and pay it off in a lump when they harvest and sell their produce. On the other hand, the flow-through households that Heyman describes are fairly poor and if they want to buy anything substantial, they do so on credit. Thus, they tend to acquire debt in a lump and pay it off gradually. Debt, then, is part of their continuous and predictable expenditures and the need to pay off this debt makes wage work all the more important for them.

The ideal-typical flow-conserving household has to live off the proceeds of one harvest until the next one comes in. Of course, life in the Sonora highlands was more complex than this idealization. Few households relied only on their crops. Instead, they had other, if less significant, economic resources; wage labour and the sale of a farm animal or items of household manufacture could generate income at other times of the year. Also, they had another important economic strategy, indicated by the point that their ratio of purchase to self-provision varied markedly over time. While these households were relatively prone to provide for themselves at all times, self-provisioning increased as debt rose over the course of the year. Worn objects were repaired rather than replaced, or were replaced by what the household made rather than what they bought; people used candles and firewood for light and heat when they were too indebted to afford paraffin; they carried water from streams rather than buy it from water-sellers.

This indicates that their consumption strategy was not linked only to their income pattern. In addition, it was linked to their relationship to economic resources. Specifically, they had to have fairly free access to things like water and wood, mud and sand and so forth. Also, they had to have relatively free access to their own time; they had to be able to devote hours of it to collecting wood and water or days of it to repairing roof and wall.

Rural life in Sonora was no idyll. E.P. Thompson's point that pre-industrial peasants work to their own regime of time should not blind us to the fact that they could work a lot and that the work could be onerous.[22] So, while the spreading loss of free access to material resources in Sonora may have driven people to the towns and cities, it is also certain that the restricted work regime in those towns and cities was attractive in many ways, as was the range of objects available in them. However, ensconced in towns, these households found it difficult to maintain their old flow-conserving strategies. This was because the economic relations that had underpinned that strategy had disappeared. If free firewood and water were getting harder to find in rural areas, they were effectively impossible to find in town. Perhaps even more important, the three or four hours of time required to get them had disappeared. The husband and older children were at work; the younger children were in school; the basic household maintenance fell more purely on the wife, even though her available time was reduced by her own wage work.[23]

In these circumstances, people were obliged to forgo the older self-provisioning that had facilitated the flow-conserving strategy by allowing a periodic refusal to buy. Increasingly, shirts and shoes had to be bought rather than made. With no access to wood and no time to gather it, wood-fired cooking gave way to gas and electricity. The flow-conserving strategy gave way to the flow-through strategy. Sonora villagers became not just urban residents but urban consumers, reliant on regular work and regular wages to pay their regular bills.

The title of the paper in which Heyman describes this process in greatest detail begins with 'The organizational logic of capitalist consumption' and he calls the change in strategy described here 'consumer proletarianization'.[24] As these phrases might indicate, he is not describing the emergence of consumption, for certainly rural households consumed and it is not clear that they consumed significantly less than urban households. Equally, he is not describing the appearance of the market in people's lives, for rural households depended on market transactions for the selling of the goods and labour power that they produced as well as for the buying of much of what they consumed. Rather, what Heyman is describing is a change in pattern, brought about in large part by the loss of the room to manoeuvre that confronted these families most starkly when they moved to town and found jobs, though it was beginning to confront them in rural areas as access to free resources was reduced.

Heyman's work points to some of what was missed by those anthropologists who embraced the culturalist approach to consumption. What he portrays is people whose consumption choices and strategies are shaped in basic ways by their positions in households that are themselves positioned in the political-economic order. Moreover, the points he makes do not reflect only the changing condition of a set of people in the northwest of Mexico. This much is apparent from concern in Britain about what is called 'work–life balance'. While this phrase has a range of meanings reflecting the changing nature of work, some of its salience arises from the fact that a growing number of people and households confront a common situation. Faced with jobs that look increasingly insecure, they send more people out to work for more hours. One consequence is that their expenditure rises, as they find themselves having to buy what they used to do and make for themselves. For these households, it is not a matter of the loss of the time required to gather firewood and water, but the loss of the time required to look after small children rather than pay for a child-minder, of the time required to prepare meals rather than buy them microwave-ready from a shop. Like Heyman's *maquiladora* workers, these households find themselves increasingly proletarianized consumers.

Certainly, British households with two wage earners, like Sonoran households working in assembly plants in border towns, make decisions about the objects around them that reflect things like sign value and cultural structures of meaning. However, Heyman's work shows the kinds of question we can ask and the kinds of issue we confront, if we attend to more than the moment of culturalist truth, meaningful choice in a world of goods.

National Consumption in the Caribbean

The next case resembles in some ways the culturalist approach I have described, for it is concerned with the meaning of objects in consumption. However, it locates those meanings in temporal and historical processes that are shaped by, and hence transmit, the sort of political-economic forces that the culturalist approach tends to ignore. This case is concerned with consumption in the Caribbean, capitalist territory but hardly the core of the developed world. The anthropologists are Daniel Miller, who has done fieldwork in Trinidad, and Richard Wilk, who has done fieldwork in Belize.

As with much of the Caribbean, an important issue in these two countries is what used to be called nation-building, what now might be called the creation of a post-colonial national self-conception. While there are many aspects to building a nation, the one that concerns Miller and Wilk is what people eat and drink. Their descriptions of the link between consumption and identity, albeit national identity, help complicate the culturalist approach to consumption. They do so by showing some of the institutions and forces that shape the meaning of objects and people's consumption decisions, institutions and forces that can be affected by the consumption decisions of outsiders. They do so as well by showing how these decisions, institutions and forces can affect legitimacy and political power.

For both Trinidad and Belize, independence and nation-building took place during a time when they confronted a growing array of global commodities, overwhelmingly produced and marketed by companies from elsewhere. In spite of the claims that creolisation is ubiquitous in countries such as these,[25] so that global commodities acquire significant local meanings, the flood of brands marking globalization would seem to be stony ground for developing a distinctive national identity. While the ground is not as fertile as it might be, Miller's research in an advertising agency in Trinidad suggests that more complex processes are at work than either the flood or the creolisation image implies,[26] processes that lie beyond the view of an approach focused on people's consumption decisions.

Miller found that the capitalist commercial logic that drove this advertising agency encouraged it to facilitate the development of a distinct Trinidadian identity, a 'Trini way'. We would expect this for objects manufactured locally. However, what makes Miller's discussion intriguing is that he shows how this happened clearly with truly global companies and their brands. To simplify somewhat the process that Miller describes, when a global company decides to try to expand its sales in Trinidad, it will approach a local advertising agency. However, as this is a global company, it will have its advertisements prepared centrally and engage the Trinidadian advertising agency only to place them in effective times and places. This reduces the agency to just a buyer of time on local stations and space in local print media, which would profit the agency much less than producing the advertisements themselves. With an eye to their profits, advertising agencies argue that the Trinidadian market is distinctive and that the advertising campaign requires a local orientation.[27] Often enough, this strategy works; the local agency gets the creative job; their advertisements enhance an image of the Trini way, as well as the agency's profit figures.

The advertising strategy that Miller describes indicates that the relationship between national identity and imported commodities is problematic; it takes a persuasive advertising agency to get the chance to make an international commodity resonate with the Trini way. In some sense, this is familiar territory, the complex relationship between the local and the global. But what Miller's description points to is the way that the meaning of objects of consumption is shaped by forces that operate well beyond the local realm of cultural values; there is nothing distinctively 'Trini way' about the desire to increase your profits, whether you are a global manufacturing company or a local advertising agency. And as the balance of this Caribbean case makes clear, those forces and meanings impinge upon and reflect important political-economic concerns and interests.

This impinging is a recurring theme in Wilk's writings on Belize.[28] When he first went to British Honduras (as it was then) as a student in 1973, his hosts served him tinned corned beef, white bread, tinned sardines and a 7-Up. These were suitable as a meal for a foreign visitor because they reflected what local people took to be English taste, which was high-status taste in this British colony. Local foodstuffs, on the other hand, were seen to be the foods of the poor and of the local population, two categories that overlapped significantly during the colonial era. With the gradual growth of nationalism, however, the better off in British Honduras changed their tastes, moving away from the sort of things shipped out, at least in popular imagination, from the mother country. They still, however, denigrated local foods. Rather, they adopted what was called 'Spanish' food, food that reflected what was thought to be eaten in Mexico and other independent countries in Central America. Only later did Belizean food emerge as an identifiable category.

This emergence was not, however, a straightforward consequence of the drive to independence or even the pressure by local firms to differentiate a local market, the process that Miller describes. Rather, Wilk says that an important factor was the development of tourism in the country. The growing number of foreigners coming on holiday wanted a taste of the local cuisine. Tamales or tinned beef with 7-Up would not do. So, restaurants catering to tourists borrowed or modified local foods, or invented dishes that echoed them. Real Belizean food was born. This cuisine was, of course, no more really Belizean than what is on offer at my neighbourhood take-away is really Chinese. Rather, its origins lay in ethnic and subregional cuisines, some of which were elevated to national status and some of which were ignored, in what was an historical process of trial and error undertaken by cooks seeking to attract tourists to restaurant tables.

Like Miller's description of multinational advertising campaigns and the Trini way, Wilk's description of the emergence of Belizean food points to the ways that people's understandings of the consumables that they confront are shaped by outside forces. Of course, the outsider status of these forces clearly is not absolute; local account executives, hoteliers and restaurant owners are crucial to what happened in Trinidad and Belize. However, it remains the case that what was going on outside these countries significantly affected what was going on inside them. Further, these outside influences and the ways that they shape the local meaning of objects can constrain local people. At the level of the meaning of consumables, this is clear in Belize, where the development of tourism meant that the consumption expectations of tourists, primarily from North America, were instrumental in generating a national cuisine.

However, when a national cuisine is created, more is at issue than the Belizean dish of the day at a tourist hotel in Ambergris Cay or Belize City. As I said, the creation of Belizean food affects different groups differently; those who have elements of their cuisine adopted are granted a national legitimacy that is denied to those whose cuisines are passed over and who remain merely local, or even invisible. Group identity and national politics, then, are affected by what goes on in these restaurants' kitchens and in the imaginations of the tourists who eat at their tables.

Miller's work on Trinidad describes the nature of this effect and the complexities that can lurk in a soft drink.[29] Trinidad is divided roughly equally between those of South Asian descent (Indo-Trinidadians) and those of African descent (Afro-Trinidadians) and much of national politics in the country revolves around the tension between these two blocs: their claim to be true Trinidadians and hence their claims to political legitimacy.[30] This cleavage does not play itself out only at the level of party politics. As one might expect, it also plays itself out at the level of consumption. Thus, Miller notes that the carbonated soft-drink market is divided between two generic products. One comprises black sweet drinks, colas of various sorts, the other red sweet drinks, largely indistinguishable from colas except by their colour. The black sweet drink is memorialized in 'rum and coke', a common festive drink; the red sweet drink is memorialized in 'a red and a roti', a common snack. While all Trinidadians are familiar with both of these drinks, the black sweet drink is considered to be more Afro-Trinidadian and the red sweet drink is considered to be more Indo-Trinidadian. Thus, while Afro-Trinidadians commonly go out for a red and a roti, they are likely to see that food as characteristically Indo-Trinidadian.

However, the meanings of the red and the black and the political cleavages and tensions they reflect, are not just a local affair. As was the case with the emergence of real Belizean food, outsiders' tastes and assumptions and consumption preferences are important as well. To the outside world, the Caribbean drink is rum and coke; the red and a roti are invisible. In this, Indo-Trinidadians are marginal with regard to what constitutes the Caribbean in general and Trinidad in particular. Were Trinidadians left to themselves, this might be fairly unimportant stuff. However, with the growing importance of tourism, these outside identifications are fed into Trinidad. What tourists want and what they expect to see affect what local people think and do.

The influence of outside tastes and consumption preferences is apparent with Carnival. Carnival or something like it is common in much of Europe and the New World.[31] However, in the North American tourism industry it appears to have its most significant forms in New Orleans, Rio de Janeiro and Trinidad. In these three places, tourists flood in to satisfy what is, after all, their consumption preference for the music, the parades, the dance and the drink. In Trinidad, as tourism becomes more important, the state and commercial bodies that seek to attract tourists have increasingly identified Trinidad with Carnival. And this identification seems to have worked; a lot of tourists want Carnival and see Trinidad as Carnival-land.

In all three of its most visible forms, Carnival is dark-complected to the point of being Black. In Trinidad this creates tension. As the salience of Carnival becomes greater in the public perception of the country, so the Afro-Trinidadian sector of the population has become more secure; its claims to be authentically Trinidadian, and hence legitimate, are buttressed. For Indo-Trinidadians, on the other hand, whatever their actual participation, symbolically they are absent, and their authenticity and legitimacy suffer in comparison.[32] If Indo-Trinidadian complaints about the carnivalization of the country are any indication,[33] tourist consumption preferences influence political legitimacy and power in Trinidad, just as they seem to do in Belize.

Ecotourist Consumption in Papua New Guinea

The last case extends the point about Belize and Trinidad, that outsiders' consumption preferences can affect people's lives. This case concerns ecotourism, particularly with regard to a set of people who live in an area on the borders of the Gulf, Chimbu and Eastern Highlands provinces in Papua New Guinea (PNG). These people have been studied by Paige West,[34] and I will present this case at greater length than the other two. This is because the mechanisms by which these preferences are transmitted in this case are less familiar than they are in Belize and Trinidad. Hence, it is important to show those mechanisms rather than simply point to them.

Being a tourist is about as close as one can get to being a pure consumer; tourism is a huge business and ecotourism is routinely said to be the fastest growing sort. Ecotourism has many definitions, but most revolve around two points. It involves travel in order to experience attractive parts of the world defined as 'nature', in a way that benefits nature or at least disrupts it as little as possible. As well, though not signalled in its name, it involves travel to experience attractive people who are exotic for the tourist, usually people construed as 'primitive' or 'simple'. Again, this travel should benefit these people or at least disrupt them as little as possible.

In many of the tropical, developing countries where ecotourists go, the business is seen to be extremely important economically. In part this is because of the general growth in tourism over the past fifteen or twenty years. In part also this is because changes in aid and trade policies in the closing decades of the twentieth century have meant that the economic position of many of these countries has become more precarious, as has the economic position of rural people in them. Consequently, attracting tourists, especially ecotourists, has come to be seen as a key way for these countries to generate foreign exchange and it has become an attractive way to generate wealth for people in rural areas.

One such set of people comprises the Gimi speakers in the area around Crater Mountain, in the PNG Highlands. They were attracted to the idea of ecotourism after the Crater Mountain Wildlife Management Area (hereafter simply 'Crater Mountain') was established by the PNG government in 1994, following sustained political agitation by a set of Australians who had spent time in that part of the country. The PNG government handed the management of Crater Mountain over to the Research and Conservation Foundation of Papua New Guinea (RCF), which was the organization that pushed for its establishment and which had received support from the Wildlife Conservation Society, which is the international conservation arm of the New York Zoological Society and the Bronx Zoo.

PNG had no money to support Crater Mountain once the Wildlife Management Area was established and the RCF was left to find its own resources. They applied for conservation funding, which came as a grant from the Biodiversity Conservation Network (BCN), about US$490,000 between mid-1995 and mid-1998, with a further US$77,000 from the Wildlife Conservation Society. Following BCN advice, the RCF's grant application stressed the development of ecotourism and requested funds for ecotourism infrastructure.

The BCN not only provided support but also encouraged a particular orientation to environmental conservation at Crater Mountain, an orientation that reflected the institutional matrix in which it operated. The BCN received funding from the Biodiversity Support Program, a consortium of the World Wildlife Fund, the Nature Conservancy and the World Resources Institute, funded in part by the United States Agency for International Development (USAID). The consortium was 'partnered' with two global agencies of the US government, which meant that staff from the two agencies worked with consortium staff in shaping funded projects. One of the agencies was the United States–Asia Environmental Partnership. This is run by USAID and promotes 'sustainable development' in Asia through public and private initiatives. The other was the US Commercial Service, the international arm of the US Department of Commerce. It works to help US businesses compete in the global market by promoting the export of American goods and services and by working to protect the interests of those businesses internationally.

In the case of the BCN, 'sustainable development' meant encouraging 'enterprise-oriented' approaches to conservation. The BCN and the US agencies behind it proposed that if rural people were given business strategies that relied on the sustainable use of the environment for success and if they were linked to a 'community of stakeholders' (effectively purchasers) outside their rural areas, then enterprise-oriented conservation would be successful. People would work to conserve their environs because they would profit by doing so. Put differently, the BCN effectively induced local people to set up programmes that would cater to consumer demand of one sort or another. The most obvious type of consumer demand was ecotourism and local people agreed.

This agreement was a complex and significant event. To understand why, it is necessary to describe the social organization of the Gimi-speaking people in the area. These people are members of one or another of six clans and though clan membership was somewhat dispersed, all significant parts of the area were considered to belong to one or another of those clans. In addition, relations between clans are occasionally antagonistic and often uneasy. In such a situation, as one might expect, clans keep an eye on each other and are anxious not to see one clan gaining resources, wealth or prestige at the expense of another. There are mechanisms for defusing tension and generating a degree of cooperation, such as an ecotourism project would require. These mechanisms revolve around protracted and careful negotiations between clans. Often this is accompanied by the transfer of wealth between them or the allocation of future wealth among them in ways that reduce inequalities or redress grievances.

In such a situation, the anticipation of any activity that looks likely to generate wealth raises concerns about clan relations. The prospect of ecotourists certainly did so, which made the initial agreement to proceed with an ecotourism project a significant event. But of course, the initial agreement was a relatively easy one to secure; in the absence of concrete plans that would raise concrete concerns, the vision of a stream of wealthy tourists was an attractive one. When the decisions to be made became more concrete, things became more difficult.

The first concrete decision concerned where to build the lodge where the ecotourists would stay. An obvious spot was at the small airstrip in the area. The airstrip and the area around it belonged to one particular clan, which West calls Namabu, and people were concerned that if the lodge were built on Namabu land, then this clan would get the bulk of the wealth and status that the lodge would bring. This was a particular matter of concern because the Namabu clan had already benefited a great deal from dealings with outsiders and the uses to which their land had been put. For instance, a member of Namabu was the salaried agent for the missionary air services to the village. Several RCF-owned houses were on Namabu land and Namabu gained rental income and status from having RCF employees stay on their land. The Namabu had a storage shed at the landing strip and charged other villagers when they stored coffee there. As well, the local school and houses for teachers were on Namabu land, which meant that Namabu children had almost no walk to school, while others had as much as a half-hour walk and that the teachers, all from other parts of the country, had formed close relationships with the Namabu.

Given the Namabu's privileged position in the village, placing the ecotourist lodge next to the airstrip on Namabu land would cause significant tension, as that clan would get the bulk of the benefit. Conscious of this, the committee of elder men in charge of the issue decided it would be best to place the lodge at a hamlet about half an hour's walk from the airstrip. Four clans had a significant number of residents at this hamlet, so that placing the lodge there would spread the anticipated benefits more equally among the local clans. It took the committee almost two years to reach this decision, but it was accepted by everyone, including the Namabu elders.

The village elders had made a decision about the location of the lodge that reflected both their desire to have ecotourism and their wish to avoid the antagonisms that would follow from placing the lodge at the airstrip. In short, they pursued the interests of local people as a whole and used their own decision-making mechanism to arrive at the decision. However, the conservation biologists and other outsiders working at Crater Mountain assumed that the decision would be a purely commercial one, shaped by the consumption preferences of outsiders. That is, they assumed that the location would be selected to attract the greatest number of ecotourists. This meant that the important issues were the ease of access to the airstrip and to the projected village artefacts shop and the attractiveness of the view of the forest from the lodge. Events proved them right.

Early in 1997 the expatriate director of the RCF was visiting the area, and the decision on the location of the lodge was presented to her. She listened to the explanation for the choice and walked to the proposed location to see it. She walked back to the airstrip, where the committee of elder men were waiting, together with most of the villagers, who had turned up in celebration of her arrival. She told them that their proposed location was not acceptable. It was 'too far from the airstrip and tourists will not want to walk that far' and 'the view from the airstrip is so much better'. The lodge's location at the airstrip was fixed, and the case was closed. Two years of delicate negotiations among villagers were dismissed with a five-minute discussion.

The director's decision caused much anger, but the committee of elders put their resentment aside and worked together to proceed with building the lodge. The promise of the project was so great; all those rich, foreign tourists who would be interested in Maimafu villagers and their natural surroundings. But the decision to proceed with the lodge raised another concrete question: who would cook and clean for the tourists and benefit thereby? After more intense negotiations that took months, the committee decided that the benefits should be spread among all the clans. As each new set of tourists arrived, a set of people from a different clan should work at the lodge and act as guides. Again, however, they were thwarted. The expatriate advisors to the RCF said that there was a better way. One person would be chosen and paid to run the lodge; several would be trained by a foreign expert in how to lead tourist treks, cook 'bush dinners' and interact with ecotourists and would become paid ecotourism guides. The visible and equitable dispersing of benefits from the lodge was abandoned in favour of a commercial construction of what consumers wanted.

The situation that West describes shows again that it may be worthwhile to shift our focus away from the culturalist concern with people's choices within a field of meaningful objects. Instead, as with the Caribbean cases, it can be revealing to focus on how people can be constrained by the choices made by consumers elsewhere. In this village in the Highlands of PNG, justifiable concerns about encouraging fairly equitable and amicable relations among sets of local people induced leaders to cater to ecotourist consumers in particular ways. However, their decisions were overturned because they were seen as commercially undesirable.

Of course, there are no actual ecotourist consumers in this tale, only their surrogates, the senior staff of the RCF. And these staff members doubtless would have argued that, in acting as surrogates, they were making decisions that would increase the attractiveness of the site, increase the number of ecotourism visitors and so increase the financial benefit to local people. Similar arguments could be made by restaurateurs in Ambergris Cay producing a Belizean cuisine and by travel agents advertising Trinidad and Carnival. They may all have been right. And certainly the RCF staff were conforming to the policies of the organizations, based in the United States and supported by the US government, that were supporting and advising on the project. In doing so, however, they were demonstrating the ways that the past decisions of a body of Western consumers, ecotourists, created a set of expectations among the advisors that constrained the villagers of Maimafu and led to a set of decisions that looked likely to increase the inequalities between clans and also the tension and perhaps even conflict among local people.

Conclusion

I said at the start that the anthropological work on consumption that is most visible is culturalist, concerned with the relationships among objects, their meanings and the identities of consumers in the moment of consumption choice. While work in the discipline has become more diverse than the relatively semiological models contained in the key writings described previously in this chapter, much of that work still echoes the culturalist orientation of these classic publications. Here I have presented three cases, in order to make one, simple point. There is much to be gained from looking at other anthropological work that approaches consumption in other ways and that locates objects and consumers in different worlds.

This does not mean that the culturalist orientation has been fruitless, for it has led to interesting and intriguing work. However, it has the weakness of its strength: the intense focus that is revealing is also restricted and constricting, reflecting, perhaps, the increasingly culturalist orientation, the increasing concern with meaning, in the discipline as a whole in the closing decades of the twentieth century. That culturalist orientation not only emerged at about the same time that neoclassical economics was becoming predominant in Western societies. As well, in its focus on meaning and choice in the present moment, it echoes the common neoclassical construction of the world as the result of people's allocation of limited resources to unlimited wants, most visible in market transactions. And this happened during a period when many people's hold on resources and hence ability to choose were becomingly markedly less secure, as was their level of consumption.

The constrictions of the culturalist view can be overcome, if we turn to work that is concerned with more than the here and now of meaning and choice, whether the choice of villagers contemplating a possible marriage or the choice of consumers in a department store. Just as mainstream anthropology of consumption has taken objects and consumption and used them to get at a larger context of meaning, so other anthropologists have taken objects and consumption and used them to get at other larger contexts. However, such is the dominance of the culturalist approach that this other work often does not look like anthropology of consumption, especially to those outside the discipline. Consider the people who are central to the cases presented here; there are no structures of desire and no choice in a world of goods; there are not even identities to be adopted or families to be shopped for.[35]

There are many reasons for this absence. An important one is that the researchers whose work I have used arrived at consumption through routes other than the conventional one. Heyman arrived at it through an interest in the political-economic forces at work in Sonora; Wilk went to Belize, then British Honduras, as an arch-aeologist; West went to PNG with an interest in anthropology of the environment; even Miller, known for his work on consumption, wanted to study modern capitalist society in a region that lacked the historical depth and baggage of Western Europe. Arriving at consumption via routes other than those of the culturalist anthropology of consumption, they situated it in the context of questions other than those of choice, meaning and identity. In doing so, they help to show the breadth and depth of what anthropologists have to say about consumption, its corollaries and consequences.

My own biases are, I suspect, clear. If the anthropology of consumption is defined primarily by the culturalist approach, and a case can be made that it is, then its limits are such that it might be time to abandon it, or to recognize that it has little new to tell those who are not part of its internal debates; the constraints and restrictions seem to outweigh the insights. This does not mean that anthropologists should ignore consumption, for it is too pervasive and important for that. It does mean, however, that attending to consumption and those who consume may be most rewarding if we approach them in other ways and in terms of other issues. The most rewarding future seems likely to be one in which consumption in anthropology becomes something like what kinship used to be.[36] That is, for a small number of specialists, a primary interest; for the rest of us, a part of the lives and processes we study and an influence on the other issues we address.

Notes

* Without Frank Trentmann's invitation, the chapter would never have been written. He has my thanks. Although they did not know it, extensive conversations with Joe Heyman, Danny Miller, Rick Wilk and Paige West contributed greatly to what you see here. The opening sections of this chapter draw on J.G. Carrier and J. McC. Heyman, 'Consumption and Political Economy', *Journal of the Royal Anthropological Institute*, 2 (n.s.) (1997), pp. 355–73.

1. F. Trentmann, 'Beyond Consumerism: New Historical Perspectives on Consumption', *Journal of Contemporary History*, 39(3) (2004), pp. 373–401.
2. Some of these echo the approaches and issues described in B. Fine's chapter in this volume.
3. See, for example, D. Silverman, *Selling Culture: Bloomingdale's, Diana Vreeland and the New Aristocracy of Taste in Reagan's America* (New York, 1986).
4. US Department of Labor, Bureau of Labor Statistics, *Handbook of Statistics: Bulletin 2340* (US Government Printing Office, 1989), tables 83, 85, 113; *Employment and Earnings* (1991) 38:5, Table C–1.

5. J.B. Schor, *The Overworked American* (New York, 1991), pp. 80–1.
6. J. McC. Heyman, *Life and Labor on the Border: Working People of Northeastern Sonora, Mexico 1886–1986* (Tucson, 1991), pp. 176–8.
7. J. Baudrillard, *For a Critique of the Political Economy of the Sign* (St. Louis, 1981); M. Sahlins, *Culture and Practical Reason* (Chicago, 1976); M. Douglas and B. Isherwood, *The World of Goods* (Harmondsworth, 1978); P. Bourdieu, *Distinction: A Social Critique of the Judgement of Taste* (London, 1984).
8. Sahlins, *Culture and Practical Reason*, p. 181.
9. The description of Bourdieu's work here condenses the longer discussions in James G. Carrier, 'Social Aspects of Abstraction', *Social Anthropology*, 9 (2001), pp. 239–52 and in Carrier and Heyman, 'Consumption and Political Economy'.
10. In, for example, M. Schudson, *Advertising: The Uneasy Persuasion* (New York, 1984).
11. D. Miller, '"The Young and the Restless" in Trinidad: A Case of the Local and the Global in Mass Consumption' in R. Silverstone and E. Hirsch (eds), *Consuming Technologies: Media and Information in Domestic Spaces* (London, 1992), pp. 163–82.
12. This stress on the moment of choice is apparent in the legal constructions of the consumer described in M. Everson's chapter in this volume.
13. M. Perry, 'The Brand – Vehicle for Value in a Changing Marketplace', Advertising Association, President's Lecture, 7 July 1994, quoted in Y. Gabriel and T. Lang, *The Unmanageable Consumer* (London, 1995), p. 36.
14. Compare D. Miller's use of Hegel's notion of objectification in his *Material Culture and Mass Consumption* (Oxford, 1987); in a different way, consider J.G. Carrier and D. Miller, 'From Public Virtue to Private Vice: Anthropology and Economy' in H. Moore (ed.), *Anthropological Theory Today* (Cambridge, 1999), pp. 24–47 and F. Trentmann and V. Taylor's chapter in this volume.
15. Consequences for producers are important for the activists described in M. Chessel's chapter in this volume.
16. For instance, Miller, *Material Culture*; J.G. Carrier, *Gifts and Commodities: Exchange and Western Capitalism since 1700* (London, 1995).
17. For instance, S. Mintz, *Sweetness and Power* (New York, 1987).
18. For instance, R.J. Foster, 'Making National Cultures in the Global Ecumene', *Annual Review of Anthropology*, 20 (1991), pp. 235–60; this finds echoes in Ina Merkel's chapter in this volume.
19. D. Miller (ed.), *Worlds Apart: Modernity through the Prism of the Local* (London, 1995).
20. J. McC. Heyman, 'The Emergence of the Waged Life Course on the United States–Mexico Border', *American Ethnologist*, 17 (1990), pp. 348–59; 'The Organizational Logic of Capitalist Consumption on the Mexico–United States Border', *Research in Economic Anthropology*, 15 (1994), pp. 175–238; 'Imports and Standards of Justice on the Mexico–United States Border' in B. Orlove

(ed.), *The Allure of the Foreign: Imported Goods in Postcolonial Latin America* (Ann Arbor, 1997), pp. 151–83.

21. Heyman, 'Organizational Logic', pp. 179–83.
22. E.P. Thompson, 'Time, Work Discipline and Industrial Capitalism', *Past and Present*, 38 (1967), pp. 56–98.
23. This echoes the argument made in N. McKendrick, 'Home Demand and Economic Growth: A New View of the Role of Women and Children in the Industrial Revolution' in McKendrick (ed.), *Historical Perspectives: Studies in English Thought and Society* (London, 1974), pp. 152–210.
24. Heyman, 'Organizational Logic', p. 180.
25. As in, for instance, U. Hannerz, 'The World in Creolization', *Africa*, 57 (1987), pp. 546–59; Miller, 'The Young and the Restless'.
26. D. Miller, *Capitalism: An Ethnographic Approach* (Oxford and New York, 1997).
27. Miller, *Capitalism*, pp. 79–83.
28. Especially R. Wilk, 'Learning to Be Local in Belize: Global Systems of Common Difference' in Miller, *Worlds Apart*, pp. 110–33; 'Real Belizean Food: Building Local Identity in the Transnational Caribbean', *American Anthropologist*, 101 (1999), pp. 244–55.
29. Miller, *Capitalism*, pp. 146–9.
30. This is described in V. Munasinghe, *Callaloo or Tossed Salad? East Indians and the Cultural Politics of Identity in Trinidad* (Ithaca, NY, 2001).
31. See D. Miller, *Modernity: An Ethnographic Approach* (Oxford and New York, 1994), pp. 107–13.
32. In fact, the nature and position of public festivals in Trinidad are more complex than the salience and image of Carnival would indicate; see F.J. Korom, *Hosay Trinidad: Muharram Performance in an Indo-Caribbean Diaspora* (Philadelphia, 2003); Miller, *Modernity*, chap. 3.
33. For instance, R. Ramcharitar, 'The Caribbean's New Colonialism: The Art of Power', *Society for Caribbean Studies Annual Conference Papers*, 3 (2002): www.scsonline.freeserve.co.uk/olvol3.html
34. P. West, 'The Practices, Ideologies and Consequences of Conservation and Development in Papua New Guinea', Doctoral dissertation, Rutgers University, 2000; 'Environmental Non-Governmental Organizations and the Nature of Ethnographic Inquiry', *Social Analysis*, 45(2) (2001), pp. 55–77; P. West and J.G. Carrier, 'Ecotourism and Authenticity: Getting Away from It All?', *Current Anthropology*, 45(4) (2004), pp. 483–98.
35. As in D. Miller, *A Theory of Shopping* (Cambridge, 1998).
36. This is a perverse echo of Miller's assertion that, for anthropologists, consumption should take the place of kinship as the key route to understanding the organization and operation of society, in D. Miller, 'Consumption Studies as the Transformation of Anthropology' in D. Miller (ed.), *Acknowledging Consumption: A Review of New Studies* (London, 1995), pp. 264–95.

–13–

Addressing the Consumer*
Ben Fine

Knowledge and identity of the consumer are heavily bound to consumer culture, attributes of which are discussed in the following section in terms of its being contextual, construed, chaotic, constructed, contradictory and conflictual. This leads in section 3 to the argument that an understanding of capitalist commodity relations offers an appropriate starting point for addressing consumer culture (even where consumption is not directly dependent on market provision). The corresponding approach to the culture of consumption is illustrated by examples in section 4 (although a wide variety of case studies is referenced throughout). The closing remarks bring out some of the implications for consumer politics.

Consumer Culture

It is twenty years since the study of consumption became the object of intensive study across the social sciences. It is an opportune moment to take stock and offer some necessarily partial assessment of what we know about that elusive object/subject of this collective endeavour – the consumer. Our knowledge, however, has not sprung anew from nowhere, for the consumer has long been studied for a variety of purposes from marketing through to social commentary. At one extreme stands the discipline of economics and its fabled *homo economicus*, rational economic man rarely acknowledged as female.[1] He sets about maximizing utility subject to budget and other constraints, increasingly across all activities of which consumption choices are but the most prominent.[2] A simple, single-minded calculus of pleasure (spending money) and pain (earning it) is presumed to suffice to explain consumption, essentially understood as equivalent to market demand. Otherwise we learn nothing about consumer and consumed. Indeed, these key categories are inevitably designated in the most anonymous form as algebraic rather than semiotic symbols, as in the standard utility function of elementary microeconomics, $u_i (x_1, x_2, \ldots, x_j, \ldots, x_n)$, where individual i gains utility from goods x_j. Further, in the virtual world of perfect competition, the humble consumers become noble sovereigns, dictating what is produced and setting in place the efficient allocation of resources for society as a whole.[3]

As a discipline, economics has not participated in the academic consumer revolution, confining itself to ever more sophisticated methods for estimating demand on otherwise unchanging assumptions of the sort laid out in the previous paragraph. Economics has exhibited scant regard for concerns around the nature of the consumer and of the consumed, part of a more general neglect by economics of the post-modernism that has ripped across other disciplines.[4] So, at the other extreme to economics stands old-time consumer studies. It has been eclectic in method and wide in scope, closely aligned to the study of marketing and advertising and more concerned with the psyche of the consumer and with *her* spending power. Given a radical twist, the sovereign consumer is deposed and becomes victim to the manipulative hidden persuaders in pursuit of what are deemed to be artificially created, even false, needs.[5]

To a large extent, consumer studies remains ignored by the new literature. With some justification, it has been perceived as predominantly middle-brow compared to the high theory of post-modernism. Yet, within its own vernacular, consumer studies offered lessons that came to be re-invented by post-modernism. First is the idea that consumers have multiple identities. This is not simply a matter of socio-economic status, varied though this is by class, age, race, gender, location, income, education, household characteristics, etc. The individual is interpreted as incorporating and acting upon an equally varied set of attributes, although the attempt is made to aggregate these into identifiable and targetable lifestyles. A modest list of factors in identifying the consumer includes:

> High or low involvement, arousal, attitude, affect, attributes, intention, reaction, learning, satisfaction, expectation, atmospherics, environment, context, convenience, memory, familiarity, judgement, choice, impulse, generics, cues, status, brand, impression, class, time, age, inference, endorsement, stereotypes, community, socialisation, norms, knowledge, lifestyle, enthusiasm, materialism, culture, self-perception, routinisation, stimulus, sentiment, role-playing, psychographics, mood, encoding, focus, situation, adaptivity, opinion, leadership, imagination, variety, scripts, vividness, disconfirmation, precipitation, persuasion, reinforcement, reminder, seduction, aesthetics, humour, etc.[6]

Not surprisingly, Lord Lever could claim that 50 per cent of his advertising works, but the problem was that he did not know which 50 per cent!

Second, by the same token, not only the consumer but also the consumed takes, or appears to take on, multiple lives of its own. In extreme form, Appadurai suggests:

> Focusing on the things that are exchanged, rather than simply on the forms or functions of exchange, makes it possible to argue that what creates the link between exchange and value is *politics*, construed broadly. This argument ... justifies the conceit that commodities, like persons, have social lives.[7]

On a more mundane level, before adverts came to be deconstructed, they had to be constructed. There is no reason to believe that the one has been handled with any greater degree of sophistication and complexity than the other. Objects of consumption, by whatever means, are endowed with the qualities construed by consumers, in part through a system of signs. These can float free from the material properties of the objects themselves – as in the idea of Coke as the 'real thing', an imaginary reality that is shifted to suit time and place. Reflexively, consumers and consumed reinvent themselves or are reinvented by others on their behalf. For mainstream economics, objects of consumption serve a given (and limited) identity represented by a utility function through their given material properties. For postmodernism, consumption is a source of shifting and multiple identities grounded in symbolic properties. Indeed, Baudrillard's simulacrum of desire can be interpreted as a nightmarish restoration of consumer sovereignty through collapsing the material to a symbolic world within the mind.

No doubt I oversimplify and exaggerate to the point of parody. But I do so for a particular purpose, to learn a third lesson. For, in recognizing that the consumer/consumed has multiple identities, like culture, ideology, systems of belief or whatever, it is necessarily subject to what I have dubbed the six Cs. Thus, the culture of consumption is contextual, construed, chaotic, constructed, contradictory and conflictual. It is worth elaborating on each of these.

By contextual is meant that the consumed is not only located in specific circumstances (high or low price, good or bad quality) but that these are associated with particular and variable meanings to the consumer. The meaning of the same dress is very different according to time and place, as has been recognized in the past through sumptuary laws and in the present by virtue of power (and casual) dressing, with jeans and varieties of footwear moving flexibly between work clothes and fashion items. The consumer is far from a passive recipient of the meaning of objects of consumption and is active in creating that meaning. But the consumer is not liable to be able to command a monopoly in doing so, not least because that meaning is both internalized from without (what does consumption mean to the consumer?) and interpreted by others (experts and retailers and not least in consumption for display).[8]

Thus, consumption is construed. But the process of construal is heavily influenced by a multiplicity of factors derived from context. This is illustrated by the shifting meanings over time, place and people (and objects of consumption) of the distinction between luxuries and necessities. It is not simply a matter of shifting the boundary between the two, in favour of the former with rising affluence. For the meaning of the two and the distinction, changes over time. Just as one person's meat is another's poison, so a luxury to one is a necessity to another.

One reason for this is that there is a tension between tying the distinction to what can be commonly afforded and to attaining a socio-economic status (that cannot be reduced to income alone except possibly at a point in time). This leads to the recognition that the meaning of consumption is not necessarily coherent, as different meanings are articulated together. A cream cake for someone on a diet can be both a luxury and 'naughty but nice', simultaneously reward and punishment.

The source of such inconsistent or chaotic attributes is not entirely or predominantly internal but derives from how the item of consumption has been both materially and culturally constructed, something that runs deeper than construal. The 'sweetness' of chocolate, for example and its different meanings to men, women and children, depend upon the material properties of chocolate itself (and what is manufactured as such) as well as the gendered and other meanings of sweetness.

The construction of the consumer is also contradictory in the dialectical sense of being deeply rooted in social forces, structures and processes that interact with one another to give rise to complex and shifting outcomes. This is well illustrated in the peculiarly modern pressures both to diet and to eat. These have given rise to what are termed the diseases of affluence, as their influence is felt at the level of the individual – not only in heart disease but also in obesity, anorexia and bulimia.[9]

Not surprisingly in view of these other attributes, the consumer/consumed is subject to conflict in the making of meaning. In a way, this is how the ideologies of consumer sovereignty/manipulation can be interpreted, an attempt at persuading consumers how they should perceive of themselves. But conflict over meaning is not confined to the relations between producers and consumers. Conflict over consumption can be initiated by those who are neither producer nor consumer, as is sharply brought into focus by campaigns against particular consumption goods in light of the way in which they have been produced – to the detriment of the environment or wages and working conditions.

Capitalist Commodities and the Consumer

On the face of it, appeal to the six Cs would appear to render the consumer even more elusive. How these attributes interact with one another is highly complex and diverse. But this does not mean that there is no place for generalities, although general theories are bound to fail. The latter tend to take one of two forms. One is horizontal theory, usually drawn from within a discipline and applied across all consumption.[10] This is true of the demand theory of mainstream economics that treats all consumption as a theory of choice in the satisfaction of preferences and of theories of emulation and distinction (stratification) within sociology. Otherwise, as with the notions of consumerism, consumer society or consumer revolution, aspects of consumer behaviour are (over)generalized as socially driven and historically specific characteristics.

The problem with such generalities is the extent to which they are empirically more observed in the breach. This is hardly surprising in view of the complexity and diversity of the determinants of consumption. On the other hand, it is too nihilistic to draw the conclusion that there are no regularities. Surely, when Ritzer points to McDonaldization,[11] he has achieved some purchase on the nature of contemporary consumption, even if everything is not and cannot be hamburger-like (quite apart from whether all hamburgers are themselves the same). Analytically, though, the problem of starting with McDonald's is that it sets a standard against which both theories and other consumption goods can be judged, but it does not and cannot justify that theoretical norm.

There is, however, a more general property of the humble hamburger that points to an appropriate starting point in the study of the consumer: that it is a capitalist commodity. Its appeal as point of departure in studying consumption and the consumer rests on the following arguments, with objections anticipated both to strengthen the case and to elaborate and refine it. First, the contemporary consumer is heavily embroiled in the world of commodities, as is acknowledged by notions such as consumer society, globalisation and McDonaldization. This does not, however, mean that all commodities are produced, distributed and bought and sold in the same way. Much of the current understanding of the consumer is based upon a putative shift from Fordist to post-Fordist ('flec-spec') modes of provision. Such ideal types are simply too crude and empirically questionable as generalities.[12] Commodities are highly diverse in how they reach the consumer, let alone in how they are consumed.

Nor does emphasis upon the commodity lead to an undue restoration of consideration of production over consumption, of material over cultural factors. This is to see the commodity as unduly reduced to its property as exchange value, as price. But classical political economy and especially Marx, defines the commodity as both exchange *and* use value. This implies that qualitative social relations are in part formed and expressed quantitatively. What you consume and what it means to you, are heavily bound by how much you can afford, a sort of consumer democracy in which some have more votes and freedoms than others. Thus, for example, there is a major tension between meeting the requirements of mass production and sustaining distinctiveness for commodity and consumer (lifestyle for sale means access for all). But it necessarily follows that consumption patterns and meanings, cannot be legitimately derived from class relations of production, although this does not mean that such class relations in their broader context are irrelevant to consumption.[13] But class, production and exchange value are readily left behind in embracing the pertinence of sign value. Whilst the leading villain in this respect has been Baudrillard, his stance on the rejection of Marx has continued to be readily accepted even though much else of his work has now been rejected as too extreme.[14]

But if social relations and culture (of consumption), are only partly and indirectly expressed and formed through commodity relations, how well does commodity analysis confront the fuller picture? An answer depends on how the classic Marxist concept of commodity fetishism is understood. On a narrow interpretation, it refers to the fact that the commodity form as such does not directly reveal how the commodity has been brought to the market (especially in its dependence on class relations of production). More broadly, though, commodity fetishism can be viewed in terms of how consumers' access to products via the market reveals little or nothing about how the use value of the commodity (in material *and* cultural properties) has been endowed, from child labour and environmental degradation to the application of science and tariffs.[15]

This broader interpretation is certainly consistent with Marx's own approach. As Carruthers and Babb put it: '[I]n Marx's analysis, commodities consist of much more than just a set of useful features: they embody social relationships'.[16] Further, for Marx, social relations merely appear as what they also are, as relations between things on the market – quantitative, uni-dimensional and monetized. To emphasize that these appearances are not necessarily false, Marx draws the contrast with religious fetishism for which exploitative social relations are expressed as a supposed (false) relationship with the deity. It follows that the nature of use values is constructed on the basis of *all* the social relations that accompany the commodity to market, each of these being fetishized by the monetary form.

In this respect, Burke's outstanding study of the consumption of cosmetics in Zimbabwe, from colonial times forward, is instructive, not least because of its strength as an exemplary case study of the relationship between the material and cultural properties of commodities.[17] He investigates how the selling and the meaning of cosmetics have been dependent upon both the strategies of capitalist manufacturers and the intersection of their advertising with shifting meanings of race, gender, cleanliness and so on. When soap is advertised with an image contrasting the cleanliness of the skins of black and white children, we know in retrospect that such commerce is situated in racist, colonial society whose concealed levels of oppression penetrate far deeper than those of personal hygiene (and the false idea that black faces cannot be made clean even by soap). So soap is about cleanliness and colonialism and the material and cultural meanings of both. Consequently, Burke appropriately poses the question of the relationship between the material and cultural properties of commodities:

> Goods are *not* pure free-floating signifiers; they are not blank slates upon which history and power can write freely. They have concrete material qualities which limit and prescribe their uses and their nature. On some level, food is for eating, soap is for washing, clothes are for wearing.[18]

He acknowledges the problematic but useful work of Baudrillard in positing the critical role of sign value in serving 'modern capitalism's ability to generate and control surplus value' and he is particularly appreciative of Haug's 'masterly treatment of "commodity aesthetics"'.[19] But Burke also displays an ambivalence towards Marx and his notion of commodity fetishism, one that is characteristic of the literature as a whole. On the one hand, he welcomes the idea that 'relations between things … accompany, conceal, or displace the actual state of relations between people'.[20] However, he concludes that:

> Marx's definition of commodity fetishism does not leave sufficient room for the complexity of the relations between things and people, room for the imaginative possibilities and unexpected consequences of commodification, room for the intricate emotional and intellectual investments made by individuals within commodity culture.[21]

Neither evidence nor argument is given for this conclusion. I suspect that it reflects a more widespread tension in wishing to recognize both that capitalistic imperatives are crucial for the nature and meaning of consumption and that they are not purely determined by them. In extremis, as Burke recognizes, this tension has often been incorrectly resolved by drawing a distinction between met and (bad) false and unmet and (good) real needs, blame for which resides somewhere between commodity fetishism and a conspiracy of the ruling classes to gain working-class acquiescence. Further, this tradition identifies false needs with appearances rather than with the supposedly deeper realities of unmet needs.

But there is nothing in Marx's definition of commodity fetishism that warrants such an interpretation or that precludes the meeting of Burke's analytical demands. His own case study demonstrates how relations of domination other than in production are concealed (and in a sense, if through reflection, revealed) by the meanings attached to cosmetics, which themselves differ by time, place and consumer. It is necessary to acknowledge that such social relations structure, without absolutely determining, the way in which commodities can be used and understood at the level of the individual – what it is to be clean or beautiful (that is white, until black is beautiful can assert itself and be, first, politicized and then itself commercialized).

In short, Marx's theory of value, of which commodity fetishism is a corollary, sustains an irreducible connection between production (for profit) and exchange (for use). In contrast, post-modernist critics of Marx discount production, depart from exchange and (re)construct use value alone. It is worth recalling, however, that Marx's early writings focused heavily on alienation.[22] To a large extent, such concerns were set aside in later works 'in order to retain the concept of *surplus-value*' and explore the material basis within capitalism for our main sources of consumption and its meanings and practices.[23] In other words, never lose sight of (someone else's) profit motive as underpinning our consumption.

In this context, Haug's much-neglected notion of the aesthetic illusion is instructive, as he argues that the shifting products and productions in pursuing profitability create a tension between the material character of commodities and the way they are perceived.[24] In a nutshell, Haug argues that commodities tend to be degraded in their material properties in pursuit of profitability through cheapened production. To guarantee sale, this is veiled by endowing them with a sexual content through advertising. Significantly, Haug establishes a shifting connection between how commodities are produced and how they are construed. But his analysis is too narrow in presuming that commodities are always worsened (a nostalgia for craftmanship and authenticity) and that compensation for that cheapening degradation only comes in the form of sexuality and advertising.

Commodities pick up their highly diverse meanings from a variety of sources, whatever their shifting quality. Mass produced and distributed frozen dough, for example, gains its appeal by being marketed as French sticks.[25] Nor is it a matter, though, of adding more meanings and content than sexuality to the making of use values. For this leaves open to a large extent the systemic source of initial meanings and whether and how these are reproduced, transformed or set aside rather than simply supplemented. What Haug neglects, then, is that production and other moments in delivering commodities do not simply strain the bounds of the received notions of properties, they are also positively constitutive of consumer culture alongside consumers themselves.

This has been recognized in the circuit of culture approach to consumption.[26] Correctly, it observes that the culture of commodities derives from different passing points in the passage to consumption. This can be deliberate, as corporations, for example, launch not only (the images of) the commodities they produce but also themselves as ethical and civic agents, of science and progress and, especially, the American way of life across a range of charitable and other interventions.[27] This suggests that the metaphor of circuit is inappropriate, or incomplete, in identifying the culture attached to commodities. For it conjures up the image of a game of Chinese whispers in which the meaning of the commodity is changed as it passes from hand to hand in gaining access to the consumer. The idea of a cultural *system* around each commodity is better able to incorporate the structured movement in the meaning of consumption as social relations are formed, expressed and acted upon in the passage from production to consumption and in reproduction.

As those familiar with my earlier work will recognize, this is to complement an approach based on commodity-specific 'systems of provision' with corresponding cultural systems. The fashion system creates clothes and culture in ways that are inextricably linked. But, in starting with the commodity, how well is the approach able to accommodate those non-commercial aspects of the culture of consumption, not least those actively practised by consumers themselves? Here it is important to reject the idea that approaching consumption through commodities in some sense heavily reduces the potential cultural content of consumption – a point emphasized by post-modernism in its focus on the bewildered consumer. It is precisely because the commodity is flattened in its meaning as exchange value, expressed in monetary terms, that it is capable of such flexibility – almost a blank cheque – in meaning as use value. When consumption is delivered other than through the market, it inevitably carries meaning through that mode of delivery (and the same remains true of market delivery where interpersonal connections are established) – home-cooking, for example. But attempts can be made to appropriate such properties by commerce in some form of as good as home-made. Further, for example, whilst critics of consumer society deplore its single-minded hedonistic ethic, itself a possibility because of the monetization of consumption, the potential for ethically driven sustainable commodity consumption is also its consequence.

In short, the richness and diversity of meaning that attaches to the consumed/ consumer derive from the commodity form – it is able to express almost all social relations[28]– although it necessarily imparts an influence of its own. It is commonplace to contrast the commodity with the gift in consumption (and otherwise), as if the one denudes society of the complexity offered by the other. But the world of commodities expands the world of gifts and the meanings that can be attached to them. Japan, for example, the society most famed for its culture of gift giving, is the most successful capitalist commodity producer (of commodity gifts) in the twentieth century.[29] This is not to suggest that consumer culture exhausts, reflects or explains all culture or, indeed, that it is the most prominent and influential source of culture. Thus, Wilska finds that Finnish consumers do not primarily create and maintain their personal identities through consumption.[30] Further, the gendering of consumption is associated with motherhood, domestic responsibilities more generally, nation-building, emancipation, sex appeal and so on, none of which is primarily determined by, let alone reducible to, the culture of consumption.

But how appropriately does the commodity as starting point serve in an understanding of non-commercially-sourced consumption, something that is common even within advanced capitalist economies (through household provision, leisure, etc)? Despite its removal from the immediate influence of the market, much of such consumption is determined by it, not least as consumers themselves internalize its impact. Cost–benefit comparisons are made with market provision (how much do I save/lose by relying upon own provision?) and with the nature and quality of results (as good as you can get from the shops or better or authentic for being home-made).

The relationship between commodity and non-commodity provision shifts the location and meaning of consumption in complex ways, as is recognized by reference to commodification (and de- and re-commodification). As capitalism cheapens commodities through productivity increase, so it undermines the capacity of consumers to 'compete'. But it can also raise incomes and leisure-time, cheapen the cost of consumer 'inputs' and widen the range of consumer activity. There is a dialectic between commodity and non-commodity consumption that does not allow the latter to float analytically free. This is strikingly illustrated by the burgeoning literature on consumption and identity in transitional economies, where the shift to embrace capitalist commodity production is part and parcel of more general material and cultural transformations.[31] And the same applies to 'westernisation' and how it is received in former colonies – as an assault on independent culture or as modernisation and elite distinction.[32] Inevitably, such confrontation with commodities restructures the gendering of consumption, prodding masculinity, for example, either to emulate 'female consumerism' or to seek to consolidate its supposedly traditional and national distinctiveness.[33] As Karlin concludes of Japan at the beginning of the twentieth century:

> The Japanese gentleman with his cosmopolitanism and stylistic promiscuity emerges in Meiji representations as the embodiment of superficiality and imitation. Such caricatures suggested that this image of feminized masculinity was somehow inauthentic and unnatural because it explored the performative and mobile categories of identity.[34]

But the contradictory logic of commodity provision takes permanent root, howsoever initial skirmishes are resolved in redefining cultural traditions. This is so not least in the restructuring of activity in and around the house – for food (decline of family meal, rise of takeaway and convenience foods), transport (private car versus public transport), entertainment (personal electronics) and so on.

Focus on the commodity as starting point necessarily questions why and how non-commodity consumption persists and with what implications for the meaning and activity of the consumer. Thus, for example, the phenomenal rise of DIY in the UK, in particular, is a consequence of the relative advantages of owner-occupation, its associated capital gains and the stretching of personal housing finance to achieve them, the poor and uncertain quality of casualized building work, the highly concentrated retail sector and its use of superstores and the mass production of commodities to serve non-commodity home improvements.

As has been emphasized, capitalist commodity production prodigiously expands and extends the scope of the material and cultural relations that it governs (and which govern it) despite, or even because of, its one-dimensional commercial imperative. But, necessarily, it cannot range historically to pre-capitalist societies other than in the more shadowy presence of the market form. Once again, the commodity as starting point is judicious, albeit for different reasons and in different ways. Commodity consumption does not reduce to capitalist commodity production and the latter's dependence on profitability is of at most marginal direct significance to the consumer. Consequently, the presence of markets in pre-capitalist societies induces characteristics from the perspective of consumption that are more developed and pronounced and hence recognizable, in capitalist societies, including the projection of commodity meanings in consumption where the commodity is absent, as discussed above. Payment and gifts, in kind prevail across pre-capitalist and capitalist societies but are equally amenable in principle to commercial valuation. Contemporary consumption often prides itself on the exclusion of the commercial, not least in the 'personal' (love, marriage, friendship and family), often more commercialized in pre-capitalist societies (and certainly so for slavery).

How, then, can an understanding of consumption starting with the commodity shed light on non-commodity consumption in non-capitalist societies? It is not appropriate to treat such consumption as if a market were present, as in the economic and social history of mainstream economics for which rational choice and the costs and benefits of comparative advantage prevail in all circumstances.[35] But the investigation of pre-capitalist consumption must start somewhere and, inevitably, it does so with categories of analysis drawn from present-day consumption and capitalist society. As far as pre-capitalist societies are concerned, these range over the questionable extrapolation of divisions between production and consumption themselves; the nature of the household; and the entirely different ways in which the material culture of consumption is generated through class, gender, power and conflict. Understanding of consumption under capitalism provides investigative tools for what should be the acknowledged basis for reconstructing the notion of consumption to reflect the material and cultural realities of non-commodity consumption.

The Approach Applied

The understanding of consumption and the consumer in terms of material systems of provision and cultural systems around specific commodities is the position *from* and not *to* which my own approach has evolved. Crewe comments:

> The importance of this approach is that it points to the possibility of 'a more balanced treatment of the relationship between production and consumption', one which also acknowledges the symbolic significance of commodities.[36]

To some extent, then, the approach has previously been recognized as such and has even been followed explicitly by others. Hansen understands the international provision of second-hand clothing to Zambia in these terms, how and where the clothes come from and the reworking of fashion systems, often bizarrely into local representations of identity.[37] Lemire deals in both first- and second-hand clothing around the UK industrial revolution. She suggests, in her second study of the system of provision approach, that no category of goods better illustrates this hypothesis than does dress.[38] A similar view is found in the edited collection of Burman on the sewing machine, for which the complex relationship between (de-)commodification and fashionability is central.[39]

But Narotzky finds the perspective wanting insofar as it does not address non-commodified consumption and its relationship to the commodified.[40] Similarly, Pennell suggests,[41] 'Fine and Leopold leave unquestioned a further, related assumption; their analysis is dependent upon an understanding of consumed objects as *always being* commodities'. This is a reasonable observation of Fine and Leopold, but the deficiency has been addressed, hopefully redressed, in the new edition through early chapters both on the commodity and on its false antithesis with the gift and by the discussion above.[42] Even so, the original contribution reflects two, possibly implicit, stances now made explicit: the heavy dependence of contemporary consumption upon (capitalist) commodity production and the need to understand the latter in comprehending the distinctiveness of non-commodity consumption.

Far more extensive than direct reference to the approach offered here are those studies that can be interpreted as having contributed to it, necessarily unwittingly and possibly unwillingly. From the cultural side, Appadurai's treatment of consumer society leads him to adopt a commodity-specific stance because of different genealogies and histories:

> Multiple processual flows that underwrite any given conjuncture ... [result in] the processes implied by history and genealogy creating multiple temporalities for any given practice. It further follows that in studying the consumption practices of distinct societies, we must be prepared to encounter a host of different histories and genealogies present at the same 'moment'. Thus, in France, the consumption of perfume may, in 1880, be underpinned by one kind of history of bodily discipline and aesthetics, while the consumption of meat may respond to wholly other histories and genealogies.[43]

Thus, for him, consumption is self-effacing, habituated and highly specific to the individual; 'in all social contexts, [consumption] is centered around ... the body [that] calls for disciplines that are repetitious, or at least periodic'.[44] As a result, 'all socially organized forms of consumption seem to revolve around some combination of the following three patterns: interdiction, sumptuary law and fashion',[45] not least, in consumption as the pursuit of pleasure, the tensions between nostalgia and fantasy as opposed to fantasy and utility (as an interpretation of Campbell's romantic ethic) and between individual desire and collective disciplines (as for Rojek). These are all thrown in, together with consumption as work in the household and as the commodification of time (with reference to E.P. Thompson and the impact of industrialisation).

As Moeran perceptively observes of Appadurai,[46] 'like others in sociology and anthropology ... he is concerned not so much with the way in which commodities form a *system* but with the meaning of different elements in the "cultural construction of value"'. Yet, Appadurai is drawn to commodity-specific analysis, as is Moeran himself, for whom there are six types of value – use value (however subjectively or socially constructed), technical (its physical or design properties), appreciative (aesthetic or cultural) and social (ethical, status, etc.). These four are perceived as encapsulating Bourdieu's social and cultural capital. They coalesce to form the two other kinds of exchange value – commodity and symbolic. As a critique of Appadurai, is this not a case of a fuller pot calling the kettle black? As far as conclusions are concerned, they do end up in the same commodity-specific pot:

> It is, then, by taking account of these six types of value, by analysing how specific objects or commodities are given particular values over and above their material properties, that we can begin to understand consumption practices throughout the world.[47]

Similarly, Carruthers and Babb judge that the differences in the ways that meaning is attributed to commodities suffice to warrant a commodity-specific approach:

> The kinds of meanings that get attached to commodities draw on a small set of recurrent themes: social status, attractiveness, gender, age, social relationships, ethnicity, group membership. These core meanings get deployed in different ways as they are connected to different commodities.[48]

Such commodity-specificity is necessarily notable for the highly diverse case-study literature. Rogers' account of the Barbie doll constructs it as icon, as a collector's item, as glocalisation (as Americanisation), the fortunes of corporate Mattel Inc., the tensions around race, class and gender, as deplored for stereotyping and praised for socializing, as experienced, remembered and socially and subjectively reconstructed.[49] It is rooted in (doll) history, fantasy, bodies, intellectual property rights, Disneyisation, the social reproduction of children, domestic production (of clothes for grandchildren), etc. and theming with 100 different Barbie dolls around three themes, hair, lifestyle and glamour – each with corresponding accessories. But Barbie is only made possible through its dependence on the international division of (child and slave) labour, for which Roger, provides telling insights.[50] No less harrowing is the account by Bishop and Robinson of the Thai sex industry as an unacknowledged system of production, with attached cultural systems on both sides of the commercial divide, Western tourist and Eastern sex worker.[51] Arce and Fisher examine how totally different narratives are attached to Bolivian coca and Tanzanian honey, as illegal drugs and fair trading, respectively, through the global chains of meanings and provision, albeit locally integrated.[52]

Beng-Huat focuses on clothing as an illustration for:

> the 'idea' of consumption as a phenomenon. Visually it is ubiquitous and indubitable, but conceptually its 'unity' is highly problematic. Each item in the constantly expanding array of goods and services which modern urban individuals and households have to consume routinely in order to reproduce their daily life is surrounded by its own systems of production, distribution, marketing, procurement and, finally, consumption. Each of these systems is in turn constituted by its own multifaceted and segmental economies in an increasingly globalised capitalism.[53]

Equally, in the context of clothing, Jirousek observes that 'a mass fashion system is a result of economic factors relating to the development of the textile industry ... substantial means of production, an effective distribution system that includes the ability to disseminate rapidly changing fashion ideal and a mass consumer public that has both the income and the social mobility to support such a system'.[54] Crane demonstrates how the fashion system is no longer subject to trickle-up or down (if it ever were) because of its dependence upon multiple sourcing in supply and targeting in demand.[55] As a result, elite fashion creates clothes that are not designed to be worn but to raise commercial publicity so that profit can be made from both segmented and mass markets.[56] Further, the attempt to address horizontal factors such as gendering can also be interpreted as needing to descend to systems of provision, as in Mort's study of clothing and masculinity (although he is explicitly concerned about leakage across systems of provision).[57]

For the rise of yuppie (reimagined speciality) coffees and the reimagination of class in the United States, Roseberry traces the material and cultural systems involved to conclude:

> Proper understanding of the proliferation of specialty coffees requires consideration of the experiences and choices of the consumer in the coffee shop and at the dinner table, but it also requires consideration of the methods, networks and relations of coffee production, processing and distribution and sale in the 1980s, as well as placement of those methods, networks and relations within a wider history.[58]

And Auslander's study of French furniture is exemplary in allowing for:

> a dialectic between analysis of stylistic change, on the one hand and of political and economic changes, on the other. The specific use of materials, the historical repertoire of forms and the products of distance culture emerged out of a set of perpetual dialogues between the culture of production, the system of distribution and the culture of the court.[59]

She concludes:

> All acts of consumption were also acts of production, but some modes of consumption were defined as almost exclusively masculine. This gendering of forms of consumption was not stable across the century, however, nor were the boundaries between the masculine and the feminine impermeable at any given moment.[60]

This is an appropriate conclusion to draw from a historical study of French furniture; it should provide a lesson for future studies.

The Politics of Consumption and the Consumption of Politics

The commodity form of consumption and the specificity of commodity and cultural systems have profound implications for consumer politics. Under contemporary capitalism, the construction of the politics of consumption tends to be subject to severe limitations as a result of the following aspects. First and foremost there is the absence of social stratification, whether by class, gender or race, etc., except as an afterthought, not least because we are all equally consumers (although some are more equal than others). Second, the politics of commodity consumption begins with individual as opposed to collective perspectives. Putting these two aspects together, consumer politics is about every*one*. Third, consumer politics tends to lack ambition in the depth and scope of targeted social change, essentially seeking to correct some form of market imperfection, to make the market deliver different or differently rather than to deliver other than through the market on the basis of capitalist production. Fourth, consumption is often falsely counterposed to production, failing to recognize the heavy weight of consumption, of inputs, that is required by production.[61] Fifth, the politics of consumption through the citizen consumer serves as the counterpart to the voter citizen, with elected government reflecting political preferences just as the market reflects consumer preferences. But there is much more to the politics of consumption than the participation as consumer, just as there is much more to politics than voting. Arguably, much more goes on behind the scenes of electioneering and shopping than is revealed by them.

The limitations on consumer politics are not just constraints by virtue of the position of the potentially isolated consumer at the end of chains of material and cultural provision. The politics of consumption as a process does itself have a tendency to be self-limiting. For, as individuals rebel against being confined to the role of simple consumers, as purchasers, some will inevitably escape from preoccupation with intrinsically constructing their own identity and extrinsically engage with the more distant determinants of consumption. This is apparent in the green consumer concerned with the environment, the ethical consumer with child or sweated labour and the boycott of apartheid goods.

The point is that these issues tend to become removed from the realm of the consumer to the realm of the citizen, an equally elusive term but not one that necessarily associates itself with the consumer and the consumed. So the engaged consumer becomes the politicized citizen.[62] As has been seen, the culture of consumption is extremely complex and diverse in origin and content. The key issue in whether and how it is engaged politically depends on how consumption and the consumer are explicitly attached to the structures, relations and processes of provision. In short, the politics of consumption depends upon how and how far it is removed from consumption itself. In other words, the consumer tends to become something else, as does consumption as its material and cultural determinants are consciously exposed, pursued and transformed. This is most notable in the case of the sorely neglected issue of 'public' or 'collective' as opposed to private consumption that dominates most of the literature.[63] In part (and not just because of post-modernism's cultural turn and preoccupation with the creative ad and consumer), public consumption has been overlooked because its active pursuit transforms it into something else, the welfare state, whether for education, health, welfare or utilities.[64]

More generally, it follows that there is a tension in the politics of consumption between containing its content to the more or less private and individual practices of consumption and extending it to questions of (collective and public) provision, power and conflict.[65] This is why collective or public consumption appears to be so limited (not least in a literature that has primarily been about *private* and *individual* consumption). For pursuit of collective provision, almost inevitably through the state, has been perceived and pursued politically other than as consumption, the more so the more it is attained. In becoming the welfare state, for example, it incorporates entirely separate sets of practices, structures and ethos.

So the politics of consumption tends to become the politics of something else as the associated issues are pursued back along the chain of provision. In addition, as the consumer engages collectively with other consumers, there is necessarily a tension with other forms of stratification, identity and interests. The homogenizing and illusory, notions of *the* consumer and of *the* consumer interest will tend to come up against differences of income, gender, race, region, nationality, class, etc. Can the discourse of the politics of the consumer be held together despite these potentially disintegrating differences across consumers? The answer, equally for the previous consideration of the transformation of consumption into something else, is that it can. And there is plenty of historical and contemporary evidence that confirms this, the more so as the consumption turn has now turned to a culture of the active consumer in material as well post-modernist cultural terms to address the politics of consumption. However, for the consumer to persist and be significant as a social agent, a dual resolution must be found to the disintegrating aspects identified. These are the tendency for issues surrounding consumption to be transformed into something else other than consumption and the difficulty for the consumer to remain a focal point despite differentiation across consumers with an appeal to correspondingly different, possibly more compelling, sources of identity.

One consequence of these limiting elements in forming a politics of consumption as such is that it is liable to be limited in its radical content. This is unless it succumbs to being transformed into something else more progressive by virtue of the nature of its shifting focus and the more targeted interests that it represents. This is illustrated in a perverse way by the current wave of privatisation of public consumption. The language of the welfare state and its citizens reverts to that of consumer and client, if not necessarily without resistance, as the pseudo practices of the market have been adopted for (welfare) provision even where the market is at most immanent.[66] For this to succeed, the politics of consumption must be contained within narrow confines, not least and most notably in the substitution of Third Wayism for socialism/Labourism. This is associated with a change in the nature of politics itself, that it should become more consumed than practised, a matter of choice over policies delivered by politicians to consumer citizens who are, other than when voting, little more active than in their weekly trip to the shopping mall.[67] Thus, the contemporary rise of consumerist politics in part reflects an imploding politicisation of consumption and a corresponding consumerisation of politics. In short, putting politics into consumption can serve to focus on the individual at the expense of the collective and immediate delivery at the expense of the broader parameters of provision and provisioning.

Notes

*For further discussion and references, see B. Fine, *The World of Consumption: The Cultural and Material Revisited* (London, 2002). Thanks to Frank Trentmann and conference participants for comments on earlier drafts.

1. For a critical appraisal of such individualism from within economics, see J. Davis, *The Theory of the Individual in Economics: Identity and Value* (London, 2003). He usefully draws the distinction between the social science critique (individual preferences are conditioned externally) and the post-modern critique (they are internally generated).
2. Gary Becker is the leading economist seeking to understand all aspects of human behaviour in terms of the 'economic approach'. See B. Fine, 'Playing the Consumption Game', *Consumption, Markets, Culture*, 1(1) (1997), pp. 7–29, for a critique.
3. B. Barry, 'Capitalists Rule OK?: Some Puzzles about Power', *Politics, Philosophy and Economics*, 1(2) (2002), pp. 155–84, cleverly makes the argument that the case for consumer sovereignty (and for voter power over government) is no stronger than that for the power of capitalist producers over government (and consumers).
4. See S. Cullenberg, J. Amariglio and D.F. Ruccio (eds), *Post-modernism, Economics and Knowledge* (London, 2001) for a rare account of economics and post-modernism.
5. See D. Miller, 'The Poverty of Morality', *Journal of Consumer Culture*, 1(2) (2001), pp. 225–43 and R. Wilk, 'Consuming Morality', *Journal of Consumer Culture*, 1(2) (2001), pp. 245–60, for the relationship between (affluent) consumption and morality.
6. B. Fine and E. Leopold, *The World of Consumption* (London, 1993), p. 59.
7. A. Appadurai, 'Introduction: Commodities and the Politics of Value' in A. Appadurai (ed.), *The Social Life of Things: Commodities in Cultural Perspective* (Cambridge, 1986), p. 3.
8. See the chapters by Trentmann and Taylor, Rappaport, Spiekermann and Gamble in this volume. See also S. Kates and R. Belk, 'The Meaning of Lesbian and Gay Pride Day: Resistance through Consumption and Resistance to Consumption', *Journal of Contemporary Ethnography*, 30(4) (2001), pp. 392ff.
9. See B. Fine, *The Political Economy of Diet, Health and Food Policy* (London, 1998).
10. Fine and Leopold, *World of Consumption*.
11. Initially, G. Ritzer, *The McDonaldization of Society: An Investigation into the Changing Character of Contemporary Social Life* (Thousand Oaks, CA, 1993).

12. See P. Scranton, *Endless Novelty: Speciality Production and American Industrialisation, 1865–1925* (Princeton, NJ, 1998).

13. For further discussion, see Fine and Leopold, *World of Consumption*, chapters 18 and 19 and B. Fine, M. Heasman and J. Wright, *Consumption in the Age of Affluence: The World of Food* (London, 1996), chapter 11.

14. Interestingly, a recent translation of earlier work, J. Baudrillard, *The Consumer Society: Myths and Structures* (London, 1998, orig. 1970), reveals that he had yet to break with a heavy, if simplistic, dose of economic determinism as monopoly capitalism is seen as homogenizing people and products, thereby creating a cult of differentiation, pp. 89f. Moreover, the view from this perspective that only the idea and not the fulfilment, of consumption has been created becomes very different within a post-modernist framework in which the economic determinism has fallen away and only subjective notions of consumption remain.

15. It has been popular to discuss such commodity fetishism in terms of lack of knowledge of the consumed by virtue of increasing 'distance' from production. However true this might be in strictly spatial terms, it is questionable insofar as direct connection to producers does not necessarily guarantee more knowledge of the product (as opposed to different knowledge); today's schoolchild may know more about distance commodities than their counterparts and adults of yesteryear.

16. B. Carruthers and S. Babb, *Economy/Society: Markets, Meanings and Social Structure* (Thousand Oaks, CA, 2000), p.18.

17. T. Burke, *Commodification, Consumption and Cleanliness in Modern Zimbabwe* (London, 1998).

18. T. Burke, *Commodification*, p. 8. Of course, eating, washing and wearing, etc. do themselves have shifting content and meaning.

19. Burke, *Commodification*, p. 6.

20. Burke, *Commodification*, p. 5.

21. Burke, *Commodification*, p. 6. Note that, in later work, Burke seems more favourably inclined to Marx and, in studying commodity rumours, adopts an approach consistent to that developed here, 'Cannibal Margarine and Reactionary Snapple: A Comparative Examination of Rumours about Commodities', *International Journal of Cultural Studies*, 1(2) (1998), pp. 253–70.

22. See R. Miklitsch, *From Hegel to Madonna: Towards a General Economy of 'Commodity Fetishism'* (Albany, NY, 1998), pp. 84f.

23. Miklitsch, *From Hegel to Madonna*, p. 93.

24. W. Haug, *Critique of Commodity Aesthetics: Appearance, Sexuality and Advertising in Capitalist Society* (London, 1986).

25. M. Marguin, 'La Vision de la France à l'Etranger à travers la Baguette de Pain', *Relations Internationales*, 101 (2000), pp. 107–22.

26. See, for example, P. du Gay and Open University, *Doing Cultural Studies: The Story of the Sony Walkman* (London, 1996).

27. See especially W. Leach, *Land of Desire: Merchants, Power and the Rise of a New American Culture* (New York, 1993).

28. The exceptions are the invaluable, inalienable or sacrosanct, what money cannot buy, although attempts will still be made to sell them.

29. C. Brumann, 'Materialistic Culture: The Uses of Money in Tokyo Gift Exchanges' in M. Ashkenazi and J. Clammer (eds), *Consumption and Material Culture in Contemporary Japan* (London, 2000).

30. T. Wilska, 'Me – a Consumer? Consumption, Identities and Lifestyles in Today's Finland', *Acta Sociologia*, 45(3) (2002), pp. 195–210.

31. See, for example, J. Patico, 'Chocolate and Cognac: Gifts and the Recognition of Social Worlds in Post-Soviet Russia', *Ethnos*, 67(3) (2002), pp. 345–68 and other contributions in the same special issue of *Ethnos*.

32. See R. Goh, 'Textual Spaces, Social Identities and Race in Singapore Advertising', *European Journal of Cultural Studies*, 6(2) (2003), pp. 131–56.

33. See J. Greenfield, S. O'Connell and C. Reid, 'Fashioning Masculinity: Men Only, Consumption and the Development of Marketing in the 1930s', *Twentieth Century British History*, 10(4) (1999), pp. 457–76, on the 'heroic masculinity' of *Men Only*, first published in Britain in 1935 and interpreted as an attempt to define the male as opposed to the female consumer. Contrast this with the current redefinition of masculinity (and consumption) through the likes of the soccer player David Beckham.

34. J. Karlin, 'The Gender of Nationalism: Competing Masculinities in Meiji Japan', *Journal of Japanese Studies*, 28(1) (2002), pp. 66f.

35. See, for example, J. de Vries, 'Between Purchasing Power and the World of Goods: Understanding the Household Economy in Early Modern Europe' in J. Brewer and R. Porter (eds), *Consumption and the World of Goods* (London, 1993), and H. Voth, 'Work and the Sirens of Consumption in Eighteenth-Century London' in M. Bianchi (ed.), *The Active Consumer* (London, 1998).

36. L. Crewe, 'Geographies of Retailing and Consumption', *Progress in Human Geography* 24(2) (2000), p. 281, citing D. Leslie and S. Reimer, 'Spatializing Commodity Chains', *Progress in Human Geography*, 23(3) (1999), p. 402.

37. K. Hansen, *Salaula: The World of Secondhand Clothing and Zambia* (Chicago, 2000).

38. B. Lemire, *Fashion's Favourite: The Cotton Trade and the Consumer in Britain, 1660–1800* (Oxford, 1992) and *Dress, Culture and Commerce: The English Clothing Trade before the Factory, 1660–1800* (New York, 1997).

39. B. Burman (ed.), *The Culture of Sewing: Gender, Consumption and Home Dressmaking* (Oxford and New York, 1999).

40. S. Narotzky, *New Directions in Economic Anthropology* (London, 1997), p. 102.

41. S. Pennell, 'Consumption and Consumerism in Early Modern England', *Historical Journal*, 42(2) (1999), pp. 553f.

42. Fine, *World of Consumption*.

43. A. Appadurai, 'Consumption, Duration and History' in D. Palumbo-Liu and H. Gumbrecht, *Streams of Cultural Capital* (Stanford, CA, 1997), p. 33.

44. Appadurai, 'Consumption, Duration and History', p. 24.

45. Appadurai, 'Consumption, Duration and History', p. 29.

46. B. Moeran, *A Japanese Advertising Agency: An Anthropology of Media and Markets* (Richmond, 1996), p. 284.

47. Moeran, *Japanese Advertising Agency*, p. 296.

48. Carruthers and Babb, *Economy/Society*, p. 44.

49. M. Rogers, *Barbie Culture* (London, 1998).

50. Rogers, *Barbie Culture*, pp. 102–8.

51. R. Bishop and L. Robinson, *Night Market: Sexual Cultures and the Thai Economic Miracle* (London, 1998). See also N. Wonders and R. Michalowski, 'Bodies, Borders and Sex Tourism in a Globalized World: A Tale of Two Cities – Amsterdam and Havana', *Social Problems*, 48(4) (2001), pp. 545–71.

52. A. Arce and E. Fisher, 'The Accountability of Commodities in a Global Market Place: The Cases of Bolivian Coca and Tanzanian Honey' in R. Fardon, W.M.J. van Binsbergen and R. van Dijk (eds), *Modernity on a Shoestring: Dimensions of Globalization, Consumption and Development in Africa and Beyond* (Leiden, 1999).

53. C. Beng-Huat, 'Consuming Asians: Ideas and Issues' in C. Beng-Huat (ed.), *Consumption in Asia: Lifestyles and Identities* (London, 2000), p. 4.

54. C. Jirousek, 'The Transition to Mass Fashion System Dress in the Later Ottoman Empire' in D. Quataert (ed.), *Consumption Studies and the History of the Ottoman Empire, 1550–1922* (Albany, NY, 2000), p. 234.

55. D. Crane, 'Diffusion Models and Fashion: A Reassessment', *Annals of the American Academy of Political and Social Science*, 566 (1999), pp. 13–24.

56. D. Purdy, *The Tyranny of Elegance: Consumer Cosmopolitanism in the Era of Goethe* (Baltimore, MD, 1998), cites Ambrose Bierce, *The Devil's Dictionary*, 'Fashion – a despot whom the wise ridicule and obey'.

57. F. Mort, *Cultures of Consumption: Masculinities and Social Space in Late Twentieth-Century Britain* (London, 1996) and 'Paths to Mass Consumption: Britain and the USA since 1945' in M. Nava *et al.* (eds), *Buy This Book: Studies in Advertising and Consumption* (London, 1997).

58. W. Roseberry, 'The Rise of Yuppie Coffees and the Reimagination of Class in the United States', *American Anthropologist*, 98(4) (1996), p. 763.

59. L. Auslander, *Taste and Power: Furnishing Modern France* (Berkeley, CA, 1996), p. 33. See also her 'The Gendering of Consumer Practices in Nineteenth-Century France' in V. de Grazia (ed.), *The Sex of Things: Gender and Consumption in Historical Perspective* (London, 1996), p. 101:

> To adequately explain the gendering of consumer practices in the nineteenth century one must ultimately locate that process within the dynamics of making nation and state and of capitalist expansion in the post-revolutionary era ... and the

political and social ... of everyday life, including the acquisition, use and disposal of goods.

60. Auslander, *Taste*, p. 277.
61. See K. Hobson, 'Competing Discourses of Sustainable Consumption: Does the 'Rationalisation of Lifestyles' Make Sense?', *Environmental Politics*, 11(2) (2002), pp. 95–120, in the context of sustainable consumption tending to be about what consumers do (too little too late) rather than what producers do (also finding that consumers can be more concerned with social justice for others than a new sustainable lifestyle for themselves).
62. In this light, not surprisingly, those who participate in consumer politics are also more active in other political activity, D. Hyman and J. Shingler 'The Hierarchy of Consumer Participation and Patterns of Economic, Social and Political Participation', *Journal of Consumer Affairs*, 33(2) (1999), pp. 380–407.
63. For a critical exposition of 'collective consumption' ranging from Saunders' forms of housing tenure to Castells' urbanism, see Fine and Leopold, *World of Consumption*, chapter 17. See R. Keat *et al.* (eds), *The Authority of the Consumer* (London, 1994) for a rare exception in looking at welfare provision from the perspective of public consumption.
64. Fine, *World of Consumption*, chapter 10.
65. As indicated by the limited politics associated with owner-occupation of housing as a form of empowerment. See A. Dávila, 'Barrio Dreams: Housing and Gentrification in El Barrio', *Immigrants and Minorities*, XV(1) (2003), pp. 113–37 and R. Rowlands and C. Gurley, 'Young Peoples' Perceptions of Housing Tenure: A Case Study in the Socialization of Tenure Prejudice', *Housing, Theory and Society*, 17(3) (2000), pp. 121–30. See also Mort's chapter in this volume.
66. See J. Harris, 'State Social Work and Social Citizenship in Britain: From Clientelism to Consumerism', *British Journal of Social Work*, 29(6) (1999), pp. 915–38; for example, M. Doel and J. Segroll, 'Self, Health and Gender: Complementary and Alternative Medicine in the British Mass Media', *Gender, Place and Culture*, 10(2) (2003), pp. 131–44; J. Crinson, 'Putting Patients First: The Continuity of the Consumerist Discourse in Health Policy, from the Radical Right to New Labour', *Critical Social Policy*, 18(2) (1998), pp. 227–39 and A. McLean, 'From Ex-Patient Alternatives to Consumer Options: Consequences of Consumerism for Psychiatric Consumers and the Ex-Patient Movement', *International Journal of Health Services*, 30(4) (2000), pp. 821–48.
67. For this in the context of the top-down consumer citizenship of the nationless European Union, see M. Everson's chapter in this volume, as well as A. Burgess, 'Consumption: Creating a Europe of the Consumer', *Journal of Consumer Culture*, 1(1) (2001), pp. 93–117 and A. Cronin, 'Consumer Rights/Cultural Rights: A New Politics of European Belonging', *European Journal of Cultural Studies*, 5(3) (2002), pp. 307–24.

Index